Co DCCW

PQ
6032

A History of Spanish Literature

A History of
Spanish Literature
by Guillermo Diaz-Plaja

Translated, Edited, and with
a Preface, Introductory Chapter, Selective Bibliography,
and Addendum on Contem-
porary Literature

by Hugh A. Harter

Professor of Romance Languages
Ohio Wesleyan University

1971   *New York:* New York University Press

© 1971 by New York University
Library of Congress Catalog Card Number: 70-124524

ISBN: 8147-1775-6 (cloth)
ISBN: 8147-1776-4 (paper)
Manufactured in the United States of America

Pour Paul et Lucille et "notre" Rue Debrousse
où cette version anglaise a été terminée

Acknowledgments

The translation of the poems of Jorge Guillén done by Richard Wilbur appear through the courtesy of Harcourt, Brace & World.

The selections from Elisha K. Kane's translation of the *Book of Good Love* are reprinted through the courtesy of Mrs. Elisha K. Kane.

The translations by Eleanor Turnbull appear here through the courtesy of the Johns Hopkins Press.

The passage from the *Celestina* is from the translation by J. M. Cohen, reprinted through the courtesy of the New York University Press.

The translations of the poems of Antonio Machado which appear here were done specifically for inclusion in this volume by Willis Barnstone.

Contents

Translator's Preface

A translator must necessarily be, at least to some extent, a traitor. Some passages come quickly, easily, and accurately into the "step-tongue"; others never seem quite right in the second language, and this is true of prose translation as well as poetry. The latter, however, as one might suppose, usually presents far greater problems because of rhythm, rhyme, imagery, and the like, for structure and word only rarely coincide in two languages even when content can readily be transposed.

Consequently I have taken some liberties with the passages that Guillermo Díaz-Plaja included as illustrative material in the original version. This has been primarily in the poetry. Where a good translation exists of a poem other than the one originally used in the Spanish volume, I have opted for the good English version, so long, of course, as the illustrative passage still serves the point being made in the linear text.

I have also added some selections. For example, I have included two additional translations of poems by Gustavo Adolfo Bécquer. Conversely I have retained only one short poem of Bécquer's contemporary, Ramón de Campoamor. This was due to the existence of better translations of the former as well as to the greater importance accorded to his work. Likewise the reader will find two poems, rather than one, by Jorge Guillén. Both translations were made by Richard Wilbur and thus the greatest living Spanish poet of this century can be seen through the eyes of one of the finest contemporary poets writing in English. Many of the translators' names which appear under both prose and poetry passages will be familiar to the English-speaking reader. I have chosen these both for their intrinsic excellence and for their literary interest. When an English version by a Byron or a Longfellow was available, I have included it both for its excellence and to illustrate the long and fecund relationship between the Spanish and English literatures. However, I have avoided adding to, eliminating, or seriously modifying the textual commentary of Señor Díaz-Plaja as much as possible. This work, after all, is his history of literature and in those places where I have found room for disagreement as to point of view or emphasis, I have tried to remain faithful to the critical opinions presented in the original.

The reader who is already acquainted with Spanish literature in translation or who is inclined to become so on reading this history may wonder at encountering titles of works that do not coincide with those used here. There is a simple explanation for this. Sometimes two or three different translations of a title of a work have been made by individual translators. This, for example, is true of Quevedo's *Buscón* which has been entitled *The Spanish Sharper* and *The Life of the Great Rascal,* among other things, while I myself did a version entitled *The Scavenger.* None of these titles is a fully accurate translation of the work *Buscón;* although each carries something of the sense of the original consequently it is not inconceivable that some future translation of this stylistically intricate novel may carry still another title.

Special mention should be made of the Antonio Machado poems of which Willis Barnstone, with characteristic thoughtfulness, made translations for inclusion in this volume. Special thanks are also due to Professor Robert J. Clements and to Robert T. King for invaluable editorial suggestions and to my mother, Georgiana Harter, and my wife Frances, for their patient proofreading.

Unless otherwise identified, all translations of literary or historical excerpts, whether prose or poetry, are my own.

Introduction

Language

"Spain," says the *Encyclopaedia Britannica,* "can boast that she supplied Rome with almost her whole literature in the silver age. The Augustans had been Italians. Their successors were Spaniards—the younger Seneca, Lucan, Martial, Quintilian, besides a host of lesser lights."

Civilization has very ancient roots in Spain, and the Spanish contribution to European literature has been vast and various. The subject of the present book, however, is the literature of the Spanish language, which, in about the eleventh century, emerged as a recognizable idiom from the "vulgar" Latin that had been spoken in the Peninsula for a thousand years. For the most part it is the literature of the Castilian dialect, although we shall also review the literature of the Galician and Catalan dialects. These dialects, together with the Portuguese language (which Galician very closely resembles), are closer to their Latin original than is Italian, which emerged about the same time. Possibly this is because there had been fewer foreign slaves in the Iberian peninsula, and perhaps also because changes of fashion did not take place as rapidly in the provinces as in Rome.

During the eleventh and twelfth centuries the central kingdom of Castile developed into a vigorous community with a growing sense of its own individuality, as the *Poem of the Cid* demonstrates. It eventually became the political, economic, spiritual, and linguistic focus of the Spanish nation. Its writers crucially affected the drama and the novel of England and France; its Renaissance lyrics were studied and imitated by Wyatt and thus contributed to the very foundations of English metrics.

The Spanish language today shares with English and Chinese the distinction of being one of the three most widely spoken languages in the world. Like those languages also, it has a relatively simple grammar and an extraordinarily plentiful vocabulary, having acquired many words of Arabic or Amerindian origin. Moreover, it has been the most stable of the three; it has not changed as much over the centuries as English, and its dialects are not as drastically different from one another as those of Chinese. American Spanish is closer to Castilian than American English is to British English. In Castilian the letter "z" is pronounced with a "th" sound; a charming but dubious tradition has it that Philip II of Spain, who reigned from 1556 to 1598, had a lisp and his loyal subjects adopted it as correct pronunciation, out of deference to His Majesty. In the New World this letter is usually pronounced as an "s."

Geography

Spain and Portugal make up the Iberian Peninsula, the area south of the high Pyrenees Mountains that was known in Roman times as Hispania. Covering some five-sixths of the Peninsula, Spain has a total area of 193,671 square miles if we include the Balearic and Canary Islands. Occupying as she does a twentieth part of the Continent, Spain is Europe's third country in size, only Russia and France having larger land areas.

The Peninsula faces both the Mediterranean and the Atlantic, the Straits of Gibraltar being the traditional gate to the West for Mediterranean civilizations; but the northern coast borders the notoriously stormy Bay of Biscay and relates Spain to Northern Europe. The most striking characteristic of the Peninsula, however, is its altitude. At an average height of 1,950 feet above sea level, Spain is the second highest country of Europe, only Switzerland being higher, and mountain ranges form natural barriers in many parts of the land, dividing the nation into several *patrias chicas,* or "little fatherlands."

The rivers of Spain are generally sluggish and dry except after rains, and only one of the major rivers, the Ebro, enters the Mediterranean. It is 465 miles long, rises in the north, and flows past the City of Saragossa in Aragon to the sea.

Many people think of "sunny" Spain as having a warm, semitropical climate, but Spain is above all a land of topographical and climactic contrasts. Galicia, in the northwest, is rainy and humid; the green, softly rolling hills and the pious Catholicism of the people suggest Ireland, and the people are, in fact, of Celtic origin, their favorite musical instrument being the *gaita* or bagpipe. In some parts of Spain, especially in the north, one finds forests, wheat fields, vineyards, and olive trees.

But the bare, arid central plateau, swept by a severe wind called the *cierza* in winter and scorched by the sun in summer, prompts the Castilian to describe the climate of his region as nine months of winter and three months of hell. The Texas Panhandle must have seemed like home to those of the early explorers who hailed from Castile.

"The Count is neither sad, nor sick, nor merry, nor well; but civil, count,—civil as an orange, and something of that jealous complexion," says Beatrice in *Much Ado About Nothing,* and Shakespeare's audience would have recognized the pun on "Seville" at once. It is now the truck farming area around Valencia that is famous for oranges, producing as it does most of Spain's citrus fruits and vegetables and a good deal of the rice. The fertile acres of this coastal plain are aptly called *huertas* or gardens.

It is in the far south that one sees the palm-lined boulevards of the tropics.

History

The 1960 census of Spain lists over thirty million inhabitants. The origins of these people are lost in the remote times before there were any written records. We do know, from the impressive cave paintings near Altamira in the north, that an intelligent and gifted people already lived in the Peninsula as early as the Upper Paleolithic Age, some fifteen thousand years before Christ.

By the time of the coming of the Phoenicians to Spain—they founded Cadiz around 1100 B.C.—there were peoples inhabiting the Peninsula known as Iberians and Tartessians. We know little about them, though Greek historians do speak of them. That they developed a fairly high level of civilization is evidenced by the sculptured bust of the famous Lady of Elche. We know that they had contact with the Phoenicians, and then later on with the Greeks, who brought arts, crafts, industry, trade, and written language to Spain. They also built roads, aqueducts, theaters, schools and other structures, the remains of which can still be seen, along with numerous Roman ruins throughout the land.

While the Phoenicians and Greeks were colonizing the southern and southwestern coasts, large numbers of Celtic peoples were invading the northern and central regions and forming a racial mixture known as Celtiberians.

In the sixth century B.C. another ethnic strain that was to play an important role in this early period came to Spain, the Carthaginians. They too established cities and slowly extended their power over most of the Peninsula before they in their turn were superseded by the Romans, who crushed Carthaginian power in Spain in the Second Punic War (216 B.C.).

The Romans were to remain some six hundred years in the Iberian Peninsula and during that time they completely transformed the land and the way of life. Rome brought its laws and

administrative procedures, its culture, architecture, roads, aqueducts, theaters, and social behavior to the conquered area. Even
more important for our present purposes she brought her language. Spain also became a Catholic nation during Roman times,
a fact we must not forget if we are to understand Spanish
civilization.

In her turn, Spain "hispanized" her conquerors. Some of
the greatest figures of Roman history, in political life and in
letters, were Spanish or of Spanish blood. These included four
of her best-known emperors—Trajan, Hadrian, Marcus Aurelius,
and Theodosius—and some of her greatest writers and thinkers.
The great Stoic philosopher Seneca, who was born in Cordova,
was tutor and later adviser to the Emperor Nero.

Spain also produced noted Christian authors who wrote in
Latin during the period of Roman domination: the churchmen
Juvencus, St. Damasus, and Prudentius.

Early in the fifth century A.D. the Germanic invasions
brought an end to Roman dominance of the Peninsula. The
Vandals, Alans, and Suebians were followed by the Visigoths,
who were Christians. The latter established a monarchy in
Spain that lasted for three hundred years. The chaotic centuries
of Visgothic rule would have left little real imprint on Spanish
life had it not been for the unifying force and the spiritual and
scholarly contributions of the Church. Several noteworthy authors lived in this period and wrote their works in Latin. The
most famous of these are Orosius, who wrote a universal history
from the Christian point of view, St. Isidore of Seville, whose
twenty-book *Etymologies* was a sort of medieval encyclopedia,
and St. Ildefonso.

The Visigothic kingdom ended when the Moors invaded
Spain in A.D. 711. Within a few years the Arabic conquerors con-
trolled all but a few isolated fastnesses in the mountainous north.
At least part of Spain was to remain under Moorish rule for almost eight hundred years, until the taking of Granada by Ferdinand and Isabella in January of 1492.

Spain became a center of Arabic learning. Great cities with
beautiful palaces and impressive libraries grew up; literature

flourished. Moorish architecture and culture, after the Roman influence, were to leave a deep and abiding mark on the life, language, and thinking of the Spaniard.

During the twentieth century it has been recognized that traces of pre-Christian paganism have never been entirely eradicated in Christendom, but in Spain paganism had two foes: Christianity and Islam. As a result, pagan customs and beliefs were more thoroughly erased or "Christianized" in Spain than in Italy. Another consequence of the Moorish centuries was that the Spanish Christian was forced to become self-conscious about his religion and zealous to convert others; Christianity was not something he could take for granted.

The Battle of Covadonga in 718 is usually considered the beginning of a long struggle to reclaim Spain for Christianity. The pitiably small bands of Christians in the north took back their land acre by acre, village by village, and in the ninth century small Christian kingdoms began to form. Catalonia gained its independence in 865, in 946 Castile became independent under Count Fernán González, but the reconquest took four more centuries to complete, and the pride, personal courage, and devotion that it required have left a permanent imprint on Spanish literature. Do we not admire these very qualities in Don Quixote even as we laugh at his folly and pity his suffering?

The people of the various regions are almost as different from each other as the regions themselves. The Basques of the Pyrenees speak an ancient language that has long been an enigma to philologists and that is utterly unintelligible to most Spaniards. The Castilians, who have given us the language normally known as Spanish, are reserved, introspective, and somewhat somber when compared with the exuberant and talkative Andalusians of the south. The inhabitants of the industrial area around Barcelona have a reputation for business acumen and their lives, as might be expected, are more similar to those that are lived in Milan, Lyons, Hamburg, Manchester, and Pittsburgh than to the lives of Gallegans, the "Irishmen" of Spain, known for their love of wit and eloquence.

Generalizing about national temperaments is always a dan-

gerous pastime, and a man who knows Spain has good reasons
for resisting any temptation to generalize about this fascinating
country. Certainly we can say that Spanish intellectual life has
not been characterized by great achievements in the kind of
philosophical theorizing that we find in France and Germany,
but in painting, music, and literature the Spanish genius has
excelled. And the achievements of Spanish explorers are legendary.

The Spaniard's reactions to the world are the emotional
reflexes of an individual, not expressions of principles or ideas.
In politics this often leads to anarchy, as the tragic history of
modern Spain has shown. Laws are regarded as abstractions,
while justice and government are personal matters. The system
of *compadrazgo* or *enchufe,* that is, of obtaining something
through the good offices of relatives or friends rather than
through legal right as in Anglo-Saxon countries, is common in
Spain and Latin America. The whole concept of honor, and
consequently the tradition of the duel or of personal revenge,
also stems from this intense individualism and the emotional
base from which the Spaniard acts. The individual feels it as his
right, and even his duty, to avenge what he considers an offense.
This attitude has produced some colorful and compelling figures
in history and literature, but it has also hindered the development of a general sense of the good of the community.

The Spaniard draws most of his personal friendships from
his own relatives, rather than from outside the family. That is
to say, he belongs to what psychologists are now calling a "kin-
ship" family, feeling a very close loyalty to his uncles and
cousins, rather than to a "nuclear" family (one in which the
husband feels close family ties only to his wife and children),
such as is normal in England and Germany. Visitors to Spain
often notice the public displays of very warm affection between
father and son, and this is one of the characteristics of Spanish
culture that has been established wherever the Spanish language
has taken hold.

The Spaniard has proved himself capable of extraordinary
heroism and of almost superhuman energy; a remarkable example of the latter is the immense output of Lope de Vega, the

great poet and playwright of the seventeenth century. On the other hand, Spain is one of the few countries where the pleasures of sociable indolence are still highly valued and widely enjoyed.

It has been said that in Spain even the atheists are Catholic, and it is true that Catholicism colors all the thinking and all the perceptions of the Spaniard, whether he be a mystic or a realist. His literature inevitably reflects and grows out of his character, and the effects of this steeping in Catholicism have been incalculable.

In the blending of Spanish sherry each year's vintage is mixed with that of the preceding year to produce the final blend, so that every sherry contains traces of original wines that may be centuries old. Similarly, we may see in Spanish poetry—even as recent as Lorca's—traces of a civilization that goes back to pre-Christian and even pre-Roman times.

1.

The Middle Ages

The Juglares *or Minstrels*

The first literary monuments that have come down to us belong to the Minstrel School or *mester de juglaría* which shared the traditions of the *jongleur* in France and of the earlier Anglo-Saxon "scop" who sang of such heroes as Beowulf.

The minstrel, *el juglar,* earned his living entertaining people either in the town square or in the castle of a noble. He was at one and the same time acrobat, musician, and reciter of poems and songs. At first he moved from place to place but later on he often established himself in populous cities or in the castles of the nobility. He is not, however, to be confused with the troubadour who was the artistic creator of what he recited and who did not earn his livelihood by performing.

Sometimes accompanied by musical instruments, the *juglar* dealt with subjects often heroic in nature and of a collective character that would be of interest to all of his audience. The feats of heroes formed the theme that most delighted the uneducated public and the poems in this category are called *cantares de gesta* or gests.

The art of the *juglar* is fundamentally uncomplicated. Ignorant of the finer points of meter, he limited himself to the stringing together of various lines of verse written in assonant rhyme and without precise count or measure. The verse line varied from ten to twelve syllables (epic verse) and later on gave rise to the *romances* or ballads.

The Spanish used by the *juglar* was quite different from that of today inasmuch as it was a language only half formed which included numerous Latinisms and vacillations of expression.

While most of the *cantares de gesta* have been lost to us or are known only as fragments, the earliest major work of Spanish literature we possess belongs to this tradition. It is the *Cantar de mío Cid* whose date of composition is set in the year 1140. This does not mean, however, that there were no poems written previous to this time. Although none has come down to us, we can deduce their existence from facts we do know: i.e., that the *juglares* themselves did exist; that certain short ballads which treat a more ample theme still exist, like the fragmentary branches that have split away from their parent trunk which is lost to us today; and that legends of an epic character have been incorporated into early chronicles and pseudohistorical works. Not only can we be certain that the epic *cantares* existed, but we can also classify them as belonging to several major cycles, such as:

1. Those concerning Rodrigo, the last Visigothic king, and the invasion of Spain by the Infidels in 711, a major preoccupation of Christian Spaniards in the subsequent Reconquest. The legends recount Rodrigo's sins and the divine retribution they incurred, the strange and mysterious death of the king, the treacherous acts of Count Julian and the Battle of Guadalete.

2. Those concerning the Infantes de Lara. This cycle tells of the terrible revenge taken by Ruy Velázquez against his nephews, the seven princes of Salas (or of Lara), whom he blames for an offense against his wife on the day of his wedding. Ruy Velázquez sends Gonzalo Gustios, the father of the seven princes or *infantes,* to Cordova with a secret message in which he requests that the Moorish king Almanzor kill his supposed enemy. Meanwhile he prepares an ambush for the sons. The Moors take the princes unawares and kill them, carrying back the severed heads to the anguished father. The latter, in the cell

where he has been imprisoned by Almanzor, speaks one by one to the severed heads of his sons in a moving and pathetic lament. The cycle ends with the terrible revenge of the last son of Gonzalo Gustios, Mudarra, who challenges and kills the traitor Ruy Velázquez.

El cantar de mío Cid

The Poem of the Cid, as we have said, is the earliest major work of Spanish literature that has come down to us. Happily it is an ample and human work, full of passages of great literary artistry. It is also wholly representative of the places and times in which it was created, a work fully worthy of its position at the beginning of a literature as great as the Spanish.

It has been asserted that the poem literarily shows traces of the influence of the French *chansons de geste,* but some scholars, such as the Spanish critic Menéndez Pidal, are of the opinion that this first epic poem is of Germanic inspiration. However this may be, we do know with certainty that the *Cantar de mío Cid* offers unmistakable characteristics of the Castilian spirit that was developing at that time in the Iberian Peninsula.

The author of the *Poem of the Cid* is not known to us. At the end of the manuscript there is a statement, in both Latin and Spanish: "qui me scripsit scribat—semper cum Domino vivat, i.e.—Per Abbat wrote it," but as the manuscript that we possess is a copy made in 1307 from a much earlier manuscript, it is probable that the Per Abbat mentioned was no more than a copyist.

According to Menéndez Pidal, the poem was composed about the year 1140. This was the date of the betrothal of Doña Blanca of Navarre, the great-granddaughter of the Cid, to Sancho the Well-Beloved. It is this event which causes the minstrel to exclaim joyously in the work that his hero has become related to royalty through marriage: "Today the kings of Spain are his relatives."

The language of the poem is full of Aragonese expressions. It is due to this that scholars have supposed that the work was written in a part of Castile close to Aragon, very probably

Medinaceli. In support of this there is also the curious fact that, whenever the opportunity presents itself, the poet describes the area around that town with numerous and precise details. Conversely, in other parts of the work he writes of much larger and more important areas in a wholly summary manner.

The versification, as can be expected of a poem of the Minstrel School, is irregular and lacking in skill.

The manuscript of the *Cantar* is a small volume of seventy-four pages in quarto, of thick and coarse parchment, from which the first pages and several on the inside are missing. Its existence was unknown until 1779 when a scholar named Eugenio Llaguno found it in a monastery at Vivar. The discovery has been followed by numerous printed editions. The manuscript is in a fourteenth-century script and was written in 1307. We can suppose that this copy made a century and a half after the work's composition was the property of a *juglar*. The lapse of time has given rise to numerous problems, namely those of determining whether a certain linguistic form is the one used by the original author or one which is the result of a "modernizing" correction by the final copyist.

The *Cantar de mío Cid* is characterized by its realism. Almost everything in the work is historically verifiable from the characters it presents and the landscapes it describes to the events it narrates. The Cid himself, his exploits, the geography and the descriptions of the territories he travels through, all belong to historical fact. When we read the work we can see how the Spaniards of the eleventh century lived and fought, how they dressed and were armed, what their customs were and how they spoke and felt. In this sense the Spanish epic is more realistic, generally speaking, than the French and German epics, which are full of miracles and imaginary and fantastic happenings.

The Cid of history is a characteristic figure of medieval Castile, heroic and magnanimous, for whom struggle is an integral part of life. Rodrigo Díaz de Vivar was historically a nobleman of the retinue of the two brother kings, Sancho II of Castile and Alfonso VI of Leon. He took part in the fratricidal wars brought on by the ambitions of the former, but after Sancho's death at the hands of a traitor he recognized the brother as rightful sovereign when he ascended to the throne of Castile. Due to circumstances not very clearly known, Rodrigo was later exiled by King Alfonso. He left Castile to enter the service of the king of Saragossa and defeated the latter's enemy, the king of Lerida, earning for himself the title of Cid [from the Arabic *Sidi* or Lord] by which we know him today.

By the time of the Cid's death in 1099 his fame had spread far and wide. As his story was told and retold, fictitious data were added to the actual facts and the Cid's legendary fame took shape, first in the books of Moslem historians and later on in those of Christian writers. The minstrels sang of him in the castles and public squares, in wayside inns and the marketplace. The *Cantar* was one of those works through which the *juglar* kept alive the memory of the hero.

The following is an outline of the events described in the work's three major divisions:-

1. The first *Cantar:* "The Exile." Rodrigo Díaz de Vivar, sent by King Alfonso to collect tribute from the Moorish kings of Andalusia, fights and defeats the Castilian Count García Ordóñez because the latter has attacked an ally of his king. The Cid, on his return, is accused by envious nobles of having withheld a portion of the tribute money. The king condemns the Cid to exile; a group of friends and vassals elect to follow him. As the first fifty lines or so have been lost, this first part has been reconstructed from prose sources, notably medieval chronicles.

Subsequently the knight sets out from Castile, first leaving his family with the monks of the monastery of San Pedro de Cardeña and then going on to the Moorish territories where he must earn his way by the sword. He conquers a number of small towns such as Castejón and Alcócer, makes tributaries of the Moors of Lower Aragon, and even joins battle with the Count of Barcelona whom he defeats, makes prisoner, and then generously sets at liberty.

2. The second *Cantar:* "The Wedding." Encouraged by his successes, the Cid continues on his way as far as the Mediterranean coast where, after a brilliant series of feats of arms, he takes the great city of Valencia from the Infidel. In vain, first the king of Seville and then the king of Morocco attempt to re-

capture it. The Cid is again victorious and with each triumph sends a part of the splendid booty which falls to him to King Alfonso who has acted so unjustly against him. Meanwhile the news of these victories excites the greed of two courtiers, the princes of Carrión. They wish to marry the Cid's two daughters, Doña Elvira and Doña Sol, who with their mother, Doña Jimena, have been reunited with the hero in Valencia. They ask the king to arrange the marriage. As a reconciliation has already been brought about between himself and the king, the Cid accedes to the monarch's request.

3. The third *Cantar:* "The Affront of Corpes." When the princes of Carrión give evidence of their cowardice on the battlefield and in their father-in-law's palace, they become the objects of the mockery of the Cid's men. To avenge their humiliation, the brothers decide to take their wives to their estates in Carrión and request permission of the Cid to do so. Once on their way the princes lead Doña Elvira and Doña Sol into a small wood named Corpes where they beat the young women and abandon them, half dead and covered with blood. Fortunately the daughters are discovered and given aid. The Cid now has ample evidence of the villainy of his sons-in-law. He asks justice of the king who, in the *cortes,* grants his request. The dispute is brought to a satisfactory end in a tourney in which the warriors of the Cid defeat the princes in combat. Doña Elvira and Doña Sol marry the princes of Navarre and Aragon.

The Cid has thus been raised to the status of a national hero. The minstrel waxes enthusiastic as he evokes him, describing him as full of energy and of majestic bearing. In the battle scenes, he depicts him as strong, bearded, and smiling: "My Cid also turned back; his coif was wrinkled, and you might see his full beard; the hood of his mail hung down upon his shoulders, and the sword was still in his hand."

He is also a deeply religious man. He commends himself to heaven and gives thanks for his victories: "And the Cid turned his horse's head toward St. Mary's, and with his right hand he blest himself on the forehead, and he said, God be praised! Help me, Saint Mary!"

Throughout the events of the poem, the Cid has remained

a loyal and steadfast vassal of the king, an important fact in considering the over-all significance of the work. Rodrigo Díaz de Vivar represents, on the one hand, the spirit of the independence of Castile as opposed to the power of its older neighbors, the kingdoms of Leon and Asturias, which followed in the traditions of the Visigothic monarchy. It is from the latter that the Germanic spirit of these monarchies derived, a conception according to which the king and his subject are united by a bond of vassalage which may be broken. In such event the vassal goes into exile or, as it is expressed, he can "denature himself." It is precisely this which happens between Alfonso VI and Rodrigo de Vivar.

The hardship with which this order of exile is carried out is clearly evident in the following lines from the poem:

My Cid Ruy Díaz entered Burgos, having sixty streamers in his company. And men and women went forth to see him, and the men of Burgos and the women of Burgos were at their windows, weeping, so great was their sorrow; And they said with one accord, God, how good a vassal if he had but a good Lord! and willingly would each have bade him come in, but no one dared to do so. For King Don Alfonso in his anger had sent letters to Burgos, saying that no man should give the Cid a lodging and that whosoever disobeyed should lose all that he had, and moreover the eyes in his head. Great sorrow had these Christian folk at this, and they hid themselves when he came near them because they did not dare speak to him; and My Cid went to his Posada, and when he came to the door he found it fastened, for fear of the King. And his people called out in a loud voice, but they within made no answer. And the Cid rode up to the door, and took his foot out of the stirrup, and gave it a kick, but the door did not open with it, for it was well secured; a little girl of nine years old then came out of one of the houses and said unto him: O Cid, the King hath forbidden us to receive you. We dare not open our doors to you, for we shall lose our houses and all that we have, and the eyes in our head. Cid, our misfortune would not help you, but God and all his saints be with you. And when she had said this she returned

into the house. And when the Cid knew what the King had
done, he turned away from the door and rode up to St.
Mary's, and there he alighted and knelt down, and prayed
with all his heart; and then he mounted again and rode out
of town. . . .

—Translated by Robert Southey

In place of the Germanic concept of law in force in Leon,
Castile followed the criterion of Roman law according to which
the king was a natural lord. This entailed a bond of vassalage
which could not be broken by mere agreement. In accord with
this, the Cid declares time and again that, despite the ill treatment he has received, he will not attack his king ("With Alfonso
my king I have no wish to contend," he says). In spite of being
in exile, the Cid sends the monarch a portion of the booty he
captures. Later on when the Counts of Carrión make him the
object of their effrontery he does not resort to personal vengeance in the Germanic tradition but to the juridical norms
established by the king, the Roman tradition.

In spite of the elements of harshness we have seen, there are
also scenes of great tenderness in the poem. The Cid is a man of
human emotions and proportion. His leave-taking as he prepares
for his exile brings tears to his eyes: "When he saw his hall
deserted, the household chest unfastened, the doors open, no
cloaks hanging up, no seats in the porch, no hawks upon the
perches, the tears came into his eyes. . . ."

When the Cid has to leave his wife and daughters at the
monastery, tears once more cloud his eyes. The pain and grief
of separation is expressed by the poet in the following lines:
". . . and the parting between them was like separating the nail
from the quick flesh." The Cid whom the poet depicts for us is
thereby a hero who laughs and weeps like any other human
being. For this reason he is a hero who is of interest to all of us.
The following is the scene of familial leave-taking:

Then Doña Jimena came up and her daughters were with
her, each of them borne in arms, and she knelt down on both
her knees before her husband, weeping bitterly, and she

would have kissed his hand; and she said to him, Lo now you are banished from the land by mischief-making men, and here am I with your daughters, who are little ones and of tender years, and we and you must be parted, even in your life time. For the love of Saint Mary tell me now what we shall do. And the Cid took the children in his arms, and held them to his heart and wept, for he dearly loved them.

Please God and Saint Mary, he said, I shall yet live to give these my daughters in marriage with my own hands, and to do you service yet, my honored wife, whom I have ever loved, even as my own soul.

—Translated by Robert Southey

The descriptive value of the poem is considerable. As a proof of the realism of the work, there is an excellent example in the description of a battle. The horsemen attack with their lances in socket, the adversary is pierced through and out of his back sticks the bandoleer, red with blood. The victor then unseats his wounded enemy and with a single tug pulls out the lance which, once he holds it vertical again, drips blood until it covers the horseman's hand.

The Origins of Castilian Lyric Poetry

We have discussed the *Cantar de mio Cid* as the earliest extant major work of literature in the Castilian tongue. No earlier complete epic poem has been preserved. Does this mean, however, that no others had been written? It would indeed be a most unusual stroke of luck if the first major work written in Spanish were the same one that has come down to us and it may well be that the grandiose character of the work with its profound sense of nationality was decisive in its preservation.

Nevertheless, Castilian manuscripts antedating 1140 have not yet been discovered. It is logical to suppose, however, that the incipient Castilian tongue must have had some kind of poetic expression preceding the creation of any poem of length and importance. What was this poetic expression? Where was it produced? Why? These are three questions which remained unanswered until relatively recently.

In 1948 several texts of Mozarabic *cancioncillas* or little songs, some one hundred years older than the *Poem of the Cid,* were brought to light. Their discovery moves the history of Castilian literature back a whole century and places it, because of its antiquity, at the head of the Romance literatures. In fact when scholars copied out some Hebraic and Arabic poems of this period they encountered great difficulty in comprehending the final lines. In Hebrew as in Arabic only the consonants are written down. The vowels are placed in the text in the manner of accents. Accordingly the written texts are similar to riddles called "flights of vowels" which make interpretation difficult. Soon, however, the scholars realized that the problem was caused by the inclusion of popular verse lines called *jarchas* or *kharjas* which were in the Romance tongue. The following are an example of one of these:

> Des cand meu Cidello venid
> itan bona albixara!
> Com' rayo de sol exid
> En Wad-al-hayara.

> Since Cidello has arrived
> what joy he has brought
> like the light of the sun he has come
> from the town of Guadalajara.

The problem of how these lines in Romance happened to be included in a Hebrew text is a relatively simple one to solve. As we know, the Spain of the Middle Ages was a cultural crossroads. In the south of the Peninsula, Moors and Jews lived together with those Christians who had remained in their native cities at the time of the Islamic invasion. These Christians, called *mozárabes,* continued to speak their Romance tongue even while under Moorish domination. It was in that tongue that these short songs or little couplets were written. Unprepossessing as they are, they doubtlessly would have been lost had not some Jewish poets taken the trouble to write them down at the end of their poems and thus bequeath them to posterity.

Some Jewish poets, like the famous Jehudah Halevi, include couplets in the Romance tongue which are supposedly recited by a young girl, as in the following example:

> Vayse meu corachon de mib
> !ya Rab! ¿si se me tornarad?
> !Tan mal meu doler li-l-habib!
> Enfermo yea ¿cuándo sanarad?

> [My heart has almost leapt away
> Oh Lord, will it return?
> Such pain for my beloved felt!
> So ill is he.
> When will his health return?]

The word *habib*, which means "friend," appears in many compositions of this type which is the precursor of the famous "friendship lyrics" or ·*canciones de amigo* popular in early Galician and Portuguese poetry. We should also keep in mind that this Mozarabic forerunner may also have influenced the incipient Provençal poetry.

The theory of Arabic influence on poetry in the Romance tongues was initiated in studies by J. Ribera who, on analyzing the *Cancionero de Aben Guzmán*, encountered a series of compositions called *zejeles* and *muwassabas* written in the Romance idiom which the lower classes had continued to speak even after the Moslem invasion.

It is clear that along with this form there must have appeared, timidly at first and with a surer expression later on, a lyric poetry in Castilian, although we have only indirect allusions to this expression. For example, we suppose that there existed

May songs or *canciones de mayo* which exalted springtime and this we deduce from allusions in both epic poetry and the ballads.

Menéndez Pidal has also traced other genres in this early lyric expression: songs of harvesting or *de siega,* of tillage or *de labor,* of milling or *de molino,* and of pilgrimage excursions or *de romería,* as well as love songs in the form of rounds or *rondas* or serenades such as this one:

> Awaken now my eyes of green,
> in early morn you'll have your rest.

Still others can be interpreted as derivations of the *cantigas de amor* and *de amigo* [songs of love and of friendship] from Gallego-Portuguese literature.

In short, Menéndez Pidal concludes, there are two principal forms of the early peninsular lyric, "one which more properly belongs to Gallego-Portuguese poetry and the other to Castilian. The Galician form has uniform strophes which end with an *estribillo* or refrain. The expression of a graceful monotony, moves along slowly in continuous repetitions. The form the Castilian takes is that of an initial *villancico* or short carol which is varied in subsequent strophes and at the end of which there is usually the repetition of all or part of the *villancico* as a sort of *estribillo* or refrain." This latter form is highly suitable to the narrative expression into which it frequently develops due to the collective character which is typical of it.

As we would suspect, these lyrics influenced each other reciprocally. Galician became the poetical language of Castilian writers and even Alfonso X wrote the lyrical part of his work in that tongue, i.e., his *cantigas.* On the other hand, the expansive impetus of Castile imposed some of its thematic material. For example the Provençal *pastorela,* a love debate between a shepherdess and a gentleman, becomes a *cantiga de serrana* which is more rigorous and rustic than its Provençal counterpart. The heroine is a simple farm girl who rudely rejects her bold suitors, if necessary by the use of her *dardo pedrero* or sling. That is how the Archpriest of Hita's *serranas* or mountain girls protect themselves. In the *serranillas,* or pastoral poems of the Marquis of Santillana, both literary types are to be found.

The first major lyrical works of Spanish poetry date from the early twelfth century. In that period a work appeared with the title of *Razón de amor con los denuestos del agua y del vino* [*An Account of a Love Tale Plus the Arguments Between Water and Wine*]. The poem contains, on the one hand, the description of a love idyl between a lady and a student-scholar; on the other, it is the dispute between water and wine over their respective excellences, a typical form of medieval debate. The work is anonymous.

A similar type of dispute or debate is contained in the *Dialogue of Elena and Maria,* a forty-line fragment, and in the *Dispute of the Soul and the Body* [*Disputa del alma y del cuerpo*], also a fragment of a longer work.

There was also early poetry of a narrative character, including such works as the *Libre dels tres reys d'Orient* [*Book of the Three Kings of Orient*], anonymous, which relates an episode of the flight into Egypt, and the *Vida de Santa María Egipciaca* [*Life of Saint Mary the Egyptian*], the story of a great sinner repentant, also anonymous. Both poems show French or Provençal influence.

The Thirteenth Century

I. Poetry—The Priestly School

Alongside the bustling and busy segments of society which were uneducated, including both the nobles and the common people whose life is reflected in the works of the *mester de juglaría* or School of the Minstrel Craft, there existed the calm and quiet life of the monasteries, far removed from the hardships of war and of heavy labor.

Only in the monasteries could one find the quiet and the time necessary for spiritual matters. As a result they became centers of culture, even more so after Saint Benedict ordered his monks to devote themselves to intellectual pursuits. The monastery was a school where the monks taught, a library where books were kept, a repository of culture, and a center for the work of copying manuscripts and for advancing knowledge.

It is highly probable that without these centers of intellectual endeavor the cultural heritage of Greece would have been lost to a great extent, even though we now recognize that frequently the knowledge then held about the classical world was faulty.

These are the words of Friar Justo Pérez de Urbel:

First of all, the monks are champions of the heroic life which man should always admire and respect however much his ideas about moral laws may vary. Furthermore, they do not lead isolated lives but take part in Councils, intervene in doctrinal disputes, rise to the highest post of the Ecclesiastical hierarchy, participate in the advisory bodies of kings, mix with the masses of people in city and town, teach, preach, give counsel, write, sustain society, defend orthodoxy, create the arts, found schools, are poets, historians, theologians, painters, calligraphers and architects; in short, their influence is of capital importance in the religious, social, political and cultural life of our Native Land.

The Mester de Clerecia *or School of the Priestly Craft*

This culture and this tradition necessarily had a strong influence on the literary output of the clerical classes. Consequently along with the craft known as the School of the Minstrels there was created another, designated the School of the Priestly Craft or *mester de clerecía*. It had clearly definable characteristics.

1. In matters of form, the School of the Priestly Craft had precise rules controlling its metric structure. This was known as the *cuaderna vía* or fourfold way. Unlike the juggler who created his verse without careful metric count or measurement,

the master of the priestly craft used what was called the *tetrastrofo monorrimo*, a strophe of four lines of alexandrines with a single rhyme scheme (14A, 14A, 14A, 14A). Furthermore the poet was conscious of the resultant importance of his style. This is clear in the following strophe in which the poet speaks with pride of his art and his metric precision in lines which in themselves are an example of the *cuaderna via:*

> Mester traio fermoso, non es de ioglaría,
> mester es sen pecado, ca es de clerecía,
> fablar curso rimado per la cuaderna vía
> a silabas cunctadas ca es gran maestría.

The above is found in the *Libro de Alexandre* [*Book of Alexander*].

2. In subjects, the School of the Priestly Craft was not limited to the narrating of frontier combats as was the minstrel. The poet found his sources not primarily in reality but in literary works on religious and imaginative subjects. Among religious subjects, the cult of the Virgin and the saints was a theme of their poetry whose goal was the inspiration of devotion, as in the case of Gonzalo de Berceo. Imaginative subjects from which the works of the priestly craft were drawn include a number of poems that are related to novelistic tales, such as the *Libro de Apolonio* [*Book of Apolonius*], or the semi-novelistic *Libro de Alexandre* [*Book of Alexander*].

3. In the matter of language, the clerics abandoned the use of Latin since their works were aimed at the general public which did not understand that tongue. However, the lexicon they used was consistently more cultivated than that of the *juglares.*

Gonzalo de Berceo (1195?–1265?)

Gonzalo de Berceo is the first poet of the Castilian tongue whose name has come down to us. His work dates from the thirteenth century. We know little of his life except that he was

born in Berceo (Rioja) and that he was attached to the Benedictine monastery of San Millán de la Cogolla. He died sometime
in the second half of the thirteenth century. He speaks of himself
in the following passage:

> Gonzalo is the name of the man who wrote this piece,
> In San Millán we mentioned, the same the child was
>   reared,
> A native of Berceo, where Saint Millan was born.

The following works are attributed to Berceo:
1. Three lives of the saints: *Santo Domingo de Silos, San
Millán de la Cogolla,* and *Sancta Oria.*
2. Three works dedicated to the Virgin Mary: *Loores de
Nuestra Señora* [*Praises of Our Lady*], *Duelo de la Virgen en el
día de la pasión de su Hijo* [*The Anguish of the Virgin on the
Day of the Passion of Her Son*], and the *Milagros de Nuestra
Señora* [*Miracles of Our Lady*].
3. Three religious poems of varied subject matter: *El
martirio de San Lorenzo* [*Martyrdom of Saint Lorenzo*], *El sac-
rificio de la Misa* [*Sacrifice of the Mass*], and *Los signos que
aparecerán antes del juicio* [*The Signs That Will Appear Before
the Final Judgment*].
In addition, three hymns are attributed to him.

The most personal aspect of Berceo's work appears in his
lives of the saints which furnished a familiar model of energy
and sanctity, and above all of Castilian saints belonging to the
Benedictine Order whose deeds were a part of the daily conversation of the monks with whom Berceo lived. This is true
of his magnificent *Life of Saint Domingo of Silos,* the humble
saint who was a shepherd when he was a "little peasant," then a
"little monk," and finally, once the bishop learned of his saintly
ways, a priest. After a period of retirement in a hermitage, he
went to the monastery of San Millán until he undertook the
establishment of a convent in a small house called "Saint Mary."
His fame spread and he was eventually named prior of the
monastery of San Millán. When the king Don García attempted

to take possession of the monastery's treasure, the saint's defense
of it was remarkable.

La estoria del Sennor San Millán [*History of the Life of
Saint Millan*] shows analogous characteristics. To a certain extent, the life story parallels that of Saint Domingo. Saint Millan
was pastor-hermit, confessor, and worker of miracles, but the
circumstances of his life seem to have been more suitable to the
poet's creative sensitivities. The narrative is not without historical interest in passages concerning the expedition of Abder-
raman, the "Lord of the Pagans," and the Christian victory over
him through the mediations of Saint Millan.

The story that Berceo enjoys telling is one that he identifies
with his own life and beliefs, and with the familiar countryside
of Castile—Silos, Burgos, Castro, Carrión, which are crossed by
the historic rivers Arlanza, Esgueva, Duero; with the glories of
the Benedictine Order—its monastic independence as opposed
to royal power; its reflection of saintliness in humble and devout
lives similar to his own.

The following passage is from *The Life of Saint Millán:*

And when the kings were in the field, their squadrons
    in array,
With lance in rest they onward pressed to mingle in the
    fray;
But soon upon the Christians fell a terror of their foes,—
These were a numerous army, a little handful those.

And whilst the Christian people stood in this
    uncertainty,
Upward toward heaven they turned their eyes and fixed
    their thoughts on high;
And there two persons they beheld, all beautiful and
    bright,—
Even than the pure new-fallen snow their garments
    were more white.

They rode upon two horses, more white than crystal
    sheen,

And arms they bore such as before no mortal man had
    seen;
The one, he held a crosier, a pontiff's mitre wore;
The other held a crucifix,—such man ne'er saw before.

The Christian host, beholding this, straight-way took
    heart again;
They fell upon their bended knees, all resting on the
    plain,
And each one with his clenched fist to smite his breast
    begins,
And promises to God on high he will forsake his sins.

And when the heavenly knights drew near unto the
    battleground,
They dashed among the Moors and dealt unerring
    blows around;
Such deadly havoc there they made the foremost ranks
    along,
A panic terror spread unto the hindmost of the
    throng. . . .

Now he that bore the crosier, and the papal crown
    had on,
Was the glorified Apostle, the brother of Saint John;
And he that held the crucifix, and wore the monkish
    hood,
Was the holy San Millán of Cogolla's neighborhood.
                                    —Anonymous translation

The Life of Saint Oria was written by Berceo when he was
quite old. It gives us the same portrayal of devotion characteristic of the poet. It may have been through a process of artistic
maturity that Berceo decided to attempt to describe a series
of supernatural visions. It is these that form the core of the work
rather than the biographical information one might have
expected.

Finally, *The Martyrdom of Saint Lorenzo,* written in imitation of the *Peristephanon* of Prudentius, relates the famed tor-

turing of the saint who was burned alive on a griddle. The traditional note of humor connected with the story is not lacking in Berceo's version. The martyr asks his torturers to turn him over saying, "It's time to turn me over. On one side I am done."

Berceo's most interesting work from a poetical point of view is the *Milagros de Nuestra Señora* [*Miracles of Our Lady*]. Its structure is limited to presenting cases of hardened sinners who invariably are saved by the divine piety of the Virgin. These miracles are narrated with an ingenuous realism. The most notable passages are "La Casulla de San Ildefonso" ["The Chasuble of Saint Ildefonso"], "La iglesia robada" ["The Church that was Robbed"], "El milagro de Teófilo" ["Theophilus' Miracle"], "El niño judío" ["The Jewish Child"], and "El labrador avaro" ["The Miserly Farmer"].

The *Miracles* begins with a poetical allegory: man is a pilgrim who moves toward God. In his moments of fatigue man can find rest in a field of green which is representative of the Virgin Mary. In this field are found four fountains which symbolize the four Gospels. The birds that sing there are the voices of the fortunate fathers of the Church, and so on. The poem begins with the following passages:

I, Gonzalo de Berceo, in the gentle summertide,
    Wending upon a pilgrimage, came to a meadow's
        side;
All green was it and beautiful, with flowers far and wide,
    A pleasant spot, I ween, wherein the traveler might
        abide.

Flowers with the sweetest odors filled all the sunny air
    And not alone refreshed the sense, but stole the
        mind from care;
On every side a fountain gushed, whose waters pure and
    fair,
        Ice cold beneath the summer sun, but warm in
        winter were. . . .
                . . . . .
The verdure of the meadow green, the odor of the
    flowers,

The grateful shadow of the trees, tempered with
    fragrant showers,
Refreshed me in the burning heat of the sultry noontide
    hours!
    O, one might live upon the balm and fragrance of
    those bowers!
                              —Anonymous translation

Berceo is not, generally speaking, a notably original writer.
He utilized materials from other medieval writers who had
written in Latin. He himself tells us the sources from which he
took the tales he wrote and candidly confesses to his audience
when certain information is lacking: "I have not read this and
thus cannot tell it. . . ."

The *Life of Saint Domingo of Silos* is taken from Grinaldo;
that of Saint Millan from the *Vita Aemiliani* of Branlio, Saint
Oria's from Munius. The *Martyrdom of Saint Lorenzo* is an imitation of the *Peristephanon* of Prudentius and the *Miracles of
Our Lady* coincides, in large part, with the *Miracles* of Gautier
de Coincy, the prior of Vie-sur-Gisne in France, although both
authors probably drew on earlier Latin source material.

What characterizes Berceo is his devout ingenuousness. For
Berceo the world is a struggle between celestial spirits—God,
the Virgin, and the angels—against the infernal—demons, Moors,
and Jews. His whole work is designed to show a pious Catholic
population the examples of virtue furnished in the lives of Jesus,
the Virgin, and the saints. To this purpose he utilizes formulas
borrowed from the *juglares* in his poems, such as "Gentlemen, if
you wish to be patient a moment. . . ." He even imitates the
minstrels in his request for recompense: "What I shall recite is
well worth a glass of wine."

As Menéndez y Pelayo has written:

The realism of the narrative, the delicate candor of the style,
notwithstanding a certain cunning and innocent malice, has
always been very Castilian and is found in the works of the
most devout and ascetic authors; the disagreeable mixture of
monkish and popular elements leaves a special and distinctive

imprint on the art of Berceo. One's mind takes pleasure in representing him as one of his German admirers has imagined him: seated at eventide at the door of his monastery recounting the miracles of the Blessed Virgin or the good deeds of Saint Millan to the burgers of Nájera and to the shepherds of the district of Cañas and drinking with them a glass of good wine from the vineyards bordering the Ebro. More instruction and even more pleasure is to be derived from his poetry than from almost the whole of the balladry of the fifteenth century.

El libro de Apolonio [Book of Apolonius]

This work also dates from the thirteenth century and belongs to the priestly craft. It relates the novelistic adventures of Apolonius, the king of Tyre, who lost his daughter Tarsiana in a shipwreck. After a series of adventures, the king finds his daughter who has become a performing minstrel. The subject matter of this work is derived from the so-called Byzantine novels which characteristically included narration of this type. Who the author was we do not know. The minstrel art of the daughter later on reappears in such figures as Preciosa in Cervantes' *Gitanilla* or *Gypsy Girl,* one of his *Exemplary Novels* of the seventeenth century, and in the Esmeralda of Victor Hugo's *Notre Dame de Paris* in the nineteenth century.

El libro de Alexandre [Book of Alexander]

This work also belongs to the priestly craft. It has been attributed to Juan Lorenzo Segura of Astorga who, like Per Abbat, may have been no more than a copyist. The work dates from the mid-thirteenth century.

Its subject is the life of Alexander the Great, a very popular figure in the Middle Ages. Paradoxically, however, his life was very incorrectly known, a serious study of antiquity not becoming feasible until the period of the Renaissance. It is not surprising, therefore, that the author surrounds Alexander (who lived in the fourteenth century B.C.) with a wholly anachronistic court of counts, bishops, peers, and knights errant, nor that he makes of his protagonist the hero of fantastic adventures such as his descent to the bottom of the sea enclosed in a cask or his flight through the air drawn by two monstrous birds.

The Thirteenth Century

II. Prose

Alfonso the Wise

Alfonso X (1221–1284), known to his contemporaries as "el Sabio" or "the Wise," has the distinction of being responsible for the beginning of Spanish prose literature.

Although Alfonso the Wise was king of Castile and a writer in his own right, his fame rests primarily on his importance as one of Spain's greatest patrons of learning. Consequently his life must be considered from the standpoint of the intellect as well as from that of politics. The political life of the monarch was marked by the failure of his aspirations to the throne of the Holy Roman Empire, a position at the pinnacle of the medieval hierarchy of Europe and as such coveted by Christian rulers who, once elected, could consider themselves heirs to the ancient Roman emperors and the political leaders of Christianity. He also had to contend with the rebellions of his son, the future Sancho IV. Alfonso was the son of the famous warrior king Ferdinand III the Saint, but he did not inherit the military spirit that brought his father the impressive triumphs of the recapture of Cordova and of Seville from the Infidel. He was, as a matter of fact, hard pressed militarily by the Moors of Granada.

Nevertheless, although Alfonso failed in the realms of the military and the political, his intellectual life was of tremendous benefit to science and letters. He gathered around him the finest minds of his time, without regard to race, origin, or religion. His court became one of the great centers of learning in the civilized world of his day. Furthermore, Alfonso X and the intellectuals who surrounded him tended to make of Spain the center of a universal political and cultural outlook. Educated men of every land, united under the cultural impulse of the king, collaborated in the writing of works.

While the king undoubtedly took some part in writing the works attributed to him, it is obvious that Alfonso himself did not actually create all the works that appear under his name. Except for the *Cantigas de Santa María* [*Songs to the Virgin Mary*] which, in their intimate and personal lyricism came directly from the pen of the monarch, the bulk of the literature attributed to him could not have been produced by a man who was busily occupied with affairs of state.

In one of his works, the *General Estoria* [*General History*], the king speaks to this point: "The king is said to have written this book not because he writes it with his own hand, but because he set forth the general outline, has made corrections and various changes and has shown how the work was to be composed. . . . It is just as when it is said that the king has built a palace; this is not said because the king has built it with his own hands but because he has commanded it to be constructed and has provided the materials to do so."

In addition to directing the composition of the works, Alfonso also intervened in matters of style. He tells us this in the Prologue to the *Libro de la Octava Esfera* [*Book of the Eighth Sphere*]: "And afterwards the aforesaid king made corrections and supervised the composition and eliminated repetitious phrases and expressions that were not in good Castilian; he substituted other expressions wherever necessary and adjusted the language himself and also had for collaborators Master John of Mesina, Master John of Cremona, the aforementioned Yehuda and Samuel. . . ."

The preoccupation with man—his past, his present, and his future—is a predominant theme in the extensive work of the king and his collaborators:

1. Man's past is studied in the historical works, the *Crónica General* [*General Chronicle*], a history of Spain up to the period of Ferdinand the Saint, and the *General e Grande Estoria* [*General and Great History*], an attempt at writing a universal history.

These books are of exceptional interest for several reasons. One is because the king drew on the Bible and on historical works then extant but produced earlier, and on legends and oral traditions that had come down to his own time. The latter are of particular importance as they have permitted a partial reconstruction of *cantares de gesta* which have been lost. Alfonso's history, however, was not a critical one in our present sense, but rather a narration of historical events with a moral and didactic purpose.

The historical event described in the following passage depicts the Battle of Guadalete:

> King Rodrigo and the Christians were vanquished and killed; the noble Goths who in many battles had vanquished and overcome other kingdoms were in their turn vanquished and overcome and their proud banners cast into the dust . . . the people that had struck fear in the hearts of men as does the thunderclap frighten; that people that had been so valiant and prized was crushed by the power of Mohammed. . . .

Once the author has given the description, however, he proceeds to draw a moral lesson from the event:

> From this we can learn that one must avoid vanity and false pride: the rich man shall not preen himself on his riches, nor the powerful man on his power, the strong man on his strength, the wise man on his wisdom, the man of rank on his position nor on his possessions. He should take pride in serving God, for it is He who wounds and He who binds up and cares for and cures, for all the earth is His. All people, all lands, all languages are altered and change, but God the Creator lasts forever and is in His glory.

Another point of interest is that we find in the historical books an exalted and eloquent sense of nationality expressed in prose that, despite some usages that are now archaic, is much more easily understood by a modern Spaniard than is the prose, say, of Chaucer by a modern Englishman. Consider, for instance, the following passage from *Loor de España* [*In Praise of Spain*] in which Alfonso speaks of the entire Peninsula as under the name *España:*

Spain is like God's paradise. It is watered by five major rivers which are the Ebro, Duero, Tajo, Guadalquivir and Guadiana, and between them there are high mountains and extensive lands. The valleys and the plains are wide and be-cause of the goodness of the earth and the waters of the rivers there are many and abundant fruits. Most of Spain is irrigated by streams and fountains and there are wells wherever they are needed.

Spain abounds in grain, is delectable in fruits, swarms with fish. It savors of milk and the products thereof, is filled with deer and game, covered with cattle, luxuriant in horses, well-provided with mules, secure and well-supplied with cas-tles, fortunate in its wines, abounding in bread, rich in metals, in lead, in tin, in mercury, in iron, in copper, silver, gold, precious stones, all manner of marbles, in salts from the sea, from the earth and from the mountains, and many other minerals, blue pigment, ochre, alum and many others that are not found in other countries, plenteous in silk and the products thereof, sweet with honey and sugar, well-lighted with wax, copious in oils and favored with saffron.

Spain is above all resourceful, fearless and strong in bat-tle, quick and eager, loyal to the Lord, cultivated through its studies, refined in its language, accomplished in all ways. No land on earth can equal it in abundance or in fortresses and few are larger in territory. Spain is far advanced in great-ness and is prized for its loyalty. Oh Spain, there is no tongue or intelligence that can truly recount your worth!

2. Man's present is regulated by juridical works which make up the *Partidas* [*Districts*], a book which is both a code of laws and a series of counsels and norms for the regulating of the life

of one's subjects in various aspects such as education, horseman-
ship, clothing, customs, and so on. For example, the following
passage advises on matters of education:

> *On the manner in which teachers should divulge knowl-
> edge.* . . . Well and loyally should teachers divulge their
> knowledge to their students by reading them books and by
> explaining things to them to the best of their ability. And
> once they have begun the study of a book they should con-
> tinue until they have finished the books they have begun.

The matter discussed below has a somewhat more practical aspect:

> *How all universities should have a messenger boy.* . . .
> There should be a messenger boy, or what is called a "bidel-
> lus" in Latin, at the university. It shall be his responsibility
> to go through the school announcing holidays and festivities
> by order of the director of studies. Furthermore if there are
> those who have books to sell or who want to buy them, he
> shall so announce and tell what books there are and where to
> go to get them. . . .

In the field of politics, the *Partidas* tended to strengthen the
royal authority, substituting Germanic law in which the king
and nobles signed a pact which could be broken (as in the case
of the Cid) for Roman law in which the king was a natural lord.
Also of great interest for what they reveal of the customs of
the epoch are the *Libros de ajedrez, dados et tablas* [*Books of
Chess, Dice and Gaming*].

3. Man's future is deciphered in the *Libros del saber de
astronomia* [*Books on the Science of Astronomy*], a treatise on
astrology which instructs in ways of divining the future according to a good or bad star and through the consultation of constellations. Many of the books of Alfonso the Wise on astronomy
do, however, have a scientific value as they translate the works
of great Oriental astronomers and thus incorporate the most advanced knowledge of the times. The most notable are the *Cuatro*

libros de las estrellas [*Four Books of the Stars*] which are a study of the constellations.

The Fourteenth Century

I. Bourgeois and Realistic Literature

The first major works of Castilian literature may be separated into two groups: works that exalt the warrior and those that exalt religion. The Schools of the Minstrel Craft and of the Priestly Craft responded to the needs of both Christian groups of the twelfth and thirteenth centuries. As we advance toward the fourteenth century, however, we observe that along with the illiterate classes, the nobles and the serfs, and the cultured ones, the clergy, there appears a new social element: that of the middle class, largely merchant, which inhabited the nascent towns. As a consequence, a bourgeois literature, lacking equally in military enthusiasm and in religious fervor, came into being for this new element in society. It was a literature whose primary aim was to entertain these people whose tastes were not very highly developed and who had a predominantly practical view of life; a literature that was bourgeois, realistic, and satirical and whose only purpose was the diversion of the public for which it was created, although it did frequently have a sententious and educational tone. It was the age of Boccaccio, of Chaucer, and of the French *fabliaux*.

In Castilian literature, the realistic and satirical tone appears in the great poets of the second period of the School of the Priestly Craft, the *Arcipreste* or Archpriest of Hita and the Chancellor López de Ayala.

The Archpriest of Hita

The scant data which we possess on the life of Juan Ruiz, the Archpriest of Hita, come, in large part, from what we deduce from his work. We have little information about the man himself.

We know, for instance, that he was a native of Alcala: "A man it is from Alcala, and greetings warm he sends." We also know that he was the Archpriest of Hita and that he died around 1350. His literary work appeared in a "book of songs" which he and posterity have entitled the *Libro de buen amor* [*Book of Good Love*].

The documentary value of the work is considerable. In it, as Menéndez y Pelayo has pointed out, the whole of Spanish society of the fourteenth century may be studied. The protagonist of the *Libro de buen amor* is the Archpriest himself who represents himself in the work under various guises. His appearance is not an enviable one, as we learn in the following passage:

> His figure is uncommon tall, with members large and
> stout;
> He's hairy, with no little head; his bull neck bulges out.
> Although it's short, his hair is dark, and long ears fom
> him sprout.

We cannot always be certain that the vices which appear in these pages are those of the author himself. however, for he is constantly censoring them. The freedom and naturalness with which he recounts various episodes, plus the fact that he was imprisoned by the order of the Archbishop of Toledo, Don Gil de Albornoz, has led to the belief that the Archpriest was a libertine and woman-chaser. Today we believe that the *Book of Good Love* is a compendium of vices and virtues, some of which the author exemplifies himself and others by real or allegorical characters.

The *Libro de buen amor* is an amalgamation of very diverse material among which narrative episodes predominate. Of these it is the major one, autobiographical in form, which has the Archpriest as its protagonist. He tells of his love affairs and of Trotaconventos, an old woman without morals and given to intrigue, who helps things along for him. In spite of the coarseness of his language, however, the Archpriest wishes to present himself in the guise of a moralizer. He explains that he has written his book with the aim of convincing his readers of the vanity of worldly love:

Wherefore, I with my small understanding and much and great rudeness perceiving how much wealth can cause the soul and body to be lost, and the many evils that accompany it and bring to pass the foolish love of the sins of the world, choosing and loving with good intentions salvation and the glory of paradise for my soul, I made this little writing for the glorification of the good and I prepared this new book in which are written some of the manners and masteries and deceitful subtleties of the foolish love of the world which some persons follow in order to sin.

—Translation by Elisha K. Kane

Indeed, throughout his work and especially in his fables he moralizes, although he does it within the strictures of his joyous satire which often is in sharp contrast to his didactic intent, as we see in this passage on money:

Certain Examples of the Power
Which Sir Money Possesses

Much power, indeed, Sir money has and much for him
we dabble,
He makes the dolt a man of worth and sets him o'er the
rabble,
He makes the lame leap up and run, he makes the deaf-
mute babble;
Why those who have no hands at all will after money
scrabble!

Suppose a man's an utter fool, a farmer or a boor,
With money he becomes a sage, a knight with prestige
sure,
In fact the greater grows his wealth the greater his allure,
While he not even owns himself who is in money poor.

. . . . .

Sir Money breaks those mortal bonds that chain a man
for life,

He empties stocks and prisons grim with noisome
    vermin rife,
But one who has no gold to give must wear the iron wife;
All up and down throughout the world Sir Money
    causes strife.

Myself have seen real miracles occur through money's
    power
As when a man condemned to die is freed within the hour
Or when those innocent the gallows presently devour
Or when a soul is prayed to heaven or damned in hell
    to cower.

Sir money often confiscates a poor man's goods and lands,
His vines, his furniture and all the things his toil
    commands,
The world has got the itch and scab of money on
    its hands;
When Money winks his golden eye, there justice stock-
    still stands.

Sir Money makes a knight presumptuous from a village
    clown
And out of peasant farmers chooses coronet and crown;
With money anyone can strut in gilt and broidered gown
While all his neighbors kiss his hands and bow their
    bodies down.

                —Translation by Elisha K. Kane

As a poet the Archpriest has an unquestionably great power.
His style is direct, vigorous, full of color, and of considerable
variety. On the one hand we find songs of the types popular with
blind men and with students, or the crude *cantigas de serranas,*
songs of mountain girls. On the other hand, *The Book of Good
Love* contains a number of lovely and delicate poems written in
praise of the Virgin Mary. They show a deep and sincere religious fervor as can be perceived in the following example:

Hail Mary, glorious as the sun,
Hail Virgin, holy, precious one,
How wide Thy blessed mercies run
    On us for Aye.

Thou full of grace and spotless being
    Mine advocate,
  In mercy work most gracious Queen,
This miracle before my seeing
    With kindness great;
Do Thou with kind and gracious mien
Protect me all unharmed, serene,
  From shameful death, so that I can
  Give unto Thee the praise I plan
    By night and day.

God dwells in Thee, resplendent star
  Who art the balm and sure of woe,
    Thy features, beautiful and bright
All glorious are;
    No stain of sin doth in Thee show.
    Then in the name of each delight
    Thou hadst, to Thee I humbly cry,
    Oh spotless rose, guard lest I
    In folly stray.

Thou art most blest, and without peer,
  Who still a Virgin, gavest birth.
    By all the angels art Thou praised
In heaven clear.
  By him Thou broughtst into the earth,
    And by that grace where Thou art raised,
    Oh blessed flower, oh rose divine,
    Most pious one, I beg Thee, shine
    Upon my way.

—Translation by Elisha K. Kane

In style the *Libro de buen amor* belongs to the School of
the Priestly Craft, although more flexible and highly developed

forms appear in it, denoting tendencies in the direction of subsequent poetic attitudes and expression.

Chancellor López de Ayala

López de Ayala was born in Vitoria in northern Spain in
1332. He led a very agitated and stormy existence because of
various political changes. He was in the service of five different
kings. He was twice imprisoned, once by the Black Prince and
once by the Portuguese. He served as the ambassador of Juan I
and of Enrique II to France and became chancellor of Castile.
He died in 1407.

In character Ayala is a moralist. He attacks the defects of
the society in which he lives. The abuses of lawyers, merchants,
moneylenders and Jews, and the scandal of the religious schism
all receive due reproach in his *Rimado de palacio* [*Palace
Rhymes*]. His own life, however, is not without its reprehensible aspects. In his political life, the way in which he confesses
to having laid down the arms of King Don Pedro to take up
those of Enrique de Trastamara when the latter ascended to the
throne ("because the affairs of Don Pedro were not going well")
demonstrates his lack of loyalty and his opportunism.

López de Ayala was a serious student of the political ideas
of the Roman Empire. He was a firm believer in a strong state
presided over by firm moral authority. In his *Rimado,* he outlines the nine factors he considers necessary in the making of a
great monarch. The first three, dealing with embassies, letters,
and monies, may be adjudged from outside the kingdom. The
second three stem from within the kingdom: well-regulated cities,
adequate inns, and able governors. Last of all he speaks of the
Court itself: the great monarch must distinguish himself through
his palace, his counselors, and the table he sets. The *Rimado de
palacio* is a long and very complex composition. Part of it is
didactic in intent and expounds the principles of the Christian
religion; another part contains political and social satire. Still
another is fundamentally moral in outlook and discusses at
length questions of vice and virtue.

Another part of López de Ayala's poetical work consists of a fragmentary work entitled *Deytado sobre el cisma de Occidente* [*Treatise on the Schism in the West*]. It is an interesting and agonizing commentary on the schism of Avignon which at that time was dividing Christianity. It includes lyrical passages and religious songs and was probably written during one of the Chancellor's imprisonments.

Ayala, like the Archpriest of Hita, gives a satirical portrayal of the society of his times. The Chancellor's satire, however, is bitter and austere, whereas that of Juan Ruiz is joyous and full of good humor.

Aljamiada or Morisco Literature

The term *aljamiada* is applied to the literature of the Moriscos, Moors who lived in Christian territory and whose works were written in the Romance tongue but utilized Arabic script. An example is the *Poema de Yuçuf* [*Poem of Yusuf*] which gives a Koranic version of the Old Testament story of Joseph.

Tales and Apologues

The most popular form of this type of literature, written for entertainment and realistic and bourgeois in outlook, are the short stories and apologues, some of which were of Oriental origin. Already around the middle of the thirteenth century the translation of Oriental tales and stories from the Indian, Persian, and Arabic literatures had begun. These swiftly and easily found their way into Castilian literature. Given the proximity of the Moslems who at that time still occupied major areas of the Iberian Peninsula, this was a natural development. Such was the case of the book called *Calila y Dimna* which Alfonso the Wise had translated while he was still crown prince. The work is a collection of fables from India, first translated into Persian, second into Arabic, and then into Castilian. The title is taken from the names of two brother wolves who are the shrewd counselors in the court of a lion. They are the protagonists in the first of a lengthy series of stories and fables of moralizing intent in which humility, temperance, friendship, and the love of God are held up as the highest good. Consequently the stories were immediately accepted in the Christian world whose moral precepts were so similar.

Other works of this tradition which were widely read include the *Sendebar o Libro de los engannos e asayamientos de las mugeres* [*Book of the Wiles and the Shrewdness of Women*] and the book of *Barlaam y Josafat,* a Christian adaptation of a legend based on the life of Buddha. Still another collection of stories of Oriental origin, written in Latin however, was compiled by Pedro Alfonso, a converted Aragonese Jew, with the title of *Disciplina Clericales.*

Other stories were of classical or French origin. During the Middle Ages the fables of Phaedrus and of Aesop, also known under the name of Isopete, had wide circulation. Also some Spanish writers—the Archpriest of Hita in particular—wrote realistic and satirical stories after the style of the French *fabliaux,* short tales marked by realism and satire.

Don Juan Manuel

Don Juan Manuel was the most characteristic prose writer of the fourteenth century.

He was born in Escalona in the year 1282. He was the nephew of Alfonso the Wise and the grandson of Ferdinand the Saint. He is considered one of the most representative figures of his time. From his youth on he fought in the wars against the Moors and in the domestic struggles motivated by ambitions of the nobility during the reigns of Ferdinand IV and Alfonso XI. He died around 1349.

Both by reason of his birth and by virtue of his activities as a warrior, Don Juan Manuel participated fully in the political life of his times. He saw himself as a representative man of his epoch and wrote at length on problems of government. He conceived of Spain as a single entity presided over by Castile. He dreamed of the Holy Roman Empire which his uncle King Alfonso had sought in vain. He recognized the supreme authority of the Papacy which he believed, in accord with the ideas of his day, should be in harmony with the Holy Roman Emperor; he wrote that "they should be in close agreement."

In the main, his political ideas are to be found in his *Libro de los estados* [*Book of States*], a work of philosophico-didactic bent. The work is structured on the so-called legend of Barlaam and Josephat and tells the story of a prince named Joas whose father, the pagan king Morovan, has him educated by the pagan sage Turin. Any idea of human suffering is hidden from the prince. One day, however, Joas and Turin have a dramatic encounter with a burial group and the prince thus discovers what had been so carefully hidden from him. The questions which Prince Joas raises as a result of this experience are satisfactorily answered only by a Christian holy man who subsequently converts the people of the story to Christianity.

Don Juan Manuel's social concepts and ideas about the society of his day are contained in the *Libro del caballero et del escudero* [*Book of the Knight and the Squire*]. The work is divided into two parts: one in which the knight tells the squire what a knight's mission in society should be and another which is a curious encyclopedic section on theology, astronomy, and the natural sciences in all of which the idea of the omnipresence of God is paramount. The work also sets forth a hierarchy of class structure for society:

> For the estates of this world are three in number: *oradores* (clergy), laborers and defenders (knights) . . . I consider the highest estate to be that of the priest who is officient at mass . . . (Chapter XVII). . . . the greatest and most honorable estate is that of the layman in the ranks of the knights . . . for the duty of the knight is the defense of others (Chapter XVIII). And the grace of God will give him succour and the intelligence to know his duties and the avoidance of evil deeds (Chapter XIX).

The didactico-moral work of Don Juan Manuel consists of the *Libro de Patronio,* more frequently known as the *Libro del Conde Lucanor* [*Book of Count Lucanor*]. The work is a collection of apologues in which the youthful Count Lucanor receives the wise counseling of his prudent tutor Patriono. The following selection, consisting of a narrative with a moral at the end, is typical of the book:

> Sir Count, there was once a woman called Doña Tru-hana who was more poor than rich. One day she went to the market carrying a container of honey on her head. As she walked along she would buy herself some eggs. From the eggs she would hatch chickens and these she would sell and with the money buy herself some ewes. She went on that way buying with her earnings until she had become richer than any of her neighbors. With all that wealth she expected to get she imagined how she would marry off her sons and daughters and how she would walk along the street with sons-in-law and daughters-in-law and how everyone would comment on her good luck at becoming so rich after having been as poor as she had been. The idea pleased her so that she began to laugh over her good fortune and as she laughed she slapped her hand to her head and forehead. With that the container of honey fell to the ground and broke, and great was her grief that she had broken the container of honey. . . .
>
> And you, Sir Count, if you want what is told you and is of concern to you to become a reality, take good care that things are well done and not just ephemeral and dubious promises.

Didactic Poetry: Sem Tob

The Jewish writer Sem Tob (1290?–1369?) was a rabbi from Carrión. He is the author of the famous *Proverbios morales* [*Moral Proverbs*] which he dedicated to King Pedro the Cruel. The work is composed of 686 quatrains into which the author has compressed a universal morality drawn from various sources rather than from a single specific religion.

The Fourteenth Century

II. The Romancero or Ballad Tradition

One of the most characteristic elements of Spanish literature and one which has lasted into our own times in an oral as well as a written tradition is the immense number of brief poems of a narrative type known as *romances* or ballads. The body of this enormous production is known as the *Romancero*. This all-inclusive designation incorporates various categories and divisions according to subject matter and origins. Metrically the ballad is composed of an indefinite number of octosyllabic lines which have assonant rhyme in the paired lines and are unrhymed in the odd lines. Originally predominantly epic and heroic, the form later took on a lyrical tone as well. The fourteenth and fifteenth centuries mark the beginning and high point of the early *romances*.

The *Romances viejos* or "old ballads" have come down to us in an oral tradition and are anonymous. What is their origin? The theory, now outmoded, that the ballads were the creation of the common people and had existed before the first *cantares de gesta* or epic poems, in which case these long poems supposedly derived from the shorter ballads, has been disproved. The contrary is now generally accepted, i.e., that the *romances* are nothing more than fragments of the best-received and best-known of the *cantares de gesta* recited by the minstrel-poets. The audience would remember the moments of greatest excitement of a performance, applauding the recitation and then frequently learning and reciting the favorite passages themselves. Thus the first ballads are fragmentary portions of epic poetry from Castile which were transmitted independently by word of mouth; the octosyllabic lines are the hemistichs into which the longer lines of the epic poems were divided.

Consequently the author of the ballad and of the *cantar de gesta* was one and the same. The general public did not con-

tribute to the creation of the ballad except in distorting it as the
oral transmission from person to person gave rise to variations. A
number of different versions of the same poem, according to the
regions and the epochs in which they were to be found, were produced by this process.

In some cases texts were distorted until they became almost
unintelligible. One of the well-known ballads originally depicted
the Emperor Nero standing on the Tarpeyan rock contemplating
the burning of Rome. The poem began as follows:

> Mira Nero de Tarpeya
> a Roma como se ardía.

> Nero from the Tarpeyan rock
> at burning Rome did look.

The public, however, through ignorance and the similarities of
sounds, joined "mira" with "Nero" and got the word *marinero*
with the resultant first line: "Marinero de Tarpeya" [Sailor from
the Tarpeyan rock].

One of the ballads, *Durandarte,* has been made world famous
by Don Quixote's references to it. It is a part of the Arthurian
cycle and chivalric in theme:

> Durandarte, Durandarte
>
> Durandarte, Durandarte,
> Son of fame, and heir of praise;
> Durandarte, if thou love me,
> Let us talk of former days.
> Tell me if thou hast forgotten
> Thy enamor'd time of youth
> When with sports and songs of music
> Thou didst show thy love, thy truth;
> When the Moors retired before thee
> When my smile conducted thee;
> Now, alas!—am I forgotten:
> Why hast thou forgotten me?
> Words are all deceitful, warrior!"

THE MIDDLE AGES 39

"Lady! if I broke my vow,
Thou wert treacherous,—Thou unfaithful,—
Thou didst break thy pledge,—even thou.
Lady! Thou didst love Gayferos
When I roam'd in exile drear;
And was not the love I sigh'd for;
Though thou hadst been far more fair,
Rather than submit to insult,
I would die in lone despair.

—Translation by John Bowring

Romances juglarescos *or Minstrel Ballads*

As a result of the enormous popularity of the ballads, the *juglares* or minstrels built their performances around the *romances*. Even when the earlier epic poems had gone out of style, they created short narrative poems that imitated them. These works are known as *romances juglarescos* or minstrel ballads as they are already separate and distinct from the epic poetry. Their subject matter is lighter and more sentimental, their heroes may be Frenchmen such as Charlemagne or English such as Lancelot, and they frequently narrate fictional love stories and adventures. The following ballad of the minstrel tradition has been particularly popular, probably because of the air of mystery the tale creates:

Count Arnaldos

Oh, who could have such fortune
    On the sea so far away
As once had Count Arnaldos
    On the morn of St. John's Day,
He was hunting on that morning
    With a falcon on his hand;
When he saw a small ship coming,
    Coming to the land,
Its sails they were all silken,
    And its rigging lace, but strong,

And the captain on the foredeck
    Was singing such a song
That it made the sea all quiet,
    And it lulled the wind to sleep,
And it lured the silver fishes
    To swim up from the deep.

It drew the birds from Heaven
    To rest upon the mast.
Then up spoke Count Arnaldos,
    Then up he spoke at last;
"For God's sweet sake, oh Captain,
    A boon I crave of thee;
For I never heard such singing
    On land or on the sea.
Oh, teach me that strange chantey!"
    Then the Captain said, said he:
"I do not sing that chantey
    Save to him who goes with me."

—Translation by Nicholson B. Adams

Other ballads, however, were based on historical events
familiar to the Spaniard, such as the following poem which recounts the death of King Pedro the Cruel of Castile in 1368 at
the hands of his half-brother, Henry of Trastamara:

The Death of Don Pedro

Henry and King Pedro clasping,
    Hold in straining arms each other;
Tugging hard and closely grasping,
    Brother proves his strength with brother.

Harmless pastime, sport fraternal,
    Blends not thus their limbs in strife;
Either aims, with rage infernal,
    Naked dagger, sharpened knife.

Close Don Henry grapples Pedro,
    Pedro holds Don Henry strait,
Breathing, this, triumphant fury,
    That, despair and mortal hate.

Sole spectator of the struggle,
    Stands Don Henry's page afar,
In the chase who bore his bugle,
    And who bore his sword in war.

Down they go in deadly wrestle,
    Down upon the earth they go;
Fierce King Pedro has the vantage,
    Stout Don Henry falls below.

Marking then the fatal crisis,
    Up the page of Henry ran,
By the waist he caught Don Pedro,
    Aiding thus the fallen man.

"King to place, or to depose him,
    Dwelleth not in my desire,
But the duty which he owes him
    To his master pays the squire."

Now Don Henry has the upmost,
    Now King Pedro lies beneath,
In his heart his brother's poniard
    Instant finds its bloody sheath.

Thus with mortal gasp and quiver,
    While the blood in bubbles welled,
Fled the fiercest soul that ever
    In a Christian bosom dwelled.

—Translation by Sir Walter Scott

Romances Fronterizos y Moriscos *or* Frontier and Moorish Ballads

The final period of the Reconquest is characterized by its great number of truces which gave birth to a series of incidents, tourneys, and adventures of a chivalric nature which the minstrels converted into the subject matter of their frontier ballads. Much of the narrative material made reference to the Moslems who were no longer seen as the fanatical enemy but as a high-spirited and chivalrous people who became the protagonists of a new type of ballad, the *romance morisco* or Moorish ballad, as in the following passage from "The Ballad of Abenamar."

> Abenamar, Abenamar,
> O thou Moor of *Moreria*
> There were many signs and aspects
> On the day that thou wert born,
> Calm and lovely was the ocean,
> Bright and full the moon above.
> Moor, the child of such an aspect
> Never ought to answer falsely.
> Then replied a Moorish captive
> (you shall hear the Moor's reply):
> Nor will I untruly answer,
> Though I died for saying truth.
> I am son of Moorish sire,
> My mother was a Christian slave.
> In my childhood, in my boyhood,
> Often would my mother bid me
> Never know the liar's shame. . . .

> —Translation by Robert Southey

In the following ballad from "Ay de mí, Alhama," the loss of the town of Alhama and the foretelling of the taking of Granada by the Christians is the central theme:

The Moorish King rides up and down,
Through Granada's royal town;
From Elvira's gates to those
Of Bivarambla on he goes.
        Woe is me, Alhama!

Letters to the monarch tell
How Alhama's city fell;
In the fire the scroll he threw,
And the messenger he slew.
        Woe is me, Alhama!

He quits his mule and mounts his horse,
And through the streets directs his course;
Through the street of Zacatín
To the Alhambra spurring in.
        Woe is me, Alhama!

When the Alhambra's walls he gained
On the moment he ordained
That the trumpet straight should sound
With the silver clarion round.
        Woe is me, Alhama!

And when the hollow drums of war
Beat the loud alarm afar,
That the Moors of town and plain
Might answer to the martial strain,
        Woe is me, Alhama!

Then the Moors, by this aware,
That bloody Mars recalled them there,
One by one, and two by two,
To a mighty squadron grew.
        Woe is me, Alhama!

Out then spoke an aged Moor
In these words the King before,
"Wherefore call on us, O King?
What may mean this gathering?"
        Woe is me, Alhama!

"Friends, ye have, alas, to know
Of a most disastrous blow,
That the Christians, stern and bold,
Have obtained Alhama's hold."
　　Woe is me, Alhama!

Out then spake old Alfaqui,
With his beard so white to see,
"Good King! thou art justly served!
Good King! this thou hast deserved.
　　Woe is me, Alhama!

"By thee were slain, in evil hour,
The Abencerrage, Granada's flower,
And strangers were received by thee
Of Cordova the chivalry.
　　Woe is me, Alhama!

"And for this, O King, is sent
On thee a double chastisement;
Thee and thine, thy crown and realm;
One last wreck shall overwhelm.
　　Woe is me, Alhama!

"He who holds no laws in awe,
He must perish by the law;
And Granada must be won,
And thyself with her undone!"
　　Woe is me Alhama!

—Translation by Lord Byron

There were also *villancicos* or songs like the following one
about three Moorish maidens:

Three dark maids,—I loved them when
In Jaën,—
Axa, Fátima, Marién.

Three dark maids who went together
Picking olives in clear weather,
My, but they were in fine feather
In Jaën,—
Axa, Fátima, Marién.

There the harvests they collected,
Turning home with hearts dejected,
Haggard where the sun reflected
In Jaën,—
Axa, Fátima, Marién.

Three dark Moors so lovely they—
Three dark Moors so lovely they
Plucked the apples on that day
Near Jaën,—
Axa, Fátima, Marién.

—Translation by Thomas Walsh

Ballads and legendary material about the Cid, and in particular the hero's youth or *mocedades* and episodes which are not a part of the *Poema de mio Cid* that portrays, as we have seen, the mature man, also belong to this period. Passages like the one reproduced below were the source of such plays as Guillen de Castro's *Mocedades del Cid* [*Youth of the Cid*] from which, in turn, Corneille's later drama was drawn.

The Cid's Courtship

Now, of Rodrigo de Bivar great was the fame that run,
How he five kings had vanquished, proud Moormen
    every one;
And how, when they consented to hold of him
    their ground,
He freed them from the prison wherein they had
    been bound.

To the good King Fernando, in Burgos where he lay,
Came then Ximena Gomez, and thus to him did say:—
"I am Don Gomez' daughter, in Gormez Count was he;
Him slew Rodrigo of Bivar in battle valiantly.

"Now am I come before you, this day a boon to crave,—
And it is that I to husband may this Rodrigo have.
Grant this, and I shall hold me a happy damosell,
Much honored shall I hold me,—I shall be married well.

I know he's born for thriving, none like him
        in the land,
I know that none in battle against his spear may stand;
Forgiveness is well pleasing in God our Saviour's view,
And I forgive him freely, for that my sire he slew."

Right pleasing to Fernando was the thing she
        did propose;
He writes his letter swiftly, and forth his foot-page goes,
I wot, when young Rodrigo saw how the King
        did write,
He leapt on Bavieca,—I wot his leap was light.

With his own troop of true men forthwith
        he took the say,
Three hundred friends and kinsmen, all gently born
        were they;
All in one color mantled, in armor gleaming gay,
New were both scarf and scabbard, when they went
        forth that day.

The King came out to meet him, with words of
        hearty cheer;
Quoth he: "My good Rodrigo, right welcome
        art thou here;
This girl Ximena Gomez would have thee for her lord,
Already for the slaughter her grace she doth accord.

"I pray thee be consenting, my gladness will be great;
Thou shalt have lands in plenty, to strengthen
        thine estate."

"Lord King," Rodrigo answers, "in this and all beside,
Command, and I'll obey thee, the girl shall be
    my bride!"

But when the fair Ximena came forth to
    plight her hand,
Rodrigo gazing on her, his face could not command.
He stood and blushed before her;—Thus at the last
    said he:
"I slew thy sire, Ximena, but not in villany;

"In no disguise I slew him,—man against man I stood;
There was some wrong between us, and I did shed
    his blood,
I slew a man, I owe a man,—fair lady, by God's grace!
An honored husband thou shalt have in thy dead
    father's place."

—Translation by J. G. Lockhart

Early Medieval Theater

During the Middle Ages the traditions of the classical drama
of antiquity had dropped out of sight. As a result a type of drama
popular with the general public, one which had no direct relationship to the Greek and Latin theater, slowly took form. It
was an ingenuous and primitive drama whose beginnings lay in
the works of the minstrel-poets or *joculatores* who entertained the
public with their recitations and performances. Nevertheless its
first real expression came in the presentation of religious scenes
which the Church used as part of the festivities of the liturgical
calendar. These performances were first given in the church itself
but later on took place in the town square.

The scenery for these plays was extremely simple and their
subjects usually were the Nativity or the Passion. Occasionally
an episode from the life of one of the saints was presented. The
different parts of the performance took place in various "places"

or against a small section of the backdrop which was marked off for this purpose.

At the same time that this liturgical drama was flourishing, there was also a secular theater that was burlesque and satirical in nature. No examples of these *juegos de escarnio* or plays of mockery are extant, but their existence is attested in various writings of the period. The form corresponds to the *jeux* in medieval France and marks the genesis of the short play known down to the present day in Spain and called by various names such as *paso, entremés* and *sainete*.

As the Castilian medieval drama developed it centered on two principal categories or cycles, the Nativity and the Passion of Our Lord. The first of these includes the *misterio* or mystery play known as the *Auto de los Reyes Magos* [*Biblical Play of the Magi*] which is the earliest dramatic text in Spanish to have come down to us and the only example of liturgical drama in the Peninsula. It is dated by some scholars as early as the middle of the twelfth century.

Although the manuscript is incomplete, it contains enough for us to comprehend the ingenuousness and devout simplicity of this type of literature. In the beginning scenes, Melchor, Gaspar, and Baltazar each have a monologue in which they tell of their astonishment at seeing the star announcing the birth of the Christ Child. They meet and undertake the journey to go to adore Him. Because of the disappearance of the star, the Magi go to Herod to ask him to tell them the birthplace of the Messiah. Herod hides his wrath and makes a pretense of wanting to go to adore the new-born Child also. Then he calls together his rabbis for consultation. At this point the manuscript comes to an end.

The work is characterized by the puerility of its expression and the exaggerated portrayal of its characters, such as the skepticism of the kings, the anger of Herod, and the bad faith of the rabbis. In short, it is a drama for an uneducated and immature public whose religion is fervently and deeply felt. The following are the principal scenes from the *auto*:

Scene I

The Kings Tell of the Discovery of the Star.
MELCHIOR (*alone*):
Oh Lord Creator, there afar
I see the marvel of Thy star,
Now for the first time in my sight,
Its time of birth has been this night.
Born then is the Saviour dear,
The Lord of all both far and near?
Can this be true then what I say
Or foolish prattle then, I pray?
I'll take a look another night,
For then I'll know if 'tis still bright.

Am I then right in what I say?
In everything, in all I see this day.
Another sign it could not be?
No, this it is and this must be!
Into the world of our Lord of woman born
In cold December's time forlorn.
To Him I'll go and Him adore,
The Lord of all forevermore.

(GASPER and BALTAZAR repeat, in monologues of their own, the same discovery. They decide to present themselves before HEROD.)

Scene III

(The Meeting with Herod.)

GASPAR: . . . I am called Gaspar,
            This man is Melchior and the other, Baltazar,
            The King of Kings is born and Lord of all
            Whose reign of peace shall bring war's fall.

HEROD: Is this the truth in everything?

GASPAR: My faith it is, oh mighty king.

HEROD: How then do you know all this?
            What proof do you have of this?

GASPAR: Oh king, the truth we tell to you,
            For proved it is and wholly true.

HEROD: Then go forth and find Him,
            And there adore Him,
            And return to me
            That I may see
            And go adore Him.

Scene IV

(Herod's Wrath)

HEROD: Another king to bring great joy,
            What sorrow is mine and what annoy!
            Who ever of things has heard,
            Their rightful king not yet interred!
            Another king to take my place?
            Let him never show his face!
            An age comes to its end
            But I to times shall never bend;
            In truth I do not feel 'tis so
            Until these very eyes do know.
            Majordomo, come thou here,
            May my counselors draw near.
            Go thou my good abbots find,
            Court Officials close behind,
            Call the scriveners in . . . .

            They shall speak the truth, if in their book it lies,
            And whether they of this do know and what has
                come before their eyes.

The Medieval religious theater developed into two distinct
types, the Mystery and the Morality Play. First of all there was

a marked amplification of the subject matter of the two cycles already mentioned, the Nativity and the Passion. New material from the Bible—the life of the Virgin, lives of the saints, and so on—was introduced and the existence of two clearly delineated directions in Medieval religious drama became established. One, which is primarily realistic in nature, the *misterio* or mystery play, presented scenes from the lives of Jesus or of the saints. Further on we shall refer to these works as *autos históricos* or historico-religious plays. The other, which is fundamentally symbolic, is the Morality Play. The characters in this type of drama were personifications of such abstract qualities, values, or other elements as, for example, the Virtues. The plays were presented in the form of parables and allegories and for this reason were called *autos alegóricos*.

It is important to keep in mind the existence of these two developments of medieval drama as later on they give rise to two significant theatrical genres in the Golden Age. The Mystery Play evolves into the *Comedia de Santos* which are plays based on the lives of saints, while the Morality play provides the point of departure for what later was to be called the *Auto Sacramental*, a short Biblical play.

One genre, although strictly speaking a type of poetry, the *Danza de la muerte* [*Dance of Death*] may be considered a sort of compendium of medieval theater as it contains both religious and profane elements as well as philosophic and popular material. In a sense it partakes of both the Mystery Play and the Morality Play and also of satire. Usually there is a series of dialogues between Death and the mortals he seeks out. The latter run the gamut from Pope to Emperor, from beggar to child, and thus include the whole of medieval society. This implies a feeling of social equality and of social criticism in a highly dramatic and effective form.

The following passage from the *Dance of Death* illustrates the macabre sense of this literature of the late Middle Ages:

Lo! I am Death! With aim as sure as steady,
   All beings that are and shall be I draw near me.
I call thee,—I require thee, man, be ready!

Why build upon this fragile life?—Now
    hear me!
Where is the power that does not own me,
    fear me?
Who can escape me, when I bend my bow?
I pull the string,—thou liest in the dust below,
Smitten by the barb my ministering angels
    bear me.

·   ·   ·   ·   ·

Come to the dance of Death! Come hither even
    The last, the lowliest,—of all rank and station!
Who will not come shall be by scourges driven:
    I hold no parley with disinclination.
List to yon friar who preaches of salvation,
    And hie ye to your penitential post!
For who delays,—who lingers,—he is lost,
    And handed o'er to hopeless reprobation.

·   ·   ·   ·   ·

I to my dance—my mortal dance—have brought
    Two nymphs, all bright in beauty and in bloom.
They listened, fear-struck, to my songs, methought;
    And, truly, songs like mine are tinged with gloom.
But neither roseate hues nor flowers perfume
    Will now avail them,—nor the thousand charms
Of worldly vanity; they fill my arms,—
    They are my brides,—their bridal bed the tomb.

·   ·   ·   ·   ·

And since 'tis certain, then, that we must die,—
    No hope, no chance, no prospect of redress,—
Be it our constant aim unswervingly
    To tread God's narrow path of holiness:
For He is first, last, midst. O, let us press
    Onwards! and when Death's monitory glance
Shall summon us to join his mortal dance,
    Even then shall hope and joy our footsteps bless.

—Anonymous translation

The Fifteenth Century

Poetry
The Poets of the Cancionero

The fifteenth century was a period of transition. It was the time of the waning of the Medieval spirit and the birth of the world of the Renaissance. Feudal society was fighting its last rebellions against a monarchy that would, after undergoing a time of weakness during the reign of Enrique IV, soon absorb it. The literature of the time reacted sensitively to these periods of crisis. It clearly reflects the dissolution and corruption of political life. It also, however, incorporates elements symptomatic of the dawning of the Renaissance.

Political and social change were coming about. The gradual transformation of Medieval society was rooted in politics and jurisprudence. Germanic law conceived of the king as a peer of the nobility who formed, through a series of pacts, a·system of feudal vassalage. This concept was slowly replaced by Roman law which considered the king the natural lord over his subjects. The appearance of a middle class or bourgeoisie in Spain, in which the monarch found an ally, facilitated the consolidation of the king's power.

The most evident external sign of this new and growing prestige of the king was the ever-closer relationship between nobility and royal court to which the nobles came in increasing numbers and where, during the Renaissance, he became a courtier. The progress made in the refinement of customs and culture is clearly discernible. A whole series of activities of an artistic nature, in music, poetry and art centered on the figure of the king and formed an integral part of palace life. The nobility became familiar with games involving the mind and soon tourneys matching intelligence and wit took their place alongside military exercises. Two courts in particular acquired renown, that of Don Juan II of Castile and that of Don Alfonso V of Aragon whose palace was in Naples.

The works of the poets who gathered together in the Courts were published together in volumes or collections which were known as *Cancioneros* or ballad collections. The best known of these is the *Cancionero de Baena.* Juan Alfonso de Baena, who compiled the collection, may be considered the prototype of the poets of the *Cancionero.* He is satirical, sharp-tongued, vain, fond of quarreling, servile, and constantly asking for favors. He was well acquainted with Provençal and Galician poetry, but his own poetic work lacks the stamp of individual personality and is restricted to the manipulating of established thematic material and to commentaries on the intrigues of the court.

The *Cancionero de Baena* has several distinctive poetic tendencies:

a That of the Galician-Provençal school which inherited the tradition of the troubadours of the *Cantigas de amor.* The best known poets of this group are Alfonso Alvarez de Vallasandino, Macías el Enamorado (who became a sort of literary hero whose legend survived into the Romantic period) and Rodríguez del Padrón.

b An independent Castilian tendency which is characterized by a philosophical and ascetic sense and whose best known poet is Ferrán Sánchez de Talavera.

c The new Italianate school which will be discussed later on and whose major figure is Micer Francisco Imperial.

The other important compilation or collection of this type, the *Cancionero de Stuñiga,* mirrors the Neapolitan court of Alfonso V. The volume includes a group of Castilian and Catalan poets such as Carvajal, Torrellas, Juan de Valladolid, and Lope de Stuñiga himself whose name identifies the collection which he put together. All of these writers were influenced by the Italian Renaissance.

The thematic material of these *Cancioneros* was first and foremost love. Life had become more refined and subsequently more frivolous in the courts of the nobility. The great themes of the past were slowly forgotten. The Reconquest had come to a halt and war-like tales and stories had gone out of style. Religious fervor had lost the force it had exerted earlier and consequently there was much less poetry on devout matters and subjects. Poets devoted their talents, frequently for monetary recompense, to the praising of certain ladies of the court. In addition, they often wrote *recuestas,* which were intimations or discussions in which the writers hypothesized on such puerile themes as the relative advantages of loving or of being loved, a preference for blue or for green, for winter rather than summer, and the role of Fortune in human life.

Satire also plays an important role in the literature of the times. Three types of satire are possible: the collective, the personal, and the allegorical.

a Collective satire: the *copla* of political satire first appears in Spain in the fifteenth century during the reign of Juan II and is extensively cultivated under Enrique IV. The prototype of this sort of literary satire is the *Coplas de Mingo Revulgo,* 1464, in which a symbolic character, a shepherd named Mingo Revulgo, represents Spain and the Spanish people. He explains to a sort of soothsayer-prophet, another shepherd named Gil Arribato, the causes of the misfortunes of his flock, i.e. the people. The latter have fallen on evil days due to their abandonment by their shepherd Candaulo who is, by implication, the king Enrique IV, and owing to their own growing lack of concern for Christian virtues.

Satire of a collective and political character also appears in the *coplas* entitled *¡Ay, panadera!* [*Oh, Baker's Wife!*], an anonymous work containing various individual allusions which were directed against the cowardly nobles who allowed themselves to be defeated in the rebellion against the king Juan II and his favorite Don Alvaro de Luna.

b Personal satire: the prototype of personal satire are the so-called *Coplas del Provincial,* a particularly stinging work of court gossip in which abound the worst kind of insults against the principal members of the court.

c Allegorical satire: the well known *Diálogo entre el amor y un viejo* [*Dialogue Between Love and an Old Man*] written by a converted Jew from Toledo named Rodrigo Cota (1405?– 1470?) is a dialogue or "debate" in a highly dramatic style and of satirical intent. An old man "in a humble little shack in the middle of a dry and outworn field to whom Love and her ministers suddenly appeared, entered into bitter argument with her until she (Love) finally conquered him." The old man, after considerable protestation, allows himself to be seduced by attractive promises in which Love assures him that she will act toward him and be to him:

> Just as I was
> When you were a handsome lad.

At that moment, however, Love abandons him.

During this time, the influence of Italy had been constantly growing. It was clearly discernible in the fifteenth century. Such poetic forms as the hendecasyllabic line and the sonnet came into vogue, as well as styles that utilized symbols and allegories similar to those employed by Dante in the *Divina Commedia*.

Micer Francisco Imperial, a Genoese who lived in Seville, was the first poet to introduce Italian styles into Spain. He was the author of *Un decir de las siete virtudes* [*Remarks on the Seven Virtues*]. In the work, Imperial hurls invectives at the administration of Seville, a city he surrounds by the Seven Mortal Sins, represented allegorically by seven serpents, in a manner paralleled only by Dante in his attack on the city government of Florence. In the work, the poet falls asleep and has a dream. On awakening, he tells us that he has found a copy of the *Divine Comedy* in his hand, thus consciously affirming the close affinity with Dante. Imperial also introduced the Italian hendecasyllabic line into Spanish.

The Great Poets, Santillana, Mena, Manrique

These poets of the *cancionero,* the polemicists, the satirists and the hirelings, are not the only representatives of the poetry of the fifteenth century. In addition, there are three major poets in this period: the Marquis of Santillana, Juan de Mena, and Jorge Manrique. It is these, rather than the former, who mark the real transition from Medieval to Renaissance poetry.

The Marqués or Marquis of Santillana, Don Iñigo López de Mendoza, Lord of Hita and of Buitrago, was born in Carrión de los Condes in 1398. He fought in the uprisings of the nobility, joining sometimes the king and at others, the nobles. He also campaigned against the Moors. He laid waste to the plains of Granada and subdued the population of Huelma in the province of Jaén. He died in 1458.

Hernando del Pulgar has left a verbal portrait of the Marquis, describing him as "a man of medium height, well-proportioned physically, and handsome of face." There is ample evidence of his vast and universal culture in the Marquis' library, the contents of which are known to us. Greek and Latin works, Italian, French and Portuguese, Provençal and Catalan authors, all those who were known in his times, are represented in the catalogue. His literary production reflects the influences of this broad cultural background.

The Marquis was proudly conscious of his role as a scholar. He stresses the superiority of the works of classical antiquity, the mediocrity of the Provençal poets and what he calls the inferiority of popular poetry such as the ballads "with which people of lowly and servile condition are regaled." He also defines poetry, saying that it is "a simulation of useful things under the guise or cover of beauty, composed with discrimination and restraint, with a fixed count, balances and measure." It can be readily seen from this that Santillana sees poetry as something requiring a study and capability far removed from everything non-aristocratic.

Santillana's *Carta-Proemio* [*Prefatory Letter to the Constable of Portugal Sent as an Introduction to His Poetry*] has come down to us. It is invaluable for understanding the Marquis' literary opinions. The letter represents, furthermore, the first attempt in Hispanic letters to formulate a history of literature. It includes discussions of Greek, Latin, Provençal, Portuguese, Italian, French and Castilian poetry. The highest praise is reserved for the French and the Italians and their influence on Santillana can be noted. Given this it is not surprising that the couplets of *¡Ay, panadera!* seem to the Marquis to be written in a "speech that is almost foreign—closely resembling the French."

Santillana's Italianate works form the most extensive group of his poems. They fit into the category of the allegorical-Dantesque school described earlier in speaking of Imperial. This is the case of the *Comedieta de Ponza* in which the poet has recourse to the device of presenting the description of factual reality, the loss of the fleet of Alfonso V near Gaeta, along with a dream in which the principal characters are Fortune, the poet Boccaccio (who speaks in his native Italian) and four women in mourning who were members of the king's household. The work ends with an augury of Fortune which predicts the reestablishment of the power of the defeated monarch.

The imitation of Dante is even more in evidence in Santillana's *El infierno de los enamorados* [*Inferno of the Lovers*]. The Marquis, like the Dante of the *Divine Comedy*, is lost in a forest where wild beasts attack him. Like the great Italian poet, Santillana has a guide and helper, his Virgil, whose name is Hippolitus and with whom he visits the Inferno and sees such famous lovers as Dido and Aeneas, and Hero and Leander.

In the *Defunsión de Don Enrique de Villena* [*The Death of Don Enrique de Villena*], nine young virgins sing the praises of the dead writer of the title.

Forty-two sonnets also form an important body within Santillana's poetic creation. The poet himself tells us that he wrote them in the Italianate manner. His principal model was Petrarch and he uses the hendecasyllabic line, though without notable skill. The poems themselves have lost considerable interest for us today because of the excessive accumulation of literary and mythological references found in them.

Santillana's fame rests primarily on those works which are fundamentally lyrical, including many poems that show evidence of Provençal influence. These include the *serranillas, canciones,* and *decires*. Without being a poet of genius, the Marquis does appear in these works divested of those cultural trappings which sometimes make him seem pedantic. He offers us in these works poems of a light and pleasant nature, similar to ones found in Provençal literature. These are made up of love poems and of bucolic poems whose setting is the highland ridges called *serranillas*. In these works we can discern how Santillana follows his model of the artificial bucolic poem, of which we spoke earlier, in which only occasionally does the harshness of the traditional highlands appear.

Political and didactic writings make up a third group of works in which Santillana's intention was to divulge his knowledge. Among them, in addition to *The Prefatory Leter to the Constable of Portugal,* of which we have already spoken, is his *Diálogo de Bías contra Fortuna (Bias's Dialogue Against Fortune),* a lengthy work whose major theme is the fugacity of life. There are also the *Doctrinal de Privados (Catechism for Court Favorites),* which is a severe condemnation of Don Alvaro de Luna, written after his death, and the *Proverbios* or *Proverbs,* a compilation of proverbial sayings of ancient philosophers.

The Marquis of Santillana is the author of the first collection of Spanish folklore. This curious work is entitled *Refranes que dicen las viejas tras el fuego* [*Refrains Old Ladies Tell Beside the Fire*]. It is one more sign of the author's universality and his curiosity in literary matters.

Juan de Mena is the prototype of the humanistic writer of his times. He is also the first literary figure who is neither of the clergy or a soldier. "Pure man of letters" is how Menéndez y Pelayo described him. His life is that of an intellectual who studied in Cordova, Salamanca, and in Rome, the most authentic center of culture of the Renaissance. He was the secretary of Latin letters and chronicler to Juan II but did not take part in the struggles of his epoch. He was born in Cordova in 1411, and died in Torrelaguna in 1456. One contemporary author described him in the following terms: "of a palid face, consumed in study, but not broken and patched by lance thrusts."

Juan de Mena was a humanist. His work cannot be studied without taking into account the author's profound knowledge of Greek and Latin classical literature and of the Italian writers of the early Renaissance. Juan de Mena even undertook the translation—"into the crude and unembellished Romance tongue," as he himself tells us—of Homer's *Iliad,* using the title of *Homero romanceado* [*Homer in Romance Tongue*], a work which is an example of his rather heavy prose style. Virgil and his compatriot, Lucian, are both imitated directly in the *La-berinto* [*Labyrinth*].

Like the latter Latin author and like Góngora, another Cordovan, Juan de Mena followed the tradition of authors who are characterized by their cultured and cultivated style, which is to say, by their creation of a poetry which is studded with neologisms and metaphors. Consequently, we find not only a large number of Latin words which have been Hispanized in Juan de Mena's poetry, but also the influence of classical syntax (hyperbaton).

The renovation which Juan de Mena undertook failed because it was premature. The Castilian language was still in a state of formation and was not capable of assimilating so many cultured expressions. On the other hand, Góngora, in the seventeenth century, was able to introduce numerous neologisms into what had become by his time a much more cultured and flexible language.

The utilization of classical elements causes Juan de Mena's style to be artificial and, in final analysis, tiring. At the same time, his literary ambitions moved him to attempt work of an epic and erudite nature. This saved him from being one of the many superficial poets who swarmed about the Court.

Mena's major work is *Fortune's Labyrinth* or the *Trescientas* [*Three Hundred*] (this was the number of strophes in the work). In *Fortune's Labyrinth* we may distinguish the following elements:

a A general theme, mythological, in which the poet, who is in the chariot of the goddess Belona, is taken to Fortune's palace. There he sees three wheels, two of which are immobile and represent the past and the future, and the third which is moving and represents the present. Each wheel contains seven circles presided over by the gods Diana, Venus, Mercury, Phoebus, Mars, Jupiter, and Saturn. It is there that mortals receive their rewards and punishments. Dante's influence is clearly apparent.

b A series of episodes of an historical nature which are interspersed throughout the poem and are brought to life by the poet's imaginative powers. The protagonists of these episodes are of various types. They include writers like the troubadours,

Macías and Enrique de Villena, soldiers like the Count of Niebla who died in the conquest of Gibraltar, and Diego de Ribera who was the victor of Alera.

In these historical episodes of the poem, the author writes with much more personal freedom.

c In addition, the *Labyrinth* has a national character. Juan de Mena's Renaissance education led him to dream of a great Spanish empire comparable to the Roman empire. His loyalty to the monarchy causes him to conceive this empire as the extirpator of the Moors under the scepter of the king whom he describes in a well-known passage:

> Don Juan the Second, he of great strength,
> The noble Caesar and of Spain great king,
> To him whom Fortune so has blessed,
> In whom are found all virtue's best,
> To him on bended knee his praises sing.

(Strophe I)

Jorge Manrique was a courtier. He was both poet and soldier. He took part in the armed struggles of his times including those on behalf of Queen Isabella, whose defense was undertaken by the Order of Calatrava. He died in battle, near the Castle of Garci-Muñoz in the year 1478.

The major part of his poetry belongs to the school of the troubadors of Provençal origin. Following their models, he wrote a series of love songs which are light in tone, full of gallantry and expressive of a mundane spirit which includes subtle amorous concepts and even some burlesque and satirical verses.

The *Coplas a la Muerte de su Padre* [*Verses Written at the Death of His Father*]: The light-hearted and courtly nature of much of his poetry is usually overlooked in favor of his *Verses Written at the Death of His Father*. This work is serene and reflective poetry, deeply felt and perceived, which is wholly distinct from the superficial tone of the rest of his literary creation. The *Coplas* is one of the major works of Castilian literature. The poem is in fact what would normally be called an Ode. The word *copla* normally was used rather freely to mean almost any brief metrical unit, such as a couplet or a ballad "verse."

a   The Medieval Spirit: Jorge Manrique begins the poem with a concept already well-established in the Christian tradition and taken from the Bible, one which had a major importance during the Middle Ages, namely that human life is a transitory passage to death. "Our lives are rivers, gliding free—To that unfathomed, boundless sea,—The silent grave."

The Church, whose influence on Medieval life was so pronounced, constantly affirmed the same idea: "Man is dust and ashes;" life is a "vale of tears." The *Dances of Death* teach the faithful the vanity of worldly glory; everything is related to the Great Beyond, the Eternal World which in forms of either punishment or reward waits implacably.

Henry Wadsworth Longfellow's translation begins as follows:

> O, let the soul her slumbers break!
> Let thought be quickened and awake,
>   Awake to see
> How soon this life is past and gone,
> And death comes softly stealing on,—
>   How silently!
>
> Swiftly our pleasures glide away:
> Our hearts recall the distant day
>   With many sighs:
> The moments that are speeding fast
> We heed not; but the past—the past—
>   More highly prize.
>
> Onward its course the present keeps,
> Onward the constant current sweeps,
>   Till life is done;
> And did we judge of time aright,
> The past and future in their flight
>   Would be as one.
>
> Let no one fondly dream again
> That Hope and all her shadowy train
>   Will not decay;

Fleeting as were the dreams of old,
Remembered like a tale that's told,
    They pass away.

Our lives are rivers gliding free
To that unfathomed, boundless sea,
    The silent grave:
Thither all earthly pomp and boast
Roll to be swallowed up and lost
    In one dark wave.

Thither the mighty torrents stray,
Thither the brook pursues its way,
    And tinkling rill.
There all are equal. Side by side,
The poor man and the son of pride
    Lie calm and still.

The typical medieval theme of *Ubi sunt?* is expressed in these lines:

Where is the King Don Juan? Where
Each royal prince and noble heir
    Or Aragon?
Where are the courtly gallantries?
The deeds of love and high emprise,
    In battle done?

Tourney and joust, that charmed the eye,
And scarf, and gorgeous panoply,
    And nodding plume,—
What were they but a pageant scene?
What but the garlands, gay and green
    That deck the tomb?

Where are the high-born dames, and where
Their gay attire and jewelled hair,
    And odors sweet?
Where are the gentle knights, that came
To kneel, and breathe love's ardent flame,
    Low at their feet?

Where is the song of Troubadour?
Where are the lute and gay tambour
    They loved of yore?
Where is the mazy dance of old,—
The flowing robes, inwrought with gold,
    The dancers wore?

And he who next the sceptre swayed,
Henry, whose royal court displayed
    Such power and pride,—
O, in what winning smiles arrayed,
The world its various pleasures laid
    His throne beside!

But, O, how false and full of guile
That world, which wore so soft a smile
    But to betray!
She, that had been his friend before,
Now from the fated monarch tore
    Her charms away.

The countless gifts,—the stately walls,
The royal palaces, and halls
    All filled with gold;
Plate with armorial bearings wrought,
Chambers with ample treasures fraught
    Of wealth untold!

The noble steeds, and harness bright,
The gallant lord, and stalwart knight,
    In rich array;—
Where shall we seek them now? Alas!
Like the bright dew-drops on the grass,
    They passed away.

   b   The Renaissance Spirit: Nevertheless, coinciding with a
slackening of religious fervor there appeared, toward the end of
the Middle Ages, a phenomenon which is reflected in the *Coplas*.
The earthly world, the world of festivities and of the beauties of
the flesh, doubtlessly is ephemeral. Man, however, can acquire

here on this earth something more durable and spiritual which can be bequeathed to his decendants; fame, honor, glory. This "third life," distinct from both the earthly and the divine, is a cry of optimism and of faith in human existence which provides insight into the man of the Renaissance who proudly set out to make of life a field of glory and not just a brief period of transition as was the case with the man of the Middle ages.

> By his unrivalled skill, by great
> And veteran service to the state,
>   By worth adored.
> He stood, in his high dignity,
> The proudest knight of chivalry,
>   Knight of the Sword.
>
> He found his cities and domains
> Beneath a tyrant's galling chains
>   And cruel power;
> But, by fierce battle and blockade,
> Soon his own banner was displayed
>   From every tower.
>
> By the tried valor of his hand,
> His monarch and his native land
>   Were nobly served;—
> Let Portugal repeat the story,
> And proud Castile, who shared the glory
>   His arms deserved.

The Fifteenth Century Theatre

As we move on into the fifteenth century, the popular element of medieval drama acceeded to the new literary currents of the Renaissance. Contacts with Italy which grew in frequency and importance facilitated the adoption of the new tendencies. Alongside the simple religious drama of the Middle Ages appeared a theatre of humanistic orientation. Nevertheless, as was to be expected, during much of this time the new drama alternated with the medieval. Most of the authors of this period of transition exhibit both tendencies in their works.

a   Medieval survivals: Gómez Manrique is a fifteenth century author in whom the medieval spirit predominates. One of his dramatic works, *La representación del Nacimiento de Nuestro Señor,* the *Representation of the Birth of Our Lord,* belongs to the Nativity cycle while another, *Laments for Holy Week,* is an example of the cycle of the Passion. In the first of these, a *Canción de cuna para callar al Niño (Lullaby to Quiet the Christ Child)* with which the work ends, illustrates the author's ability as a lyric poet; this may also be noted in the love poems which he wrote in the tradition of the *cancionero.*

b   Transitional authors: Juan del Encina, who was born in Encina de San Silvestre in 1469, best illustrates the tendencies of transition in this period. Encina studied at Salamanca and later served as a musician in the court of the Duke of Alba. He went to Rome where he was a singer in the Pontifical Chapel. He also journeyed as a pilgrim to Jerusalem and later returned to Spain where he died in 1529.

Two wholly distinct atmospheres are discernible in his drama. One is that of Salamanca where he spent much of his youth. The shepherds of his early short works on the Nativity and the Passion, the *Autos de Natividad y de la Pasión,* and his plays on the carnival period before Ash Wednesday, speak the rustic dialect of the peasants of the Salamanca region just as his shepherds and students in the *Auto del Repelón* play gross practical jokes. This atmosphere follows in the medieval popular tradition.

The other tendency clearly reflects Encina's stay in the Rome of Renaissance culture. These are the years of maturity during which the author's contact with the bucolic Greco-Latin tradition brings about the transformation of the shepherds of his earlier plays into refined courtiers who discuss the primacy of divine love and human love. It is the latter that wins out in two of the Eclogues which Encina wrote in this period, his *Plácida and Victriano* and his *Cristino and Phoebe.* In his *Eclogue of Philenus, Zambardo and Cardonio,* profane love causes the suicide of the luckless Philenus whom the others wish to canonize. In all of these works the Renaissance exaltation of the pagan world triumphs over the religiosity of the Middle Ages.

Consequently Encina is, as we have already indicated, a transitional playwright who partakes of both the medieval and renaissance worlds. His very beautiful lyrical works still retain the ingenuousness of medieval poems. The following passages illustrate the two styles of Encina. The first is of the medieval popular tradition:

Don't Shut Your Door

Don't shut your door,—don't shut your door:
    'Twill be no use at all.
    If love should come and call,

If love commands, you'd best obey,—
    Resistance will but hurt you,—
And make, for that's the safest way,
    Necessity a virtue.
So don't resist his gentle sway,
    Nor shut your door if he should call,—
    For that's no use at all.

I've seen him tame the wildest beast,
    And strengthen too the weakest:
He loves him most who plagues him least;
    His favorites are the meekest.
The privileged guests who grace his feast
    Have never opposed his gentle call,
    For that's no use at all.

He loves to tumble upside down
    All classes, all connection;
Of those who fear or wear a crown
    He mingles the affections,
Till all by love is overthrown;
    And moated gate or castle-wall
    Will be no use at all.

He is a strange and wayward thing,—
   Young, blind, and full of malice;
He makes a shepherd of a king,
   A cottage of a palace.
'Tis vain to murmur; and to fling
   Your thoughts away in grief and gall
   Will be no use at all.

He makes the coward brave; he wakes
   The sleepy with his thunders,
In mirth he revels, and mistakes,
   And miracles and wonders;
And many a man he prisoner makes,
   And bolts the door:—you cry and call;
   But 'tis no use at all.

       —Translation by John Bowring

The action of the play, *Plácida y Vitoriano,* begins, after an introduction by a rustic comic type, with the lament of the heroine, Placida, whom Vitoriano has supposedly abandoned:

Poor heart of mine, by sorrow torn.
What ills and sadness have you bourne,
What evil times, all undeserved.
What love could he have felt for me
And what compassion did he show
To leave me so?
Alas, what will become of me?
Unlucky day the one we met.

   Indeed no lamentation would I make
If on occasion for my sake
He'd show himself less silent and withdrawn.
This pulsing mortal wound of mine
Would heal if only I could see him now.
But should I if
He treats me thus with such short shrift?
It's better that he go his way,

And take his leave! But wait, what heresy
Has fury uttered through my lips?
Oh pain that cuts so sharp and deep!
How did I ever think such things?

A madness holds my brain in sway.
Away! Away!
May God protect me from such thought.
Without my lover, life is naught.

Six farces and eclogues of a pastoral nature and rustic in tone
by another playwright, Lucas Fernández, have also come down
to us. The realism of his *Auto de la Pasión* is especially noteworthy. Nevertheless, although he is similar to Encina in his use
of the country idiom of the Salamanca region, Fernandez is closer
to the medieval tradition than that of the Renaissance.

The major work of the period, and one of the greatest masterpieces of Spanish literature, the *Tragicomedy of Calisto and
Melibea,* better known as the *Celestina* and also translated into
English under the title of *The Spanish Bawd,* appeared in Burgos
in 1499. It is usually categorized as a novel in dialogue form "in
which are contained, in addition to its agreeable and pleasing
style, numerous philosophical axioms and necessary advice for
young people." The plot is the tale of two young lovers, Calisto
and Melibea, the victims of the evil arts of Celestina, a perverse
old woman who makes her living by arranging rendezvous between men and women desirous of meeting each other. The action
ends in tragedy. Calisto falls headlong from the wall of Melibea's
garden where the two have secretly met, and the heroine, as a
result, commits suicide. The work purportedly has the moralizing
intent of warning "foolish" lovers of the perils of worldly at-
tachments. Celestina is a literary descendent of Trotaconventos
of the Archpriest of Hita's *Book of Good Love.*

The *Celestina* gives us excellent insight into the social strata
of the epoch, the aristocratic world of the young lovers and the
picaresque world of Celestina and the servants. The work includes
an extensive gallery of portraitures which may be grouped in the
folowing categories:

a. The protagonists, Calisto and Melibea, who are motivated by the illicit love that brings about their deaths. Their actions reflect the two philosophies of ancient times which the Renaissance had brought into vogue, the epicurean which counsels the enjoyment of the senses, and the stoic which finds suicide acceptable.

b. The servants and Celestina, who are motivated by their greed for money.

The protagonists and the servants form a contrast which is typical of Spanish literature. In the drama, the hero, who is concerned only with his amorous adventures, appears in the play in the company of his servants who are preoccupied with material things. This paradoxical pairing of characters will, of course, find definitive form in the immortal relationship of Don Quixote and his inseparable companion, Sancho Panza. The rogues, ruffians and prostitutes of Celestina's world will be imitated later in the picaresque novel. The work has been extremely influencial not only on Spanish literature but on French and English literature as well.

The following passage presents the plot summary for Act I and the lovers:

From Act I:

Calisto enters a garden in pursuit of his falcon, and there finds Melibea, with whom he is deeply in love. He begins to address her, but is sternly dismissed, and returns home very sad. He confides in Sempronio, one of his servants, who with some difficulty persuades him to enlist the help of an old woman called Celestina, in whose house lives Sempronio's mistress Elicia. When Sempronio arrives there on his master's errand, the girl is entertaining Crito, another of her lovers, who is quickly concealed. While Celestina and Sempronio are negotiating, Calisto talks to Parmeno, another of his servants; and their conversation lasts until Sempronio returns with Celestina. The old woman recognizes Parmeno, and tells him at some length of his mother's character and exploits. She persuades him to make friends with Sempronio.

CALISTO: In this I see God's greatness at work.
MELIBEA: In what, Calisto?

CALISTO: In that he has empowered nature to endow you
with perfect beauty, and granted me the undeserved favour of finding you in this favourable
spot where I can at last declare my secret passion.
I have prayed and sacrificed to him, and I have
performed pious works, all in the hope that he
would grant me this opportunity. But the reward
is a thousand times greater than my deserts. Was
ever living man so blessed as I am now? The
saints in their glory cannot know such joy as I
feel in conversing with you. But alas, how unlike
them we are! Being purest, they rejoice without
fear of falling from their happy state. But I, a
creature of matter and spirit, even as I rejoice,
fear the tortures I shall suffer when you are gone.

MELIBEA: So you think of this as a great reward, Calisto?

CALISTO: So great that if God were to seat me above
his saints in heaven, I should count it a lesser
felicity.

MELIBEA: I shall reward you yet more fittingly if you
go on.

CALISTO: How blessed are my unworthy ears to hear that
promise!

MELIBEA: Not blessed but cursed, you'll say when you've
heard me out. I'll make you regret your au-
dacity. This speech of yours is true to your
character, and has only one purpose, to dis-
honour me. But on virtue like mine your words
are wasted. Go away, you wretch! Go away! It
is intolerable that any man should dare to make
wicked advances to me.

CALISTO: I will go as one pursued by cruel fate with
special hatred.

In the following monologue, Celestina, who has just left the
home of Melibea, mutters about the encounter with the young
woman whose seduction she now knows is assured through her
astute handling of the situation:

CELESTINA: That was a dangerous moment! But I was wise
to be so bold, and I was very patient. I should

have been very near to death if I hadn't been
cunning enough to lower my sails in time. How
that virtuous creature threatened me! What an
angry young lady! But the devil I conjured up
kept his word and did all I asked. I'm indeed
grateful to you, Devil! You tamed that female
fury, and you provided me with my opportunity
to talk to her by sending her mother out of the
way. Old Celestina has reason to be happy, because well begun is half done, you know. O my
fine snake-oil and my white thread, you worked
everything in my favour. If you hadn't I'd break
all my bonds, past, present, and future, and
stop trusting in herbs, charms, and spells. Rejoice, old girl, for you'll make more out of this
than out of fifteen patched maidenheads. Damn
these long, cumbersome skirts! How they ham-
per me when I'm in a hurry to tell my news!
Fortune favours the brave and foils the timid.
A coward can't escape death by running away.
How many would have failed where I've just
succeeded! What would the new mistresses of
my profession have done if they had found themselves in such a tight spot? They'd have answered
Melibea back, and so lost all that I gained by
keeping silent. No wonder they say, leave the
lute to the man who can play it; and that in
medicine experience counts for more than learning, and that skill comes with caution and practice, as it has to this old lady, who's wise enough
to lift her skirts when she's crossing a ford.

The style and language of the *Celestina* give ample evidence
of the broad classical background of its author who imitates in
his prose the richness of vocabulary and the elegance of construction which are characteristic of Latin. Neologisms abound, especially in the speech of Calisto and Melibea. On the other hand,
everyday expressions and even coarse language are used in the
speech of Celestina, the servants and the prostitutes.

The principal author of the work, Fernando de Rojas, was a

university graduate who was born in Puebla de Montalban in the province of Toledo. He tells us his name in an acrostic poem in the preface of an edition of 1500. While the author of the first act is unknown to us, it is now generally acceptable that de Rojas was the principal writer of the other twenty acts of the work as we know it today. He also states that he encountered the first act while at the university and that he was excited by this to continue the writing of the work. The accuracy of this declaration has long been open to question and it has been speculated that this explanation may well be little more than a literary pretext on the part of de Rojas. Literary scholars are still debating the problems of authorship.

The work itself is in the form of prose dialogue. Although abridged versions have been staged, the work has not been presented on the stage in its entirety as it is very lengthy and some of its outspoken language has shocked Spanish sensitivity.

The *Celestina* represents a spirit and a period of transition. For the first time in Spanish literature, human love in both its phyical and its spiritual manifestations is the focal point of action. In this sense the work has a Renaissance vitality. Its author, however, shows a basically medieval tendency of bringing his love affairs to a tragic end and drawing a moral lesson from them.

We can distinguish the following component parts in the *Celestina:*

a A comedy of love, imitative of Terence, the Latin dramatist who was much in vogue in the Renaissance, and

b A series of maxims and proverbial sayings which are interspersed throughout the play and have a moralizing effect. As Ramiro de Maeztu wrote in the early years of this century:

Rojas' book portrays for us the tragic tale of two young lovers, of the evil and shrewd old woman who brings them together in the whirlwind of their passions, and of two false and insidious servants. All come to a violent end, the good lovers and the evil mediators and servants. The spectacle of their disastrous end makes manifest the purification which the soul of man achieves through tragedy, for moral suffering, just like physical, indicates to us those things which are dangerous to us and which we should avoid.

Prose

The didactic prose of this period now utilizes the Romance tongue as its vehicle of expression and thus marks a movement away from Latin which, nevertheless, continues to influence the sintax and lexicon of the new idiom.

One of the writers of the period, Enrique de Villena, or Enrique de Aragón, as he is also called, was a curious person. He was from a noble family, although he was not a marquis as some have claimed. He first lived in Castille and later moved to Aragon where he was under the protection of Fernando of Antequera. The latter named him President of the *Juegos Florales,* a type of literary festival held in Barcelona, which, in imitation of those of Provence, had become customary in that city. When the king died, Villena withdrew to Torralba where he lived surrounded by books on alchemy, enchantments and mythology. His enormous curiosity led him to write such varied works as the following:

a on poetry: the *Arte de trovar* or *Art of Composition,* a very interesting work for comprehending the precepts of the epoch and for the descriptions of the *Juegos Florales* of Barcelona which it contains.

b On the art of cutting with a knife: the *Tractado del Arte de cortar del cuchillo o Arte cisoria* or *Treatise on the Art of Cutting with a Knife,* which is a book of etiquette which sheds much light on the customs, and particularly the eating habits, of the society of the times.

c On the art of avoiding the evil eye: *Libro de aojamiento o fascinología* or *The Book of the Evil Eye or Bewitching,* a work which is a mixture of medical science and superstition.

d On mythology: Villena also wrote a book called *Los doce trabajos de Hércules* or *The Twelve Labors of Hercules,* of Classical inspiration.

Satirical prose works also appear in the epoch. The most important writer in this vein is Alfonso Martínez of Toledo, better known as the Archpriest of Talavera, who was born around 1398 and died around 1470. We know that he resided in Toledo and in Barcelona and that he was the Archpriest of Talavera. In addition to historical and religious writings of relatively small importance, such as the *Atalaya de Crónicas* or *Lighthouse of Chronicles* and the *Vida de San Isidoro y de San Ildefonso* or the *Life of Saint Isidoro and of Saint Ildefonso*, the Archpriest's lasting fame comes from a single work, *El Corbacho o Reprobación del amor mundano* or *The Whip or Reproach of Worldly Love*, in which he castigates the vices and the evil ways of man.

By this time, the writing of history had undergone considerable development since the period of Alfonso the Wise. Historical figures were being studied both in their external and their psychological aspects. We have, for example, the impressive verbal portraits of Fernán Pérez de Guzmán (1576?-1460) in his book of *Generaciones y semblazas* or *Successions and Portraits* which inaugurates literary biography in Spanish letters. In a similar vein, Hernando del Pulgar (1436?-1493?) wrote his *Claros varones de Castella* or *Eminent Men of Castile* in which we see his considerable gift of observation. His portrayal of the Marquis of Santillana is perhaps the best known.

Chivalry and Humanism

The end of the fifteenth century is best described as a period of transition during which two significant genres appear, the books of chivalry which symbolize the medieval tradition and the first humanistic works which mark the dawn of the Renaissance.

During the Middle Ages, the feudal world organized collective security in its own way. Chivalry was an institution which partook of both the religious and the military. The knight was admitted to an order after having stood watch over his arms. He was solemnly invested with knighthood and swore to devote himself to the service of God, woman, and the weak. Knighthood lost its importance when, during the Renaissance, the great monarchies organized armies and systems of security.

Meanwhile, the novel of chivalry had come into being. Throughout Europe, and particularly in France, fictional narratives appeared. They recounted the fantastic adventures of knights who were without fear or blemish. These *romans courtois* or courtly novels gave birth to the great heroes of chivalry— Lancelot, Ivain and others—who came into the Spanish tradition as the heroes of novels and of ballads.

In Spain the literature of chivalry began with the *Amadís of Gaul* which may have appeared first in either Spanish or Portuguese. The oldest edition of the work is one from Saragossa dated 1508. It is in Spanish and the author named is one Garci-Rodríguez (or Garci-Ordoñez) de Montalvo. We do not know, however, whether this work is original or merely a reworking. There may have been an earlier edition in Portuguese. These questions have still not been satisfactorily answered. We do know, however, that references to the work can be found as early as the fourteenth century. They are sufficiently vague to leave us in doubt as to which edition they refer. As we know it, the *Amadis* contains four major divisions or books. A fifth one, which was added later, is entitled *Las sergas de Espladián* [*The Exploits of Espladian*]. The endless series of successors and continuations of the original began with the latter work. Amadís remains, nevertheless, the prototype of the knight without blemish, the conqueror of giants, monsters, evil spells, and enemies, the loyal guardian of his love of Oriana the lady of his heart.

In Spain the literature of chivalry multiplied prodigiously. Each knight errant became the founder of a dynasty. His sons, grandsons, nephews and so on became the heroes of new adventures in subsequent books which became more and more confusing and absurd. Cervantes, in his immortal *Don Quixote,* brought into vivid focus the ridiculousness of so many preposterous adventures.

At about the same time that the books of chivalry appeared, i.e., toward the end of the fifteenth century, the sentimental novel also came into vogue. Diego de San Pedro wrote what is considered to be the best known work of the genre, the *Cárcel de amor* [*Prison of Love*]. It came out in 1492. The work is a curious one. The characters in it are to a certain extent symbolic. The author meets the youth Leriano in a mysterious castle. The latter begs the author to tell his lady love, Laureola, of the torments he is suffering because of her. Leriano is successful in escaping from the castle. Meanwhile his beloved is imprisoned by her father who is the king of Gaul. Leriano succeeds in freeing her, but Laureola decides not to see her lover again. As a result of this Leriano lets himself die bit by bit. The influence of Ovid and Boccaccio is discernible in the work.

Another famous sentimental novel, the *Cuestión de amor* [*Question of Love*] was written by Juan de Flores. It appeared in 1513. Two Spanish gentlemen, Vasquirán and Flamiano argue about which one of the two has suffered most over being rejected by their lady loves.

In addition there is another novel of this type called the *Siervo libro de amor* [*Book of Love's Slave*] written by Juan Rodríguez de la Cámara. The presentation of love as a tragic and sorrowful theme and as a strange allegorical and mysterious atmosphere is characteristic of this work.

Humanistic studies flourished in the court of Ferdinand and Isabella. As the Middle Ages progressed, royal power began to acquire strength and form. The passing from Germanic to Roman law is evident in the work of Alfonso the Wise and of López de Ayala. This tendency toward a consolidation of power in the state remained purely theoretical up to the latter part of the fifteenth century. If we are to judge from the reigns of Enrique III, Juan II, and Enrique IV, it was very difficult to establish. Nevertheless the necessity for a unifying political system had become apparent.

Throughout Europe the first writers to begin to rediscover the ancient world, the Humanists, took their ideas from the Roman Empire of the Caesars as this embodied a political unity. What these men lacked was a concept for the practical application of the idea. This evolved under Ferdinand and Isabella, known as the Catholic Kings. It was they who consolidated royal power, ended the rebellions of the nobles, and established a court in which the Queen gave reign to her thirst for culture by the study of Latin in the company of the ladies of her household.

It was in this setting that Elio Antonio de Nebrija gained stature. He was born in the province of Seville and had studied the humanities—i.e., classical culture—in Italy. He proposed to "dispell the barbarism so widely spread throughout Spain." He made his way to Salamanca which was then the principal seat of medieval learning and which he considered, with considerable reason, to be a "fortress conquered not without a struggle." He also said of Salamanca that "all the other towns of Spain should show it homage." As a matter of fact, he taught Humanities for some twelve years at the University of Salamanca until, acclaimed for his learning by Cardinal Cisneros, he went to Alcala for the purpose of revising the Latin and Greek texts of the Polyglot Bible. He died in Alcala in 1522.

Nebrija was closely involved in the politics of the reign of Ferdinand and Isabella. In the year 1492 when the Moorish Kingdom of Granada finally fell into Christian hands and America was discovered, Nebrija published his famous *Gramática castellana* [*Grammar of Castilian Spanish*] which was the first of its kind to be published in a modern tongue. The work was dedicated to Queen Isabella who gave a major impulse to humanistic studies. The book's dedication contains a statement in which Nebrija asserts that "language has always been the traveling companion of empires." He elaborates on this by using classical references and states that language so follows empire that "together they began, grew and flowered, and later fell into decay." Accordingly one of the purposes of the grammar was the preparation of the linguistic instrument for the dominion over the Empire which Nebrija represented.

Regional Literatures of Medieval Spain

Galicia

Galician-Portuguese lyrical poetry appeared early. The Provençal troubadours brought their lyrical poetry into Spain by two main routes. One of these was direct, namely by means of politico-cultural relations between Catalonia and southern France. The other was the so-called "French route" which passed through Burgos, Leon, and Astorga on the way to Santiago de Compostela in Galicia. It was the second of these which had the greater impact on the formation of early Castilian lyrical poetry.

A series of types or genres of composition characterizes this poetry. Some are cultural in nature, namely the *cantigas de amor* or love songs, which are supposed to be recited by the lover. The others are popular in character. They are called *cantigas de amigo* or songs of friendship and were presumably recited by an admirer. In these poems there are frequent allusions to the countryside and the sea of Galicia.

The first of these two types was modeled on poems of the troubadours. They have the least originality and genuine feeling. Conversely the *cantigas de amigo,* in both Galician and Castilian versions, offer all the enchantment and deep sadness of Galicia. A third genre completes the tableau of this primitive lyric, the *cantigas de escarnio y de maldecir* or songs of mockery and backbiting. All of these compositions utilize, in general, a parallel strophe.

The examples of this primitive Spanish lyric poetry which we possess are contained primarily in three collections entitled *cancioneros de Ajuda, de Vaticana,* and *de Colocci-Brancutti.* In the first of these three the style and form are cultured and suggestive of Provençal poetry. In the other two collections indigenous forms predominate and the tone is primarily popular and sincere and of outstanding beauty.

Among the numerous Galician poets of the period, Martín Codax, who lived in the court of Ferdinand the Saint (1199–1252), is the one who stands out most clearly. Seven of his "songs of friendship" have come down to us. The theme of the sea, as well as that of love, appears in his poetry.

Payo Gómez Chariño was both military man and poet. It was he who, as admiral of the sea in the fleet that went up the Guadalquivir, completed the conquest of Seville. His poetry unites themes of sentimentality and landscape.

As we know, Alfonso X, the Wise, who had the historical and scientific works in his court written in Castilian Spanish, utilized Galician for his famous *Cantigas de Santa María* [*Songs to the Virgin Mary*]. The latter are of special interest to us, first of all, as an example of the value of Galician as a vehicle for lyrical poetic expresion, inasmuch as Alfonso the Wise had his prose works written in Castilian and reserved Galician for poetry. Second, they serve as an example of the influence of the literature of devotion to the Virgin Mary in Spain. This type of writing was widespread throughout Europe and in this respect Alfonso X was not original in his choice. An example of this collection is the following "Song to Our Lady":

> Lady, for the love of God,
>   Have some pity upon me!
> See my eyes, a river-flood
>   Day and night, oh see!
> Brothers, cousins, uncles, all,
>   Have I lost for thee;
> If thou dost not me recall,
>   Woe is me.

> —Translation by Thomas Walsh

Third, they served as a collection of pious legends which later on gave birth to further developments. The following passage is an example of this:

A nun who was put in charge of the valuables of a convent runs off with a young man. Before leaving, however, she has left her keys on the Virgin's altar and entrusted herself to her Protectress. Some years later the nun repents and returns to the convent. She finds that no one has replaced her as the Virgin Mary has carried out her duties during her absence. In the seventeenth century Lope de Vega utilizes this story in his *Buena guarda* [*Faithful Guard*], while in the nineteenth Zorrilla bases his *Margarita la Tornera* [*Margarita the Doorkeep*] on this legend.

In another tale a woman from Segovia whose livelihood was the making of silk had forgotten the offering of a garment which she had promised to make for the Virgin. She goes home, and to her surprise, finds that the silkworms have set themselves to the task of weaving the mantle.

In still another story a monk asks the Virgin to give him some idea of what life after death is like. The Virgin grants his request. He hears the song of a little bird and is so enchanted by it that three hundred years go by without the monk's realizing it.

One of the troubadours of the court of Juan II, Macías, is a historical figure of the early fifteenth century who found a place in numerous subsequent works and has become a sort of archetype of romantic love. Macías was known as "The Lover" who gained fame because of his tragic death at the hands of the Lord of Porcuna while singing a love song to the latter's wife, Doña Elvira.

The decline of Galician literature was rapid and decisive. It did not recover its vigor until the mid-nineteenth century.

Catalonia

During the Middle Ages Catalan literature acquired an outstanding individuality and splendor and as a consequence added greatly, as did Galician literature, to the diversification of Hispanic letters. The Catalonian tongue attained sufficient maturity to be utilized in books of philosophy and in both didactic and historical prose.

In the latter category there are four major chronicles. They are rich in historical and in literary aspects. Their respective authors were Jaime I, Bernat Desclos, Ramón Muntaner, and Pedro the Ceremonious. Equally famous for his writings of religious polemics and his knowledge of medicine was Arnán de Vilanova, who lived in the last years of the thirteenth and the early part of the fourteenth centuries.

The best known figure of Catalonian medieval literature was Ramón Llull whose interests covered a wide range that included poetry, philosophy, and mysticism. He was born in 1232 on the island of Mallorca where he lived as a layman and married a woman named Blanca Picany. At the age of thirty, however, he abandoned his home and former life and took the habit of a Fransciscan monk. From that time on he devoted himself to study and meditation. Nevertheless he was a tireless traveler and made trips to Rome, Santiago, Montpellier, and Paris. He also went repeatedly to Africa and, according to legend, was stoned in Tunis. Badly injured, he returned to Mallorca where he died in 1316. His life is described in his book entitled *Blanquerna*.

Llull was obsessed with the idea of unity of belief among men. As a part of his attempt to realize his aims he wrote works such as the *Art general* and the *Art demostrativa*. He also proposed the formation of councils and such things as preaching to the Infidel. To the latter end Llull founded a school of Oriental languages at Miramar de Mallorca.

Llull wrote various works in which his mystical tendencies are apparent. In this vein are such writings as *Els cent noms de Déu* [*Hundred Names For God*], the *Cant de Ramón* [*Song of Ramón*], the *Plant de Sants María* [*Plaint of the Virgin Mary*], the *Libre de contemplación in Déu* [*Book on the Contemplation of God*], the *Libre de l'Amicid e l'amat* [*Book of the Beloved and the Lover*], and so on. The following passage is from the last of these works:

> The paths along which the lover searches for the beloved are long and dangerous, peopled with thoughts, sighs and pain, and lighted by love. The Beloved said to the Lover: "You who are radiant as the sun, fill my heart with love." The Lover answered, "Without love's fulfillment, your eyes would not be wide with suffering nor would you have come into the presence of your Lover."
>
> "Tell me, Beloved," said the Lover, "will you be patient if I experience once again my sufferings?" The Beloved replied, "Yes, my Lover, if you will experience once again your Love."

Among the Catalan Humanists several are worthy of mention. Fra Antoni Canals is an author who, in imitation of Petrarch, wrote a *Raonament entre Escipió e Aníbal* [*Dialogue Between Scipio and Hannibal*]. Another is Antoni de Vilarguet who translated Seneca, while Juan Roís de Corella is noteworthy for his writings on mythological themes.

The major figure of Catalonian poetry of the fifteenth century is the Valencian Ausías March. He was born in Gaudía in

1393. He took up the profession of arms and fought with the expedition to Cerdeña in 1420. He spent most of the rest of his life in his native city and in Valencia, dying in 1459.

Ausías March's cultural formation came from a profound knowledge both of scholastic philosophy—Saint Thomas in particular—and of classical Latin literature, of Dante, and of Petrarch. These influences are perceptible in his poetic works. March's love poetry, which recalls Petrarch, has a theological and moral basis. His hundred *Cants d'amor* [*Songs of Love*], in which he analyzes his own feelings, were dedicated to Teresa Bon with whom he was in love. When Teresa died, the poet dedicated his seven *Cants de Mort* [*Songs of Death*] to her memory. In his *Cants morals* [*Morality Songs*] he makes a philosophical study of man's hunger for God, Truth, and Beauty. Finally, his *Cant espiritual* [*Spiritual Song*] is a fervent supplication to God. All in all, March is a very individualistic and personal poet whose work is characterized by emotional sincerity and vigor of thought.

March had considerable influence on subsequent Castilian poetry. In the sixteenth century Juan Boscán was to write of him as follows:

And to the great Catalonian who was love's king,
Ausías March, who in his verse did place his heart,
With strength and beauty's plaint in every thing,
Whose pen has left its imprint on our art.

Garsilaso de la Vega imitated him and Jorge de Montemayor translated his works into Castilian.

The novel also was cultivated in this period. The famous *Tirante lo Blanc* dates from this time. It was a novel that had extensive influence in Castile and throughout fifteenth-century Europe. Readers of today will recognize it primarily through the following passage from *Don Quixote* in which Cervantes highly praises the work both for its excitement and for its "realism":

When the Curate and the Barber are finishing the examination of Don Quixote's library, they encounter the novel.

"Great Heavens!" said the Curate in a loud voice. "Why here is Tirante the White! Hand it over to me, friend. I realize that here we have a treasure in content and a wealth of pastimes. Here is Quirieleison of Montalban, that doughty knight, and his brother Thomas of Montalban, the knight Fonseca, with the battle which brave Tirante had with the mastiff and the sorrowings of the Lady Placerdemivida and the love affairs and tricks of the Widow Reposada, and the Lady Emperatriz who was in love with Hypolitus, her squire. I tell you the truth, my friend, that for style there is no better book in the world. Here the knights eat and sleep and die in their beds and make their testament before their death, with numerous other things that are missing from other books of this type.

The novel itself has two clearly discernible components. First of all, it is a novel of extraordinary adventures whose protagonist is Tirante lo Blanc. He is a heroic knight who sallies forth at the head of his warriors to save the Isle of Rhodes from a siege by the Turks. Later on he goes to the aid of the Emperor of Byzantium, receiving as a reward for his deeds of valor the hand of Princess Carmesina in marriage and the throne of Byzantium.

The second component is a series of amorous episodes which are full of humor and sensuality. What sets the work apart from others of its kind, however, is the fundamental realism of the episodes and stories it includes, in sharp contrast to the excessive fantasy often found in other books of the genre. Conversely, the realism and large numbers of episodes included are sometimes considered a serious flaw.

The author of *Tirante lo Blanc* is the Valencian Joanot Martorell, a man who during an adventure-filled life made numerous trips and fought many a battle. He undoubtedly drew heavily on his own experiences in the composition of his novel.

In drama, the so-called Mystery of Elche has come down to us. It is presented every year in the Basilica of Santa María in Valencia as a curious reminder of Medieval drama which still holds interest. The work has as its theme the death of the Virgin Mary and her Assumption. Its presentation lasts two days. On the first day, the Virgin laments her solitude. An angel descends from the skies and announces to her the coming of death and presents her with a palm leaf. Mary dies surrounded by the Apostles. On the second day, after songs are sung before the Virgin's tomb, the burial, which the Jews noisily try to prevent, is prepared.

The *Araceli* ascends to the roof of the church with angels who carry a picture of the Virgin. The presentation comes to an end on a note of humor. Saint Thomas arrives late and makes his excuses saying, anachronistically, that he has been busy in the New World. The work is sung throughout the performance and this, of course, adds considerably to the interest of this example of early drama in the Iberian Peninsula.

2.

The Golden Age

The period of the greatest achievement in Spanish literature is known as the Golden Age. Its importance and complexity can best be comprehended by observing its esthetic tendencies which fit into different historical periods. These may be compared to the four epochs of human life and to the four seasons of the year: adolescence, youth, maturity, and age or decline, or, springtime, summer, autumn, and winter. This works out as shown in the following chart:

The Renaissance in Spain coincides with the appearance of the political phenomenon of the establishment of strong monarchical power. In discussing Ferdinand and Isabella, we saw that the monarchy was tending to consolidate power. This tendency reaches its culmination in the reign of Charles I (better known as Charles V, of the Holy Roman Empire). In addition to a strong monarchy based on the absorbing and realistic views of Machiavelli, Spain also looked to the Holy Roman Empire as the supreme form of organization. This imperial aspiration, based on the concept of the Empire and consequently founded on the idea of the Catholic hierarchy, became a concept of universal monarchy with the king of Spain cast in the role of Defender of Christianity.

A famous sonnet of Hernando de Acuña entitled *Al Rey Nuestro Señor* or *To Our Lord the King,* clearly expressed this

THE GOLDEN CENTURIES
The Four Great Periods of Castilian Literature

Sixteenth Century

Reign of Charles V
1517–1556

Springtime: Early Renaissance

Introduction of
Italianate Forms .... Garcilaso
Erasmistic Ideas .... Valdés

Reign of Philip II
1556–1598

Summertime: Later Renaissance

Incorporation of
Italianate Forms ....
{ in Salamanca   Luis de León
  in Seville   Herrera
  Saint Teresa
  Saint John of
  the Cross }

Catholic Reform ....

Seventeenth Century

Reign of Philip III
1598–1621

Autumn: Period of Plenitude

The Greatest Creators .... { Cervantes
Lope de Vega }

Reigns of Philip IV
and Charles II
1621–1700

Winter: Period of Decline

The Great Baroque Authors

"Culteranos" .... { Góngora
Calderón }

"Conceptistas" .... { Quevedo
Gracián }

attitude. For the poet, Christ's "banner" has passed to "One Monarch, One Empire and One Sword." With the Roman Empire in mind, Spaniards of the sixteenth century spoke of Charles V as Caesar.

We can discern in Spain both an early and a later Renaissance. The period cannot be considered a homogeneous movement, nor was there a single fixed epoch. Different levels of intensity and attitude in the new forms of culture are apparent. Consequently we must consider the expression "Siglo de Oro" or "Golden Century" which has long been utilized in describing this period in Spanish literature as inadequate. First of all, the "classical" period of Spanish letters lasted longer than one century. It actually extended a century and a half, from the works of Garcilaso de la Vega in 1530 to the death of Calderón de la Barca in 1681. Furthermore, the expression "Golden Century" presupposes a period of time characterized by spiritual homogeneity whereas, as we have pointed out, the situation is precisely the opposite; several different periods can be distinguished.

The Early Renaissance

The early Renaissance corresponds to the first half of the sixteenth century. It is a period of incorporation, which is to say that formulas which come from abroad are absorbed into the Spanish spirit. Some, notably those of Italian origin, it accepts and makes its own. Others, principally those of the Protestant Reformation, it rejects, instituting instead formulas commensurate with Catholicism and the Counter Reformation.

By the seventeenth century the Italianate forms have been wholly assimilated and are important in the creation of a national literature in Spain. The period of plenitude, is represented by the two major figures, Cervantes and Lope de Vega; in the period of the baroque two major tendencies, *Culteranismo* and *Conceptismo,* appear.

Poetry

Juan Boscán made a major contribution to the period of the early Renaissance. He was born in Barcelona and belonged to a part of the nobility known as "honorable citizens." He studied in the university of his native city and became the tutor of the Duke of Alba. He married Ana Girón, who published his works after her husband's death in 1542.

Boscán, in his education and in his works, is clearly a humanist. He studied with the great Latin scholar Lucius Marineo Sículo and was thoroughly acquainted with the classical works of Greek and Latin antiquity, as can be seen in his *Hero and Leander* which he wrote in imitation of Museus, Ovid, and Vergil, as well as with the Spanish authors of the Middle Ages whom he studied and commented on in his *Octava Rima* [*Eighth Rhyme*]. He is consequently a representative figure of Spanish Renaissance culture.

In addition, through his knowledge of the Italian authors whom he imitated, he brought to the Spanish Renaissance a translation of Balthasar de Castiglione's *The Courtier*. This work alone would have earned him a place among the best prose writers of his time. A version of a tragedy of Euripides done by Boscán has been lost to us.

Boscán wrote in Castilian. He was, nevertheless, a Catalonian and one of the first of his people to abandon his native tongue for Castilian Spanish. This fact is interesting historically as it reflects the absorption of languages not in a privileged position in the center of the country into the tongue of the dominating Castilian monarchy. However, this did not keep Boscán from feeling love for his home land, as can be discerned in his praise of Barcelona in his *Octava Rima*.

Boscán's metric innovations are of far-reaching importance. In a letter to the Duchess of Soma, he explains the impact of his meeting in Granada with Andrea Navagero, the Ambassador of the Republic of Venice. The latter urged the poet to change from the short verse line customarily employed in the *cancioneros* as well as by Boscán himself for "sonnets and other poetic forms used by the best writers of Italy." It should be noted that the sonnet and, more generally, the hendecasyllabic line had been utilized earlier, notably by the Marquis de Santillana in the fifteenth century. Boscán, however, attempted to acclimate both the hendecasyllabic line which was accented on the sixth syllable or on the fourth and eighth, accentuation typical of the Italian metrics, and, in addition, strophes which had not been used in Spain before that time such as the *canción* or song, the *octava rima,* the *estancia,* the *epistola en tercetos* or epistle in tercets, and the *verso suelto* or blank verse.

The following passage is from the letter to the Duchess of Soma:

One day while I was in Granada with Navagero (who having been so venerated recently I wished to mention to your Ladyship) conversing with him on creativity and literature, and especially on the variety of languages, he asked me why I did not try my hand in Castillian at composing sonnets and other poetical forms used by the best authors of Italy. Not only did he not say this to me lightly, he even entreated me to follow his advice. Several days later I left for home. On the long and lonely journey I thought over what Navagero had said to me. It was in this manner that I began to try this type of verse. At first I found many difficulties as the forms were very different from those to which we are accustomed. Somewhat later, perhaps with the love that grows for one's own things, it seemed to me that the writing began to go well. I set myself at my task with enthusiasm. This would not have sufficed for me to have progressed successfully, however, had it not been for Garcilaso and his wisdom. In my opinion and everyone else's, it was he who held my endeavors to be of a certain precept and who confirmed me in my undertaking.

Boscán and Garcilaso de la Vega were good friends. They are the creators of the Spanish poetry of the Renaissance. The following sonnet by Boscán, written on the occasion of the untimely death of Garcilaso, gives a good idea of the deep feeling between the two poets:

On the Death of Garcilaso.

Tell me, dear Garcilaso,—thou
    Who ever aim'st at Good,
And, in the spirit of thy vow,
    So swift her course pursued,
That thy few steps sufficed to place
The angel in thy loved embrace,
    Won instant, soon as wooed,—
Why took'st thou not, when winged to flee
From this dark world, Boscán with thee?

Why when ascending to the star
    Where now thou sitt'st enshrined,
Left'st thou thy weeping friend afar,
    Alas! so far behind?
O, I do think, had it remained
With thee to alter aught ordained
    By the Eternal Mind,
Thou wouldst not on this desert spot
Have left thy other self forgot!

For if through life the love was such,
    As still to take a pride
In having me so oft and much
    Close to thy envied side,—
I cannot doubt, I must believe,
Thou wouldst at least have taken leave
    Of me; or, if denied,
Have come back afterwards, unblest
Till I, too, shared thy heavenly rest.

—Translation by J. H. Wiffen

In addition to the original works we have cited and his translation of *The Courtier,* Boscán wrote a series of sonnets in the style of Petrarch that show the influence as well of Ausías March. One work, the *Mar de amor* [*Sea of Love*], is allegorical. Another work, the lengthy *Epistle to Mendoza,* is written in tercets.

Nevertheless Boscán's main contribution and accomplishment is to have brought the Renaissance forms into Spanish poetry. His own versification is frequently forced and belabored. Consequently he is known more for his role in the history of the development of Spanish literature than for the intrinsic value of his work.

Garcilaso de la Vega's case is different in that he is important both for his role in the history of Spanish letters and for his poetic genius. He became acquainted with Boscán as a youth. The two poets met at the home of the Duke of Alba where Garcilaso was a tutor. The friendship that developed between the two men had a major literary importance. Of the two it was Garcilaso who perfected the metrical innovations which Boscán put into practice.

Garcilaso's life is an interesting one. He was born in Toledo in 1503. He came from a noble family. After completing his education in his native city in 1520 he entered the service of the Emperor. He accompanied him to Galicia and participated in the Wars of the Communes. He was wounded in 1521. He also took part in the expedition to the Isle of Rhodes and the campaign in Navarre in 1522–1523. His friendship with Boscán took shape during these years of court life. He married Doña Elena de Zuñiga in 1525. His poetic love, however, was a lady of the suite of Queen Isabella of Portugal. Her name was Isabel Freyre and she was known poetically as Elisa. Garcilaso also went to Italy where he was present at the Emperor's coronation, and to France where he was a special ambassador. On his return to Italy, he received an order from the Emperor exiling him for having attended a wedding of which the monarch disapproved. The exile was to an island in the Danube. Once he was pardoned, he went to Naples where he experienced one of the happiest and most productive periods of his life. He later made a journey to Barcelona, passing through the Vaucluse in southern France as an homage to Petrarch and then went to Tunis as part of the military expedition of Charles V in 1533. He was wounded in the mouth and in one arm. He was promoted to the position of Camp Commander. It was in this capacity that he personally carried out the assault on the small fortress of Muy (Fréjus) in southern France. Wearing neither helmet nor shield, he received a blow on the head from a stone cast by the defenders of the fortress. He fell headlong and a few days later in Nice died from the wounds he had received. He passed away in the arms of his close friend the Marquis of Lombay who later was to be venerated under the name of Saint Francis of Borja.

The spiritual world of Garcilaso is perhaps best seen in his pastoral poetry. It is all the more surprising to find the pastoral themes dominating his work when we consider that the poet's life was dominated by his military career which hardly has any place at all in his poetry. This can be comprehended if we see the pastoral theme as a sort of ingenious rejection of the poet's own life. Among the works that most clearly exemplify this are the *Eclogues* which are Garcilaso's most lengthy poems and which contain the greatest amount of autobiographical material. The principal characters of these poems, the two shepherds Salicio and Nemoroso, recount to each other the misfortunes and sorrows that love has brought them. The following selection is taken from the *First Eclogue:*

> The sweet lament of two Castilian swains,
> Salicio's love and Nemoroso's tears,
> In sympathy I sing, to whose lovèd strains
> Their flocks, of food forgetful, crowding round,
> Were most attentive. . . .
>
> Through thee the silence of the shaded glen,
> Through thee the horror of the lonely mountain
> Pleased me no less than the resort of men;
> The breeze, the summer wood, the lucid fountain,
> The purple rose, white lily of the lake,
> Were sweet for thy sweet sake;
>
> .   .   .   .   .
>
> Flow forth, my tears, 'tis meet that ye should flow!
>
> In the charmed ear of what belovèd youth
> Sounds thy sweet voice? on whose proved truth
> Anchors thy broken faith? who presses now

Thy laughing lip, and hopes thy heavens of charms,
Locked in the embraces of thy two white arms?

. . . .

Flow forth, my tears, 'tis meet that ye should flow!

Here, I remember, waking once at noon,
I saw Elisa standing at my side;
Oh cruel fate! oh finespun web, too soon
By Death's sharp scissors clipt, sweet, suffering bride,
In womanhood's most interesting prime,
Cut off, before thy time!
—Translation by J. H. Wiffen

The lamentations of the shepherd Salicio are supposedly those of Garcilaso himself. Nemoroso, his interlocutor, is believed to have been Boscán, as the word *nemus* means *bosque* or woods, which is clearly suggestive of the latter's name. There is another theory, however, that both shepherds represent Garcilaso, each being an aspect of the poet's spirit. The dialogue may be then considered as the expression of a thirst for self-analysis which is very characteristic of the Renaissance.

At the same time, the pastoral formula permitted the disguising of the Duke of Alba under the name of Albanio, of the Duchess as Camila, and of Doña Isabel Freyre, the Portuguese lady of the poet's heart, as Elisa. In the transformation of this real world into the artificial one of the shepherds, Garcilaso utilizes all of his humanistic knowledge of authors such as Theocritus, Vergil, Tibullus, Horace, Boccaccio, Petrarch, and Sannazaro.

Furthermore the pastoral theme becomes, for Garcilaso, a sort of dream of repose or escape from the fatigue of his life as a soldier. The landscapes he describes, the verdant valleys and crystalline streams, the Tajo, the Tormes, and the Danube which he calls the "divine river," constitute the most beautiful example of nature description in Spanish literature.

His neoplatonism is obvious in his works. From the times of the troubadours and Provençal literature, poets had practiced the expression of a spiritual love in which the woman was the symbol

of perfection which attracted the lover and made of him an ador-
ing slave. Garcilaso's platonic love for Elisa, which he expresses
in his *Eclogues,* is in reality, as we have already mentioned, a love
"without hope or requital," which Doña Isabel inspired. This
unrequited love filled the poet with melancholy: "They cannot
take from me the sorrowful feeling if along with life itself they
do not take all feeling," he wrote.

As a man of the Renaissance, however, Garcilaso also loved
the enjoyment of life and felt the desire to live fully and take
advantage of the moment. He wrote as follows to his belovèd:

> Of this your happy springtime take
> The luscious fruit, before swift time
> With winter's snow thy lovely summit heaps.

In number, the works of Garcilaso are relatively few. There
are one epistle, two elegies, three eclogues, five songs, and thirty-
eight sonnets, plus a group of compositions in Latin verse and
several couplets in the traditional manner. These constitute the
whole body of Garcilaso's poetic creation. These poems plus a
prologue for the translation of *The Courtier* which Boscán did
and a small number of letters and a testament are all that have
come down to us. This much, however, was sufficient to establish
the poet's spiritual physiognomy as we can see in the following
passage by the twentieth-century writer Azorín:

> Garcilaso loves water, trees and flowers. These are three
> supreme delectations. In his verses the poet paints the clear
> water that crosses a fresh and verdant field; the pure and
> crystalline water; the trees that are reflected on the terse sur-
> face of the rivers and fountains, the flowering and shaded
> valleys; the gentle wind that softly moves the trees; the tinted
> clouds that appear bordered with gold as the sun sets; the
> murmur of water from mountain springs; the robust and
> verdant oaks; the lofty beech trees; the flowering glens, thick
> and shadowy; the silence broken only by the gentle noise of
> the bees; the green and tranquil fields.

In addition, certain aspects of the life of Garcilaso may be seen in the poems. For example, the following passage is called "Written in Exile":

> With the mild sound of clear swift waves the
>   Danube's arms of foam
> Circle a verdant isle which peace has made her
>   chosen home;
> Where the fond past might repair from weariness
>   and strife,
> And in the sunshine of sweet song consume
>   his happy life.

—Translation by J. H. Wiffen

The following sonnet reminds us of the poet's friendship with Boscán:

The Sonnet to Boscán

> Boscán, you are now revenged upon my play
> Of past severe unkindness, who reproved
> The tenderness of that soft heart which loved
> With such excessive warmth; now, not a day
> Passes, but for the things I used to say
> With so much rudeness, I myself chastise;
> Still, times there are when I at heart despise,
> And blush for the abasement I betray.
> Know that, full grown, and armed against desire,
> With my eyes open I have veiled my plume
> To the blind boy you know,—but soft, my lute,
> Never, oh never did man's heart consume
> In so divine and beautiful a fire;
> If you her name solicit, I am mute.

—Translation by J. H. Wiffen

A description of war may be found in the *Second Eclogue:*

Next, angry Mars, imperious to behold,
Advancing, gave the youth a crown of gold!
Threatening the illustrious youth, a knight was seen,
Of a fierce spirit and insulting mien.

Wallowing in blood; some silent dying; some
Yet breathing free, not wholly overcome,
Showed palpitating bowels, strangely gored
By the deep gashes given by his sharp sword.

—Translation by J. H. Wiffen

Garcilaso's love of his own native land, and especially the area
of Toledo and the Tagus River, may also be found in his works:

The glorious Tagus therefore she designed,
There where he blesses with his sinuous train
The happiest of all lands, delightful Spain!
.   .   .   .   .
On the highest mountain's airy head was placed
Of ancient towers a grand and glorious weight;
Here its bare bosom white-walled convents graced,
There castles frowned in old Arabian state;

In windings grateful to the eye of taste,
Thence the smooth river, smilingly sedate,
Slid, comforting the gardens, woods and flowers,
With the cool spray of artificial showers.

—Translation by J. H. Wiffen

The *Ode to the Flower of Gnido,* one of Garcilaso's best known
works, combines the theme of war with that of love:

Think not, think not, fair flower of Gnido,
    It e'er should celebrate the scars,
Dust raised, blood shed, or laurels dyed
    Beneath the gonfalon of Mars;
    Or borne sublime on festal cars,

The chiefs who to submission sank
    The rebel German's soul of soul,
And forged the chains that now control
    The frenzy of the Frank.

No, no! its harmonies should ring
    In vaunt of glories all thine own,—
A discord sometimes from the string
    Struck forth to make thy harshness known;
    The fingered chords should speak alone
Of beauty's triumphs, Love's alarms,
    And one who, made by thy disdain
    Pale as a lily clipped in twain,
    Bewails thy fatal charms.

                    —Translation by J. H. Wiffen

In résumé we might say, then, that being genteel and of a noble family, Garcilaso de la Vega was the perfect "courtier" in the manner of Castiglione. He was proud and a gentleman. He was educated to arms and to letters in the court of Charles V. Greco-Latin classical culture held no secrets for him. Vergil and Horace above all captivated him. He himself wrote poetry in Latin, but later on, in his period of greatest maturity, he preferred to saturate himself with Italian poetry, with Petrarch, Bembo, and Sannazaro who are the poets whose influence on his works is most marked. It was from this that his attachment to such Italian metric forms as the *lira, silva, canción* and the sonnet stemmed.

Despite the relatively small number of compositions, Garcilaso is called the "prince of Castilian poetry." His influence was considerable.

Gutierre de Cetina is the best known of the poets who formed a sort of school of Garcilaso, following in the footsteps of the latter in the Italianate vogue. Cetina was born in Seville in 1520 and is known as the poet of love. He died around 1557. His madrigals are justly famous, and especially the one reproduced below:

Clear eyes, so lovely and serene,
if for your gentle gaze you're so much praised,
why, if you look my way are you in anger raised?
If when with kinder glance
more lovely do they seem to him on whom they're cast,
let not this look of anger last,
Oh raging, tortured trance!
lest in that moment thus your charm and beauty chance.
Oh, raging, tortured trance!
Clear eyes, so lovely and serene,
Even though you look askance, let me not go unseen.

Other poets who wrote in the Italianate vein were Hernando
de Acuña, whose imperial sonnet praised the King as Defender
of Christianity, and Francisco de Aldana, the spirited singer of
war and an exalted neoplatonist in matters of the heart.

There was a reaction of traditionalism by poets who opposed
the new Italianate forms and meters. Not everyone accepted the
innovations of Boscán and Garcilaso. A vigorous opposition to
them was begun by Cristóbal de Castillejo, who represents the
resistance which the medieval spirit made to the new forms of
the Renaissance.

Cristóbal de Castellejo lived from 1490 to 1550. He was born
in Castel Rodrigo. He became a monk of Saint Martin of Val-
deiglesias. Later on he acted as secretary to Don Fernando of
Bohemia, the brother of Charles V, and bettered his fortunes
with a post in the collegiate church of Ardegge. He died in
Vienna. His private life left much to be desired. It was a mixture,
also discernible in his work, of the devout and the pagan.

Castillejo opposed the Italian meters. He defended the octosyllabic verse which had long been the traditional meter of
Spanish poetry. In his couplets entitled *Contra los que dexan los
metros castellanos y siguen los italiano* [*Against Those Who
Abandon Castilian Meters for Italian Ones*], he attacked Spaniards
who, in place of traditional forms, preferred meters which were
"foreign and new to our ears." He maintained that the hende-
casyllable was not new because that line had been utilized by
Juan de Mena and the Marquis of Santillana.

Drama

The Renaissance transformed the drama in language, ideas, and presentation. The medieval style, which was colored, of course, by the Renaissance, persisted in several authors. The new spirit, however, made substantial progress.

A major figure in the transition to the Renaissance was Gil Vicente. He was born about 1565, it is believed, in Lisbon. His works are written in both Spanish and Portuguese for, although he came from Portugal, he wrote many works in Castilian and was equally adept in both tongues.

The "facts" of Gil Vicente's life as they have come down to us are not always reliable. He was a musician, poet, goldsmith, perhaps a lawyer, and he lived in the Portuguese court. In 1502, on the occasion of the birth of Prince Don Juan III (who was the son of the king of Portugal Dom Manuel I who had married Maria, the daughter of Ferdinand and Isabella), Gil Vincente entered the royal chambers reciting his *Monólogo del Vaquero* [*Monologue of the Cowboy*] which was the "first thing to be presented in Portugal." The festivities were repeated at the request of the queen and a "canto" on the Nativity and the Three Kings was added. These works were influenced by Juan del Encina.

Gil Vicente created an ambitious allegorical drama. Taking advantage of the interest which the various versions of the "Dance of Death" had awakened, he portrayed the whole gamut of society in his famous *Trilogía das Barcas* [*Trilogy of the Ships*], two of which, the one of the *Inferno* and the other of *Purgatory,* are in Portuguese, and the other, *Glory,* in Spanish. In these works we see the social life of the times portrayed with a note of Erasmian satire, a fact which provides the traditional medieval theme with an accentuation of the new spirit of the Renaissance.

The *Auto da Barca da Gloria* [*Playlet of the Ship of Glory*] is written in Spanish and is the part of the trilogy which is most closely related to the genre of the "Dance of Death." Death calls on the potentates of this earth, on the Emperor, the Pope, the King, the Cardinal, the Duke, the Archbishop, the Count, and the Bishop, all of whom recite prayers and ask forgiveness for their sins. At the end, Christ appears and helps in the salvation of the wretched.

In the *Barca do Inferno* two ships are seen, one which is guided by an angel and goes to Heaven, and another which a devil steers and which goes to Hell. Different social types appear, such as the gentleman, the usurer, the shoemaker, and so on, who are accused by the devil of reprehensible vices, despite an outward display of devoutness. Antiecclesiastical satire is clearly evident.

The *Barca do Purgatorio,* also in Portuguese, is based on the legend that on Christmas night the devil's ship is grounded so that no one can go to hell. The literary critic Valbuena writes:

> The lyrical beauty of the work strikes us from the very beginning with its three angels rowing and singing: "A-rowing go the boatmen—ship of happiness." The presentation of the contrast between the ingenuity and simplicity of the people and the horrors of Hell is completely successful. For example, there is a little shepherd girl who fears the vision of the Enemy who appears to her at the moment of death: "Jesus! Jesus! What time is this?", and a child of few years who cries when he sees the Devil, "Look, the bogeyman is there!" The ending with its devils who carry off a blasphemous gambler with their disharmonious song and the angels who lull the child with their melodic chant is of an ingenuous poetry unequalled in any drama.

Vicente's comedies of manners such as *La comedia del Viudo* [*Comedy of the Widower*] or *Farsa dos Físicos* [*The Farce of the Two Physicians*], a satire against doctors and full of an extraordinary sense of humor and excellent verses, are noteworthy for the sharpness of their portrayals of character. Other farces in which he presents men of the people, such as his *Auto das Gitanas* [*Play of the Gypsies*], are more popular and satirical. His chivalric plays, including *Dom Duardo* and *Amadis,* have a profound poetic sense.

He was also an outstanding poet. In addition to possessing

a sense of drama and of satire, Gil Vicente was a poet of the highest quality who frequently used themes from the common people.

Lope de Rueda also made signicant contributions to drama in this period. He was born in Seville in the early years of the sixteenth century. He was both actor and author and traveled about Spain with a company of players and in the service of several noblemen.

In his work we find the following:

a *Pasos* or short dramatic sketches and popular dialogues, written in prose and in realistic speech. These works constitute the earliest national drama of Spain; they mirror the life of the lower classes—their language and their customs. The best known of his "pasos" are *Las aceitunas* [*The Olives*], *El Convidado* [*The Invited Guest*], and *La Tierra de Jauja* [*Jauja's Land*].

In this first expression, Lope de Rueda's merit is evident. He is creator of a prose drama, or, to put it another way, of a theater which permits an exact presentation of the language of everyday reality. In this respect, Rueda is an excellent collector of phrases, sayings, turns of speech, and jests which give to his scenes a truly extraordinary realism and gaiety.

b The Italianate drama, which was influenced by the works performed by companies of traveling Italian comedians who toured Spain. Rueda's most lengthy and perfected works, such as the *Eufemia, Armelina, Los engañados,* and *Medora,* belong in this category.

These are comedies of situation with many adventures, exploits, and sudden recognitions similar to those which constituted the basis of the Byzantine novel. Rueda's originality in the writing of these plays is almost nonexistent as they are actually little more than imitations of the dramas performed by Italian actors who constantly toured Spain at this time.

Cervantes, in the prologue to an edition of his own plays, wrote:

I said that I recalled having seen a performance of the great Lope de Rueda, a man outstanding both as a performer and in his wisdom. He was born in Seville and was of the

profession of "batihojas" which means that he was of those
who make gold leaf. He was an outstanding writer of pastoral
poetry and in this vein neither before nor since has he been
bested. . . . His plays were a sort of dialogue similar to
eclogues between two or three shepherds and a shepherdess.
He embellished them and filled them out with two or three
interludes, first one about a Negro, then about a ruffian,
another about a dopey fellow or a Biscayan. These four figures
plus many others were drawn by the aforementioned Lope
with as great a skill and fitness as may be imagined. When
Lope de Rueda died, he was known as so excellent and famous
a man that he was buried between the two choir lofts in the
main church of Cordova.

Bartolomé de Torres Naharro is another dramatist who
serves as an example of the progressive influence of the doctrines
of the Renaissance. Although he was from Extremadura, Torres
Naharro spent many years in Rome. He died about 1531.

It was in Rome that Torres Naharro became acquainted
with the esthetic of Horace which he incorporated in his book,
the *Propalladia* (or first gift to Pallas) in which he collected his
plays. Following the principles of Horace he established the
division of plays into five acts or *jornadas*.

His work contains several classifications. In his plays, Torres
Naharro creates a form that we might call "documentary"—
sketches of customs and the portrayal of the daily life of soldiers
(*Soldadesca*) or of cooks (*Tinellaria*)—and which he himself designated *comedias a noticias*.

There are also plays extant called *de argumento* in which
plot predominates and in which the characters take part in a
drama not involving an everyday occurrence. The best of these
comedias a fantasía is the *Himenea*. The story involves lovers'
complications. The youth Himeneo, who is in love with Febea,
enters his loved one's house. There he is taken by one of the
lady's brothers who wants to kill the suitor. This is avoided by
lengthy explanations and the marriage of the two lovers. The
work is conceived within the Aristotelian precepts of the Unities.
Others of Torres Naharro's so-called *comedias a fantasía* are the
Serafina, Aquilana, and *Calamita*.

The Sevilian Juan de la Cueva is close to Lope de Vega both in time (he lived between 1543 and 1610) and because of the similarity in the aspiration of his drama. One of his plays is considered a precedent of Tirso's play, the *Burlador*. It is the play of greatest interest to us today and is entitled *El infamador* [*The Defamer*]. In it the dramatist portrays the figure of a cynical braggart named Leucino who, enamored of Eliodora, tries, with the help of his servants, to force her will. Eliodora defends herself and kills one of the servants. Leucino then accuses her and she is condemned to death. When the real truth is established, however, it is Leucino who is executed. The interest in this work stems in large part from the theory that the figure of the "defamer" is an antecedent of Tirso's Don Juan.

These authors who more and more markedly show traits of the Renaissance are forerunners of a theater that is fully humanistic in character. By humanistic we mean a drama that develops out of the reading of works of the great Greek tragedians and of the *Poetics* of Aristotle, in addition to those of the great Latin authors—Plautus, Terence, and Seneca—and the *Ars Poetica* of Horace.

This purely Renaissance drama is written only by the humanists who were acquainted with classical literature. It is not, consequently, drama of the people but is refined and aristocratic. In final analysis it lacked real vitality and finally died out.

Didactic Prose

A new style in prose developed. We have already pointed out, as in the case of the *Celestina,* how the influence of the Renaissance brought about the vogue of using the lengthy and embellished Latin clause, difficult neologisms, and hyperbatons characterized in most cases by the placing of the verb at the end of the sentence. In the sixteenth century the excessive accumulation of Latin elements disappears. There is a tendency toward a simpler prose and one which is more flexible and balanced and more useful for didactic expression.

Alfonso de Valdés is important in the development of prose style. He was born in Cuenca, served in the Chancellery of the

Emperor and even became secretary to Charles V for whom he
wrote numerous state papers. He was a fervent friend of Erasmus
with whom he maintained an intense correspondence. He was
among those Spanish humanists who most vividly felt Erasmus'
influence.

Because of this influence and of being secretary in the service of Charles V, he wrote the famous *Dialogue Between Lactancio and an Archdeacon* in which he justifies the sack of Rome
in 1527 by alleging that the Pope had broken the peace. He also
stated that the Pope and his Cardinals were not the whole
Church, which consisted of all Christians. What happened, says
Lactancio, is that since the Church did not heed "the honest rep-
rehensions of Erasmus, and even less the dishonest injuries of
Luther, God has taken other means to bring about a change and
has permitted the soldiers to sack Rome."

The Dialogue Between Mercury and Charon is in the same
spirit of reform. In it the Emperor is defended against the challenge of the kings of France and England. It is a gallery of
satirical portraits. The great dignitaries of political life and of
the Church pass by in Charon's bark, and Valdés severely judges
them.

These works of Alfonso de Valdés follow in the vein of
Erasmian satire already noted in the *Trilogy of the Ships* of Gil
Vicente. It was this spirit that was dominant throughout Europe
at the time.

Juan de Valdés, Alfonso's brother, is also justly remembered.
He resided many years in Naples where he had a reputation for
being a great humanistic scholar. His *Diálogo de la lengua (Dialogue on Language)* is famous. In the work two Spaniards and
two Italians discuss the beauty of their respective native tongues.

With respect to linguistic ideas, Juan de Valdés is one of
the first to affirm: (*a*) That Castilian Spanish is as rich and elegant
as Tuscan Italian. He does, however, recognize its lack of a great
literary tradition comparable to Dante and Petrarch. In Italy,
nevertheless, "among ladies as well as gentlemen it is held to be
courtesy and gallantry to know how to speak Castilian." (*b*) That
the best style is the most natural one ("and without any affecta-
tion whatsoever, I write as I speak"). In his conversation Valdés

THE GOLDEN AGES   107

utilized a number of proverbial sayings for the purpose of obtaining the effect of naturalness he recommended. (c) That the model for good Spanish is Castilian.

Juan de Valdés disclaims the authority of Nebrija because the latter was from Andalusia. "Don't you see that although Nebrija was a very scholarly man . . . he was Andalusian, he spoke and wrote Spanish as they do in Andalusia and not in Castile?"

In the same period, Friar Antonio de Guevara is one of the most representative authors of the sixteenth century. He was born in a mountain district of northern Spain in 1480, educated in the court of the Catholic Kings, and was, he tells us, "more given to bad habits than to good." When Queen Isabella died he entered the Franciscan Order. During the War of the Communes he fought in the service of Charles V. Guevara's work spread throughout Europe and his ideas, which can be divided into two categories, had considerable influence on Montaigne.

On the political level, Guevara defended the existence of a great Christian monarchy, a model of which he sketched in his work the *Relox de Principe* (*Clock of Princes*). It is divided into three parts, one on the religiousness of the prince, two, on family and private comportment, and three, on his public obligations.

On the moral level, Guevara defended the simplicity and the virtues of the country in his *Menosprecio de Corte y Alabanza de Aldea* (*Scorn of Court Life and Praise of the Village*). In a chapter of the *Clock of Princes* entitled the "Peasant of the Danube," Guevara states the rights of a simple man to live his life independently and to reject the settlements which, despite their virtuous aspects, represent rapine and slavery. In this work, Guevara imagines a meeting in which the emperor Marcus Aurelius tells the following tale:

> The first year that I was consul, there came to Rome a poor peasant from the bank of the Danube to ask for justice from the Senate against a censor who had caused much trouble and hardship to his village. Truly the man outlined his case so well and the injuries that the judges had done in his native land that he presented it better than Tullius or than Homer could have.

The peasant makes a passionate defense of the liberty which "natural" peoples enjoy:

Happy and fortunate republic, not the one in which there is much friendly intercourse, but the one where many virtuous men live; not the one where riches abound, but the one where virtue is prized; not the one where many boisterous people live but where men of peace reside. From all this we may conclude that the police [i.e., the culture] of Rome, being wealthy, must be held to be blemished whereas the police of Germany, being poor, is to be envied.

Epic and Historical Works During the Renaissance

Throughout both the early and later Renaissance periods, a series of cultured epic poems in imitation of the great epopees of the Italian Renaissance, and especially Ariosto and Tasso, were written. In them there appears the characteristic strophe of the *octava real,* diverse themes, and a frequent combination of reality and fantasy.

First of all there is the use of national themes. The exaltation of the exploits which brought the Spanish Empire into existence provided this poetry with its major thematic material. For example, the emperor Charles V is exalted in an epic poem by Luis Zapata entitled *Carlo Famoso* and in *La Carolea* by Jerónimo Sempere. The war against the Moslems is celebrated by Juan Rufo in *La Austriada* (whose hero is Don Juan de Austria) and by Herrera in his famous *Oda a la Batalla de Lepanto* [*Ode to The Battle of Lepanto*]. The epopee of America was poetized by Alonso de Ercilla in his famous work *La Araucana,* doubtless the finest cultured epic poem in Spanish. In the work, Ercilla exalted the valor of the native Araucan Indians of Chile in the defense of their native land. The real protagonist-hero of the work is the Indian chieftain Caupolicán. Pedro de Oña tried to correct this interest in the Indian and as a result exalted the

Spanish conquistador Don García Hurtado de Mendoza in his
poem *Arauco Domado* [*Araucan Tamed*].

The following are passages from *La Araucana* by Alonso de
Ercilla:

The son of a cacique, whom friendship's hands
    Allied to Spain, had long in page's post
Attended on Valdivia, at his hands
    Receiving kindness; in the Spanish host
He came.—Strong passion suddenly expands

    His heart, beholding troops, his country's boast
Forsakes the field. With voice and port elate,
    Their valor thus he strives to animate:—

                .   .   .   .   .

    "On memory imprint the words I breathe,
Howe'er by loathsome terror ye're distraught;
A deathless story to the world bequeath,—
    Enslave Arauco's liberation wreath,
When fate propitious calls, and prompts high thought!
    Or in your rapid flight an instant pause
To see me singly perish in your cause!"

With that the youth a strong and weighty lance
    Against Valdivia brandishes on high;
And, yet more from bewildering terror's trance
    To rouse Arauco, rushes furiously
Upon the Spaniard's conquering advance:
    So eagerly the heated stag will fly
To plunge his body in the coolest stream,
Attempering thus the sun's meridian beam.

                .   .   .   .   .

He wounds, he slaughters, strikes down all around,
    Suddenly clearing the encumbered space:
In him alone the battle's rage is found;
    Turned all against him, the Spaniards leave the chase;

But he so lightly moves, now here, now there,
That in his stead they wound the empty air.

. . . . .

Of whom was ever such stupendous deed
    Or heard, or read, in ancient history,
As from the victor's party to secede,
    Joining the vanquished even as they fly?
Or that barbarian boy, at utmost need,
    By his unaided valor's energy,
Should from the Christian army rend away
    A victory, guerdon of a hard-fought day?

—Anonymous translation

Ercilla's "Second Canto" is as follows:

Coloculus' address to the heads of the Araucanians who
have been fighting among themselves over commands of the
army, as follows:

Caciques! defenders of your country, hear!
    It is not envy wounds my tortured sight,
When I observe these struggles, who shall wear
    Ambition's badge,—which had been mine of right;—
For see my brow in aged wrinkles dight,
    And the tomb tells me I must soon be there;—
'Tis love inspires me! patriotism! zeal!—
    Listen my soul its counsels shall unveil.

. . . .

Madden your weapons with the' enthusiast soul!
    O let them probe th'invaders' inmost breast;
He who would chain you to his proud control,—
    To slavery, insult!—O 'twere wise, 'twere best
To stay his fettering hand, nor tamely rest
    While strength and valour to your efforts call!

Your blood, chief's is your country's—guard it then
For her!—it is not yours, heroic men!

—Anonymous translation

Secondly, there is the religious epic. This genre is represented by *El Monserrate,* by Captain Cristóbal de Virués. The
work tells the legend of the Friar Garín, a great sinner who
finally obtains God's pardon through harsh and lengthy penitence.
A similar work is *La Cristiada,* by Friar Diego de Hojeda, which
is a poem of the Redemption.

Thirdly, there is the novelistic epic. This genre is the one
most influenced by Italian models. One of its best known works
is *Las Lagrimas de Angélica (Angelica's Tears)* by Barahona de
Soto.

Finally, there is the burlesque epic. Among the works of this
sort are *La Gatomaquia (Catfighting)* by Lope, *La Perromaquia
(Dogfighting)* by Nieto de Molina, and *La Mosquea (The Fly-
swatting)* by José de Villaviciosa.

For a long time, history was written as a literary work. Today
we think of history as a science which proves the facts under
consideration. However, history used to be, above all, a work of
art from which a lesson or an experience was to be derived.
History and legend moved along in similar fashion in two directions: The cultural, followed by the humanists, who attempted
to imitate the style and manners of the Greek and Latin historians, and the popular, inherited from the medieval chronicles
and from the epic *canciones de gesta,* in which the historian
recounted in a direct and lively manner what he knew of the oral
and written tradition.

In the work of Father Mariana, a Jesuit, who wrote the
monumental *History of Spain* beginning with the arrival in Spain
of Tubal, the son of Jafet, we have an example of history as a
cultured art. The work's value is purely literary. The work of
Bernal Díaz del Castillo exemplifies history as a popularized art.
When we read this writer's *Verdadera historia de los sucesos y
conquista de la Nueva España (True History of the Events of
the Conquest of New Spain),* we can comprehend the popular,

direct, "journalistic" flavor of his history. The great American epopee has historians of a "cultured" type as well, such as Fernández de Oviedo, López de Gómara, and Antonio de Solís.

History as a science began in Spain with the *Annals of the Crown of Aragon* by Jerónimo de Zurita, published 1562–1580.

The Second Renaissance

The term "Second Renaissance" is used here to designate the spirit of the second half of the sixteenth century during the reign of Philip II, from 1556 to 1598. Consequently this period falls between the early Renaissance (1500–1550) which fills the reign of Charles V (1517–1556) and those periods of plenitude in the seventeenth century under the reign of Philip III (1598–1621) and the baroque which reaches its height during the reigns of Philip IV and Charles II, from 1621 until about 1700.

The Italianate forms which had been introduced during the early Renaissance by Boscán and Garcilaso were assimilated and came to constitute two schools of poetry which, in the second Renaissance, took on the stylistic peculiarities of the regions from which they sprang:

1. The School of Salamanca, headed by Fray Luis de León, which reflects the grave and sober spirit of Castile.

2. The Sevillian School, whose leader was Fernando de Herrera and which acquired the external brilliance and the deep sonority of Andalusia.

As to content, although neoplatonic ideas were incorporated in the works of the mystics, Erasmian tendencies and leanings toward Protestantism were rejected by the powerful movement of Catholic reaction. This had been initiated by Saint Ignatius and throughout Spain had taken up the banner of the Catholic Reform or the Counter Reformation.

The School of Salamanca

Fray Luis de León is the best known writer of the school of Salamanca. He was born in Belmonte in the province of Cuenca in 1527. He studied in Madrid and Valladolid and later went to Salamanca where he received an advanced degree in Sacred Theology. He entered the Augustinian Order and became a professor in the University of Salamanca.

For having published and commented on *The Song of Songs* in Spanish, he was brought to trial by the Inquisition. Although the accusation was brought on by the envy of others, he was, nevertheless, imprisoned for four years. During this period he wrote his famous *De Los Nombres de Cristo* [*On the Names of Christ*] and some of his finest poetry. A verdict absolving him permitted him to return to his professorship.

Fray Luis finally triumphed. Once he had returned to his classes at the university, with his famous opening statement, "As we were saying yesterday, . . ." he undertook a series of new activities, and his prestige grew constantly. He was elected to the post of Provincial of the Augustinians of Castile. He died in Madrigal in 1591.

Fray Luis was one of the best educated men of his time and a man of great culture. He wrote several of his works in Latin. He translated *The Song of Songs, The Book of Job,* and various *Psalms* and *Proverbs* from the Hebrew into Castilian. He also did translations of Latin authors, including Virgil's *Eclogues* and Book One of *The Georgias,* besides works of Horace, Tibulus, and others, and of Italian writers including Petrarch, Bembo, and Giovanni de la Casa. We can see the traces of these translations in Fray Luis's original works.

Fray Luis was thoroughly acquainted with the Bible in the original Hebrew. The following works show the Bible's influence:

1. *The Song of Songs,* a translation of the *Book of Solomon* in which, under the symbolism of two lovers, the Husband (Christ) and the Wife (The Church) carry on a dialogue of love. Fray Luis wrote a commentary on each part of the book.

2. *The Book of Job* in which, utilizing the story of Job from the Old Testament as a starting point, Fray Luis de León explains how Providence makes use of the adversities which befall Job as a motive for his glorification.

3. *The Perfecta Casada* [*Perfect Wife*], a work of greater originality in which the author portrays the ideal wife in the

Christian home. One of Fray Luis's models is to be found in the strong woman spoken of in the Bible.

4. *On the Names of Christ* is a work also based on the Bible. It is a gloss or commentary on each of the names used in speaking of God in the Bible: Pastor, Father, Jesus, Lamb, Prince of Peace, Mount, and so on. The work is written in the form of a dialogue between various persons, one of whom is Fray Luis himself.

The influence of Greek and Latin authors on Fray Luis is hardly less interesting. His poetry shows a deep admiration for Horace. In the tradition of the "Beatus ille . . ." we have his famous eulogy of the man who lives out in the country, far from the traffic of the world:

Retirement

O, happy, happy he, who flies
Far from the noisy world away,—
Who, with the worthy and the wise,
    Hath chosen the narrow way,—
The silence of the secret road
That leads the soul to virtue and to God!

No passions in his breast arise;
    Calm in his own unaltered state,
He smiles superior, as he eyes
    The splendor of the great;
And his indazzled gaze is proof
Against the glittering hall and gilded roof.

.   .   .   .   .

The warbling birds shall bid me wake
    With their untutored melodies.
No fearful dream my sleep shall break.
    No wakeful cares arise,
Like the sad shapes upon another's will.

Be mine my hopes to Heaven to give,
    To taste the bliss that Heaven bestows,

Alone and for myself to live,
    And 'scape the many woes
That human hearts are doomed to hear,—
The pangs of love, and hate, and hope, and fear.

.   .   .   .   .

At ease within the shade reclined,
With laurel and with ivy crowned,
And my attentive ear inclined
    To catch the heavenly sound
Of harp or lyre, when o'er the strings
Some master-hand its practised finger flings.

—Anonymous translation

Fray Luis's bucolic poetry is purely literary and fictitious as
the poet's life was one of constant activity. He does, however,
give excellent descriptions in his work of the landscape around
Salamanca.

Fray Luis also knew and was influenced by the works of the
poets of the Italian Renaissance. He translated them and imitated
them, especially Petrarch and Bembo. He also knew the works of
the Spanish poets, such as Garcilaso, and was influenced by them.

Fray Luis was fervent in his love for the Spanish language.
He defended the use of Spanish for all literary works, including
religious ones, against those who preferred Latin. He used as
an example the *Holy Scriptures* which God "bequeathed in plain
words and a language which was natural for those to whom he
first gave them."

He recognized the danger of the Protestant desire to give
free interpretation to the Holy Scriptures. He asserted, however,
that because of the difficulty of reading them, people had begun
to read "a number of books that are not only inane but even
markedly harmful which, like the acts of the devil, have increased
due to the lack of good reading."

Fray Luis de León himself attached little importance to his
poems. He spoke of them as *obrecillas* or "trifling works"

which "sort of slipped through my fingers." This attitude was due to the fact that he was intent on his longer works of biblical character and his arduous scholarly studies in theology. Nevertheless Fray Luis owes his fame in large degree to his poems.

His poetry is more cerebral than sensory. It excites admiration rather than captivates by its charm; what one admires above all is the superb balance between poetic intention and the form of expression. There is neither excess in the concept nor exaggeration in the form.

His concept of poetry is individual. For Fray Luis poetry is something that brings us closer to God "for undoubtedly it was inspired in man's soul by God for the purpose of lifting him, through its movement and spirituality, to the skies from which it comes. Poetry is no less than a communication of the celestial and divine spirit." It is thus that the poet expounded the neoplatonic doctrine.

In his well-known ode to the great musician Salinas, he also explained the elevating power of beauty and of art. As he listens to the compositions of the noted musician, he says, in the "Ode to Francisco Salinas":

> The air grows pure and clear,
> Steeped in unearthly loveliness and light,
> When we, Salinas, hear
> Thy music take its flight,
> Pressed from the keys by hands of magic might;
>
> And, at that wondrous sound,
> My soul, that long in apathy had lain,
> New wisdom now hath found;
> And taught by thee would fain
> Of her high origin take thought again.
>
> —Anonymous translation

Thus, to rephrase the poet's words, the soul recaptures a sense of its origins at the divine sound of the music.

Fray Luis's poetry, consequently, contains a religious feeling as shown in the following ways. First he disliked the artificiality of a society motivated by ambition, envy, and falseness:

> What boots it my content
> That the vain voice of fame should favor me,
> If in its service spent
> I find myself to be
> Vexed by dull care and gnawing misery?

> —Translation by John Bowring

Secondly, he eulogized the world of nature, simple and pure. The vision of the countryside or of a starry sky awakened in him a hymn of praise for the majesty and power of his Creator. For Fray Luis, nature provided the repose for tormented souls. For example, the *huerto* or "garden" symbolized for him the simple and agreeable life while the *nave* or "shipbark" represented ambition and humanity's desire for pleasure:

> O hill, O stream, O field,
> O solitary refuge of delight;
> Since my bark now must yield
> To storm, your solace bright
> I seek and flee this sea's tempestuous might.

> —Translation by Aubrey F. G. Bell

Finally, he looked to a world better than our own for definitive happiness. This world, after all, is an exile in which mankind cries out in its separation from God:

The Quiet Night

> When yonder glorious sky
> Lighted with million lamps, I contemplate;
> And turn my dazzled eye
> To this vain mortal state,
> All dim and visionary, mean and desolate:

A mingled joy and grief
Fills all my soul with dark solicitude;
    I find a short relief
    In tears, whose torrents rude
Roll down my cheeks; or thoughts which thus intrude:—

    Thou so sublime abode!
Temple of light, and beauty's fairest shrine!
    My soul, a spark of God,
    Aspiring to thy seats divine,—
Why, why is it condemned in this dull dell to pine?

                    —Translation by John Bowring

It is curious to note that for Fray Luis eternal life is not only supreme bliss but also supreme knowledge. Like a good man of the Renaissance, he was full of curiosity concerning the mysteries of Nature. These mysteries would be divulged in Heaven:

    And there shall I behold
The pillars that prop Earth everlastingly,
    The boundary-marks that hold
    In check the angry sea,
In prison fixed for it by Heaven's decree;

    Why the Earth trembles, why
The waters of the deep sea rage and swell,
    Whence in grim strife to vie
    The north wind comes, what spell
Causes the Ocean waves to ebb and well;

    Where rise the crystal springs,
And who to the great rivers' ceaseless flow
    Their store of water brings;
    Of icy cold and snow
And summer heat the causes I shall know;

    Who in the air sustains
Water on high, the forge of lightning flash,

The dwelling of the rains
Shall I see, and how God's lash
Furls the treasured snow, and whence the thunders crash.

—Translation by Aubrey F. G. Bell

Several Castilian poets became disciples of Fray Luis. One of the outstanding of these poets was Francisco de la Torre, the creator of sonnets full of amorous melancholy who found consolation in the contemplation of nature. His poems to the night are of unusual beauty.

Another Castilian poet who was a disciple of Fray Luis was Francisco de Figueroa who wrote in imitation of the delicate melancholy of love found in Petrarch.

The School of Seville

Fernando de Herrera, known to his contemporaries as the "divine," was born in Seville in 1534. From a family of humble means, he studied for the priesthood. He was able only to obtain a position in the lower orders which did, however, permit him to receive the income of a clergyman on which he lived until his death in 1597.

Herrera was not a courtier (i.e., man of arms and letters) but a man who devoted himself exclusively to the life of the mind. He was a poet with considerable knowledge of classical culture and was strongly influenced by Petrarch.

Withdrawn and haughty, he was sometimes attacked by his contemporaries. One of them, the writer Juan Rufo, exclaimed, "If he is already not human, why call him divine . . . ?"

The lady of Herrera's love poetry was Doña Leonor de Milán, the Countess of Gelves. The poet actually met and knew her in Seville in the palace of her husband, the cultured Don Alvaro Colón, Count of Gelves, who frequently entertained the finest writers of the city in his home. This "love affair" was undoubtedly purely literary. The love of which Herrera sings in his poetry to the Countess was platonic, which is to say, devoid of all materialism, which illumined the soul of the poet. In his first poems the poet hoped for the attainment of his desires. "I dared and I feared," he tells us, expressing thus both his hopes and his fears.

In later poems, the countess "with honest fear and full of tender love," confesses her affection and the poet replies:

Now my pain has passed, I know now what life is like.

His happiness comes to a sudden end with a brusque reaction from Doña Leonor who cut off her relationship with Herrera. The poet expresses his bitter lament, saying:

and now a hostile and far friend
undoes the path of happiness I'd found.

In addition to his love poetry, Herrera has also bequeathed us an abundant series of poems on patriotic themes. He repeatedly eulogized the Spanish Empire and he immortalized the Battle of Lepanto and the Spanish victory over the pagan Turk in his famous *Ode* in which he imitated a biblical style. Herrera also had recourse to classical authors in his desire to sustain a certain grandeur of diction. Thus we find a transposition in the first strophe:

Now praise the Lord who on the watery plain
did conquer of the sea the savage Turk

(rather than "Now praise the Lord who did conquer the savage Turk on the watery plain of the sea"). Herrera used, as we can see, a structure found in Latin sentences. If we add to this the fervor which he showed for neologisms and his stress on the use of imagery, perhaps also through the influence of the Bible, we can discern that his work as a whole shows a considerable advance over Garcilaso's. In it can be seen the development and intensification of the elements in Renaissance poetry which in turn led to the baroque style of Góngora.

The following stanzas are from the "Ode on the Battle of Lepanto":

The tyrants of the world from hell's abysm
    Summoned the demons of revenge and pride,
    The countless hosts in whom they did confide,—
And gathering round the flag of despotism
    The priest, the slave, and the liberticide,—
All who had bound men's souls within their den,—
    Tore down the loftiest cedar of the height,
The tree sublime; and drunk with anger then,
Threatened in ghastly bands our few astonished men.

    .   .   .   .   .

"Earth's haughtiest nations tremble and obey,
    And to our yoke their necks in peace incline,
    And peace for their salvation of us pray,—
Cry, 'Peace!' but that means death, when monarchs sign.
    Vain is their hope! their lights obscurely shine!—
Their valiant gone,—their virgins in our powers,—
    Their glories to our scepters they resign:
From Nile to Euphrates and Tiber's towers,
Whate'er the all-seeing sun looks down on,—all is ours."

    .   .   .   .   .

For the due glory of thy righteous name,
    For the just vengeance of the race oppressed,
For the deep woes the wretched loud proclaim
    In pieces thou hast dashed the dragon's crest,
    And clipped the wings of the destroying pest:
Back to his cave he draws his poisonous fold,
    And trembling hisses; then in torpid breast
Buries his fear: for thou, to Babel sold
Captive no more on earth thy Zion wilt behold.

    .   .   .   .   .

Those who behold thy mighty arms when shattered,
    And Ocean flowing naked of thy pines,

Over his weary waves triumphant scattered
   So long, but now wreck-strewn, in awful signs,
   Shall say, beholding thy deserted shrines,—
"Who gainst the fearful One hath daring striven?
The Lord of our Salvation their designs
O'erturned, and, for the glory of his heaven,
To man's devoted race this victory hath given."

Anonymous translation

As to esthetics, Herrera's style is more cultured than Garcilaso's. He utilizes words from the Latin (neologisms), as we have seen, and structures his words in imitation of Latin syntax (hyperbaton). His vast literary knowledge is apparent in his *Annotations* of the poetry of Garcilaso in which he defends the necessity for creating new words and other poetic innovations.

Asceticism and Mysticism

As we have seen, religious literature in Spain has a long and well-established medieval tradition. The warrior themes used by the School of the Minstrel Craft, such as the story of the Cid, as well as the lives of the saints and eulogies of the Virgin of the School of the Priestly Craft, take place in a religious atmosphere.

In the medieval world the church presided over everything. With the coming of the Renaissance, however, humanistic culture developed independently from ecclesiastical culture. In the so-called Second Renaissance in Spain, we find once again the growing importance of the Counter Reformation which was given impetus by the Council of Trent which proposed to wipe out licentiousness as well as the Erasmian tendencies derived from the Lutheran heresy. The study of Spanish literature must then necessarily include, more for its spiritual effectiveness than for its esthetic qualities, the *Ejercicios Espirituales (Spiritual Exercises)* of Saint Ignatius de Loyola which appeared in 1548. This book marks the beginning of the Second Renaissance in Spain which is characterized by the splendor of its religious literature, both ascetic and mystical.

In his approach to God, man has two paths: the ascetic and the mystical. In its desire to come closer to the Divine, man's spirit has recourse either to his own efforts, which, by means of a series of exercises, mortifications, and prayer, help him to disassociate himself from mundane things and to purify himself, or to supernatural grace, by which God elevates man and permits him to experience divinely beyond his own frail limitations.

The first path is the ascetic (from the Greek for "exercise"), the second is the mystical (from the Greek for "to close," i.e., "what is closed or mysterious"). Ascetic literature is much more abundant than the mystical which is reserved for only a select few.

The *Camino de Perfección* [*Way to Perfection*] is a frequent theme. Ascetic and mystical literatures are not, however, two separate fields. In the works of many authors, examples of both are to be found. Both form part of the "path to perfection" of the spiritual life which, according to theologians, in its approach to the Divinity consists of three steps or stages:

1. *The Way of Purgation* in which the soul frees itself bit by bit of its errors and of its worldly desires.

2. *The Way of Illumination* in which the spirit is enlightened by the examples of the Passion of Our Lord and the presentiment of Glory.

3. *The Way of Unity* in which the marriage of God and the soul is effected. Only the most perfect reach the third stage.

From a literary standpoint, which is what most interests us here, we must consider three aspects of Spanish mysticism: its precedents, its importance, and its language. In the spiritual doctrines of the Orient there are several examples of pure love for the Divinity in which the believer is stripped of all earthly sensation (nirvana); platonic love, which sets aside the material world, was transformed into a religious love by the neoplatonists of the Middle Ages and was also cultivated by the Arabs. We must also keep in mind the affective love of Saint Catherine of Sienna (in Italy) and the philosophical indifference to the world of Thomas of Kempis in Germany. Spanish mysticism brings these two attitudes together. It gives harmonious unity to the affective and to the philosophical. This is its major originality. Finally we must consider the spiritual doctrines of Erasmus which influenced some of the heterodox mystics.

All of these precedents are evidence of the extraordinary importance of Spanish ascetico-mystical literature, both in quantity (there are some three thousand works which may be included in this genre) and in quality. In the latter aspect Spanish literature reaches limits of sublimity and of beauty which have never been surpassed.

Generally speaking, the language of mysticism purports to tell with words that which belongs to the realm of the ineffable. Accordingly, its statements are reduced either to exclamations of love expressed by the enamored soul or by symbols and allegories which attempt to explain the intimate colloquies between the human spirit and the Divinity.

Spanish mysticism may be divided into three epochs or periods:

1. The *Period of Initiation*, whose most representative figures are the beatified Juan de Avila and Fray Luis de Granada, and in which asceticism predominates.

2. The *Period of Plenitude*, which is personified by Saint Teresa and Saint John of the Cross and in which mysticism predominates.

3. The *Period of Decadence*, in which some heterodox mystics flourish as well as a series of authors who do no more than repeat and distort the writers of preceeding periods.

The Period of Initiation

Juan de Avila is the author of the *Epistolario espiritual para todos los estados* (*Spiritual Epistle for All Conditions*) (1578), in which he addresses himself, in plain language, whether ascetic or mystical, to various persons who ask his advice. He adjusts the tone of the epistle to each person's needs. He was a great religious orator and was known in his own times as the "Apostle of Andalusia."

Fray Luis de Granada, called in his own century Luis de

Sarria, lived from 1504 to 1558 and was of greater importance. He was born in Granada of a humble family and was a protégé of the Count of Tendilla who appointed him as page to his sons. He learned his oratorical skills and his inclination for religious rhetoric, to which he devoted himself, from his teacher Juan de Avila. He belonged to the Dominican Order.

His work is very extensive. Three treatises form the basis of it: *El Libro de la oración y meditación* [*Book or Oratory and Meditation*], *El Guía de pecadores* [*Guide for Sinners*], and the *Introducción del símbolo de la Fe* [*Introduction of the Symbol of Faith*]. The first two are devotional works. They indicate to the Christian the paths of perfection and the dangers which threaten him. *The Introduction to the Symbol of Faith* describes the beauties of this world in striking passages and from these the author deduces the existence of God.

Fray Luis de Granada also wrote a biography of his teacher Juan de Avila in addition to numerous other works and sermons which gave him considerable prestige. He translated Kempis's *Imitation of Christ*. The following is a characteristic passage from the *Guide for Sinners:*

Think about the sins you have committed and commit every day since you opened your eyes to the knowledge of God. You will find that there still lives in you an Adam with many of the old roots and habits. Consider how insolent you are before God, how ungrateful for His benefaction, how rebellious to His inspiration, how slothful in His service. . . . Meditate how hard is your heart toward your fellow beings and how merciful in dealing with yourself; how you favor your own wishes, your own flesh, your own honor and your own interests. Consider how prideful you are, how ambitious, wrathful, conceited, envious, malicious, coddled, changeable, fickle, sensuous and companion to recreations and conversations, laughter and chattering. Consider how inconstant you are in good intentions, how thoughtless in your words, how unprepared in your work, how cowardly and faint-hearted for any serious business. Think of the multitude of your sins, think then of their gravity so that you may see everywhere how your misery has grown. For this you must first consider against whom you have sinned and you will discover that you have sinned against God whose goodness and majesty is infinite and whose favors and mercies toward man exceed the sand in the sea. . . . Is it thus that one pays for the precious blood shed on the cross? Oh wretch that you are for what you have lost, and how much more so for what you have done; and still more so if with this you do not feel your perdition!

Fray Luis de Granada's style is oratorical. His works are always preachable and suggest the grandeur of the Ciceronian period. In Latin he wrote a *Retórica eclasiástica [Ecclesiastical Rhetoric]* in which he advocates clarity and the use of a large vocabulary. His influence throughout Europe was notable.

The Later Renaissance

Saint Teresa of Jesus belongs to the period of plenitude. Before she entered the religious life, Teresa de Cepeda y Ahumada (1515–1582), from Avila, a city of "song and of saints," she was a girl full of fervor for things of the mind. She read books of chivalry and of devotion. She wanted to flee with her brother Rodrigo to the lands of the Moors to be martyred.

In 1534 while still quite young she entered the convent of the Carmelites of the Incarnation at Avila. The first period of her religious life, she has told us, was spiritually of little fervor.

1515: born at Avila	1534–1556: Carmelite Nun, period of little fervor	1556–1562: period of great fervor	1562–1565: The Book of Her Life
Carmelite Reforms	1588: The Inner Castle or The Mansions	1573: The Book of Foundations	1582: died at Alba de Tormes
The Way of Perfection 1585	Works edited by Fray Luis de León 1586		

Around 1556 she felt the strong pull of religious fervor and of the mystical life. At the same time she initiated her great labors of reforming the Carmelite Order with the severest of rules. This brought her much work and countless difficulties as many in the Order looked upon the reforms with disdain. From this time on her life was one of constant activity. She died in Alba de Tormes in 1582.

Saint Teresa demonstrates her cultural background in her knowledge of the works of religious literature, ranging from the Bible to the writings of Fray Luis de Granada. The influence of this reading can be noted in her writings. Saint Teresa was not, however, of the opinion that one could forget one's immediate responsibilities for one's predilection for reading. "Heaven keep all the daughters of our Order from being Latinists," she once declared.

In addition to her writing, one of Saint Teresa's preoccupations, as we have observed, was the reform of the Carmelite Order and its extension. She journeyed throughout Castile and Andalusia founding new convents. They numbered seventeen. As a woman of a practical spirit, firm and enthusiastic, sincere and uncomplicated, she forgot no detail, no matter how insignificant. "God is even to be found near the cooking pot," she said.

Saint Teresa has left us the story of her life in a work entitled *Libro de las Misericordia de Dios* [*The Book of God's Mercies*]. Her work as the founder of convents is outlived in her *Libro de las Fundaciones* [*Book of Foundations*]. Both books give a lively portrait of the spirit and the activity of the saint. The book of her life explains primarily her inner life. She tells us of her mystical visions, of her ineffable bliss. *The Book of Foundations*, on the other hand, speaks more of her everyday life, the anecdotes and travels of her indefatigable mission, always recounted with wit and charm.

There were three sisters and nine brothers of us and we were all like our parents in being virtuous, except for me, although I was my father's favorite. . . . My brothers kept nothing from me that might help in the service to the Lord. One brother was about my age. We read the lives of the saints together. He was the brother I cared for most although I loved them all and they loved me. When I realized what martyrdom the saints underwent in their love of God, it seemed to me they paid little indeed to go on to the presence of God, and I wanted very much to die that way, not for the love I held towards Him but for the great good I had read existed in Heaven. My brother and I tried to figure out what means were available to us for such undertaking. We agreed to go off to the lands of the Moors and there to beg them for the love of God to behead us. The Lord was already giving us strength at that tender age, had we found the means, but having parents did seem to us to be a terrible disadvantage. We were greatly frightened when we read that suffering and glory were forever. It happened that frequently we spoke of this and we liked to repeat "Forever, forever, forever!"

—From *La Vida* [*The Life*]

Las moradas o El castillo interior [*The Mansions or The Inner Castle*] was the title given by Saint Teresa to her most important work. By using the customary symbolism of mystical language, she presents the human soul surrounded by seven abodes or enclosures.

These Mansions are not to be understood as being one after the other, like something strung together, but rather place your eyes in the center which is the hall or place where the King is to be found and consider how a palmetto has many layers which enclose its delicate fruit and must be passed through to reach what is edible.

—From Chapter II

In the center is God. To come to Him, however, one must use prayer to enter into one's self, conquering each abode or mansion which encloses the vices and vanities of this world. Finally one attains the immense pleasure of the union with God.

> [One feels] a great freedom from everything and the desire to be forever alone or occupied in things of benefit to the soul, and neither barrenness nor inner works but with a memory and tenderness for our Lord which wishes only to praise Him, so that when one slackens, the Lord Himself awakens us as we have said, for it can be seen clearly that that impulse, or whatever it is called, comes from the innermost parts of the soul.

—From the *Seventh Mansion*

Saint Teresa also wrote other works in prose and in verse. We have her *Conceptos del Amor de Dios* [*Concepts of the Love of God*] and the *Way of Perfection,* both devout in character and written for the religious education of those who were under her care. Some poems, notable for their simplicity and intensity, have been attributed to her, although not all of them are actually hers. There is also a lengthy series of letters (there are over four hundred of them) which tell us about her activities, her fervor, and the great liking for her which both she as a person and her work have inspired.

The following is one of her sonnets:

> 'Tis not thy terrors, Lord, thy dreadful frown,
> Which keep my step in duty's narrow path;
> 'Tis not the awful threatenings of thy wrath,
> But that in virtue's sacred smile alone
> I find or peace or happiness. Thy light,
> In all its prodigality, is shed
> Upon the worthy and the unworthy head:
> And thou dost wrap in misery's stormy night
> The holy as the thankless. All is well
> Thy wisdom has to each his portion given;—
> Why should our hearts by selfishness be riven?

'Tis vain to murmur,—daring to rebel:
Lord, I would fear thee, though I feared not hell,
And love thee, though I had no hope of Heaven!

—Translation by John Bowring

Saint Teresa's language and style are always characterized by simplicity and clarity. Her manner of expressing herself is uncomplicated and plain. She adapted herself to her reading public and despite the use of the commonest of everyday language, succeeded in expressing the most intricate thoughts.

She preferred the "style of hermits and of solitary folk who take no note of novelties and frills in their way of speech." In spite of her literary background, she wrote in a careless way which deliberately avoided the vanities of style as just one more vanity of worldliness. Archaic words only in use among the lowest elements of society are found in her works. She uses "naide" for "nadie," "auque" for "aunque," "ilesia" for "iglesia," and so on.

Saint John of the Cross marks the maximum point of fervor in Spanish mystical literature. Although younger than Saint Teresa, Juan de Yepes, who was born in 1542 in Fontiveros in the province of Avila, was also a member of the Carmelites. He knew Saint Teresa. It was she who inspired in him the same religious fervor and made him one of her collaborators. Like Saint Teresa, Saint John of the Cross founded many monasteries. Like her, he journeyed throughout Andalusia and Castile on missions of education, reform, and construction. Like her, he has left us a literary work of major importance. He died on one of his missions in Ubeda in the year 1591.

His mysticism, however, differs somewhat from Saint Teresa's. In the latter, we are constantly reminded of practical and pedagogical aspects which conform to the needs of the most humble conscience, while in the work of Saint John there is a mystical illumination of such lofty degree that it would seem to be addressed only to spirits similar to his own, ones both fervent and initiated into the mysteries of mysticism who may find in the saint's work a certain spiritual direction. Saint John of the Cross

felt himself alienated from the terrestrial world. It might be
said that he spoke in dreams with his God. The Divinity can be
attained only by elevating oneself above the earthly. "He who
can be dead to everything [human]," he tells us, "shall have life
in everything [divine]." On another occasion he wrote, "To
arrive at pleasure in everything, one must look for pleasure in
nothing."

There are four doctrinal treatises of Saint John, the *Subida
del Monte Carmelo* [*Ascent of Mount Carmel*], the *Noche oscura
del alma* [*Dark Night of the Soul*], the *Cántico espiritual* [*Spiritual canticle*], and the *Llama de amor viva* [*Living Flame of Love*].
Very frequently Saint John of the Cross condenses his mystical
thought in symbols and allegories. His prose treatises explain
the doctrines embodied in his verse.

These symbols refer to the pathway which goes from the dark
night of the soul (in which the soul, even though it so desires,
does not experience God) to the light of day which illuminates
the spirit which is "lifted from the shadows of natural knowledge
to the morning light of the supernatural experience of God."
This is, in other words, the way from the ascetic to the mystical.

The relationship between God and the soul is symbolized
by the Husband who represents the Divinity and the Wife who
portrays the soul in love with its Creator, just as Saint John had
found it in the Bible's Song of Songs. He wrote: "The order of
these songs goes from the time when a soul begins to serve God
until it comes to the ultimate degree of perfection which is a
spiritual wedding."

Saint John of the Cross also wrote *Avisos y sentencias* [*Counsels and Axioms*] and *Letters,* all in prose. These works have a
doctrinal character of religious education, in which their author
lavishes advice and teachings on the members of his Order (Saint
John was the spiritual director of many Carmelite communities).

We also have his poetry which is full of impassioned and
evangelistic fervor. It is this which makes of Saint John of the
Cross one of the most notable of all writers of lyric poetry any-
where. In the *Subida Del Monte Carmelo* or *The Ascent of
Mount Carmel*, the first poem sets down the two different types
of night which the spiritually sensitive spend according to the

two parts of man, the superior and the inferior. The poem begins as follows:

First Song

On a dark and gloomy night,
By longing and desire aroused,
Oh unspeakable delight!
Unheeded did I start my flight,
While tranquilly my household drowsed.

In this first song, the soul sings its joyous happiness and fortune in overcoming material appetites and the imperfections that come from the senses and the confusions of reason. For whose information be it known that for a soul to arrive at a state of perfection, ordinarily it must pass through two main types of nights which the spiritually sensitive call purgations or purifications of the soul, which here we denominate nights. In either one state or the other, the soul proceeds as though in a dark night. The first night or purgation is from the sensuous part of the soul . . . .

The Declaration of the Song

In short what the soul is saying in this song is that it went forth (brought forth by God) only for love of Him, aroused by His love on a dark night which is the privation and purgation of all the appetites of the senses for the material things of this world and those which delight the flesh and those which give pleasure to the will. All of this is done in this purgation of the senses. For this reason the soul speaks of flight from its tranquil household which is part of the senses. All of the appetites are quiet and drowsing, for there is no flight from the pains and anguish of the privy of the appetites until they are diminished and asleep. For this we read "unheeded did I start my flight," which is to say, without any appetite of the flesh nor other thing obstructing its path. And also because the flight was in the night, which is to be deprived of God which is night for the soul. The flight was an unspeakable delight as God, from Whom such good comes, put Himself in that night in which the soul would have trouble entering. For one does not succeed in emptying one's self of appetites all alone to go to God. This is the declaration of the song and now we must proceed to continue writing about each stanza of the poem and to declare our purpose.

The language of Saint John of the Cross in expressing these things is necessarily complex and symbolic. Of all Spanish mystics, the work of Saint John is the most difficult. He explains his mystical contemplations by means of allegories. He himself knew very well that what he was expressing was difficult to comprehend by means of the intellect, for one does not come to God through the intelligence but through one's heart.

The Sonnet to the Crucified Christ [the famous *Soneto a Cristo crucificado*], which is one of the brightest jewels of Spanish literature, has been attributed, most unconvincingly be it said, to Saint Teresa, to Saint Francis Xavier, and to Saint Ignatius de Loyola. It must be considered as an anonymous work.

To Christ Crucified

I am not moved, my God, to love Thee so,
By that fair heaven which Thou hast promised me;
Nor am I moved to fear offending Thee,
By terror of that dreaded hell below;

Thou movest me, my God; my heart doth glow
To see Thee nailed upon that shameful tree,
To see Thy body wounded piteously,
To see Thee die, with agonizing throe;

Thy love, in sooth, doth move me in such wise,
That if there were no heaven, my love would burn,
And if there were no hell, my will would bow!

I love Thee not for hopes beyond the skies,
For did my every hope to nothing turn,
I'd love Thee still, as I do love Thee now.

—Translation by James Young Gibson

Heterodoxical mystical schools were also in existence. They, like the Quietist movement championed by Miguel de Molinos in his *Guía espiritual* [*Spiritual Guide*], were persecuted by the Inquisition.

Narrative Prose

The tradition of the Orient, which began with *Calila y Dimna,* gave way to short tales and narratives which grew out of Spanish folkloric material or out of translations from the French and Italian. Among the best known are Melchor de Santa Cruz's *Floresta española de apotegmas y sentencias* [*Pleasing Maxims and Sayings*] and Juan de Timoneda's *El Patrañuelo* [*Fabulous Tales*].

Paralleling pastoral poetry there appeared in Spain a type of idealization of country life, the pastoral novel, which was often based on Italian models. The pastoral novel consists of an interminable series of episodes of a sentimental nature—unrequited passions and love laments—which take place within the framework of a Nature as peaceful as the action of the novel is false. The plot usually is brought to an end by acts of magic which enable everyone to attain his love's ideal.

The best known works in their time were the *Diana* by Jorge de Montemayor and the *Diana enamorada* [*Diana In Love*] by Gaspar Gil Polo.

The following passages give an idea of the love poetry included in the works of the authors mentioned:

I Cannot Cease to Love

If it distress thee to be loved,
   Why,—as I cannot cease to love thee,—
Learn thou to bear the thought unmoved,
   Till death remove me, or remove thee.

O, let me give the feelings vent,
   The melancholy thoughts that fill me!
Or send the mandate; be content
   To wound my inner heart, and kill me;

If love, whose smile would fain caress thee,
    If love offend, yet why reprove?
I cannot, lady, but distress thee,
    Because I cannot cease to love

If I could check the passion glowing
    Within this my bosom, if I could,
On other maids my love bestowing
    Give thy soul peace, sweet girl, I would.

But no! my heart cannot address thee
    In aught but love—then why reprove?
I cannot, lady, but distress thee,
    Because I cannot cease to love.

—Gil Polo, from *Diana*
Translation by John Bowring

What change is here, O hair,
    I see since I saw you?
How ill it fits you this green to wear,
    For hope the color due?
Indeed I did well hope,
    Though hope were mixed with fear,
No other shepherd should have scope
    Once to approach this hair.

—Jorge de Montemayor, from *Sireno's Song*
Translation by Sir Philip Sidney

The Moorish novel is a genre of refined tastes, chivalrous
and sentimental, such as the delightful *Historia del Abencerraje y
la hermosa Jarifa,* an anonymous work, or the *Guerras Civiles de
Granada* [*Civil Wars of Granada*] by Ginés Pérez de Hita.

The picaresque novel merits special consideration, as much
for its literary importance as for its spiritual significance. What
is a *"pícaro"*? There are differing etymologies of the word. Some
attribute to it the sense of "prattler" and "early riser." Some see
in it an allusion to Picardy from which many Spanish soldiers

returned after service in the wars in Flanders. A *"picaro"* (the English term "rogue" has often been used as a translation of the Spanish word) is, accordingly, a man without a set occupation who lives the life of a tramp or vagabond. He may be the servant of an aristocrat one day and the card shark in a tavern the next; that is, even when he is not really a criminal, his situation leaves much to be desired. His aspiration is to live without desiring vaingloriousness. His fortunes are almost always adverse. This causes him to be resigned to his fate and causes him to hold a pessimistic philosophy of life.

His role in society is a special one. When we studied the *Celestina* we saw two opposing worlds, the one to which the heroes or protagonists belonged and where the motivation was love, and the one to which the servants belonged where the motivation was money. These two worlds in counterpoint are to be found in all Spanish novels (as with Sancho Panza and Don Quixote) and in the drama (where the protagonist is accompanied by his servant). The idealism of the first is always countered by the materialism of the latter. The *picaro* is an antihero. He is the man who sees only with the eyes of material reality while the hero sees with the eyes of the imagination. (Thus Don Quixote sees giants where Sancho sees only windmills.)

The picaresque novel constitutes a complete reaction against the books of chivalry. Its literary characteristics may be classified as follows:

a Autobiographical narration. The Knight Errant always had a chronicler who narrated his exploits. Who, however, was to relate the poor *picaro's* life? It was he himself who was to establish for us, with tongue in cheek, the pattern of his ascendancy (*picaros* like himself), his sufferings, and his adversities. He omitted no disagreeable detail in the telling and, in the novels of the seventeenth century, embellished his exploits with lengthy and deeply pessimistic philosophical commentaries. Generally speaking, the writers of picaresque novels retained the autobiographical form.

b Satire. The *picaro* is a vagabond. His usual occupation is that of a servant. This permits him to live in close contact with those of high estate—with noblemen, military men, and clergy.

He exposes what is false and blameworthy in them all. The picaresque novel is fundamentally satirical. Society is portrayed with all its crudity and its petty wretchedness, and its moral defects are brought into the open. The *picaro* has his vengeance on the society that rejects him by exposing the ridiculous reality which hides behind a facade of grandeur.

c Style. The style of the picaresque novels is generally simple and clear. It describes the reality of things without avoiding even the most disagreeable aspects of life or allowing good taste to obstruct its exposé.

There are two main periods of the picaresque. When, in the second half of the sixteenth century, the *picaro* made his first appearance in Spanish literature it was still the period in which the desire for glory and fame were strongest (remember what was said about the *Coplas* of Jorge Manrique). The figure of the *picaro* was little noticed for he believed in nothing; he wanted only to live with as little work as possible. This early period is represented by the *Lazarillo de Tormes*, dating from 1554.

As the sixteenth century drew to an end, however, the Spanish Empire began to crumble. All of the extraordinary structure of Spanish glory began to disintegrate. It was then that the *picaro* who mocked the search for glory came into his own. His figure grew in stature and appeared in a great number of books, bringing to them his pessimistic philosophy. The representative work of this second epoch is *La Vida del picaro Guzmán de Alfarache* [*The Life of Guzmán de Alfarache*] (1599) by Mateo Alemán.

We have already alluded to the *Celestina* as a precedent of the picaresque world. In the *Book of Good Love* and in the *Corbacho, picaros* were also portrayed. In this early period the best-known work is undoubtedly the *Lazarillo de Tormes*. The author's name is unknown.

1. The autobiographical aspect. Lazarillo, or Little Lazarus, had a father who was a thief and a mother of questionable virtue. While still a small child he was put in the service of a blind man who brutally introduced him to the vicissitudes of life. "I awakened from the simplicity in which, as a sleeping child, I had

lived . . . ." he tells us. From then on he utilizes the tricks he has learned to escape from the blind man. He goes on to serve successively a clergyman, a petulent and impecunious nobleman, an unscrupulous seller of Papal Bulls, and a notary. He ends up as town crier in Toledo.

Lazarillo describes his family.

Let me tell you first, sir, that I'm called Lázaro de Tormes. I'm the son of Tomé González and Antonia Pérez, both natives of Tejares, a village of Salamanca. . . . My father (may heaven forgive him) was in charge of a grain mill which is by the river Tormes and he worked there for fifteen years. When I was a child eight years old my father was accused of certain bloodlettings in the ribs of the sacks brought there for milling and consequently he was thrown in jail, made his confession and did not react and underwent his punishment. . . . At about that time there was an expedition sent out against the Moors and on it went my father who had been exiled for the aforesaid trouble. He went as the stable boy of a nobleman and like a loyal servant died along with his master.

2. The satirical aspect. Each one of the persons whom Lazarillo serves is the target of satire. He sees the evil of the blind man, the avariciousness of the priest, the bragging of the squire. . . .

The blind man's meanness.

Let me tell you, sir, that as far as the blind man is concerned, since God created the earth, He has made no man more shrewd or wise. He was an eagle in his work. He knew a hundred prayers and more by heart. He recited in a low voice, restful and full, which made the church where he prayed fairly resound. As he did so he put on a humble and devout face and made neither gesture nor smirk with the eyes nor with the mouth as some others do. . . .

The avarice of the priest.

As I have explained, every night into my mouth I put the key to the coffer where the bread was kept and I slept without fear that the old devil my master would find it. But when troubles come, industry is fruitless. My ill luck had it, or perhaps I'd better say my sins, that one night the key got lodged in my mouth in such a position that the air was sucked through an opening in it. Unfortunately for me it began to make a very loud whistling noise. My startled master heard it and thought it must be the "snake" hissing, and it must have sounded like it.

He got up very quietly with his club in his hand. By groping along and following the noise he came up on me without a sound, so that the "snake" wouldn't hear him. When he got up close he decided the "snake" must be in the straw where I slept because of the heat of my body. He lifted up his club, and thinking he had the "snake" underneath, he let go with a powerful blow to kill it and hit me such a thump on the head that he left me senseless and badly damaged.

The swaggering squire.

Furthermore, he said, I'm not so poor as not to have ancestral lands and houses where I come from. If the buildings were still standing and the fields well tilled, all those many acres where I was born near Valladolid, I would be worth a great fortune for the soil is very rich. If my dovecote hadn't fallen apart it would easily provide a couple hundred pigeon a year. I could tell you others things too, but I won't, as I left it all behind for a matter of my honor.

Nevertheless, his satire is more ironical than bitter. He says of the petulant squire who almost let him die of hunger that he was "very fond of him and held more pity for him than enmity." Lazarus is not a hardened rogue. He is portrayed more as an adolescent buffeted by life.

"Gentlemen," say some women to the law officers who are pursuing them, "this is an innocent child. . . ." It is this innocence which is the essential characteristic of the early period of the picaresque novel.

The Period of Plenitude

Between the later Renaissance and the baroque came a period of plenitude in Spanish literature which corresponded, as we have pointed out, to the reign of Philip III. Two names define it, the great Lope de Vega and the immortal Miguel de Cervantes.

Cervantes

The plenitude of the novel comes with Cervantes who was the fourth son of the seven children of the surgeon Rodrigo de Cervantes. He was born in Alcalá de Henares in 1547. In his youth he traveled to various places with his father who was constantly on the move trying to support his family. In 1568 the young Cervantes was in Madrid as the student of the humanist López de Hoyos. He later went to Italy in the service of Cardinal Aquaviva. He enlisted on the galleon "Marquesa" on board which he took part in the Battle of Lepanto in 1571.

During that battle he fought heroically and was wounded in the chest and also in the left hand which thereafter was useless to him. Later on he began the return voyage to Spain, but his ship was assaulted by Berber pirates who carried him off to Algiers where he remained captive for five years. He was ransomed by Trinitarian monks and returned to Spain in 1580. He married Catalina Salazar four years later. He requested a post in government administration and, after a long wait, got it. An accounting error committed by one of his subordinates, however, put him in jail for a short while.

He was released on bail and went to Valladolid in 1603. It was there that another unfortunate incident, the murder of a man in front of the door of his house, brought him new legal troubles. This whole period of Cervantes' life was marked by financial difficulties. It was, nevertheless, his most productive literary period.

Cervantes passed the last years of his life in Madrid where he died on April 23, 1616.

Thus Cervantes' life was spent in highly diverse settings. His mind was formed by them and his powers of observation served him later in the portrayals in his literary works. For example, Cervantes was a soldier who was proud of his profession. He was a hero in the Battle of Lepanto and was commended by Don Juan de Austria. The pride which Cervantes had in his years as a soldier was something which lasted all his life. His crippled hand became a mark of honor. He wrote of it in the Prologue to the second part of the Quixote, in a passage in which he tells us he would prefer his wounds and his crippled hand to missing his part in these military events of his times.

Cervantes also alluded to his period of captivity in descriptions in both his plays and his narrative works. In the drama *El trato de Argel* [*The Happenings in Algiers*], he portrayed himself in the figure of the captive soldier Saavedra. His spirit during his captivity is well described in the *Epistle to Mateo Vásquez,* Philip II's secretary, in which he requested help for his situation.

Cervantes expressed his opinions of the authors of his times in the *Canto de Caliope* [*Song of Caliope*] from the novel *La Galatea* and in the *Viaje del Parnaso* [*Journey to Parnassus*]. Also, when the curate and the barber made their famous examination of Don Quixote's library, some of the volumes were saved from the flames; these are surely Cervantes' favorite books. For his own part the circumstances surrounding his literary reputation were not always pleasant. Lope de Vega wrote that of all writers "none is worse than Cervantes, nor so stupid as to praise *Don Quixote.*"

Cervantes' opinion of his own works and himself as author is interesting. Few works in Spanish literature contain passages which permit us to see an author through his own eyes. Cervantes is one who has left us several sections in which we see his self-portrait. In his Prologue to the *Exemplary Novels,* for example we see the physical portrait. Cervantes wrote:

The person you see here, with an aquiline face and brown hair, a smooth forehead, bright eyes and arched but well proportioned nose, a silvery beard which less than twenty years ago was golden, long mustaches and a small mouth . . . , the body neither very large nor very small, of high color, more fair than dark, somewhat stoop-shouldered and not very light of foot. This person, I tell you, is the author of *The Galatea* and of *Don Quixote de la Mancha*.

Cervantes at the time of writing this passage was almost seventy years old.

Cervantes repeatedly alludes to his useless hand, the consequence of his wounds in the Battle of Lepanto. These wounds "are stars which guide others to the circle of honor," he wrote in the Prologue to the second part of the *Quixote*. Mercury, in the *Journey to Parnassus*, says to the author:

Well I know that at the battle's height
You lost the movement of your left hand
For greater glory of the right.

We are also given the portrait of his character. ". . . he was called Miguel de Cervantes Saavedra. He was a soldier for many years and a captive for five and a half. It was then that he learned patience in adversity." With these words in the Prologue to the *Exemplary Novels*, Cervantes spoke of a very characteristic aspect of his life, his adversities not only in his everyday life, including prison and deprivation, but also in his literary life. It is a well-known fact that a second part of the Quixote was published apocryphally under the name of Avellaneda. It was filled with insults against Cervantes. The latter's answer to the imposter is an example of patience and dignity, as we can see in the Prologue to the second part of the *Quixote*.

If by chance you make his acquaintance, tell him for me that I am not offended. I know what the temptations of the devil are and that one of the greatest of them is for a man

to have understanding enough to write and publish a
book. . . .

Finally, there is the literary portrait. What was Cervantes'
opinion of his own work? He wished to be a innovator and a
creator. "I am the first who has written a novel in the Castilian
tongue," he tells us. The reason he says this is that he considered
the novels before his to be imitations of foreign works. In the
Journey to Parnassus, for example, Mercury calls him an "unusual
inventor."

One question is whether Cervantes understood the importance of his work. He stated of the *Quixote* that it was no more
than an "amusement for the downhearted." Posterity has seen
much more in this immortal novel. This is partially comprehensible when we realize that Cervantes always wanted to be a
poet, but was not successful in his efforts:

> I who toil and would a poet be,
> Who struggle and amends would make
> For gifts that heaven has denied to me . . .

The first works to come from Cervantes' pen were poetical.
While he was still quite young, his teacher Juan López de Hoyos
included some of his verses in a book eulogizing the late queen
Isabel de Valois. Cervantes wrote his poetry not only in separate
compositions, but also as a part of his prose works, as in the case
of *La Gitanilla* [*The Gypsy Girl*], and in the *Quixote* itself.

Cervantes was passionately interested in the theater also. In
his youth, he wrote successfully for the stage. Two of the twelve
works he wrote at that time have come down to us. They are the
Cerco de Numancia [*Siege of Numancia*] and *El Trato de Argel*
[*The Happenings in Algiers*]. These works follow the classical
models of Renaissance drama. At the end of the sixteenth century
while Cervantes was away from Madrid, Lope de Vega, with his
new and popular drama, revolutionized the public's taste in
plays. When Cervantes wanted to continue his work, he tells us,
he did not find "birds in the nests of yesteryear." At first he spoke
out in protest against the changes:

> To public theater farewell,
> There now where ignorance does reign
> And nonsense does its praises tell . . .

but later on he changed his opinion and became a disciple of
Lope. The result was a series of plays as full of life as his *entremeses* or interludes, several of which, notably *El retablo de mara-
villas* [*The Retable of Marvels*], *La Guarda Cuidadosa* [*The Soli-
citous Guard*], and *El juez de los divorcios* [*The Divorce
Magistrate*] are still performed today. A group of plays written on
the theme of captivity also belongs to this later period. It includes
El gallardo español [*The Gallant Spaniard*], *Los baños de Argel*
[*The Baths of Algiers*], and *La gran sultana* [*The Great Sultana*]
in which Cervantes portrayed a setting well known to him. There
is also a most interesting picaresque play called *Pedro de Urdemalas*.

Today we think of Cervantes primarily in connection with
the following novels:

1. His Pastoral Novel: *La Galatea*. We have seen how bucolic themes entered Spanish poetry in the works of Garcilaso and
Fray Luis de León. At the same time the pastoral novel was
introduced. It, like the poetry, had the characteristics of artificiality and of the disguising, in the form of shepherds and
shepherdesses, of known personages. Cervantes did homage to
the genre with his *Galatea* which dates from 1585. More than
seventy shepherds and shepherdesses appear in its pages, lament-
ing the cruel sufferings of love. The action takes place along the
banks of the Tagus River. Cervantes tells us in his Prologue that
"many of the persons appearing in these pages are shepherds
in costume only."

2. The Exemplary Novels. Cervantes, in the Prologue to
these twelve *novellas* which appeared in 1612, says: "I have given
them the name of exemplary and no matter how closely one
looks, there is not a single one which does not give a beneficial
example. . . ."

According to a contemporary critic, Ludwig Pfandl, the
Exemplary Novels may be classified in three categories:

   a. Those concerning love affairs and turns of fortune, in

which unusual plot situations, unlikely love affairs, en-
counters of lost lovers and abandoned sweethearts, cap-
tivities, confusions, and journeys appear. This category
includes *La gitanilla* [*The Gypsy Girl*], *La ilustre fregona*
[*The Illustrious Kitchenmaid*], *Las dos doncellas* [*The
Two Maidens*], *La fuerza de la sangre* [*Blood Ties*], *El
amante literal* [*The Generous Lover*], *La señora Cornelia*
[*Señora Cornelia*], *La española inglesia* [*The Spanish
English Woman*], *El casamiento engañoso* [*The Deceitful Marriage*], and *El celoso extremeño* [*The Jealous
Extremaduran*].

The Gypsy Girl has as its protagonist a bright and
honest gypsy girl named Preciosa. A young gentleman
named Don Juan de Cárcamo falls so deeply in love with
Preciosa that he too becomes a member of the gypsy
caravan. Falsely accused of being a thief by a woman
whom he has disdained, he kills the mayor's nephew who
has struck him. As a consequence most of the gypsies
are taken to the prison of Murcia where it is discovered
that Preciosa is the magistrate's daughter who had been
kidnapped as a child by an old gypsy woman. Don Juan's
identity is also established. He is pardoned and the tale
ends with the wedding of the two young lovers.

The Illustrious Kitchenmaid also is the story of a
humble servant girl, of an inn in Toledo, who is of
noble blood. A young gentleman named *Tomas de Ave-
dano*, who pretends to be a servant in the inn, falls in
love with her.

The Two Maidens presents the case of two young
girls who have fallen in love and who leave home disguised as men and do not return until, after many adventures, they have attained their goal.

b. Satirical vignettes, including *Rinconete y Cortadillo*,
which belongs to the later period of picaresque literature, and *El coloquio de los perros* [*Colloquy of the Dogs*].
c. Collections of proverbial sayings in novelistic form, as
in the *Licenciado Vidriera* [*The Gentleman of Glass*]—

the story of a man who went mad and believed himself to be made of glass and who astonished everyone with his axioms and proverbs.

3. The Byzantine Novel: *Los trabajos de Persiles y Segismunda* [*Labors of Persiles and Segismunda*]. In this work Cervantes brought together, in a "mosaic of remembrances from his readings and his life" (according to the critic Bonilla), a series of fantastic adventures and travels, characteristic of the so-called Byzantine novel, which happened to two lovers, Persiles and Segismunda, who marry at the story's end. The *Persiles* was the last work that Cervantes wrote.

The *Prologue and Dedication to The Count of Lemos* was written a few short days before the author's death. On April 19, 1616, Cervantes wrote, "Yesterday I was given extreme unction and today I am writing this. Time is short, my anguish grows, hope diminishes. . . ." He died on the twenty-third of the month.

4. The *Quixote* is the most famous work of Spanish literature. The story of *The Ingenious Gentleman Don Quixote de la Mancha* is that of Don Alonso Quijano, who loses his sanity from reading too many books of chivalry. In his madness he thinks he is one of the old knights errant. He sallies forth into the countryside, accompanied by a peasant from his little town— Sancho Panza, who becomes his squire. He commends himself to the love of his lady Dulcinea del Toboso and sets out on a multitude of adventures involving one squabble and calamity after another, as wherever he goes he wants to right wrongs and set everything to rights. The disaster of his final undertaking in Barcelona is decisive for his return home a beaten man who dies shortly after recovering his sanity.

In the Prologue to the book, Cervantes tells us that the *Quixote* was written to put an end to the taste for reading the "books of chivalry, disdained by some but praised by many more." Indeed, as we have seen, Don Quixote's madness stems from the reading of "books of chivalry." Cervantes points out that in his times chivalry was already a part of past history. Don Quixote was ridiculous because knights errant belonged to the Middle Ages, a period when the monarchical power was insufficient for the maintenance of law and order; the figure of the protagonist with his lance, his shield, and his armor was already anachronistic and grotesque at a time when armies had begun to fight with harquebuses and cannon. The language of Don Quixote, in keeping with this, is liberally sprinkled with archaisms ("fermoso" for "hermoso," etc.).

Nevertheless, Cervantes wanted to do something more than just write a work attacking books of chivalry. He wished to portray the overwhelming struggle between the idealism represented by Don Quixote and the materialism of Sancho Panza.

Don Quixote's aspiration is to better humanity, to restore justice and goodness, but he constantly runs headlong into the reality which is his implacable adversary. Sancho Panza, like the protagonists of the picaresque novels, sees reality as it is. He sees windmills where Don Quixote insists on seeing giants; he sees inns where the knight sees castles. He warns his master who rejects his advice, and Don Quixote is contantly knocked down, beaten and defeated, which leads us to believe that it is the materialistic Sancho who is in the right. It is strange, however, that the one time that Sancho becomes a "Quixote" himself, i.e., when he is governor of the island so long promised by his master and which he tries to govern with justice and impartiality, is when he is ridiculed and abused most savagely.

It is from all of this that Don Quixote's deep pessimism stems, since it shows the harsh struggle necessary for idealism to overcome materialism. At the same time, we feel admiration and enthusiasm for the knight's ennobling tenacity.

The widespread fame of the *Quixote* was rapid; it had an extraordinary success. It has been translated into all languages and the number of its editions is countless. Don Quixote and Sancho have become prototypes of humanity's idealism and materialism. The *Quixote* is undoubtedly the work which has given Spanish literature prestige throughout the world.

A Short Cervantine Anthology

From *The Siege of Numantia*
(*Bariatus, a boy and the last survivor of the siege, speaks.*)
BARIATUS: The whole wild fury of all those who perished

Within this town, now turned to dust and ash,
Their rage at treaties and agreements broken
And offers of submission laughed to scorn,
All of their fiery anger and resentment
Are here united in my breast alone!
I have inherited Numantia's valour—
If you think you can conquer me, you're mad!
Beloved country! O unlucky city!
Never imagine it, nor fear, that I
Would be nonplussed at what I owe to you
Being by you engendered, or that I,
For promises or fears, would flinch or falter!
Now that I have no earth nor heaven nor
    destiny
And the whole world to conquer me conspires
It is impossible that to your valour
I should not pay the duty that I owe.
If fear enticed me here to hide myself
From imminent and terrifying death,
Death now will take me forth with greater
    courage
Since I desire to follow in your wake.
For my vile fear that now has passed away
The reparation will be strong and brave;
For the late terror of my tender youth
A death of bold resolve will pay in full.
And I assure you, my brave citizens,
That your resolve within me is not dead—
That the perfidious Romans shall not triumph
But over our mere ashes. Their designs
Are all in vain, whether they strike me down
Or tempt me with their doubtful promises
To spare my life and ope wide gates to wealth.
Hold back, you Romans! Do not waste your
    strength
Or tire yourselves by swarming up the wall!
Were you ten times more powerful, your
    power
Could never hope to conquer me at all.
Now let me show you my intention. That

I loved my dear-beloved country purely
And perfectly, let this fall be the proof!

(*The boy throws himself off the wall. A trumpet sounds.*)

—Translation by Roy Campbell

. . . . .

From the Exemplary Novel, *Rinconete and Cortadillo*

(*Rinconete introduces himself to his new companion Cortadillo.*)

Well I can tell you that I am one of the least appreciated fellows you'll ever run into. Just to put Your Mercy to the obligation of unburdening yourself with me and baring yourself, I shall be the first to tell you about myself for I'd say that there's no little mystery to the fact that chance has brought us together here and I'm sure that from this day forward we'll be true friends. I, sir, come from Fuenfrida, a place that's well known for the illustrious travelers who continually pass that way. My name is Pedro del Ricón. My father is a person of quality for he is an agent of the Holy Crusade. By that I mean he's a seller of Papal Bulls, a Bull Seller as the common people sometimes say. At times I went with him on his rounds and I learned his trade so well that I'll not take second place to anyone at selling Bulls, however good he is. One day, however, when I showed more affection for the cash paid in than for the Bulls themselves, I became very attached to the money bag and off we both went to Madrid where I had soon taken the innards out of that purse and left it more wrinkled than an anxious bridegroom's handkerchief. The fellow who was responsible for the money came after me. I was caught and had no protection, but when the authorities saw how young I was they were satisfied when I was tied up to the iron ring and given a good dusting on the back and exiled from the Capital for four years. I took it all quietly, gave a shrug of the shoulders, endured the lashing and set out on my exile with such speed that I had no time to get myself a mount. I took what valuables with me I could and what seemed to be the most necessary and among them I brought these cards. (*He then pulled out a pack he had kept in his collar.*) I've earned my way with them in one inn after another from Madrid here, playing twenty-one. They may look dirty and worn to you but they have a miraculous power for the person who understands them. He'll never cut the deck without finding an ace underneath. And if you're acquainted with this game, sir, you will understand what an advantage anyone has who knows his first card will be an Ace which can be a One or an Eleven. With that much certain and with a bet on twenty-one, the money stays home. Aside from this, I learned from a certain ambassador's cook certain tricks at various card games and just as you can prove your skill at tailoring leggings so can I show you my skills in the science of gaming. That way I know I'll not die of hunger, for even though I come to a farmhouse there is always someone wanting to have a bit of a game. From now on we should carry out our tasks together. Let's prepare our net and see if one of those birds of mule-drivers over there gets caught. What I mean is we should play a game of twenty-one as if we were playing seriously. And if a third person comes along, we'll make him first to lose his cash.

.   .   .   .   .

Passages from *Don Quixote*

Don Quixote loses his sanity:

You must know then, that this gentleman aforesaid, at times when he was idle, which was most part of the year, gave himself up to the reading of tales of chivalry, with such relish that he nearly forgot all the sports of the field, and even the management of his domestic affairs, and his curiosity and extravagant fondness for them reached that pitch that he sold many acres of arable land to purchase books of knight-errantry, and carried home all of that kind he could lay hands on. . . .

In fine, having quite lost his wit, he fell into one of of the strangest conceits that ever entered into the head of any madman, which was what he thought it expedient and necessary, as well for the advancement of his reputation as for the public good, that he should become a knight-errant, and wander through the world, with his horse and arms, in quest of adventures, and to put in practice whatever he had read to have been practised by knights-errant; redressing all kinds of grievances, and exposing himself to danger on all occasions; that, by accomplishing such enterprizes, he might acquire eternal fame and renown. The poor gentleman already imagined himself at least crowned emperor of Trebizond by the valour of his arm; and wrapt up in these agreeable delusions, and hurried on by the strange pleasure he took in them, he prepared to execute what he so much desired.

And the first thing he did was to scour up a suit of armor, which had been his great-great-grandfather's, and, being moldy and rust-eaten, had lain by, many long years, forgotten in a corner. This he cleaned and furbished up: but he perceived one great defect, which was that instead of a helmet there was only a simple morion or steel-cap! But he dexterously supplied this want by contriving a sort of vizor of pasteboard, which, being fixed to the head-piece, gave it the appearance of a complete helmet.

The famous episode of the windmills:

Just at that moment they came upon thirty or forty windmills of a type that are found on these plains, and as soon as he saw them Don Quixote said to his squire: "Fortune regulates our affairs better than we could wish. Look, friend Sancho, there before us stand at least twenty great giants. I shall meet them in combat and kill them all, however many they may be. With the spoils of battle we shall begin to get rich. Besides that it is a service to God to rid the face of the earth of such a wretched breed."

"What giants?" asked Sancho.

"Those over there," his master replied, "the ones with the long arms. Some of them must be yards long."

"Take care," warned Sancho. "What we see over there are not giants but windmills, and what look to you like their arms are their wings. When the wind turns them they then turn the millstone."

"It is easy to see," said Don Quixote, "that you know very

little in matters of adventures. These are giants, I tell you, and if you are afraid, move on away and say some prayers while I meet them in a most unequal and terrible combat."

As he was speaking he gave his horse Rocinante a prick of the spurs, without paying any heed to his squire Sancho who kept shouting to him that they were indeed windmills and not giants, and was off to the attack. He was so completely convinced that these were giants that he not only did not hear the warnings of Sancho, he did not even recognize the fact, as he got closer and closer to them, that these really were windmills. Just the contrary, as he galloped along he shouted out, "Don't run away, you wretched cowards. It is only one knight alone who is attacking you."

A bit of wind just then made the wings start to revolve. and when Don Quixote saw this, he exclaimed, "Even if you wave your arms more than the great giant Briarius, you'll pay for it all the same." As he said these words, he commended himself with all his heart to his Lady Dulcinea, beseeching her to aid him in his danger and well covered with his shield and with his lance in rest, he hurtled, with Rocinante at his fastest gallop, against the first mill that stood in his path. However, just at the moment that his lance pierced the wing with a striking blow, the wind spun it upwards with such fury that it broke the lance all to pieces and carried with it both horse and rider who were tossed in a heap in the dust.

The preoccupation with fame:

In the meanwhile, Don Quixote had shut himself up in his chamber with Sancho only. When the former had closed the door, he said: "I am very sorry, Sancho, you should say, and stand in it, that it was I who drew you out of your cottage, when you know that I myself stayed not in my own house. We set out together; we went on together; and together we performed our travels. We both ran the same fortune, and the same chance. If you were once tossed in a blanket, I have been thrashed a hundred times; and herein only have I had the advantage of you."

"And good reason," answered Sancho, "for, as your

worship holds, misfortunes belong more properly to knights-errant themselves than to their squires."

"You are mistaken, Sancho," said Don Quixote, "according to the saying: *Quando caput dolet,* etc."

"I understand no other language than my own," replied Sancho.

"I mean," said Don Quixote, "that when the head aches, all the members ache also. Therefore I, being your master and lord, am your head, and you are a part of me, as being my servant. For this reason, the ill that does or shall affect me must affect you also, and so on the contrary."

"Indeed," quoth Sancho, "it should be so; but when I, as a limb, was tossed in a blanket, my head stood on t'other side of the pales, beholding me frisking in the air, without feeling any pain at all; and since the members are bound to grieve at the ills of the head, that also, in requital, ought to do the like for them."

"Would you insinuate now, Sancho," replied Don Quixote, "that I was not grieved when I saw you tossed? If that be your meaning, say no more, nor so much as think of it, for I felt more pain then in my mind than you did in your body. But no more of this at present, a time will come when we may set this matter upon its right bottom. In the meantime, tell me, friend Sancho, what do folks say of me about this town? What opinion have the common folk of me? What think the hidalgoes, the gentlemen? What discourse is there of the design I have engaged in to revive and restore to the world the long-forgotten order of chivalry? In short, Sancho, I would have you tell me whatever you have heard concerning these matters, and that without taking from the bad one tittle. It is the part of faithful vassals to tell their lords the truth in its native simplicity and proper figure, neither enlarged by adulation, nor diminished out of vain respect. And I would have you, Sancho, learn that, if naked truth could come to the ears of princes, without the disguise of flattery, we should see happier days, and former ages would be deemed as iron in comparison of ours, which would then be esteemed the golden age. Let this advertisement, Sancho, be a caution to you to give me an ingenuous and faithful account of what you know concerning the matters I have enquired about."

"That I will do with all my heart, Sir," answered Sancho, "on condition that your worship shall not be angry at what I say, since you will have me show you the naked truth without arraying her in any other dress than that in which she appeared to me."

"I will in no wise be angry," replied Don Quixote. "You may speak freely, Sancho, and without circumlocution."

"First and foremost then," said Sancho, "the common people take your worship for a downright madman, and me for a fool. The hidalgoes say that your worship, not containing yourself within the bounds of gentility, have taken upon you the style of *Don* and invaded the dignity of knighthood, with no more than a paltry vineyard, a couple of acres of land with a tatter behind, and another before. . . ."

—Translation by Charles Jarvis

Don Quixote, before dying, recovers his sanity:

"Gentlemen," resumed Don Quixote, "let us proceed fairly and softly, and not look for this year's birds in last year's nest. I was mad, I am now sober; I was Don Quixote de la Mancha, I am now, as I have said, Alonzo Quijano the Good. May my unfeigned repentance and sincerity restore me to the esteem you once had for me and let the notary proceed. Item, I bequeath to Antonia Quijano, my niece here present, all my estate real and personal, after the payment of all my debts and legacies; and the first to be discharged shall be the wages due to my housekeeper for all the time she has been in my service, and twenty ducats beside for the mourning. I appoint for my executors signor the curate and signor bachelor Sampson Carrasco, here present. Item, it is my will that, if Antonia Quijano, my niece, is inclined to marry, it shall be with a man who, upon strictest enquiry, shall be found to know nothing of books of chivalry. In case it shall appear he is acquainted with them, and my niece notwithstanding will and does marry him, she shall forfeit all I have left her and my executors shall apply her part to pious uses, as they think proper.

Item, I beseech the said gentlemen, my executors, that if good fortune should bring them acquaintance with the author who is said to have written a history handed about and entitled, *The Second Part of the Exploits of Don Quixote de la Mancha,* they will, in my name, most earnestly entreat him to pardon the occasion I have unwittingly given him of writing so many and so great absurdities as he there has done; for I depart this life with a burden upon my conscience for having furnished him with a motive for so doing.

—Translation by Charles Jarvis

The *Quixote* of Avellaneda appeared before the real second part of Cervantes' work. The first part of the *Quixote* was published in 1605. It was extraordinarily successful. An unknown writer who used the name of Alonso Fernández de Avellaneda wrote a second part to the *Quixote* which appeared in Tarragona in 1614, in order to capitalize on the success of Cervantes' book. When the latter published the real second part in 1615, he clearly stated in the Prologue the suffering caused him by the abuse heaped on him by Avellaneda.

Cervantes preserved his dignity but he wrote, "What I have not been able to pass over is his calling me an old man and a cripple as though I had it in my power to hold Time back or as if my crippled hand had come from a tavern brawl rather than the most exalted event of the past, the present, or the future. . . ."

Lope de Vega

Lope de Vega was the creator of a Spanish national drama, which is to say that once this dramatist began writing, Spanish drama acquired a definitive character. Up to this time, two tendencies, which we have already studied, existed side by side —the one, the spontaneous and magnificent medieval tradition of a religious and popular drama, the other, the solemn and passionless Renaissance renovation which was of a cultural nature. The first of these had a vitality stemming from the soul of the people, but it lacked literary prestige. The second, on the contrary, was of high intellectual quality but held little interest for the general public.

The glory of having created a drama that was literary, impressive, and of great popularity, and in which traditional and Renaissance tendencies were united in a harmonious and definitive formula, fell to Lope de Vega.

Félix Lope de Vega Carpio was born in Madrid in 1562. He led a full life. He was a precocious child. His father, who had noble blood in his veins, was an embroiderer. He wanted his son to have an education in "virtue and letters." Lope himself tells us in his *La Dorotea,* "I was sent to Alcalá at the age of ten. At that age, I already knew Grammar and something of Rhetoric." It was discovered, however, that his real talents lay in writing verse, to such an extent that "my school notebooks served me for writing down my thoughts which often I wrote in Latin or Spanish verse."

These lines mark the first of Lope's characteristics, his facility in writing.

From youth on, Lope's life was marked by his love affairs and adventures. Various names corresponding to various women whom Lope loved during his long lifetime have been preserved for posterity in his works, Amarilis, Marfisa, Filis, Belisa, Camila, Lucinda, and so on. These affairs provided themes of vehemence and passion for his writings. He also had numerous children— Antonia, Clara, Marcella, Lope Félix, and Carlos Félix—all of whom are mentioned affectionately in their father's works. Lope was a soldier in the Armada; he was exiled to Valencia for injuries caused to some actors; his whole life is full of scandalous doings and adventures.

With equal passion and the sincerity with which Lope gave himself to worldly love, he turned at various times in his life to religion and the love of God. Lope was ordained a priest in 1614. His devout works express the weight of his sins, which always returned to disturb his devotions. Nevertheless, despite his sinfulness, Lope was a profoundly religious man who died a Christian death in Madrid in 1635.

Lope's productivity was extraordinary. He was known to his contemporaries as the "Phoenix of the Geniuses" and the "Monster of Nature" because of his prodigious creativity. According to Montalbán, who eulogized him, Lope wrote eighteen

hundred plays—not counting the short works or interludes—
and four hundred religious dramas. The figure is probably exaggerated. Some four hundred plays and forty religious *autos*
have come down to us. Even though we accept a lower figure, the
number is astonishing. This is due to his aforementioned prodigious facility. He himself stated that he wrote whole plays in
a single day.

> And more than a hundred in twenty four hours
> Have left the muses for the stage. . . .

To this may be added the enormous quantity of poems, novels,
epistles, epic poetry and so on which gives us an approximate
idea of what this great writer produced.

As we have seen, Lope renovated the drama as he found it.
His genius created a drama that was both cultured and popular
and which gave form to a Spanish National Theater.

In his *Arte nuevo de escribir comedias* [*New Art of Writing
Plays*], Lope explained his system. The work should have three
acts; until the middle of act three the conclusion should not be
evident to the audience. The esthetics of Horace had earlier
established the use of five acts in a play. Later on this had changed
to four acts, and finally to three. This innovation of the three-
act play took place before Lope, however, a fact which he
acknowledges in his *New Art*. In this work also he explains that
the first act sets the theme, the second develops the action, and
the third brings—it is to be hoped, without any loss of suspense—
the conclusion.

In addition to these statements, Lope tells us that the language of the play, or of a particular situation, should fit the
character. A king, for example, should show "true gravity," while
the lackeys should not, on their part, "speak of lofty subjects."
The costume should also be suitable to the role an actor takes,
and certain verse forms Lope deems more fitting to certain frames
of mind than others: *décimas* for lamentation, the *romance* or
ballad for narration, the *redondilla* for love scenes.

In the *New Art*, Lope modestly pretended to be lacking in
culture. He wrote:

I, doomed to write, the public taste to hit,
Resume the barbarous task 'twas vain to quit:
I lock up every rule before I write,
Plautus and Terence drive from out my sight, . . .
To vulgar standards then I square my play,
Writing at ease; for, since the public pay,
'Tis just, methinks, we by their compass steer,
And write the nonsense that they love to hear.

—Translation by Lord Holland

Lope's facility caused him to touch on almost every theme imaginable. Historical themes (for example, *La creación del mundo* or *The Creation of the World*) were drawn from antiquity (*El esclavo de Roma* or *The Slave of Rome*), from the Middle Ages (*El mejor alcalde el rey* or *The Best Magistrate, the King,* and *El Caballero de Olmedo* or *The Gentleman from Olmedo*), and from his own times (*El Marqués de las Navas* or *The Marquis de las Navas*). Among geographical subjects, we find in Lope's work plays whose action takes place in Germany (*La Imperial de Otón* or *Oton's Empire*), in Italy (*El castigo sin venganza* or *The Punishment Without Revenge*), and in the capital (*El acero de Madrid* or *The Sword of Madrid*). In the case of social life, we encounter plays about noblemen (such as *El perro del hortelano* or *The Gardener's Dog*), about country people (such as *El villano en su rincón* or *The Rustic in His Corner*), or about the opposition between one and the other, i.e., nobleman versus the common man (as in *Peribáñez* and *Fuenteovejuna*).

The variety found in the thematic material also exists in the genres employed. In Lope's work we have plays of a religious nature, taken from the lives of saints, from pious legends, or from evangelical tales (such as *El nacimiento de Cristo* or *The Birth of Christ*). We also have plays of a historical nature, taken from themes in Spanish history (*El Rey Don Pedro en Madrid* or *King Don Pedro in Madrid*), or foreign history (*El gran Duque de Moscovia* or *The Grand Duke of Muscovy*). There are plays based on attitudes of the times, and these are various in theme: chivalric (*La dama boba* or *Lady Dunce*), of intrigue (*El anzuelo de Fenisa* or *Fenisa's Hook*), or picaresque (*El rufián Castrucho* or *Castrucho the Ruffian*). A fourth group comprises tragedies such as *El castigo sin venganza* [*The Punishment Without Revenge*] and *La estrella de Sevilla* [*The Star of Seville*], whose authorship is questionable.

The following is the story of the latter play:

The Star of Seville is a beautiful woman of Seville, named Estrella, who is betrothed to Sancho Ortiz de las Roelas. The King Sancho IV also falls in love with her. By means of a bribe, and incognito, he successfully gains entrance to the lady's rooms. At that moment, her brother, Bustos Tavera, comes in, argues with the king and keeps him from carrying out his plans. The king then charges Sancho Ortiz with the duty of killing a man accused of lèse-majesté. Sancho promises to do so before learning that the condemned man is Bustos Tavera. He struggles with his conflict between obedience to his king and his love for Estrella. Opting for the former, he kills Bustos. Justice intervenes but an incident causes the king to confess that Bustos' death was by his order. Sancho Ortiz is freed, the two young lovers renounce any hopes for marriage. Duty triumphs over love.

Finally, we have short plays such as *autos*, on religious works, colloquies, and interludes.

Up to now we have noted several characteristics of Lope's theater: (*a*) the productivity which is the fruit of his astonishing facility; this productivity leads us to (*b*) the universality of thematic material (in time, space, society) and in genres (religious, historical, topical and so on; to this we can add (*c*) naturalness; the rapidity with which he wrote his plays and his great literary genius permitted Lope to create works notable for their simplicity and their dynamism. These are clearly popular. (*d*) The sense of honor which consists more in the consideration of others or one's public reputation than in the individual's personal virtue. "Honor is something which comes from others," says one of Lope's characters. Dishonor may be checked by silence but it can be washed away only in blood. Honor is not the exclusive prerogative of the aristocracy as some nobles believed. In the plays *Peribáñez* and *Fuenteovejuna* Lope shows how men of low estate can energetically defend their honor against the abuses of noblemen.

The following is the final scene of *Peribáñez*. The protagonist,

whose name provides the title for the work, is an honest farmer
whose wife was approached by Don Fadrique, the knight commander of Ocaña. The latter had Peribáñez sent away by naming
him captain. He then proceeded to try to seduce the wife. Peribáñez returns in time to prevent this and kills the commander.
Once his honor has been vindicated, Peribáñez presents himself
before the king:

PERIBANEZ: I am a man
                          who, though of humble birth,
                          in family and blood remain
                          by Jew or Moor untouched.
                          I stood out first among my peers
                          and, whenever troubles came our way,
                          the villagers would give me sway,
                          and six years in office stayed.
                          To this good lass I married me,
                          as fine of blood as I, and she
                          a humble girl and virtuous,
                          if beauty's reputation can be clean.
                          Fadrique the commander,
                          of our village of Ocaña
                          Lord and Comendador,
                          as a youth did love her . . .
                          I clearly saw this man's intent.
                          One day he called me to him
                          saying that he had received
                          some letters from you gentlemen
                          with orders that a group of men
                          should do military service.
                          Finally then to me he gave
                          command of quite a squadron.

                          A captain named, I left
                          Our village of Ocaña with my men,
                          but seeing that when night did fall
                          my dishonor'd be complete,
                          by ten o'clock on horse I went
                          back to my house and hearth,
                          for often have I heard it said

that wise men keep their head
and tend to their well-being
with two good mares at home.
I found my doors wide open,
and my wife attacked
like any little baby lamb
in clutches of the greedy wolf.

Her cries I heard and did unsheath
both dagger and the sword
I had put on to serve thee,
not in so sad a feat as this.
I pierced his chest and then
he left my sheep still white
for I, as shepherd, knew what might
could keep the wolf from taking her.

KING: What do you think?

QUEEN: I have wept.
That answer then should be enough
to show that here no crime can be.
It was an act of valor.

KING: How strange!
To think a humble farmer so would hold
his name in such a high esteem!
In heaven's name, it is no reason
to condemn him. I hereby grant him
then his life. . . . But what's this I say?
It is no more than just.
And of a man so valorous
I make him here and now
the captain over all the men
he has led forth from his town.

In *Fuenteovejuna,* which is sometimes known as *The Sheep
Well,* there is a similar situation. However, in this play it is a
whole town that rises against the abuses of the Commander of
Calatrava who is killed for his crimes. When the judge asks who

is responsible for the death, the answer is unanimous; even
Mengo, the comic character, does not break under torture:

> JUDGE: Who killed the Commander?
> MENGO: Fuenteovejuna, Sir.
> The king pardons the righteous people.

Another of the characteristics of Lope's theater is the transformation of the *pastor-bobo* or stupid shepherd, a stock comic
character who made people laugh because of his stupidity, into
the figure of the *donaire* or wit, a character who amused because
of his ingenuousness. He is the protagonist's servant and accom-
panies his master on all his undertakings. Like the *picaro*, he is
a sort of counter hero or antihero to his master whose rapturous
moods he brings down to earth. Finally the manservant usually
marries a maidservant of the female protagonist by the end of
the play. His principal goal is money. Lope says he calls them
escuderos [squires]:

> because they are always
> looking for *escudos* [coins]
> and always find them . . . .

All of the aspects of Lope's powerful individuality are also
to be found vividly expressed in his lyrical poetry, in which the
principal themes are profane love, sacred love, and love of family.
   Love is celebrated in his *Rimas* with an impassioned strength
both as pleasure and as pain:

> The Varied Effects of Love
> To swoon, to dare, to anger yield,
> Harsh, tender, ever-bold, yet shy,
> In health, yet dead, alive to die,
> Brave knight behind a coward's shield
>
> And not to find a peaceful field
> Apart from love; now sad, with pride

Thy mood oft times at whim will fly,
Offended, haughty, glad, annealed.

Forgetting gain, to court defeat,
To shun the truth that breaks the spell,
To quaff the hemlock as nectar sweet:

To think that heaven fits in hell,
To give up life and soul to clear deceit:
This is love. Who tastes it knows it well.

—Translation by Marguerite Gamble

Along with this profane love there is also a sincere expression
of his religious spirit, The *Rimas Sacras* [*Sacred Rhymes*]. Lope,
who well knew the weakness of the human heart, is contrite and
hopeful in his religious fervor as he addresses God:

Tomorrow

Lord, what am I, that with unceasing care
Thou did'st seek after me, that Thou did'st wait
Wet with unhealthy dews before my gate,
And pass the gloomy nights of winter there?

Oh, strange delusion, that I did not greet
Thy blest approach, and oh, to heaven how lost
If my ingratitude's unkindly frost

Has chilled the bleeding wounds upon Thy feet.
How oft my guardian angel gently cried,
"Soul from thy casement look, and thou shalt see

How He persists to knock and wait for thee!"
And oh, how often to that Voice of sorrow,
"Tomorrow we will open," I replied,
And when the morrow came I answered still

"Tomorrow."

—Translation by Henry Wadsworth Longfellow

The fundamental thing about Lope's poetry is the expression of his profound humanity, of his sincerity made flesh and blood. The following poem is a moving elegy written on the death of his little son Carlos Félix:

> For you my child did I encage
> Bright colored birds of tender age
> To please your ear and charm your eye.
> I planted tiny shoots that vie
> In verdure and in blossoms fresh
> With the fragile beauty of your dear flesh,
> But hardly had you come
> Forth from the dawn,
> Carlos, my son, into the air,
> Still sweet, still wet with dew, so fair,
> When faded were the golden veins,
> The lily's white to ice was changed,
> To earth it fell and then toward heaven ranged.

Some of Lope's poems are narrative in character such as *La Dragontea* whose protagonist is the English pirate Sir Francis Drake. The theme of the Crusades appears in *The Jerusalén Conquistada* [*Jerusalem Reconquered*]. Others are devotional, such as *El Isidro,* or mythological, such as *Circe,* or of Italianate novelistic style, such as *La hermosa Angélica* [*Beautiful Angelica*].

Lope also wrote in the genre of the novel. He added one more pastoral novel to the list with his *Arcadia.* He also created an intricate series of adventures in his *El peregrino en su Patria* [*The Wanderer in His Homeland*].

La Dorotea is a mixture of novel and play, an "action in prose." It is an interesting work and is primarily autobiographical. In it Lope describes a youthful love affair which is frustrated by a rich man. Lope appears under the name of Fernando, the girl, Dorotea, and the rival, Don Bela.

Lope's fame and influence were so great that in his own times it was said, "I believe in the almighty Lope de Vega, poet of Heaven and of Earth . . . ."

The Followers of Lope de Vega

Gabriel Téllez, a member of the religious Order of la Merced who signed his works with the pseudonym Tirso de Molina, presents a curious enigma in his birth. The surname on the baptismal certificate is blotched. It seems that Gabriel Téllez was the illegitimate son of Don Juan Téllez Girón, the Duke of Osuna, and was born in Madrid in 1584.

As a youth in 1601 Gabriel Téllez entered the religious Order of la Merced. In 1616 he embarked at Seville for America. He taught courses of theology on the isle of Santo Domingo and returned to Spain in 1618. He was appointed Chronicler of his Order and later named to the governing committee. He died in Soria in 1648.

He began writing while still quite young. He was frequently under severe criticism from officials of the Counter Reformation who considered his works licentious.

Tirso wrote two works which imitated the Renaissance dialogues of the *Courtier*. They were the *Deleitar aprovechando* [*To Please in a Beneficial Way*], and *Los Cigarrales de Toledo* [*The Gardens of Toledo*] in which he treats many literary themes through the characters in the works.

Tirso also wrote a history of his order but he is best known for his works for the theater. In his dramas we note first his admiration for Lope de Vega. Tirso de Molina's plays follow in the footsteps of Lope's drama. Tirso wrote, in the *Cigarrales*, that Lope had given to Spanish drama "the perfection and subtlety it now possesses." He refused to believe that Lope was not aware of the precepts for pleasing the public and stated that the latter had said so "only for reasons of modesty."

The women of Tirso's plays are justly famous. They are always energetic and resolute in the attaining of their goals. They even dress as men in order to go out in search of their lovers, as in *Don Gil de las calzas verdes* [*Don Gil of the Green Breeches*]. Despite their pride, they find the means of communicating their love to men of lower station, as in *El vergonzosa en Palacio* [*The*

Bashful Lover at Court]. They are equally skilled at covering up their feelings, as in *Marta la piadosa* [*Pious Martha*]. Finally, Tirso presents an excellent portrayal of the Queen Doña María de Molina, who bravely defended her son's throne, in *La Prudencia en la mujer* [*A Woman's Prudence*].

To Tirso de Molina falls the glory of having created the figure of Don Juan who is the protagonist of his work *El burlador de Sevilla y convidado de piedra* [*The Jokester of Seville and the Guest of Stone*]. Don Juan is typical of the Renaissance. He represents the man who aspires to incessant worldly pleasure and love with no thought for life after death. The figure of Don Juan has been used by Molière, Zamora, and Zorrilla.

If, as we have said, the figure of Don Juan is typically Renaissance, he is also a character of the Counter Reformation who stemmed from the pen of a member of a religious order. Consequently Don Juan suffers the punishment of eternal damnation at the end of the play. In the nineteenth century in the Romantic period, conversely, the Don Juan of Zorrilla is saved.

El condenado por desconfiado [*The Man Who Was Damned for Lack of Faith*], whose authorship has been placed in doubt, merits a separate section in the work of Tirso. In this work, the major theme is the theological problem of predestination which had come down from the Middle Ages.

Tirso uses the story of a hermit named Paulo to whom the devil, in the form of an angel, appears. He tells the hermit that his end will be the same as that of Enrico who is a savage Neapolitan bandit. Paulo, in desperation, becomes a criminal himself. It so happens, however, that Enrico, who has the one virtue of respect and love for his father, listens to the latter's counsels and, before being put to death, repents and is saved. Paulo, on the other hand, is attacked by some ruffians, dies in his despair, and is thereby condemned to damnation.

What Tirso is showing here is that divine grace makes salvation possible for all, but only those attain it who earn it by their works. In this way he refutes the Protestant thesis wherein faith without works is sufficient.

Tirso's style is occasionally affected by "culteranismo." His theater, although it belongs primarily to the cycle of Lope, sometimes comes closer to the works of Calderón de la Barca. He may thereby be classified as a transitional writer.

Few deny Tirso de Molina the second place among the masters of our stage. Indeed there are many who categorically place him first and consider him closest to Shakespeare. He undoubtedly deserves such praise, if not for powers of inventiveness in which no one has outdone Lope who created a literature in itself, then for the intensity of his poetic vitality, for his powers in creating characters and for the unsurpassable freshness of details. . . . His relative rejection of the chivalric ideal, which was largely false and conventional, his powerful sense of reality, his frank and sincere gaiety, his healthy intellectualism, that worldly intuition of his that was so comic and at the same time so poetic, the witty freshness of his rustic muse, his mordant ingenuousness, his inexhaustible cunning that at bottom was candid and optimistic, enchants us today and has the virtue of an old and comforting balm, one that chases away all care and tedium.

—Menéndez y Pelayo.

Don Guillén de Castro y Bellvís is a contemporary of Tirso's. He was born in Valencia in 1569. He was a captain in the coastal cavalry and later was in the service of the Duke of Gandia. He was a literary follower of Lope de Vega. His best known work is the *Mocedades del Cid* [*The Cid's Youthful Exploits*], based on legends that came after the great *Cantar* and which relate the love story of the Cid and Doña Jimena.

In the play, during a heated discussion in the palace, Count Lozano, Doña Jimena's father, strikes Diego Laínez who is the father of Rodrigo Díaz, the Cid. The latter asks that his sons avenge the insult. It is Rodrigo who is best fitted for this duty, although he does not know that the offender he must fight is the father of the woman he loves. He makes the challenge and kills the Count.

In despair, the youthful Cid departs for the territory of the Moors. Meanwhile love and filial duty struggle in Jimena's heart.

Love wins out and the work ends in a happy marriage. The
French author Corneille drew on this work for his famous play,
Le Cid.

Juan Ruiz de Alarcón is another major dramatist of the
period. He was born in Mexico in 1581. Both in his studies in
Salamanca and in Seville, as well as in his work, he was fully
accepted as a Spanish writer of the Spanish Golden Age. Once
established in Madrid, he saw his works performed in the theaters
of the capital. He participated in literary polemics. His physical
defect—he was a hunchback—was mercilessly satirized by his
contemporaries. At the time of his death in 1639 he held a post
with the *Consejo de Indias.*

Probably because of the brutal attacks of which he was
the object, Alarcón turned on his colleagues with furious satires.
He was deeply bitter. Even the general public did not escape his
animosity. On one occasion he wrote, "Savage beast, to you I
speak. . . . Here are my plays, so treat them as you usually do,
not as you should, but as you please. . . ."

In his play *Las paredes oyen* [*The Walls Have Ears*], Alarcón
painted a self-portrait in the figure of Don Juan de Mendoza
(who had the author's first name and one of his family names).
He portrays himself as an unfortunate person but one whose
nobility of soul finally earned him the love of the heroine, Doña
Ana. In the play he writes, "In a man you should not see / his
handsome mien or gentleness / but rather noble actions stress, / in
knowledge let his manners be." With such statements Alarcón
combated his detractors.

There are several outstanding characteristics of Alarcón's
drama, of which morality is one. The principal characteristic of
Alarcón's major plays is their preoccupation with moralizing. For
example, in his *La Verdad sospechosa* [*The Dubious Truth*], he
demonstrates how the habit of lying costs the youthful protagonist
Don García the friendship of his best friend and the love of the
woman whose hand he seeks. In another work, *La prueba de las
promesas* [*When Promises are Put to the Test*], which was taken
from a tale in Don Juan Manuel's *El Conde Lucanor,* the ambi-

THE GOLDEN AGES   169

tions of the protagonist Don Juan are justly thwarted by a
magician, Don Illán, who leads him to believe he has obtained
the highest positions in the land for him. In *Los favores del
mundo* [*The Favors of This World*], the generosity of Don García
Ruiz de Alarcón is praised when he pardons his enemy Juan de
Luna whom he has heard praying to the Virgin . . . we must
recognize, however, that ofttimes Alarcón's morality condemns
defects of little importance.

Alarcón also tried his hand at plays involving magic and
spectacle such as his *La Cueva de Salamanca* [*The Cave of Salamanca*] which makes use of apparitions and of rapid changes of
scene. There is also a play involving spectacle, *El Anticristo* [*The
Anti-Christ*].

The critic Valbuena has written of Juan Ruiz de Alarcón's
heroic plays that in them "one finds often characters and situations which are truly romantic." The people often show greatness
of character as in the case of the protagonist who helps the man
who killed his brother in *Ganar amigos* [*Winning Friends*], and
scenes full of mystery and terror as in *El tejador de Segovia* [*The
Weaver from Segovia*].

The French dramatist Pierre Corneille made use of Alarcón's
La Verdad sospechosa in writing his *Le Menteur*.

Antonio Mira de Amescua (1574–1644) was a priest who lived
mostly in Guádix and Granada. As a poet, he was outstanding. His
Canción Real de una Mudanza [*Royal Song of Inconstancy*] appears in many anthologies of Spanish poetry. It is an excellent example of both "internal" and "external" baroque style, "external"
in lexicon and imagery, "internal" in the pessimistic lesson to be
drawn from it. The central figure is a linnet, "gay, proud, cheerful
and in love," whose delicate beauty is destroyed by an implacable
hunting arrow. In rapid succession the pretty lamb falls victim
to the voraciousness of the wolf; a haughty heron, to a greedy
eagle; a captain, to his lack of military experience; a lovely lady
is victim of smallpox; and a navigator, of a storm at sea. In the
same manner, the poet's thoughts which mount to the heavenly
presence of his lady, end in despair:

Son, go the pillar seek
That did my fortune's joy sustain
And see if there it does remain,
What bronze and marble seemed,
Now woman, and like something dreamed,
Brief wind, fleet spray that gleamed.

As playright, Mira de Amescua wrote some excellent *comedias de santos* or "saints' plays." Among the most interesting of these is *El esclavo del demonio* [*The Devil's Slave*], a curious forerunner of Goethe's *Faust*.

In this work, Don Gil, a man who leads a saintly life, falls into temptation. He signs a pact with the devil in which he exchanges his soul for the possession of a woman with whom he is in love. When he finally does possess the woman, he finds only a skeleton in his arms. He sees how he has been tricked and, in despair, calls on his Guardian Angel who struggles with the devil and succeeds in retrieving the pact which Don Gil had signed.

Luis Vélez de Guevara was born in Ecija in 1570. He studied in Osuna and established himself in Madrid. He wrote poetry, novels (his *El diablo cojuelo* or *The Crippled Devil* is one of the characteristic works of the second period of the picaresque) and drama. In the latter he is renowned for his plays of a historical-legendary type. The best known of these is his *Reinar después de morir* [*To Reign After Death*] which is is a dramatization of the macabre legend of Doña Inés de Castro.

Beautiful Doña Inés was secretly married to Prince Pedro of Portugal. There were, as a consequence of this marriage, grave disturbances in the country, instigated by Doña Blanca de Navarra who was the official fiancée of the prince. It was decided that the only way to pacify the kingdom was to put Doña Inés to death. This was done, despite the supplications of the unfortunate victim. At the same time, and quite suddenly, the king also died. The Prince was proclaimed king and immediately announced publicly his marriage to Doña Inés. It is then that Doña Blanca tells him of her rival's tragic end. The new king condemns the executioners to death and commands that the cadaver of his wife

be placed on the throne. The crown which was given to Doña
Inés during the wedding ceremony was placed on her head and
she received all the honors of a queen.

Other plays include *La niña de Gómez Arias* [*The Daughter
of Gómez Arias*], the story of a famous seducer who was condemned to death by the Catholic Kings, and *La luna de la sierra*
[*The Moon of the Sierra*] which tells the tale of a beautiful village
girl who resists the immoral advances of two noblemen.

3.

The Age of the Baroque

Classicism Gone to Excess

If, as we have said, the early Renaissance is a period of the importation of foreign forms and the later Renaissance one which is marked by the incorporation of these forms into the Spanish spirit, the period of the baroque, is characterized by the complete assimilation of these forms. With the exception of the literary values of the period of plenitude, and notably Cervantes and Lope de Vega, it is the greatest period of Spanish literature.

The age of the baroque is the period of the reigns of Kings Philip IV and Charles II. Political decadence marks the epoch. On the death of Philip II, the process of the decay of the Spanish Empire became increasingly accelerated. A long series of wars slowly diminished Spain's military power and deprived her of her position of predominance in Europe.

There was a reaffirmation of religious faith. The rulers of Spain knew that their decision to support the Catholic Reform, as in the Council of Trent and through the Jesuit Order, had greatly influenced many of the enemy Protestant European countries. Due to this, Spain, both monarchy and people, came more and more to identify themselves completely with Catholicism. Consequently religious expression, such as the cult of the Eucharist with its processions and plays, became spectacles of great popular devotion.

The consequences of political decadence and the preoccupation with religion were pessimism, an anti-European spirit, and a tendency toward art for art's sake.

Some authors felt the fatigue of so many years of struggle. They lacked confidence in the efficacy of so much expenditure of energy. Fame no longer had the motivating force it had had before. The characteristic vitality of the neopaganism of the Renaissance gave way to a melancholy contemplation of life which was spoken of in terms of "dream," "play," and the "lie." The best writers of the time comprehended that the political decline was under way.

The religious Counter Reformation, which was supported by political power, zealously closed the frontiers to the ideals which were fermenting in the rest of Europe. Consequently Spain became a sort of spiritual recluse, on the fringes of the scientific advances made in other parts of the Continent. The result of this was, of course, the strengthening of the nationalism which characterizes this period.

The previous age had provided plentiful subject matter for writers: the Empire, war, love. The pessimism and preoccupation with religion in the baroque period brought an end to the predominance of these themes. Poetry no longer served to celebrate great deeds; it was converted into a vehicle of intellectual entertainment, into a game of difficulties and of ever-increasing complexities. The literary fashion demanded more and more ingenuity. The solemn and severe art of the Renaissance became the heavily ornamented art of the baroque.

Culteranism

One of the typical manifestations of the baroque in literature was "culteranism." Dámaso Alonso explained the phenomenon of *culteranismo* as "the synthesis and the intensified condensation of the lyrics of the Renaissance." Most *cultismos* or affectedly elegant expressions had already appeared to some extent in earlier poets, including Herrera. The school of "culteranos," as the poets who cultivated this style were called, greatly intensified their use. The fundamental elements that characterize their work are the following:

a Neologisms. The "culto" poet wanted language to differ markedly from the vernacular. Because of this he used newly invented words taken from Latin or Greek which are termed neologisms. These words came under heavy fire from the opponents of *culteranismo*. Nevertheless many of them eventually became a part of everyday speech. Thus we may say that the movement considerably enriched Spanish vocabulary.

Contemporary satirists made good use of this renovation of the lexicon. Quevedo, for example, attacked Góngora for his use of such words as "fulgores," "arrojar," "flores," "presiente," "candor," "construye," "métrica," "armonía," and so on, all words in current use today. At times, the attacks got well out of hand. Góngora on one occasion, protested:

A banner in the wind and no more than a bubble,
Not a word of praise or glory do they grant
Except to criticize what they call foreign cant.

b Hiperbaton. Not content with introducing foreign vocabulary, the culteranos also borrowed Latin syntax. As a result, the word order of their poems is radically changed (hiperbaton). The normal word order in a Spanish sentences is subject-verb-predicate, Meyer-Lubke notes, and its objects, direct-indirect-circumstantial. Grandgent pointed out that the word order in Romance tongues is usually simpler than that of Classical Latin, although he also believed that certain exaggerated forms were not customary in everyday usage. Nevertheless, it is indubitably from Classical Latin that Góngora took his most frequently used hiperbatons, the placing of the adjective before the noun, the excessive separation of two elements connected by sense and by concordance, etc. Also typical of "cultismo" and to be noted far earlier in the style of the Archpriest of Talavera and of *The Celestina* in the fifteenth century is the tendency to place the verb at the end of the sentence.

c Metaphors. By means of metaphor, the culteranos were able to replace the real names of things with poetical names in which they found a certain relationship. For example they used "carnation" for "mouth," "emerald" for "grass," "gold" to designate blond hair, and similar expressions. This, of course, makes reading their poetry a difficult, though not insuperable, task.

Every metaphor grows out of a comparison. Therefore there must be some common sensorial element in the objects to be compared. In the metaphor of "carnation-mouth" it is the red color. It is sound in "voice-silver." The more daring and the less frequently used by the poets, the more beautiful the metaphor was considered to be, and, as we know, contemporary poetry also uses many metaphorical combinations.

Conceptism

Parallel to *culteranismo* there existed a school of opposing tendencies, called *conceptism,* which stressed content rather than form. Its principal elements were as follows:

a The *concept,* which consisted of expressing, as Gracián put it, "the correspondence which exists between objects." To accomplish this, antithesis, paradox, and philosophical concepts were used.

b *Concision,* which consisted of aiming, contrary to "culteranism," at expressing its ideas with a minimum of words. Gracián wrote, "What is good, if also brief, is doubly good."

A comparison between culteranism and conceptism may be made. These two schools, despite being contemporary, were different and fought each other. Culteranism was preoccupied with form. Its foundation rested on the richness and structure of its vocabulary. Its principal adherents tended to appeal to the senses. Conceptism was mainly concerned with content and ideas. Vocabulary was to be reduced to what was indispensable. Its writing aimed at more than the intellect.

The baroque style in Europe had several names: "euphuism" in England, "marinism" in Italy and the "Silesian School" in Germany. Only France was able partially to avoid these literary extravagances.

The Poetry of Culteranism

Luis de Góngora y Argote (1561–1627) was born in Cordova. He received a humanistic education in his native city and at the University of Salamanca. He became a priest and held a post in the Cathedral of Cordova. Góngora made extensive trips throughout Spain. He traveled in Castile, Andalusia, and Galicia, whose countrysides he described in his poems. He was later named private chaplain to Philip III and in 1617 became a resident of Madrid.

The poet, whose fame had already begun to spread, began his life in the literary circles of the Court. He answered with satire the attacks against his way of writing—principally by Quevedo and Lope. In the final years of his life, his culteranistic style became more exaggerated. He died in Cordova at the age of seventy-six years.

We have already pointed out that Góngora borrowed and intensified the culteranism that had appeared in such poets as Herrera and Carrillo de Sotomayor. He became in his own right the leader of the school of culteranism whose characteristics we described earlier.

It has been said that two periods and two styles can be discerned in Góngora's work: first of all, the *popular* as in his *Letrillas* and *Romances,* and a second, later culteranistic style, that of his great *Polifemo* and the *Soledades* [*Solitudes*]. This is not wholly accurate, however, as his culteranism can already be discerned in his seemingly simplest work and, in addition, it would be very difficult to mark the transition from one period to the other.

In Góngora's works it is the longer poems which provide us with the most extreme examples of the style of culteranism. In the *Polifemo* a mythological theme is developed, the love of Acis and Galatea, which is obstructed by the giant Poliphemus who changes Acis into a rivulet. In his *Panegyric* for the Duke of Lerma and in his *Sonnets* and *Canciones,* Góngora also demonstrated how exceptional a poet he was. His *Soledades* was a work of even more considerable breadth.

The *Soledades* is a lengthy but incomplete poem. It was to have four parts but Góngora left us only the first part and a fragment of the second.

The story is a simple one. A youth who has been shipwrecked reaches the shore where some shepherds give him shelter. There are descriptions of songs and dances, a rustic wedding, and athletic games. In the second part there are fishing scenes. As one can see, the plot could hardly be more slender for some two thousand verses. Actually it is little more than a pretext, allowing the poet to write descriptions, in the style of culteranism, of the landscapes which the action provides—seas, beaches, rivers, woods, mountains, and so on.

The *Soledades* does have much merit, however. The work is Góngora's most difficult one. It contains some passages of great beauty, but even Góngora's own contemporaries published explanatory commentaries on the work. In the descriptions of nature in the poem, as Dámaso Alonso has ascertained, "the ugly, the troublesome, and the disagreeable have all disappeared." Each element has been replaced by beautiful metaphor, the rivers are "crystals," birds are "citharas of feathers," and so on. There is much color and the lines contain an unsurpassable musicality.

There are several characteristics of Góngora's culteranism. The two baroque schools of culteranism and conceptism are hardly ever found in a pure state. The writers of the former frequently employ techniques supposedly reserved for the latter, and this is precisely what happens in Góngora's case. His style, as a result, rather than *culterano* is "gongoriano"—a mixture of both schools.

From the first "Soledad" or "Solitude"

It was the flowery season of the year
In which Europa's perjured robber strays—
Whose brow the arms of the half-moon adorn,
The sun the shining armour of his hide—
Through sapphire fields to feast on stellar corn,
When, fitter cupbearer than Ganymede

For Jupiter, the lovesick boy gave tears
(Absent, disdained and shipwrecked) to the tide
And winds, which moved by his complaining lays
As to a second Arion's harp gave heed.

A pitying lamb from mountain pine, opposed,
The constant enemy to Notus' strife,
Became no puny dolphine on that day
To the unthinking traveller who reposed,
Trusting to miserable boards his life,
And to an Ocean's Lybia his way.

Close by a headland, crowned
With sheltering feathers and dry rushes, he,
Engulfed before, then spewed up by the sea,
(Covered with foam, with seaweed girded) found
A hospitable rest,
Where built the bird of Jupiter his nest

—Translation by Edward Meryon Wilson

Conceptist Poetry

Francisco de Quevedo y Villegas was born in Madrid in
1580. He was of an aristocratic family which, however, had little
wealth. He studied in Madrid and in Alcalá where he acquired
a thorough foundation in Greek and Latin, sufficient, in fact, to
enable him to become one of Spain's greatest humanists. His university years also gave him an acquaintance with student and
picaresque life which he was to portray so vividly in his works.

A duel fought in the defence of a woman which ended in
the death of his opponent is said to have caused Quevedo to flee
to Italy in 1611. There he was the protegé of the Duke of Osuna
who made him his chief adviser. When Osuna became the viceroy
of Naples, Quevedo was named to the post of Secretary of the
Treasury and later went to Venice as a part of the conspiracy to
annex the Venetian Republic to Spain. When the plot was dis-

covered, Quevedo miraculously escaped with his life by disguising himself as a beggar.

When he returned home to Spain, Quevedo tried to situate himself at court, despite the ill feeling of the Count-Duke of Olivares who feared his independent and outspoken spirit and with whom his relations were always strained. Accused of having left a petition against the Count-Duke under the king's napkin at table, Quevedo was imprisoned in the Convent of San Marcos de León in 1639. He died a short two years after his release, in 1645.

The surroundings in which Quevedo spent his life, whether in Italy or in Spain, are those of the court and its politics, which at that time were characterized by abrupt and mercurial changes. Quevedo's profound skepticism before human vanities is largely due to this. He acquired a sense of stoicism from his study of Seneca.

Quevedo lived at the height of the Counter Reformation when the courtier who was a man of arms and of letters had given way to the philosophical and introspective writer. In *La hora de todos* [*Everybody's Hour*], Quevedo wrote, "The person who wrote that arms and letters were brothers knew little of what he spoke, for there are no more divergent lineages than those of 'doing' and 'telling.'"

Quevedo lived at the time when the appearance of the two literary schools of culteranism and conceptism was most stirring. His philosophical background and asperity placed him in the ranks of the conceptist school. He was subsequently militantly anticulteranism, an expression which he considered too heavily ornamented and devoid of ideas.

He had the works of Fray Luis de León and of Francisco de la Torre republished as he considered them to be models of what poetry should be. Furthermore, in satirical works like *La culta latiniparla* [*The Cult of "Speakalalatin"*] and the *Aguja de navegar cultos* [*The Compass for Navigating the "Cultos"*], he struck out against Góngora and his school. In these works he mocked the excessive metaphors of the culteranos by the use of extravagant puns that frequently defy translation.

Curiously enough, many of the words which Quevedo criticized are now a part of regular usage which shows that culteranism did enrich the Spanish lexicon.

Furthermore, in spite of the harshness of his criticism of culteranism, Quevedo's own work is not free of it. His poetry, frequently of great beauty, like Góngora's, is a strange mixture of both conceptism and culteranism.

Politically pessimistic, Quevedo is one of the men who most clearly saw the decadence of the Spanish monarchy. He implacably analyzed its causes, which he discusses in his works, as follows:

a Softness and corruption in the people's habits which caused laziness and weakness. This is the subject of his famous *Epistle* censoring the Count-Duke of Olivares.

b The turning over of the royal power to incompetent favorites—the *privado* or favorite, according to Quevedo, should have two qualities, discretion and impartiality. He even wrote a play on the subject, *Como ha de ser el privado* [*What the Favorite Should Be Like*].

c The triumph of material values over spiritual—money had conquered both virtue (as in *Poderoso caballero es Don Dinero* or *Fair and Healthy Is Sir Wealthy*) and love:

> —If you want my heart, dear Leonor,
>   To you I will entrust it.
> —Heavens, this is madness,
>   But with money we'll adjust it!

Quevedo's acute political pessimism is a consequence of experience. In his works on politics, the *Marco Bruto* and *La Politica de Dios* [*The Politics of God*], he outlines what an ideal state should be. In other works, such as *España defendida* [*Spain Defended*], he points out the perils to which the Spanish monarchy was exposed, in large part because of the growing might of France.

The major theme on which Quevedo meditates in his poetry is the passage of time, or as he expressed it on one occasion, the "collector of death's fee." The testimonials to its implacable passage, old age and ruins, appear time and time again. The roadway to death is constantly invoked, for "everything is a reminder of death."

Death Warnings

I saw the ramparts of my native land
    One time so strong, now dropping in decay,
    Their strength destroyed by this new age's way
That has worn out and rotted what was grand.
    I went into the fields; there I could see
    The sun drink up the waters newly thawed;
Their miseries robbed the light of day for me.

I went into my house; I saw how spotted,
    Decaying things made that old home their prize;
    My withered walking-staff had come to bend.
I felt the age had won; my sword was rotted;
    And there was nothing on which to set my eyes
    That was not a reminder of the end.

            —Translation by John Masefield

Nevertheless Quevedo is of special interest because he raised all the abstract pessimism of baroque poetry to a national and political plane. The crumbling of the walls of his native land is for Quevedo a clear and terrifying symptom. Spain had been able to become dominant throughout the world, but she had to maintain her vigilance:

How much easier, oh Spain, in many ways,
What you from others to yourself did take,
To take in turn from you in other days.

Quevedo was an ascetic where ethics were concerned. The pessimism that is reflected in his political writings was also projected into his life itself. There is a fundamental and constant idea at the core of his thinking: death. His asceticism caused him to think of death the better to direct one's life. He wrote, "The skull is the dead man and the face is death; what you call to die is to stop dying and what you call to live is to die living."

With such an idea at the core of his thinking, it is not surprising to encounter in Quevedo the concept of the vanity of the things of the world. Even more, he does not believe in them, even though he esteems them. For example: (a) Honor does not really exist. In *El sueño del infierno* or the *Vision of Hell* he wrote, "Once you see what honor is, you know it is nothing at all." (b) Valor is nothing more than fear that is disguised: "The man who fights to defend his soil, fights out of fear of an evil that is greater than being taken captive or killed. And the man who sets out to conquer those who stay at home sometimes does so out of fear that the other man is about to do the same to him."

These ideas appear predominantly in Quevedo's ascetic works, in *La cuna y la sepultura* [*The Cradle and the Grave*], *Providencia de Dios* [*God's Providence*], and in the philosophical works *De los remedios de cualquier Fortuna* [*Remedies for Whatever Luck*] and *Los cuatro pestes del mundo* [*The World's Four Plagues*].

Life is a suffering in which that of death begins and lasts as long as life lasts. Consider it like the day's work of a laborer, who has no rest from the time he begins until he finishes. You begin to be born and to die at the same time and it is not within your power to hold back the hours. If you were sensible, you would not try to do so; if you were good, you would have no reason to fear. You begin to die before you know what life is, and you live it without pleasure, anticipating the tears that are to come.

Uneducated people often see in Quevedo a joyous storehouse of more or less dirty jokes. There is nothing further from the truth. Of course some of his works are classified as satirical or festive, but it is no less certain that Quevedo's satire is grounded in bitterness and suffering.

In studying the picaresque novel of this period we must cite

Quevedo's *La vida del Buscón Don Pablos* [*The Life of the Scavenger Don Pablos*]. Quevedo perceived the implacable satire against everything that is exalted which is implicit in picaresque literature. Thus, in his *Sueños* [*Visions*] he has all the different figures of the social scale pass in review. Doctors, hangmen, and poets are satirized in *El sueño de la calaveras* [*The Vision of the Skulls*]; merchants, playwrights, flatterers, and government officials are portrayed in *El alguacil alguacilado* [*The Peace Officer Pacified*]; tailors, booksellers, and duennas are pilloried in *Las zahurdas de Plutón* [*Pluto's Pigsties*], and so on.

There are, nevertheless, purely festive works among Quevedo's writings. The author's wit shines to best advantage, though not always in the best of taste, in his *Cartas del Caballero de la Tenaza* [*Letters from The Gentlemen With the Claw-like Grasp*] and the *Libro de todas las cosas y otras más* [*Book About Everything and a Few Things More*].

There are also two collections of Quevedo's poetry, *El Parnaso español* [*Spanish Parnassus*] and *Las tres últimas musas españolas* [*The Last Three Spanish Muses*]. The following themes appear in them:

a   Philosophical and political themes, as in the aforementioned *Satirical and Censorious Epistle Against the Habits of Present-Day Spaniards,* dedicated to Olivares, and many more which allude to the decadence of Spain.

b   Love themes in poems which were dedicated to a lady known by the fictitious name of Lisi, with whom, it appears, Quevedo was in love.

It is touching to note that death, which was a constant obsession for Quevedo, could be conquered only by love which endures even in the grave:

> Soul in which a God enclosed has been,
> Veins which wit to so much fire did give,
> Substances that were to flame and glory kin,
> From body gone, in heedfulness shall live;
> They ash will be, though purpose shall reside therein,
> They dust will be, but dust to love still sensitive.

c Satirical themes as in the *A una nariz* [*To a Nose*], *Al mos-quito de la trompetilla* [*To a Buzzing Mosquito*], and the famous *Poderoso caballero,* a selection of which is a follows:

> Mother, I to gold am slave,
> My lover and beloved is he,
> And he so much in love with me
> That he has turned quite yellow;
> For simply dressed or full festooned
> He even hardest hearts can mellow.
> Fair and healthy
> Is Sir Wealthy.

In all of Quevedo's poetry, we can discern his vast literary background. We find traces of Anacreon, Horace and Vergil, the Italian Petrarch and the Frenchman Du Bellay.

In my opinion, Quevedo is Spain's first writer. I repeat, writer. There are classics and classics. Quevedo, like Fernando de Rojas, like Saint Teresa, like Góngora, give the impression that at every moment they are creating the language in which they are expressing themselves. The two Fray Luis's, on the other hand, seem to have found their language already set and do little more than put up with it. Cervantes occupies a position in between.

.   .   .   .   .

. . . What nervous and high-bred words, like sensitive young stallions, those words of Quevedo! What rapid and perfect couplings of nouns and adjectives! What leap in the ellipsis, what a tragic Bacchanalia in the hyperbaton!
. . . And what frenetic impulse that forces the vestal notions and makes intransitive verbs twist violently and prolifically into transitive! . . .

In the midst of this orgy of brilliant energy the intelligence abruptly becomes malice, with all the cold splendor of a Spanish blade in the tumultuous confusion of a popular fandango.

—Eugenio D'Ors

The Later Picaresque Novel

In categorizing the picaresque novel, we noted that the later period coincided with the decay of the Spanish Empire to such a point that the pessimism of the *pícaro* mirrored the broader pessimism of the nation.

1. *Guzman de Alfarache.* In the last year of the sixteenth century, in 1599, the *Primera parte de la vida del pícaro Guzman de Alfarache* [*First Part of the Life of the Pícaro Guzman de Alfarache*] was published in Madrid. Its author, Mateo Alemán, who lived from 1546 to 1614, was from Seville and had been educated in Alcalá and Salamanca. He may well have learned the picaresque life at first hand during a term in jail for irregularities in keeping certain accounts and through his journeyings and adventures which took him to Mexico where he spent his remaining years.

As in Cervantes' case, an imitator who used the name of Mateo Luján de Saavedra, wrote an apocryphal second part to the *Guzmán*.

The story, in essence, may be quickly outlined. Guzmán de Alfarache, the son of a thief and a licentious woman, educated without discipline or good example, followed the classical trajectory of the *pícaro*. He was a servant in an inn, a cook's helper —and a cheat; he journeyed to Italy where he was in the service of a cardinal. After some disagreeable experiences, he returned to Spain to become, successively, a usurer, a thief, and even worse things, until finally he was condemned to lashings and to the galleys.

The philosophy of the *Guzmán* is much more bitter than that of the earlier *Lazarillo* (1554). Idealized values such as love, justice, and goodness no longer exist or are vanquished by physical appetites. Frequently what appears to be virtue is no more than hypocritical mask. Honor and respectability are things to be purchased: "Tell me, who grants respectability to some and takes it away from others? Having more or less (money)," he says in Book VI, Chapter III. Everything that one dreams of is illusion and falsehood: "How well things turn out at night in the dark in our meditations! How quickly they melt in the dawn like a snowdrop in summer! It was all castles in the air, fantastic shapes of the imagination!"

The context of the work is the same in the *Lazarillo*, but Guzmán's life is much more extensive and complicated. He knows greater changes of fortune. He travels extensively in Italy, France, and Spain. He is more daring and his cynicism is more biting. Each episode is accompanied by long moral disquisitions in which the gloomiest pessimism predominates.

2. The *Rinconete y Cortadillo*. This work, which is basically picaresque, is one of The *Exemplary Novels* (1613) of Cervantes. The patio of Monipodio's house in Seville, which is a sort of headquarters for a group of wrongdoers, is the principal setting. The characters, according to Rodríguez Marín, may be divided into two categories—the "idlers" who include beggars of various types, false cripples, "prayers-for-hire," and trinket-sellers, and the "workers" or thieves, cardsharps, and sellers of stolen goods. The descriptions of Seville, which was then the main point of departure for the Americas and was full of opportunity for unscrupulous adventurers, and consequently for the youthful Rinconete and Cortadillo, are characteristic of picaresque literature.

On the other hand, the satirical element is missing. Cervantes, in this work, is more of an observer than critic. When we compare him with Mateo Alemán, as Menéndez Pelayo puts it, so "gloomy and pessimistic," he seems "so different, . . . that he does not appear like a contemporary."

3. *La vida del escudero Marcos de Obregón* or *Life of the Squire Marcos de Obregón*. This is the work of the musician and poet Vicente Espinel who was educated in Salamanca and who traveled in Spain, Flanders, and Italy. A native of Ronda, he had ample opportunity as a student, soldier, and squire, for acquaintance with the picaresque way of life. He was an excellent poet to whom is attributed the creation of the poetic strophe called the *décima*, a ten-lined stanza also known as the *espinela* in honor of its creator.

The *Marcos de Obregón* (1618), with all its adventures and mishaps, has an educative purpose. Espinel does not give as extensive a portrait of the lower strata of society nor of their destitution and misery as is usually found in picaresque works. Furthermore, his language, Gili Gaya tells us, is limpid and cultured, that of a man who avoided as much as possible all excess of vulgarity. Espinel himself wrote: "Those books which go to the printer should be pure and chaste in language."

Some of Marcos de Obregón's adventures later served as a model for the French writer Lesage in his *Gil Blas de Santillana.*

4. *El Diablo Cojuelo* or *The Crippled Devil.* This is the work (1646) of Luis Vélez de Guevara who is also known as an important dramatist. This work has various satirical aspects. Its protagonist, Don Cleofas Pérez Zambrillo, frees the Crippled Devil from a phial in which a magician has imprisoned him. In gratitude the Devil takes the protagonist on a tour of such cities as Madrid and Seville, lifting the roofs off houses and showing him all aspects of city life. The book has, therefore, a satirical social aspect. Nobles, students, poets, actors, lunatics and, above all, says Pfandle, "the movement of the picaresque novel," appear in its pages. It is written in a lively and natural style.

5. *La vida del Buscón Don Pablos* or *The Life of the Scavenger Don Pablos.* This is Quevedo's picaresque novel. Pablos, the son of an unscrupulous barber and a woman of little virtue, becomes the servant of Don Diego Coronel who studies in the boarding school of the terrible Domine Cabra who lets the pupils in his care perish from hunger. When his father is put to death, Pablos goes to Madrid, to Toledo, and to Seville and finally leaves for America. Pablos' travels give him the opportunity to describe student life at Alcalá, that of adventurers and opportunists in Madrid, of a troup of actors in Toledo, and of a company of beggars in Seville.

The satirical and descriptive passages acquire terrifying force in Quevedo whose portrayal of reality is often caricature.

These then are the last examples of the picaresque in this period. As the genre developed, the pessimistic philosophy emitted by the picaresque world developed independently of the novel and eventually became purely philosophical writings as in the work of Quevedo. Gracián, whom we shall soon study, expresses the same philosophy and the same pessimistic and skeptical outlook that Guzmán, the *picaro*, does. The characters, however—the gamblers, beggars, and thieves—had disappeared, as had the picaresque novel, Montesinos tells us.

Conceptist Prose

Baltasar Gracián was born of a poor but large family in Belmonte near Calatayud in 1601. He studied in Jesuit schools at Calatayud and Huesca and entered the Company of Jesus.

He made many trips to Madrid where his fame as a preacher earned connections and promotions for him. He was eventually named rector of the seminary at Tarragona. At about this time he served as military chaplain in the raising of the siege of Lérida and earned the title of "Father of Victory" (1646).

From this time onward, whether because of the curious incident in which, while preaching in Valencia, he said that he would read a letter from Hell in the pulpit, an action the ecclesiastical authorities reprimanded him for, or because of the bent of his profane works, some of which were published without the order's permission, but above all because of his independent character, he lost prestige in the Company. Finally he was exiled to Huesca. He died in Tarazona in 1658 after having tried to leave the order.

Quevedo may be the first conceptist but Gracián is both the most extreme and the one who turns the movement into literary doctrine with his book *Agudeza y arte de ingenio* [*The Worldly Art of Wisdom*]. In "Discourse LX" he writes, "Words are the leaves on the tree and 'concepts' are the fruit." Against the abuse of words in culteranism, conceptism proposed the "intense profundity of the verb." The loftiest and most philosophical concepts were to be expressed in the leanest of language. Gracián, consequently, became a master of the short saying, dry and pithy but nevertheless magnificently expressive. "Quintessence outweighs farragos," he says.

Gracián's philosophy is interesting. When we spoke of the final period of the picaresque novel in the baroque age, we said that its pessimistic philosophy took on an independent existence.

Gracián took it up, although no *pícaros* appear in his work. His pessimism shows several characteristics:

a A lack of confidence in man. Man, for Gracián, is an animal with the very worst instincts. In his *Criticón* or *Fault-finder* he tells the tale of a traveler who saved a man in the company of tigers, dragons, and serpents from a deep cave in which they had been confined. All the animals kissed their savior's feet in gratitude. The man killed the traveler so that he could rob him.

> "Believe me that there is no wolf or lion or tiger, there is no basilisk who comes up to man; he excels them all in ferocity."
>
> —*Criticón*, I, IV.

a Life for Gracián was a perpetual battle. "There is nothing that does not have an opposite against which it struggles." (*Criticón*, I III). Because of this, man must always be on guard against his enemies—"Against malice, malice."

c The things of this world all pass away, and when death comes it can be seen that they are the "machine of the wind," "coals," and "ashes." Only the treasures of the spirit, i.e., knowledge, are of value.

> . . . For the creative mind is no flattery, like a new book every day.
>
> —*Criticón*, II, IV.

d Against all this pessimism, however, Gracián proposed will power: "Everything rests with it," he tells us.

> Do you see those blind knots that Will ties with a *yes*? Well it unties them all with a *no*.

Will power and struggle are the only things which can save us and bring us to God.

Gracián makes us retrace the way toward the Divinity in his book *El comulgatorio* [*The Communion Altar*].

Gracián wanted to paint, in ideal types, portraits of model men in every aspect of human life. His books *El Héroe* [*The Hero*], *El Discreto* [*The Prudent Man*] and *El Político* [*The Politician*] give examples of all types of human activity (war, culture, government). The archetype of the politician is King Ferdinand the Catholic.

The true and magistral politics, certain and firm and which did not dissolve into fantastic absurdities, were those of Ferdinand, the Catholic King. . . . He conquered kingdoms for God, crowns for the thrones of his Cross, provinces for the Fields of the Faith and, in brief, joined earth and sky.

Capacity constitutes the person; lack of capacity engenders monsters. The former gives us a Caesar who founds a monarchy; the latter breeds a Gallienus who loses it; the former heartens a Cyrus in his glorious hour of fatigue; the latter, a Darius in his idleness and rest. Thus from one are born the virtues of a Pelayo, from the other, the vices of a Rodrigo; of one, the feats of a Romulus; of the others, the abomination of a Tarquin.

—From *El Político*

These are the axes for the prudent man's success; nature alternates them and art enhances them. Man is the famous Microcosm and the soul is his firmament. When temperament and ingenuity are joined, in a rhyming of Atlantis and Alcide, they assure, through their fortune and their brilliance, that all one's other assets will shine forth.

One without the other has been a partial felicity for many, bringing in its train either envy or negligence of fortune.

Therefore, let temperament be singular, but not anomalous; balanced, but not paradoxical. In few men does admiration satisfy their cravings, and neither is heroism to be found in every prince nor culture in every prudent man.

—From *El Discreto*

El Criticón [*The Faultfinder*] is central to Gracián's work. Gracián's philosophical ideas are concentrated in the form of maxims in his book *Oráculo manual y arte de prudencia* [*Oracular Manual or The Art of Being Prudent*]. For a thorough knowledge of his thought, however, it is necessary to read *El Criticón*, a lengthy philosophical novel full of allegories and symbols.

The *Criticón* is the story of Critilo who is shipwrecked. On the island of Saint Helena he meets Andrenio who is a man in his natural state who has grown up in isolation and knows neither his beginnings nor the language which Critilo teaches him. What Gracián is doing here is presenting the contrast between Andrenio who is the noble savage guided only by instinct, and Critilo, the educated man whose guide is reason. Both travel extensively in Spain, France, and Italy, and meet various allegorical personages, each of whom gives a corresponding commentary.

Man dies just as he should begin to live, when he has fully become a person, when he is wise and prudent, ripe with knowledge and experience, tempered and formed, brimming with perfections and of the greatest utility and authority in both the home and the fatherland. What was born a beast dies fully human. But we should not say that he has died now, but that he has just died, for life is nothing more than a dying day by day. What a terrible law of life! Death is the only one which allows not one exception, for whom no privilege exists! What debt it holds to those great men, the highly placed, the flawless prince, the consummate gentleman, with whose death perishes virtue, prudence, valor, wisdom, and often a whole city or even a whole kingdom. Indeed those heroes of great virtue and fame whose pathway to the summit of greatness cost them so dear should be immune to death, but with such frequency the very contrary is true, that often those of smallest importance last the longest, while those of greater value live the shortest time. Those who merit scarcely one full day of life go on forever while those virtuous men, shining for a moment like a brilliant comet, pass across our sky. The famous King Nestor, of whom it is told that he consulted the oracles to learn the length of his life and learned that he had a thousand years to live, had a plausible solution. He said, "Well, that means there is no use in building a house." When his friends insisted that there was time not only for building a house, but for building many, and even places, he answered them saying, "You want me to busy myself with building a house when there are no more than a thousand years of life? For so short a period I should construct a palace? A tent or a hut to shelter me in passing will be quite enough for it would be sheer madness to establish something permanent."

How well all this fits into what we were saying! Even though men live at the most a hundred years and cannot be certain of one single day, they undertake the construction of buildings that will last a thousand years hence and plan houses as if they were to last forever on the face of the earth. Among the latter, no doubt, belongs the man who said that even if he knew he would live only a year, he would build a house; if a month, he would marry; if a week, he would buy a bed and chair; if a single day, he'd make a stew. How death must laugh derisively at these stupid men seeing that while they are constructing great houses, she is opening for them a narrow sepulcher as in the proverb: "Once the house is done, the tomb is wide open." When a man sets things to rights, Death sets things awry. To finish the palace and to come to life's end is one and the same, for the seven columns of the most superb edifice are easily exchanged for seven feet of earth, or seven spans of marble, the hollow vanity of many. After all, what difference is there between rotting among porphyry and marble and among clumps of earth?

It was on this empty truth that the prudent Courtier was discoursing with our two pilgrims in Rome as they walked along. They came to a large square full of people who stood there waiting for one of their vulgar spectacles which they so much admire.

"What is this all about?" asked Andrenio.

And the answer: "Be patient and you will learn wisdom."

After a bit they saw appear a monstrous figure dancing and leaping about on a tightrope with all the nimbleness of a bird and the intrepidity of a madman. Those who watched him were fully amazed; the performer showed no fear. The crowd trembled as they watched and the performer performed so that they would watch.

"What daring!" exclaimed Andrenio. "No doubt performers like that lose their minds first and then their fear. On level ground life is never sure and here this fellow walks the narrow ledge."

"Are you frightened of him?" asked the Courtier.

"If not of him, of whom then?"

"Of your own self."

"Of myself? Why myself?"

"Because what is happening to you is childish foolishness. Do you know where you are putting down your feet? Do you know where you are going?"

"What I do know," Andrenio replied, "is that they would not get me up there on that rope for anything in this world, while that poor fool risks his neck for the lowest of reasons."

"That's fine indeed!" said the Courtier. "If you could only watch yourself walk along, not only like that performer but in even greater danger, what would you feel and what would you say?"

"Me?"

"Yes, you."

"Why?"

"Tell me, don't you walk every hour and every moment on the thread of your life and that not as thick or as substantial as a tightrope, but as thin as a spider's web, and even more so, and yet you dance and leap about on it? There you eat, there you sleep, there you take your rest with no fear whatsoever. Believe me when I tell you that all mortals are daring acrobats on the slender thread of a fragile life, with this difference, that some fall today and others tomorrow. It is on that thread that men construct splendid houses and great illusions, erect castles of air and lay the foundations for all their hopes. They are aghast to see the daring of the performer who walks on the thick and substantial rope, but show no astonishment at themselves who are held up not by a cord but by a strand of silk, less even, a hair, and even that is exaggeration, by the filament of a spider's web. But even that is something when compared to life, which is even less. When faced with facts such as these man has good reason to be thunderstruck, sufficient to make his hair stand on end and still worse when he considers the abyss of unhappiness into which the heavy burden of his errors hurls him.

Culteranism and Conceptism in the Theater

The characteristics of the baroque age appear also in the theater:

a Culteranism and conceptism influence the language of the principal characters. (The *graciosos* or servant-comics usually ridicule these literary exaggerations.)

b Scenography, which had been rudimentary in the time of Lope de Vega, becomes more elaborate. Costly settings and light changes make their appearance, and music acquires greater importance.

Pedro Calderón de la Barca, the major representative of baroque drama, was born in Madrid in 1600. His life was completely different from Lope's. He had neither adventures nor changes of spirit. He had a life of tranquillity, dedicated to study and to work, without leaving Madrid except for the period of war with Catalonia in which Calderón saw service and was wounded. At the age of fifty-one he became a priest. He obtained the chaplaincy of *Reyes Nuevos* in Toledo until he was named private chaplain to Philip IV and then took residence in the capital (1663). He died there in 1681, a very famous man.

The number of works left us by Calderón is much smaller than that of Lope. He himself fixed it, shortly before his death, at one hundred ten. On the other hand, the quality is greater, as Calderón's plays, produced less rapidly than Lope's, are much more reflectively and carefully written. He tried his hand at all the same genres that Lope did, but he excelled in two of them that were little cultivated by the "Phoenix"—mythological plays and *autos sacramentales* or short religious plays.

In comparison with Lope, Calderón's drama may be characterized as less abundant and more intense. For Calderón de la Barca, everything that makes up life can be put into two categories: *(a)* Material things, which should be at the disposal of the king, to whom one must be wholly loyal, and *(b)* Spiritual things, which are for the service of God.

He believed that honor constitutes a patrimony of the soul. Everybody, whether peasant or noble, has a right to a good reputation. In *El Alcalde de Zalamea* [*The Mayor of Zalamea*] *we see* how energetically a common man, Pedro Crespo, defends the honor of his daughter against a captain who offends her.

The story is as follows: Pedro Crespo, an honest farmer from Zalamea, billets Captain Don Alvaro de Ataide of the infantry regiment of Don Lope de Figueroa in his house. The captain falls in love with Isabel, Crespo's daughter. He carries her off and seduces her, leaving her abandoned in the woods where her father finds her and hears of her misfortune from her own lips. Pedro Crespo, who has just become Mayor, begs the captain on bended knee to save his honor by an honorable marriage, but his only reply is disdain. Crespo then takes up the staff of justice and orders the arrest and trial of the Captain. Don Lope de Figueroa orders that the prisoner be freed, but Crespo stands firm. When the soldiers are about to set fire to the town, Philip II arrives. The king recognizes the justice of Crespo's case and asks that the prisoner be turned over to him for punishment. The mayor complies with the captain's body, for the latter has already been garroted. The king accepts the punishment and names Pedro Crespo lifelong mayor of Zalamea.

The following passage illustrates the dispute between Don Lope and Pedro Crespo:

CRESPO: A thousand thanks, I give,
             For the favor you have granted me,
             The chance and possibility
             To avoid what might destroy me.
DON LOPE: What indeed
             Would now destroy you?
CRESPO: Putting to death the man
             Who has aggrieved me. . . .
DON LOPE: Great Heaven, don't you know
             He is a captain?

CRESPO:	By Heaven, yes.
	And if he were a general,
	In things that touch on me
	I'd kill him.
DON LOPE:	The man who lays a hand
	On the lowest ranking of my men
	Or even of their clothes a thread does touch,
	That man I'll hang.
CRESPO:	And anyone, I say,
	Who dares to touch one atom
	Of my honor, that man too,
	By Heaven's name, I'll hang.
DON LOPE:	Do you know that being who you are,
	A man of lower station, you must bring
	yourself
	To bend to these offenses?
CRESPO:	With what is mine,
	But with my reputation, never, no.
	For king and country, goods and life
	I'll gladly give; my honor though is not
	of this;
	It to the soul's estate belongs
	And only God can own my soul.

The theme of honor acquires tragic aspects in Calderón's drama. His plays of amorous intrigue revolve around the problem of honor, and honor can, as we saw in Lope, be tarnished by the slightest insinuation.

The remedy for dishonor is death, as in *El médico de su honra* [*The Physician of His Honor*], and *El Mayor monstruo, los celos* [*The greatest Monster, Jealousy*] or silence, as in *A secreto agravio, secreta venganza* [*Aggrieved in Secret, In Secret Revenged*]. All of these themes have appeared already in Lope de Vega's plays, but Calderón makes them more pointed and intensive.

God's presence in all human action is characteristic of Calderón's drama. Nevertheless, all human beings are creatures possessing free will and are responsible for their actions even when education or circumstances influence them.

Didactic drama is important in Calderón's work. The most characteristic drama of Calderón's philosophical thought is his famed *La vida es sueño* [*Life Is a Dream*].

In the story, Basilio, the King of Poland, learns from astrology that his new-born son, Segismundo, will deprive him of power. To avoid this, the king has his son imprisoned in a lonely tower and keeps his identity from him.

Consequently Segismundo grows up without knowing any other human beings except his jailer, Clotaldo. Finally the king decides to put Segismundo to a test and therefore has him drugged and brought to the Court. On awakening Segismundo finds himself in the palace. He shows the most savage of instincts, and bursts into anger at the slightest provocation. He even throws a courtier who argues with him over a high balcony. He makes advances to the lovely Rosaura, the first woman he has seen. Basilio is thus confirmed in his fears that his son would make a cruel and despotic king. Accordingly he has him drugged a second time and taken back to his prison-tower where he is to be told that his past experiences were only a dream. But the populace rises in rebellion in favor of Segismundo who is considered the legitimate heir to the throne. The son defeats the father who throws himself as Segismundo's feet, and thus the predictions are fulfilled. All of this is due, however, not to the inevitability set by the stars, but to the mistaken education the king had decided upon. Segismundo, meanwhile, has learned his moral lesson from all that has befallen him and treats his father with due respect.

> It is true, we must repress
> This barbarous condition,
> This fury, this ambition,
> Just in case we're dreaming.
> We'll do it so, indeed,
> For this our world is such
> That life is just a dream;
> And experience has taught me
> That the man who lives
> Dreams life until he wakes.

The king dreams he is king
And with this fantasy commands,
Disposes and holds sway;
The adulation he receives
Is written on the wind,
Unhappy sort, to ashes
All his glory soon reduced.
How then a kingdom reign
Since he, like everyman, must wake
In that other dream of Death?
The rich man dreams his riches,
For all the cares they bring;
The poor man dreams his poverty,
His misery and his wretchedness;
The prosperous man also dreams,
And he who struggles for his ends,
The man who insults and offends,
And, in conclusion, in this world,
All men dream just what they are,
Though no man can explain it.
I dream that I in prison here
Am held in heavy bondage;
I also dreamed of high estate
And felicitous surroundings.
What then is life? Illusion,
A fiction and mere shadow.
The greatest good is small,
For all of life is dream,
And dream of dream is all.

Calderón's religious plays are very significant also. His *El Mágico prodigioso* [*The Marvellous Magician*] is frequently cited as a forerunner of Goethe's *Faust*.

A student named Cipriano is preoccupied with the problem of a true God, distinctly different from the pagan deities. He is led astray by the devil who introduces him to the beautiful Justina. He promises her to Cipriano, through his magical arts, if the youth will sell him his soul. Cipriano accepts the pact, but Justine will not give herself to him and one day when he embraces her he finds only a skeleton in his arms. Subsequently

Cipriano is converted to Christianity and suffers martyrdom with Justina.

In *La devoción a la Cruz* [*The Devotion to the Cross*] we see the redeeming influence of the symbol of Redemption at the end of the life of a man of evil ways.

The *autos sacramentales* [moral-philosophical allegories] is a dramatic work of one act in length, allegorical in nature, and usually related to the Communion. The allegory of the *autos* is composed principally of the presentation of ideas or abstractions in the guise of persons. In *Los encantos de la culpa* [*The Charms of Sin*], Man appears surrounded by such personages as Understanding, Taste, Smell, Touch, Sight, and Hearing. Additional characters include Sin, Flattery, and Penitence. The dialogue between these characters portrays the struggles of Man, aided by Understanding, against Sin, which tempts the Senses. At the end, the Eucharist is eulogized as the surest means of salvation for the human soul.

One of the most famous of Calderón's *autos* is *El Gran Teatro del Mundo* [*The Great Theater of the World*] in which God appears in the figure of The Author who apportions the "roles" of this life. The action comprises the performance of each person's role, and the judgment which the Supreme Author makes of each one's comportment. This theatrical vision of the struggles of the spirit was of great interest to the profoundly religious public of the day.

The performances were usually scheduled for the Corpus Christi festivities, as these works exalted the Eucharist. They were given in the open with sumptuous settings which were mounted on wheeled vehicles.

In such works as *Eco y Narciso* and *Faetón*, Calderón cultivated mythological themes. Some of these, notably his *El laurel de Apolo* or *Apollo's Wreath* and *La purpura de la rosa* or *The Rose's Purple* were performed with music as a sort of *zarzuela*, the name of the valley near Madrid where they were staged.

Such works as *La dama duende* [*The Woman Ghost*] and *Casa con dos puertas, mala es de guardar* [*A House With Two Doors Is a Hard One to Watch*] are interesting for their complex plots, their presentation of contemporary customs, and for what they show of the author's ingenuity.

Calderón could only conceive of the drama in terms of elaborate stage settings. On the publication of one of his *autos* he stated, "Some passages will necessarily seem tepid as the written work cannot express either the sound of music nor the machinery of stagecraft."

We can comprehend Calderón's theatrical preference from the following passage:

> The first vehicle should be a globe, the largest which the surface of the vehicle will support. Its outer surface is to be painted with thickets in which there are various animals. It should also be designed with a map of the terrestrial sphere and between the lines, decorated with beautiful roses and other flowers. In front of it should be two trees of paper against which half the globe can lie, as it should be made to open up in two halves, one of which is fixed in place and from which a woman is to step, riding on a lion's back.

The eminent literary historian, Angel Valbuena, has written:

> If in addition to being the creator of a Spanish national theater, Lope represented the predominance of an extensive series of accumulated episodes and double plots, of the mixture other than the fusion of lyrics and settings, of all that is inventive, spontaneous and improvised, . . . Calderón conceived of a drama that was similar in subject matter but fundamentally different in technique, in which mature reflection, architectonic perfection, the interpenetration of poetical and dramatic elements, the unity of action, and an artist's art were paramount.

Francisco de Rojas Zorrilla is another well-known dramatist. He was born in Toledo in 1607. He studied Humanities in Toledo and Salamanca and resided the rest of his life in Madrid where he took active part in the literary polemics of the age. One

controversy was so violent that he was gravely wounded by
someone whom he had offended by his satire. He died in 1648.

The characteristic themes of his drama are (*a*) honor and
loyalty, (*b*) woman as the avenger of her honor, and (*c*) caricature.

His famous work with three titles, *Del rey abajo ninguno*
[*No One Less Than The King*], *El Labrador más honrado* [*The
Most Honorable Farmer*] and *García de Castañar*, is the story of
a loyal subject of Alfonso XI, whose responsibility it was to
avenge to the death the dishonoring of his wife, something he
cannot do as it is the king himself who has committed the offending act. The struggle between the two obligations, honor and
loyalty, is resolved when García learns that the man who entered
his wife's chamber wearing the king's insignia was not the monarch but a nobleman named Don Mendo. The husband kills the
latter because:

> . . . as long as my good head
> upon these sturdy shoulders sits,
> to no one less than king
> any wrong shall I permit.

In Rojas Zorrilla, there are some interesting female protagonists who avenge their own dishonor. In the work *Cada cua-
lo que le toca* [*To Each His Own*], Isabel kills her seducer with
her husband's sword:

> DON LUIS: So it was for this that you asked my sword?
> ISABEL: To avenge you,
> So that my arm and your stout sword
> Should share equally his punishment.

The plays of caricature are initiated with *Don Lucas de
Cigarral*. Don Lucas, an ugly and suspicious man, has arranged
to marry Doña Isabel de Contreras. He sends a cousin, Pedro d
Toledo, to see Isabel but the two fall in love with each other an

Don Lucas ends up by consenting to their marriage. They are characters, especially Don Lucas, who border on caricature.

Agustín Moreto y Cavana was born of an Italian family in Madrid in 1618. He studied in Alcalá and lived in the capital. He became a priest in 1654 and moved to Toledo where he died in 1669.

His comedies of manners give an excellent picture of life in the palaces of the nobility.

The best known of these is his *El desdén con el desdén* [*Disdain for Disdain*] in which Carlos succeeds in attracting the interest of his absent-minded ladylove, Diana, by pretending not to care for her. In *El lindo Don Diego* [*The Handsome Don Diego*], Doña Inés succeeds in winning the hand of her true lover, Don Juan, because her maid, disguised as a widow, successfully seduces her official fiancé, a vain and stupid youth named Don Diego. In all of these plays, the author's delicate ingenuity skillfully handles the events.

The Reaction Against the Baroque

We have already noted that Quevedo, with his satirical works, represents a reaction to the extravagances of culteranism. His attitude was shared by a number of poets who succeeded in simplifying form and stressing meaningful content.

Among these was Captain Andrés Fernández de Andrade whose famous *Epístola moral*, dedicated to his friend Alonso Tello de Guzmán who had a position in Madrid, appears under the pseudonym of "Fabio." The *Epistle's* counsels may be summarized as follows:

a Man should not enjoy more consideration than he deserves. If his fortunes are adverse, he should suffer with dignity. No one should look to the favor of the courtier.

> The soul, plebeian and mean-spirited,
> He, timorous, chooses rather to remain
> In state of suspense than to fall from grace,

While the upright, the true generous heart
Unto his adverse destiny will bow
Rather than bend the knee before the great.

—From *The Epistle to Fabio*
Translation by Eleanor L. Turnbull

b Life can give no more than a reasonable amount of experience. Unlike the man of the Renaissance, the man of the Counter Reformation ought not to aspire to experiencing everything.

But do you think, perchance, man was created
For thunderbolt and havoc of grim war,
To plow the salty waves of the high seas,

To measure the circumference of the earth
And the path where the sun forever circles?
Oh, how he errs who understands it so!

This our high portion here, our lot divine
Is unto greater, nobler does it end.

Alas for him, but poor is he that seeks
For gold and silver over sea and land,
In every clime, and travels far and wide!

Enough for me a corner by my hearth,
A book, a friend and a brief time for sleep
Quite undisturbed by creditors and sorrows.

Now, my dear friend, I flee and I retire
From all I, artless, loved; I broke my ties.
Come, you shall see what is that noble end
Toward which I aim, ere time die in our arms.

c The only recompense life receives is after death.

This ascetic sense of life is characteristic of the Counter Reformation.

The sobriety of style and the philosophical serenity which emanates from the fugacity of things are also characteristic of Francisco de Rioja (1583–1659), the poet of flowers who is noted for his delicate sense of the use of adjectives.

For some time the famous *Canción a las ruinas de Itálica* [*Song to the Ruins of Italica*] was attributed to Rioja, until more scholarly investigations found it to be the work of the Sevillian poet Rodrigo Caro who lived from 1543 to 1647. Caro was a humanist who knew his classical literature well, an archeologist and a collector, as his book on *Las Antiguedades de Sevilla* [*The Antiquities of Seville*], demonstrates. His *Canción*, of which variants exist, is unique in the poet's work. Caro polished it and made changes in it until the time of his death.

The Renaissance made of antiquity a relivable past. The baroque age converted it into a scholarly and sometimes melancholy remembrance. The courtier who dreamed of reliving the pagan and imperial life of a Roman citizen gave way to the scholar who drew on antiquity for stoic axioms or forms for his verses. The latter may have had less feeling of the Classical world, but he had a sounder knowledge of it. The *Canción a las ruinas de Itálica* expresses the poet's melancholy as he gazes at the ancient ruins which represent to him the futility of man's efforts. Thus "the towers which once the very air defied / by its heavy hand have died."

Two brothers from Aragon, Lupercio and Bartolomé Leonardo de Argensola present a case of parallel lives. They both came from Barbastro. Both traveled to Madrid and to Naples in the service of the Count of Lemos and both attained the fame they merited. Lope de Vega said of them that they had come from Aragon "to reform Spanish poetical language." It is true that they are outstanding among the lyric poets of the culteranists for their sober elegance and their circumspect reflections.

Lupercio, who was the elder of the two, excelled in elegant
themes of love and bitter satirical writings. He wrote tragedies
on the classical model, including *Isabela* and *Alejandra.*

Bartolomé, who was a more prolific and complex poet, presents magnificent lessons of philosophy and didacticism. A famous
sonnet of his begins with the questions:

> Father of us all, You who are just,
> Why does your Providence permit
> In prison dark sweet Innocence to sit
> While fraud has even judges' trust?

and ends with the answer:

> Blind that you are, is Earth the Spirit's goal?

We shall end our brief comments on the reaction to culteranism with the name of Estéban Manuel de Villegas who lived
from 1589 to 1669. In his poetry he imitated Anacreon, Theocritus, and Horace, all of whom he translated. Villegas decisively
renewed the taste for such pastoral forms as the *cantilena* and the
letrilla. These forms are agreeably delicate on the surface and
ingenuous in subject, but they are mannered, despite which, and
due to the boredom with culteranism, they had a greater success
than their intrinsic merit actually deserved.

Villegas left an extensive literary legacy both as poet and as
translator. His *Cantilenas* are pastoral in theme, delicate and
epicurean, childish and playful, full of graceful passages but
monotonous despite being poetically correct and agreeable. His
Odas, which are more spiritedly handled, contain similar idyllic
subject matter. Villegas' attempts at versifying in Latin forms, in
Castilian, especially in the hexameter and the sapphic verse, are
interesting. The balanced neoclassicism of the eighteenth century
may be said to appear already in Villegas' style.

4.

The Eighteenth Century

French "Classicism" in Spain*

At the outset of the eighteenth century there was a sharp change in the political and cultural orientation of Spain. On the death of Carlos II, called the "Hechizado" or Bewitched, whose pathetic and sickly figure seemed like a living symbol of the national decadence, the grandson of Louis XIV of France, Felipe V of Anjou, came to the throne, although only after a lengthy civil war.

The Spain of the House of Austria and the Counter Reformation had come to an end. The black clothes of the court at Madrid gave way to the brilliant and multicolored garments of Versailles. The politics of isolation from the rest of Europe also came to an end. Two impressive reigns, those of Felipe V (1701–1746) and Carlos III (1759–1788) filled the century, and under the encouragement of these kings everything possible was done to put Spanish culture within the circle of the intellectual currents of Europe.

---

* Despite the phrase *"el clasicismo francés,"* Spanish literary historians refer to the literature of this period as "Neoclassical," reserving the word "Classical" for the literature of Greek and Latin.

The transformation did not come rapidly, however, nor did it reach, as we shall see, all aspects of the Spanish spirit.

As a direct result of the coming of a Frenchman, Felipe (or Philip) V, to the throne of Spain, the influence of French Classicism, which had spread throughout Europe, acquired a special importance. With Felipe V the state took an active interest in cultural matters. The National Library, the Royal Spanish Academy, and the Academy of History came into being. Fine arts and the theater received special encouragement. The monarchy made of culture a motive of special splendor.

The Predominance of Reason

The eighteenth century was essentially one dominated by norms. As a reaction to the extremes of artistic liberty of the baroque period of the preceding century, the artist was subjected to rules. Art, according to Aristotelian theory, was to serve moral perfection and was to be comprehensible to all. The following rule was fundamental to classicism: *Nothing can be beautiful which is not reasonable.* Because of this the artist was to submit himself to rigorous precepts studied in Aristotle and Horace. Those which, in France, were based on the *Art Poétique* of Boileau were imitated in Spain by Ignacio de Luzán in his *Poética [Poetics]* of 1737. According to these theorists, since the goal of art is to educate, it should avoid the caprices of imagination and fantasy and adjust itself to a simple and balanced expression which came to be known as *el buen gusto,* or good taste.

Both Góngora and Calderón were excluded from the list of recommendable authors as lacking in *buen gusto.* This indicates that literary expression was subjected to rules to such an extent that poetry came to be characterized by its proximity to prose.

The Preoccupation with Science

A strong philosophical and critical influence gave to literature a marked tone of gravity which is apparent in almost all genres. Both the exact and the physio-natural sciences became distinguishable from the errors and the superstitions which had hampered them. The totality of these renovating tendencies was given the name of the Enlightenment.

The Royal Spanish Academy

Felipe V created the Royal Spanish Academy; for his model the King used the French Academy which had been founded in 1635. With the establishment of the former, the State took over the function of directing the national culture. What characterizes these academies as institutions is precisely the fact that, unlike the literary circles or groups they replaced, they were founded by the Crown. The State created them to give a certain official and obligatory character to their decisions, for example, that the conservation and the prestige of the national language had sufficient importance to be a matter reserved for public, i.e., royal, power and policy.

The Royal Spanish Academy was founded on the third of October, 1714. Its first director was Juan Manuel Fernández Pacheco, the Marquis of Villena. It consisted of twenty-four chairs marked with capital letters of the alphabet. Later on twelve more seats were added, each with a letter in lower case. Writers are named to the Academy by election and retain their chair for life. The insignia is a crucible in the fire, with the epigraph "limpia, fija y da esplendor,"—cleanses, fixes and gives splendor—which alludes to the fundamental tasks of the institution with respect to the Spanish language.

One of the first responsibilities of the Royal Spanish Academy was the preparation of a *Diccionario de la Lengua* [*Dictionary of the Language*] which was to cleanse ("limpia") Spanish of foreign terms, to indicate and fix ("fija") the form of a word which was the correct one, and to give prestige to those words meriting approval ("da esplendor"). To this purpose the Royal Academy published its first dictionary in six volumes (1726–1739), characterized by the fact that its words had attained acceptance by the use made of them by the classical writers, the authorities of Spain's Golden Age. Because of this the first edition was entitled

Diccionario de Autoridades [*Dictionary of Authorities*]. It also attempted to stem the tide of incoming *galicismos* or French words and terminology.

Subsequent editions of the dictionary have varied considerably, as each has prudently admitted new words which have come into the language through current usage. In the latest editions these include numerous "Americanisms." To make their decisions, the Academicians have a weekly meeting to discuss the validity of certain words, employing for this purpose, in addition to distinguished authors, the advice of members of various branches of knowledge such as doctors, jurisconsultants, and the like.

At the same time, and from its inception on, the Academy has published successive editions of its *Gramática* [*Grammar*], excellent among those of its type, which, even though it does not adapt to the new linguistic and grammatical currents, represents a prudent traditional criterion in questions of language.

Another area of interest to the Academy is the stimulating of the publication of works of Spain's greatest authors and studies of their writings.

Literary Salons

The artist had long been considered by the nobility as a sort of servant, but in the eighteenth century he became independent. The liberal professions such as the magistracy, the military, and the professorate gave him a certain economic freedom and a dignity he had lacked previously. The "salons"—aristocratic gatherings where art and literature were discussed—conferred on him a sense of social position. There were also numerous *tertulias,* or more informal literary gatherings, like the famous one of the Inn of San Sebastian in Madrid where the newest literary works then circulating in Europe were read.

Frequently men such as Moratín, Ayala, Cerdá, Rico, Cadalso, Pineda, Ortaga, Pizzi, Muñoz, Iriarte, Guevara, Signorelli, Conti, Benascone and other learned persons met at the old Inn of Sebastian where they took a room with chairs, tables, writing materials, fireplace, and everything necessary for holding those meetings at which, as the one rule, one could only talk about theater, bullfights, love and poetry. It was there that the best tragedies of the French stage, the satires and poetics of Boileau, the odes of Rousseau, various sonnets and songs of Frugoni, Filicaja, Chiabrera, Petrarch and some cantos of Tasso and of Ariosto were read. Cadalso gave a reading of his *Cartas marruecas* [*Moroccan Letters*] and Iriarte, some of his work.

. . . Meanwhile the literary gatherings of the Inn of San Sebastian continued to be a school of erudition, of good taste, of refined criticism. The questions which were discussed there gave the members of the group the impulse to investigate and to establish the most solid principles, applied in particular to the study and the perfection of literature.

—L. F. de Moratín

For its part, the Academy, which is a reflection of absolutism in politics, regulated taste according to universal norms and gave an official character to culture following what has been called Enlightened Despotism.

The literary art of the eighteenth century was, consequently, aristocratic and reflective, but it generally lacked vivacity and spark. Furthermore, Spanish thought, which during the Counter Reformation had been closed to all foreign influence, was Europeanized. French influence, which at first was limited to literary doctrines, extended to political and social ideas. The ideas of the Encyclopedists, which brought about the expulsion of the Jesuits in 1767, infiltrated Spanish thought which in many cases then abandoned its traditional ideas in search of an intellectual atmosphere more in accord with the movements in Europe to whose culture Spain had to be permanently united.

The Transition to Neoclassicism

The influence of culteranism and of conceptism did not disappear immediately. There were cases of loyalty to the Spanish national tradition.

Diego de Torres y Villaroel was born in Salamanca in 1693 and was a figure in the true picaresque tradition. At one time or another he was a student, gambler, dancer, bullfighter, and doctor. Due to his natural talents and the deplorable state of scientific studies in the Spain of his times, he became professor of mathematics at the University of Salamanca. He gained considerable renown through his *Almanaques* [*Almanacs*] in which he predicted the future. In one prediction he foretold, thirty-three years before the event, the French Revolution.

Torres y Villaroel's literary model was Quevedo. His *Sueños morales* [*Morals Visions*] imitate the famous *Sueños* of the seventeenth-century master. His novelistic autobiography, *Vida, ascendencia, nacimiento, crianza y aventuras del doctor don Diego de Torres y Villaroel* seems almost to have come from the pages of Quevedo's *Buscón,* for the author portrays himself mercilessly as an adventurer, a vagabound, and a cynic without shame. Torres had good reason to say that his work came into being "between dancing and guitars."

Ramón de la Cruz was a native of Madrid, born in 1731 and under the protection of the Duke of Alba and the Duchess of Osuna, and was a profound student of the life of his native city. Several things stand out in his works:

1. Tragedies and comedies of a French or Italianate type. In this group may be included translations of Racine, Metastasio, and Voltaire which constitute the least important part of his work.

2. *Zarzuelas* (a sort of musical comedy) and *Sainetes* (or short interludes) in the traditionally Spanish style. On the other hand, his typically Spanish *Zarzuelas* and *sainetes,* in which we see all of the author's graceful wit and powers of observation, are of great value.

This part of his work is characterized by fecundity. He wrote more than three hundred *sainetes* which are small masterpieces. The best known are *El fandango del candil* [*The Fandango of the Lamp*], *La pradera de San Isidro* [*The Meadow of Saint Isidro*], and *Las castañeras picadas* [*The Vexed Chestnut Vendors*].

In his sense of tradition, Don Ramón de la Cruz can be seen

as the legitimate heir of the *pasos* of Lope de Rueda and of the *entremeses* of Cervantes. These *sainetes* show a marked contrast to the official French tastes in theater, tastes radically foreign to the Spanish tradition. In these works the author displays his broad and profound knowledge of the life of the Spanish people, in particular those of Madrid. We see them dancing, singing, and speaking in a natural way.

Anyone who wishes to acquire a thorough knowledge of the customs of the Spaniards of the eighteenth century should study the drama of Don Ramón de la Cruz, the poetry of Iglesias, and the *caprichos* of Goya.

—José Somoza

Nicolás Fernández de Moratín was born in Madrid in 1737. He regularly participated in the literary reunions in the Fonda de San Sebastián which we mentioned earlier, was a professor in the Colegio Imperial, and partook of a dual character—loyal both to the Spanish traditions and to new developments in Europe.

Consequently his work, which is one of transition, offers two aspects. One is the Spanish tradition which is reflected above all in his poetry, the Moorish ballads after the manner of Góngora, descriptions and exaltation of tauromachy (*Fiesta de toros en Madrid* or *Bullfight in Madrid, Oda a Pedro Romero* or *Ode to Pedro Romero,* and so on), patriotic works on the military victories of Spain (the war in Morocco, Cortez' burning of his ships), and praises of Madrid which at this time was becoming a great capital city. In all of these works Moratín was a disciple of the great Spanish poets—Garcilaso, Herrera, Lope, Góngora—and an enthusiastic admirer of Spain's glories.

The second aspect is that of the neoclassical Francophile. In his critical works and his drama, Moratín followed the intellectual tendencies of his times. He not only avoided Spanish luster in his poetry, but in his work *Desengaños al teatro español* [*Disillusionment of the Spanish Theater*] he attacked the Spanish masters of the seventeenth century and Calderón de la Barca in particular. Nicolás Fernández de Moratín, along with other "enlightened" men of the period, were instrumental in bringing about the banning of the *autos sacramentales* in 1765.

Following these ideas Moratín wrote his dramatic works, the comedy *La Petimetra* [*The Precious Young Lady*], set in Madrid, the tragedies of *Lucrecia* on a Roman theme, *Hormesinda,* the sister of Don Pelayo who was in love with the Moor Munuza, and *Guzmán el Bueno* [*Guzman the Good*]. All of these works, written in verse, inspired by French works and rigorously heeding the three unities, lack life and interest.

To sum up, perhaps the true key to this period of transition is the struggle between European culture which begins to have an impact in Spain and the national traditions which react against it as, for instance, in the case of the uprising of Esquilache when there was a popular outbreak against a law regulating the use of traditionally Spanish hats and capes. It was a struggle of Gallic influences against traditional purity and it was, perhaps, as Eugenio D'ors claimed, the eternal battle of Spanish culture, Europe versus the purely national.

No other epoch, for example, despite its apparent lack of warmth, presents so complex an ideological gamut. Its preoccupation with ideas was such that poetic creation was relegated to second place. The eighteenth century was not propitious for lyrical poetry. Nevertheless, it was a period in which we can glimpse through the artist's vision, the formidable conflicts which even the noblest of intentions provoked and which brought about some of the most profound changes which humanity has undergone.

The Temper of Neoclassicism

A Literature of Norms

The most characteristic genres of the eighteenth century, in neoclassicism's period of plenitude, were those in which there was a predominance of the rational study of scientific and philosophical problems, such as treatises and essays, or the normative analysis of artistic and literary works, such as critical and preceptive studies.

For example, Ignacio de Luzán, in his *Poética* of 1737, established the norms or rules by which a literary work was to be governed. He was a cultured man who had studied the rules of neoclassicism in Italy under Muratoni. For Luzán, poetry was an "imitation of nature . . . for utility or for the delight of man." He did not, however, completely reject the element of fantasy in poetry. In drama he proclaimed the necessity for the three unities and characterized Lope and Calderón as corruptors of taste. All literary art was, for *Luzán,* pedagogy.

The epic was to serve for the education of kings and great military men; tragedy was to be utilized for the tempering of those of frivolous spirit, and so on. Accordingly the poet was to dispense with fantasy, and elements of marvel were to be used only with considerable care. Luzán, nevertheless, was far less extreme than his model, the French poet Boileau, who rejected miraculous elements of Christianity as poetic themes while admitting only fantastic events from classical mythology.

In the same year that Luzán's *Poetics* appeared, 1737, the publication of the *Diario de los Literatos de España* [*The Spanish Writers' Daily*], an imitation of the *Journal des Savants* of Paris, began in Madrid. It was the first periodical review of literary criticism in Spain and was important for the rigor of its judgments and the neoclassical orientation of its commentaries.

Father Feijóo introduced the popularizing of science. One of the most expressive figures of the Enlightenment in Spain, it was Benito Jerónino Feijóo who presided over eighteenth-century Spanish literature.

In Feijóo, we can discern provincial life. He was born in northern Spain, in Casdemiro in the province of Orense. In 1676 he entered the Benedictine Order and became a professor at the University of Oviedo where he remained, far from the capital, among his books and his papers. In sharp contrast to his relatively cloistered life, Feijóo presents the spectacle of an intellectual curiosity that knew neither limits nor frontiers. Everything of

interest, whether of the past or of the present, in the sciences
or in the arts, in life or in customs, was the object of the attention
of this brilliant Benedictine.

In his writings, Father Feijóo made a critical study of knowledge down to his own times, demanding of that knowledge that it
be based on logic or on experience. Thus he combated facile
routine superstition, a defect which, in his epoch, posed serious
hindrances to science. The value of his work today, consequently,
lies more in its intent and its results than in its intrinsic worth,
as frequently Feijóo explained things which in his lifetime were
either badly or confusedly known but which now have been
studied more than enough. Among other superstitions now inconceivable, Feijóo attacked the "philosophy stone," the belief
in satyrs and naiads, the faith in exorcisms and dubious miracles,
the confidence in witches and curers and, above all, the confusion
between science and fraud.

Father Feijóo did not organize his knowledge into treatises
but wrote in the form of articles or essays which were published
in seven volumes and which were entitled *Teatro crítico universal*
[*The Universal Critical Theater*] and in the four *Cartas eruditas
y curiosas* [*Erudite and Curious Letters*]. As we have said, his
work had a tremendous influence as it made readily available
to all, in a readable and periodical style, a vast area of knowledge.
Perhaps the most admirable aspect of Feijóo's work is the fact
that he handled his material, much of which up to that time had
been treated only in the most routine way or without comprehension at all, with a very modern sense of proportion and
tolerance.

The prose of the author of the *Teatro crítico universal,* while
not excessively polished, is clear and simple and serves admirably
as the vehicle for the type of popularization of knowledge which
it proposed. Feijóo himself explained his ample and compre-
hensive linguistic criterion. He felt that language should renew
itself and that imprisoning one's self in a purist's attitude was
absurd. He wrote, "Purity! One should better speak of poverty,
nudity, misery, dryness." This did not keep him from rejecting
Gallicisms when they were superfluous. For example, he criticized
the use of the word *remarcable,* which is now in use, because there

already existed the perfectly good term *notable* in Spanish. In one curious work, *Paralelo de las lenguas castellana y francesa* [*Parallel of the Castilian and French Languages*], he attacks the idea that the latter is the richer of the two tongues. His opinion was that there are many words in Castilian that have no true equivalent in French.

Feijóo's language is reasoned and simple. It is fully suited to the popularization of science and is free of neologistic exaggerations.

The only man who drank of the spirit of his times and felt it burn deep inside while still remaining faithful to the best of the Spanish tradition was Father Feijóo. He was a man of his historical moment and at the same time a Spaniard who would not be seduced by foreign influences. This person who did not believe in the miracles of man realized one himself, that of making the passion for knowledge acceptable, of exploring the reality of life with the eyes and not with preconceived doctrines, the desire to reason things out, to submit every bit of knowledge to a rigorous proof or to what was then and still is called, with puerile vanity, experimentation. All of this he made compatible, and only stupid men of his times or of those that have followed could dispute its importance.

—Gregorio Marañon

Father José Francisco de Isla wrote satire. He was born at Vidanes in 1703. As one of the Jesuits who was expelled from Spain, he went to live in Italy where he died in 1781. The fundamental work of Father Isla appeared with the title of *Historia del famoso predicator Fray Gerundio de Campazas, alias Zotes* [*The Story of the Famous Preacher Friar Gerundio de Campazas, alias Zotes*]. It is a satirical book which attacks the exaggerations of the baroque period in sacred oratory, and contrasts Friar Gerundio, a ridiculous and ignorant preacher, with the figure of Friar Prudencio who represents sobriety and reason. The work permitted Father Isla to criticize *culteranismo* whose excesses discredited Spanish pulpits.

The Literature of Neoclassicism

Literary Creativity

We have already studied the authors who characterize the normative aspects of the eighteenth century and we shall now turn our attention to the more properly literary creativity of the period. Neoclassical drama was dominant. The vogue of neoclassicism brought to the theater the cult of the three unities and the imitation of French classical drama, notably that of Racine. Nevertheless it may be said that the attempts to adapt these norms to the Spanish stage were a complete failure. What resulted was a rhetorical and affected drama written by such authors as Comella, who was ridiculed by Moratín. Despite this there are some works which, although they are not masterpieces, can still be read with pleasure and interest.

One interesting play, the tragedy *Raquel,* was written by Vicente García de la Huerta who was born in Zafra in 1734. It tells the story, which had already been utilized in the theater, of the love of Alfonso VIII for a Jewish girl of Toledo, Raquel, who was famous for her beauty and who inspired such passion in the monarch that the nobles finally killed her. On the surface, the work conforms to the rules of neoclassicism; it has, however, a dramatic power which transcends these rules and makes this work stand out among the mediocre plays of the epoch.

Leandro Fernández de Moratín was born in 1760. Unlike his famous father, he was a timid and indecisive man, influenced by the French ideas of liberalism and encyclopedism to such an extent that at the time of the Napoleonic invasion he entered the service of José Bonaparte and was named Head Librarian in 1808. Because of this he was forced to go into exile and he died in Paris in 1828.

French literary tastes dominated his works. He was preoccupied with neoclassical ideas. In his *Sátira contra los vicios introducidos en la poesía castellana* [*Satire Against the Vices Intro-*

duced into Castilian Poetry], written in verse, he extolled reason
and good taste:

> Good taste and reason, whether verse or prose,
> Do invention rectify, for without those,
> No art can come to right conclusion.

In his prose satire, *La derrota de los pedantes* [*The Pedants'
Defeat*], 1789, he attacked the poets who followed *culteranismo*
for they still represented a considerable number of writers at the
end of the eighteenth century. As the structure of his satire,
Moratín has the pedants form an army to storm the palace of
Apollo. The god is both angered and moved to laughter; he
finally decides to give battle, and aided by the good poets, defeats
the *culteranos*.

Moratín's plays are the most successful part of his literary
creation. Despite the author's slavery to neoclassical rules, Moratín's drama is sensitive and delightful. In his work *La comedia
nueva o el café* [*The New Drama or the Cafe*], Moratín continued
his satire of abuses, this time in the theater where, he found, there
were "trickery instead of craftmanship and the ornamentations
of a magic lantern rather than truly comic situations." In addition to *La comedia nueva*, Moratín also wrote *El viejo y la niña*
[*The Old Man and the Girl*], *El barón* [*The Baron*], *La mojigata*
[*The Hypocrite*], and *El sí de las niñas* [*When a Girl Says Yes*],
the last of these being the best known and the most characteristic
of his works.

The heroine of *El sí de las niñas* is a young woman named
Francisca. Her mother, Doña Irene, has promised her hand in
marriage to an elderly man named Don Diego. Francisca, however, is already in love with Don Carlos who is the nephew of
Don Diego. The young man, who is equally in love with Francisca, gives up the idea of marrying her out of respect for his
uncle. Don Diego learns the truth of the situation, however, and
realizes that the reasonable thing to do is to arrange the marriage
of the two young lovers.

The final scene of *When A Girl Says Yes* involves Don Carlos,
Don Diego, Doña Irene, and Doña Francisca, as follows:

DON CARLOS:	That, no . . . *(Don Carlos comes quickly out of a room. He has Doña Francisca by the arm and leads her upstage where he places himself in front of her as if to defend her. Doña Irene draws back in fright.)* While I am present no one will offend her!
DOÑA FRANCISCA:	Carlos!
DON CARLOS:	*(going up to Don Diego)*: Please excuse my being so outspoken, I saw she was being insulted and I couldn't hold back my anger.
DOÑA IRENE:	What in the world is happening to me? Great heavens! Who are you? What carrying on is this? What shameful conduct!
DON DIEGO:	There's no shameful conduct here. . . . This is the man with whom your daughter is in love. Separate them and you kill them; it's one and the same . . . Carlos . . . Well, no matter . . . . Kiss your bride-to-be. *(Don Carlos goes over to Doña Francisca. They kiss each other and then kneel at Don Diego's feet.)*
DOÑA IRENE:	So this is your nephew?
DON DIEGO:	Yes, Madam, my nephew who with his clapping and his serenade and his note has given me one of the worst nights I've ever passed in my life. . . . What is all this, children, what is all this?
DOÑA FRANCISCA:	Do you mean you forgive us and want our happiness?
DON DIEGO:	Yes, my dear ones. Yes. *(He has them get up).*
DOÑA IRENE:	And you are determined to make such a sacrifice?
DON DIEGO:	I could separate them forever and quietly enjoy the presence of this adorable child, but my conscience would not permit it. Carlos! . . . Paquita! . . . The effort I've just made has cost me dearly. After all I'm just a wretched and a weak old man.
DON CARLOS:	*(kissing his uncle's hands)*: If our love and our gratitude can cancel out so great a loss . . .

DOÑA IRENE: So that's our good Carlos!
DON DIEGO: He and your daughter were made with love
for each other while you and her aunts
were building castles in the air and filling
my head with illusions that have disappeared like a dream. . . . This is the result
of too much authority and of the oppres-
siveness our youth has to undergo. These
are the guarantees given by parents and
teachers, and that shows how much we
should believe her when a girl says yes. . . .
By accident I learned in time what an error
I had fallen into. . . . Pity those who learn
too late!
DOÑA FRANCISCA: Do you see how happy we are? And you,
who love me so much, you will always be
my friend.
DON DIEGO: Paquita, my dear (he embraces her), let
your new father embrace you. . . . Now I
no longer fear the terrible solitude that
comes with age. . . . You (he takes Don
Carlos and Doña Paquita by the hands)
are my heart's delight. The first fruit of
your love . . . , yes children . . . it is inevitable, he will be for me. And when I
hold him in my arms I'll be able to say
that this innocent babe owes his existence
to me. If his parents live and are happy,
it is thanks to me.
DON CARLOS: May heaven bless such goodness!
DON DIEGO: And may our Lord be praised.

Tomás de Iriarte was born in Orotava in the Canary Islands
in 1750. He resided most of his life, however, in Madrid and died
there in 1791. He participated in the literary polemics of his
times. He wrote various satirical folios such as his *Los literatos en
Cuaresma* [*Writers During Lent*], and a didactic poem entitled
La Música [*Music*].

Iriarte was a writer of fables. His *Fábulas literarias* [*Literary
Fables*] which appeared in 1782 are of a satirico-esthetic nature.
In them the writer attacks literary excesses in accord with the

norms of neoclassicism—for example, the disproportionate use
or archaic words and expressions in *El retrato del golilla* [*The
Ruff Collar's Portrait*], erudition without order or discretion in
La urraca y la mona [*The Magpie and the Monkey*], the abusive
inclusion of French words in *Los dos loros y la cotorra* [*The Two
Parrots and the Parakeet*], and the need for rules in artistic creation as in *El burro flautista* [*The Ass and the Flute*], which we
reproduce below:

The Ass and the Flute

This little fable heard,
    It good or ill may be;
But it has just occur'd
    Thus accidentally.

Passing my abode,
    Some fields adjoining me,
A big ass on his road
    Came accidentally,

And laid upon the spot,
    A flute he chanced to see,
Some shepherd had forgot
    There accidentally.

The animal in front
    To scan it nigh came he,
And snuffing loud as wont,
    Blew accidentally.

The air it chanced around
    The pipe went passing free
And thus the Flute a sound
    Gave accidentally.

"O then," exclaimed the Ass,
    "I know to play it fine;
And who for bad shall class
    This music asinine?"

Without the rules of art,
Even asses, we agree,
May once succeed in part,
Thus accidentally.

—Translation by James Kennedy

Félix Samaniego is another writer of fables. Born in La Guardia in the province of Rioja in 1745, he participated in the founding of the Sociedad Vascongada de Amigos del País (or Basque Society of Friends of the Country), a group of intellectuals and economists presided over by the Count of Peñaflorida, the author's uncle and a typical figure of the Enlightenment. He was at first a friend of Iriarte but later became his rival and attacked his works.

Samaniego wrote his famous *Fábulas morales* [*Moral Fables*] for the students of a school founded by his uncle. The poems themselves have an ample educative and didactic sense. They attack such vices as pride, laziness, ambition, evil, hypocrisy, just as other writers of fables, including Aesop and La Fontaine, had done. The fable given below, *El ciervo en la fuente* [*The Stag's Reflection*] is an example of his work.

The Stag's Reflection

A stag one day himself did spy
Reflected in a placid pool;
Great was the joy that he thereby
Felt looking at his antlers fine,
But staring at his gangling legs
He said aloud with quite a sigh,
"Great gods! With what intent in mind
Have you this handsome head of mine
On such a base foundation put
That does all sense of grace defy?
Oh woe is me! Oh smarting pain!
Is there no beauty in this world?"
And speaking on in such a vein
He saw a savage greyhound nigh.

To save himself from death
Into the woods he quickly ran.
His horns, however, held him back
For stuck they were on branches high.
But once from danger he was free,
He said, still shuddering with fear,
"Despite my horns if now I'm safe,
'Twas by these legs, I certify;
The devil take my lovely horns
And blessèd these my legs let be."
For thus it often happens man
Will praise an object to the sky.
He sees the surface and no more,
He takes what wise men would deplore;
So let him get this through his head,
Let use and beauty share one bed.

The Plenitude of Neoclassicism

First School of Salamanca

The plenitude of the neoclassical school of Spanish poetry
was attained by a group of poets known as the First School of
Salamanca of the Eighteenth Century. The lyrical output of this
group of writers, almost all of it on bucolic themes, is without
major redeeming grace. It is the monotonous repetition of pastoral scenes in which the poets sing the graces of their shepherdess
lady-loves, their Filis, Mirta, Belisa, and Cloris, all placed within
a setting of green fields filled with equally artificial flocks of
sheep. One of the few of these poets of some small merit is Fray
Diego Gonzáles.

Of more interest and talent was the poet José Iglesias de la
Casa, who was born, lived, and died in Salamanca (1748-1791).
His works may be grouped as follows:

a Poetry of a pastoral bent. In these Iglesias imitates the
graceful rhythms of the *tonadillas* of the people.

b Humorous poetry. These short works are of a festive and
amusing nature.

The following is illustrative of his poetry:

Song

Alexis calls me cruel;
    The rifted crags that hold
The gathered ice of winter,
    He says, are not more cold.

When even the very blossoms
    Around the fountain's brim
And forest walks, can witness
    The love I bear to him.

I would that I could utter
    My feelings without shame;
And tell him how I love him,
    Nor wrong my virgin fame.

Alas! to seize the moment
    When heart inclines to heart,
And press a suit with passion,
    Is not a woman's part.

If man comes not to gather
    The roses where they stand,
They fade among the foliage;
    They cannot seek his hand.

—Anonymous translation

Juan Pablo Forner is another poet worthy of recognition. He was born in Merida in 1754. He was a thorough student of the humanities and of jurisprudence but owes his fame to his poetry and his polemics. His poetry may be grouped in the following categories:

a The idyllic-pastoral, in which the poet takes part under the pseudonym of Aminta and writes in the style of Anacreon and Villegas.

b The satirical and epigrammatic, which serves as an outlet for Forner's polemical and critical ideas.

c The philosophico-moral, of less value literarily than the poems of the other categories; they treat themes such as man, immortality of the soul, and so on, which are little suited to lyric expression.

Juan Pablo Forner is above all a polemicist. He was a man of considerable vigor in literary conflicts and published numerous works of satire and attack. These fall into three groups:

a Assaults against persons, i.e., Iriarte, Huerta, Vargas Ponce, and so on.

b Critical attack on literary abuses of a type found in the poets who imitated Góngora and Quevedo. He did, nevertheless, criticize Calderón de la Barca, for having based his dramas on "fanciful things." It is his imitators, however, who receive the brunt of the assault.

c Defense of Spanish culture and its contribution to other lands in which he was notably outspoken. In his *Oración apologética por España y su mérito literario [Argumentation on Behalf of Spain and Her Literary Merits]*, he brilliantly refuted the French writer Masson who had asked, "What contributions has Spain ever made?" He not only defended the intellectual life of Spain in the past, but demonstrated irrefutably that in many cases French literature was deeply indebted to the Spanish. Spanish culture, he pointed out, had always tended to the betterment of man rather than to abstract philosophical elucidations.

Juan Meléndez Valdés was the poet of the greatest prestige in Spain in the eighteenth century. He was born in Ribera del Fresno in 1754. He held a chair of Humanities in Salamanca and was a magistrate in Zaragossa and Valladolid. He was a Francophile and was named President of Public Instruction by King José Bonaparte. When the French troops withdrew from Spain, Meléndez Valdés had to go into exile with them and he died in France in Montpellier in 1817. He wrote of the anguish of his exile in a poem entitled *Los suspiros del proscrito [The Sighs of a Man Proscribed]*, a part of which we reproduce below:

> Oh woe! All gone the ties which once
> Did bind me to my native land.
> My honor and my fortunes stand
> By malice and by cares impaired.

I roam about on foreign soil,
By loved ones, family, forgot,
By friends betrayed, I want them not;
Their mockery, at least, I'm spared. . . .

There are two aspects to the poetry of Meléndez Valdés. On
the one hand he follows the poetical school of Salamanca, writing
bucolic poetry for which by temperament and artistic background
he was well prepared. On the other hand, his own feelings, stirred
by adversity and by a series of profound preoccupations, motivated him to compose a number of works of a philosophical and
moral tone which presaged a new turn in the literary directions
of the period.

a Bucolic poetry. The bucolic or pastoral tendency is
clearly within the traditions of the eighteenth century. Neoclassicism placed high value on poetry which was tranquil, sensuous,
and pleasant, which sang of life that was conceived of in terms of
sensuous pleasures. The poet created an intoxicating world of
exquisite beauty populated by shepherdesses named Filis, Dorila,
and Lisi. All the senses are excited. There are verdant fields, the
perfume of flowers, savorous fruits, shining silks, and lovely music
which create an environment of refined beauty and of amorous
gallantry. Perhaps the most famous of this neoclassical aspect of
his work is the poem *Rosana en los fuegos* [*Rosana in the Flames*].

b Philosophical and sentimental poetry. In addition, there
existed the poet's own thoughts and preoccupations. Under the
influence of such writers as the Frenchman Rousseau and the
English poet Edward Young, Meléndez Valdés began to write of
his emotions, of solitude, of night, pain, disillusionment, and the
nearness of death. The following is part of the poem *La noche
y la soledad* [*Night and Solitude*], which illustrates the tendency:

Your celestial favor I implore,
Come, give comfort to this weary breast,
Oh solitude sublime, and free me from
The confusing throng around me.
Alas, why then does man, insane,
When seeing at his feet, blind fool,
The tomb that waits, delight in thee?

Neoclassic Preoccupation with Spain's Destiny

Although they also participated in the stylistic and esthetic outlook of the other neoclassicists we have already studied, two poets stand apart in their profound preoccupation with the historical problems and the destiny of Spain.

José Cadalso y Vásquez was one of the most interesting and likable figures of the eighteenth century in Spain. He was born in Cádiz in 1741. He studied with the Jesuits. He traveled throughout Europe and had a military career in which he advanced to the rank of colonel in the cavalry.

Cadalso was so deeply in love with the actress María Ignacia Ibáñez that when the latter died suddenly, the poet was so distraught that he attempted to disinter the body of his loved one. Fortunately the Count of Aranda prevented him from doing so and finally had to exile the desperate poet to Salamanca. The poet described these happenings in an autobiographical work which he entitled *Noches lúgubres* [*Lugubrious Nights*], of which several versions exist, none of them of a certainty from the hand of the author.

He was on intimate terms with the poets of Salamanca and notably with Meléndez Valdés. As a colonel he went to fight against the English at Gibraltar. Despite warnings of the danger he ran, Cadalso remained at his post and was killed by the fragment of a grenade. He died at the age of forty-one in 1782.

With the exception of the *Noches lúgubres* which must be classed with the preromantic works of Young and which is distinctly different from the rest of his works, Cadalso's literary production is typical of the neoclassical epoch in which it was written.

1. Lyrical poetry. In a book of poetry entitled *Ocios de mi juventud* [*Pastimes of My Youth*], Cadalso wrote of his love for the actress María Ignacia Ibáñez whom he called Filis in his verses.

2. Drama. His play, *Sancho García*, a tragedy, was an imitation of French drama and is without real spark of life.

3. Critical works. The most interesting part of Cadalso's writing are the critical works. Cadalso was a contemplative man who was acutely aware of what went on around him. In his work, *Los eruditos a la violeta* [*The Wise Men Without Wisdom*] which appeared in 1772, Cadalso satirized pedants who, without any real knowledge, pretended to be erudite. He described the book as a "course in all the fields of knowledge, divided into seven lessons to correspond with the seven days of the week. It is published for the sake of those who pretend to know a great deal but learn nothing."

The major work of Cadalso, his *Cartas marruecas* [*Moroccan Letters*], was published in 1793. Imitating the formula of Montesquieu's *Lettres Persanes,* the author invented a correspondence between an Arab named Gazel who had come to Spain as part of a diplomatic mission and a Spaniard named Nuño Núñez. A third intermediary was an elderly counselor called Ben-Beley. None of these personages has what could be considered a real personality; they are mere pretexts utilized by the author to expound his theories and ideas.

All of the work of Cadalso is pervaded with his preoccupation with things Spanish. He praises the riches of his native land and defends its history, in particular the colonization of America which was being severely·attacked at that time. Nevertheless, he assailed false and misplaced patriotism which "rather than a virtue becomes a ridiculous defect and often is even harmful to one's country."

Cadalso described the Peninsula as an entity of considerable diversity. He saw the Cantabrians as a people lacking in complexity but good navigators, the Gallegans as robust and patient, the Castilians as loyal and proud, the Extremanians as conquerors and soldiers, the Andalusians as arrogant and astute, and the Catalonians as very industrious. Despite this variety, he recognized a fundamental sense of unity, particularly in time of war.

Cadalso lamented Spain's decadence. He saw his native land as a country which had risen to its highest glory at the time of the Catholic Kings Ferdinand and Isabella, and which by the time of Carlos II was no more than "the skeleton of a giant." Cadalso saw this decadence as the result of the continuous wars, the booty thereof, and especially the treasures of the New World which brought about a feeling of contempt for manual labor and engendered a vain and ineffectual aristocracy.

Thus far, my friend Nuño. From all this you may infer, as do I, first of all, that this Peninsula has known no peace for a good two thousand years and, consequently it is a miracle that there is still a blade of grass in the fields or a drop of water in the wells. Second, since religion has been the cause of so many wars, and in particular against the Moors, it is not surprising that it should play so important a role. Third, having arms continually in their hands has made the population learn to scorn commerce and industry. Fourth, from this it follows that every nobleman of Spain is proud of his nobility. The fifth thing is that the treasures so rapidly acquired in the New World have brought the mechanical arts into disrepute. . . .

—From *Moroccan Letters, III*

In spite of his being an officer in the army, Cadalso hated war and saw it as a calamity which supposedly brought fame to the soldier but which in actuality brought only death.

With equal clarity and sense of purpose, Cadalso assailed the vices of the society of his time, the lack of culture, the pedantry and habits of people with little character, and the disproportionate regard for things foreign.

In *Letter LVI*, Cadalso wrote:

Everyone was aghast at hearing such lamentations. "What in the world?" said some. "What can the matter be?" asked others. The three couples continued with their complaints and their groaning, one trying to outdo the other. I myself was upset to hear so much misfortune and although less in-

terested in the fortunes of the nation than the others present,
I asked just what was the cause of all this commotion.

"Is it, by any chance," I asked, "because the Algerians
have invaded Andalusia and laid waste to that lovely
province?"

"No, no," one of the ladies replied, "No, no, it's far
worse than that."

"Has some new savage tribe of Indians appeared and invaded Mexico from the North?"

"Not that either, but far, far worse," said another of our
patriots.

"Has some plague killed off all the flocks in Spain and
left the nation without any wool to clothe itself?" I said
uneasily.

"That wouldn't make much difference compared to what
is happening," said one of our zealous citizens.

I kept on mentioning a whole list of calamities that can
occur in a nation, asking if one of them was the cause of all
the tears, sobs, sighs, moans, groans, lamentations and curses
against the stars and heaven itself, when finally one of the
women, one who had said nothing and seemed the most
sensible of the lot, exclaimed in a dolorous voice: "Can you
imagine, Gazel, that in all of Madrid there was not a single
piece of ribbon of this color no matter how hard or where
we looked?"

Gaspar Melchor de Jovellanos was born in Gijón in 1744 and
was a judge in both Seville and Madrid. He was exiled to the
province of Asturias when his protector, the politician Cabarrús,
fell out of favor, but when he recovered his influence he was
named Minister of Justice. He was, however, an enemy of Godoy
and when the latter became Prime Minister he exiled Jovellanos
to Mallorca where he stayed from 1801 to 1808.

When Napoleon's troops took control of Spain, José Bonaparte, thinking that Jovellanos would accept a post in his administration because of his exile, offered him the position of
Minister of the Interior. Jovellanos patriotically refused the post
and instead became a member of the *Junta Central,* a group which

was strongly anti-French. Due to his membership in this group he was forced to flee to Asturias where he died in 1810. He became known as the "Father of His Country" because of his patriotic attitude against the French invaders.

Jovellanos is the prototype of the philanthropist, of the man whose major interest was the well-being and the progress of his compatriots. All his talent, his interests, and his culture were at the service of feeling.

The sentimental and reflective character of Jovellanos is clearly apparent in his poems which, unlike the poetry of his friends and contemporaries of the Salamancan School, contain little of the anacreontic tendency. Jovellanos preferred to write of friendship, night, solitude, and of sadness. Several of his compositions are well known, including *the Himno a la luna* [*Hymn to the Moon*] and *A Arnesto*.

For Jovellanos poetry was a vehicle for the expression of feelings and above all of sadness, of tender affections, of moderated sorrow and lamentations as in the poem, *Al cumpleaños de Galatea* [*On Galatea's Birthday*] below:

> Perhaps in shame among the myrtles
> She her face does hide, that face
> That is a throne of modesty and joy,
> And now is bathed in tears?
> Do tell me, Galatea, why you hide.
> Since when, my Galatea so divine,
> Has natural feeling been a crime?
> Could the most prying eye discern
> Upon your breast the tears you've shed
> For friendship without blot or stain?
> Those who from others hide their pain
> Have fear of showing they are weak,
> But the tender heart before the flame
> Of friendship, open, unafraid,
> Why should it of its feeling be ashamed?

In his play, *El delincuente honrado* [*The Honest Offender*], Jovellanos expressed the same idea: "Yes, tears are the result of the sensitivity of the heart. Unhappy he who is incapable of shedding them!"

He was highly patriotic. When Spain was invaded by the troops of Napoleon in 1808, Jovellanos wrote an inspiring poem called the *Canto guerrero para los asturianos* (*War Chant for the Asturians*), in which he exhorted his compatriots to resist the tyranny of the French emperor and his brother José who had been placed on the Spanish throne. He also explained his point of view in a letter which he wrote to a French general:

> I do not follow any party. I follow the sacred and just cause which sustains my Native Land, which those of us who have received from her hand the august duty of defending and directing her and which we have all sworn to follow and sustain at the cost of our lives. We do not fight, as you have ascertained, on behalf of the Inquisition nor for imaginary preoccupations, nor for the interests of the Grandees of Spain; we are fighting for the precious rights of our king, our religion, our constitution and our independence.

Jovellanos wrote a tragedy entitled *El Pelayo* in hendecasyllabic verse and neoclassical style. The aforementioned *El delincuente honrado,* which was an imitation of the *comédie larmoyante* then in vogue in France, written in prose, is of greater interest. It tells the story of a gentleman who kills another man in a duel and later marries the widow. When an innocent man is accused of killing the dead man, the gentleman confesses that it was he who did it. The judge who condemns the young man to death learns that it is his own son he has sentenced, but the innocent man is pardoned.

Preromanticism in Spain

The crisis of neoclassicism occurred in the second half of the century. The rigorous requirements of neoclassic style gave birth to a literature which, while proper and carefully composed, lacked the breath of life. Rationalism produced works that were lacking in human warmth. The boredom with neoclassical works was already apparent in the second half of the eighteenth century and a change of taste could be discerned long before the triumph in the nineteenth century of what we know as romanticism.

Some of the authors we have studied—notably Meléndez Valdés and Jovellanos—seem to have been moved not only by the mechanism of their intellect but also by the impulses of the heart. The influence of some of the French writers, Rousseau in particular, made something sacred of human feelings and placed sentiment above social norms. Through the influence of the Englishman Edward Young, who dedicated poems to his little dead daughter, the Spanish poets began to write of solitude, night, and anguish, as in the case of Cadalso with his *Noches lúgubres*.

The "rational man" of neoclassicism was replaced by the "sensitive man" who presages the triumph of romanticism.

Rhetorical ostentation began to replace the impassive and descriptive language of the neoclassicists which was insufficient for the expression of the sentiments of the heart. The poet adopted a more moving and energetic style better suited to lamentation and to eulogy. He made use of exclamations and vehement expressions. More and more he insisted on a maximum freedom of expression as opposed to oppressive norms in his creativity.

Furthermore, the pastoral and didactic themes of neoclassical rationalism became increasingly unproductive and insufficient. Worlds of fantasy and dreams of idealized and distant places became subjects of poetry and novel alike. Translations of the works of the Frenchman Chateaubriand brought into vogue such subject matter as the North American Indian, while other works popularized the color and exoticism of Oriental courts. The Count of Norona made translations of Arab and Persian poets, and Moorish and African tales came into vogue.

These tendencies in literature were accompanied by political ideas advanced by the French Encyclopedists. The entry of liberal thought was a part of the thirst for novelty and the taste for things from beyond the Pyrenees.

All these characteristics which pointed toward the dissolution of neoclassicism became more accentuated and finally reached their plenitude with the triumph of romanticism.

Second School of Salamanca

There was a Second School of Salamanca of the Eighteenth Century. Because of the chronological difference, and above all a difference in outlook, a group of poets including Nicasio Alvarez de Cienfuegos, Juan Nicasio Gallego, and Manuel José Quintana is usually classed as the Second Salamancan School.

Nicasio Alvarez Cienfuegos was born in 1764 and lived until 1809. In his poetry, as he himself tells us, "faithful to the expression of his sensitivity, of his tenderness and his melancholy," Cienfuegos exploited almost all the themes of the preromantic period. We find sentimentalism in his *Mi paseo solitario de primavera* [*My Solitary Walk in Spring*], exoticism in his Moorish songs, exaggerated rhetoric and funereal themes in his *La escuela del sepulcro* [*The School of the Sepulcher*].

Juan Nicasion Gallego, 1777–1853, was a patriot during the wars against Napoleon and a liberal in politics who wrote most of his work in a neoclassical style. It is due to the enthusiasm and the vehemence of expression in such poems as his *El dos de mayo* [*The Second of May*], which commemorates the execution of Spanish patriots by the French on that date, that the poet is often classified with the preromantics. He also wrote a number of elegies.

Manuel José Quintana, who was born in 1772, was the outstanding poet of the group. Imbued with the ideas of the Encyclopedists, he was the exalted singer of progress. Like Gallego, he was a patriot and a liberal and held various political posts of importance. At the height of his fame, Queen Isabella II crowned him poet laureate.

The liberal outlook of Quintana is directly traceable to the French Encyclopedists, who saw Spain as a land which was inherently free and democratic in spirit until the period of Charles V when despotic oppression vilified and disfigured her character.

From this concept stemmed the popularity of the Commune movement which was considered to be strongly liberal. Quintana began the vogue for eulogies.

When Spain was invaded by Napoleon, Quintana reacted patriotically and nostalgically, recalling the Imperial Spain that was so far-flung that, as he wrote, the ocean "wherever she her waves unrolled, her fury thus to break, encountered Spanish coasts." The following is a part of the famous poem *A España, después de la revolución de marzo* [*Ode to Spain After the Revolution of March*]:

> War, awful name and now sublime!
> The refuge and the sacred shield in time
> To stay the savage Attila's advance
> With fiery steed and lance!—
> War! War! O Spaniards, on the shore
> Of Guadalquivir, see arise once more
> Thy Ferdinand the Third's imposing brows!
> See great Gonzalo o'er Granada rear!
> Behold the Cid with sword in mad carouse!
> And, o'er the Pyrenees the form appear
> Of brave Bernardo, old Jimena's son!
> See how their stormy wraiths are interspun!
> How valour breathes from out their hollow tombs
> Where "War" upon the mighty echoes booms!

> —Anonymous translation

In another work called *El Panteón del Escorial* [*The Pantheon of the Escorial*], Quintana expounded the Black Legend of Spain, calling Philip the Second a monster of evil and the monarch responsible for the decadence of Spain.

Quintana also wrote numerous poems on philosophical themes such as *En la muerte de un amigo* [*On the Death of a Friend*], and didactic compositions such as *Las reglas del drama* [*The Rules of the Drama*] in which he expounded neoclassical rules for the theater.

In his dramatic works Quintana followed the rules he had laid down in such plays as the tragedy *El Duque de Viseo*, 1801, and the patriotic drama, *Pelayo*.

Among his works in prose, Quintana wrote a book of biographical sketches of famous Spaniards—including the Cid, Guzmán the Good, Roger de Lauria, Alvaro de Luna, and Pizarro—entitled *Vidas de españoles célebres* [*Lives of Famous Spaniards*].

School of Seville

At the end of the eighteenth century there was a group of noteworthy poets in Seville, known as the school of Seville, who took the name of the *Academia de Letras Humanas* or *The Academy of Humane Letters*. The group accepted as its norm "good taste" and "literary principles," i.e., neoclassicism. They left a margin for "genius," however, and for the free expression of one's own personality. Consequently much of the poetry of the group may be classified as preromantic.

Alberto Lista y Aragón is the best known writer of the group. Because of his personal prestige as well as for his literary works, Lista is considered the most important member of the Sevillian school. He was born in Seville in 1778, studied humanities and taught in Seville, in Cadiz, and in Madrid. He went into the priesthood and was a man of vast culture.

In his literary ideas Lista inclined to neoclassicism. Those poets which influenced his output were primarily of the Classico-Renaissance tradition—Horace, Petrarch, Garcilaso, Fray Luis de León. He advised against following Góngora and satirized baroque poets. He always tried to find an equilibrium between form and content. He wrote religious poetry in the vein of Fray Luis de León—for example, *La muerte de Jesús* [*The Death of Jesus*]—and ballads of a preromantic type such as *La cabaña* [*The Cabin*] and *El puente de la viuda* [*The Widow's Bridge*].

Félix José Reinoso, who was born in Seville in 1792, was a friend of Lista, member of the Academy, and a priest. His work in the neoclassical style is of little originality or interest. On the other hand, his poem *La inocencia perdida* [*Innocence Lost*], which takes up the biblical theme of original sin, is important in that it, like Milton's *Paradise Lost,* utilized fantasy to glorify the "marvels of Christianity," something which neoclassic norms prohibited.

José María Blanco was born in Seville in 1775. He was a restless man who left his country and the priesthood and went to England where he became a Protestant. He translated Shakespeare and Pope into Spanish and even became quite adept at writing English, publishing under the English translation of his name, White. His poem *Una tormenta nocturna en alta mar* [*A Nocturnal Storm on the High Seas*] is the immediate percursor of the famous *Al faro de Malta* [*To the Lighthouse at Malta*] written by the man who initiated romanticism in Spain, the Duque de Rivas, or Duke of Rivas.

José Marchena is another writer of this group. He was born in Utrera in 1768. He took minor orders, but before finishing his studies for the priesthood, he became imbued with the ideas of Voltaire. He left Spain and went to France at the height of the Revolution and joined the Girondists.

In 1808 he returned to his native land as a secretary to the French general Murat. He was made archivist to the Ministry of the Interior, a post which, naturally, he had to give up when the French withdrew. In 1820 he returned once more to Madrid, but his collaboration with the French caused him to be treated badly. He died in 1821.

Marchena was a revolutionary poet. In his *Epístola a José Lanz sobre la libertad política* [*Epistle to Jose Lanz, on Political Liberty*], Marchena attempted to minimize the evil effects of the French Revolution. He thought that philosophy would redeem all peoples and he spoke in one of his works of the "divine Rousseau." His ideological extremism unfortunately frequently marred the undoubted talent which Marchena had.

One independent, Cabanyes, deserves mention. The last of the poets, fully in the nineteenth century, to maintain the superiority of neoclassicism was Manuel de Cabanyes. He was born in Villanueva y Geltrú in 1808 and died quite young. His only book of poetry, *Preludios de mi lira* [*Preludes from My Lyre*], show him to be a faithful disciple of such classical models as Horace and such neoclassical poets as Fóscolo and Alfieri. Nevertheless, in his anguished melancholy and his spiritual restiveness he is clearly a poet of transition who stands between neoclassicism and romanticism.

5.

The Nineteenth Century

Classicism Overcome: Romanticism

The triumph of the literary and artistic ideas which were being forged during the second half of the eighteenth century is called romanticism. Its period of triumph is the first half of the nineteenth century.

In contrast to neoclassicism which, throughout Europe, was a product of the diffusion of French classicism, romanticism represents the reaction of a national spirit in the countries formerly influenced by France in opposition to the all-absorbing power of Napoleon. Thus everything which in the classical canon had been founded on unity, since all literary works reflected common models, came to be based on the principle of variety. Independence became prevalent.

Each nation, each people, each individual was capable of creating something unique. From this idea stemmed the cult of national values and the interest in folklore and in anything that was considered typical and picturesque. This, of course, gave an impulse to travel.

This "right to diversity" which took the place of the neoclassical uniformity culminated in the esthetics of individualism. The cult of the ego became the foundation of romanticism. The growing importance of individualism dates back to the Renaissance when there was a true "rebellion of man." This was accentuated in the eighteenth century when a total spiritual independence in religion, politics, and literature developed.

In opposition to the authority of norms and of academic rulings, complete liberty was proclaimed. As the ego, one's self, was the sole base of inspiration, everything that was spontaneous and sincere was sanctioned. No moral hindrance, any more than any academic norm, was to impede freedom of expression.

Whereas neoclassic literature had been based on reason and addressed itself primarily to a refined, select audience, the fundamentally sentimental character of romanticism gave it an appeal to less educated classes of society as well. Consequently romanticism was enormously popular. The rational man of the eighteenth century was replaced by the man of feeling.

The romantic cultured love of nature in all its immensity offered the writer a vision of infinity and a sort of mirror of his soul. Whereas the classicists had loved the geometrically planned gardens and parks in which nature was thus "rationalized," the romantics adored nature in her freest state, tangled forests, melancholy ruins, the wide uncharted sea, the night full of mystery and of sadness.

In their flight from all that was commonplace and plebeian, the romantics took refuge in scenes of far-away places, in remote islands, virgin forests, and fantastic cities. The interest in the exotic increased. The Orient, which had already enjoyed considerable vogue through the translation of the *Thousand and One Nights,* became a fashionable literary topic. The picturesque Spain of Moorish palaces and ancient walls became a favorite subject of writers throughout Europe, and in America with Washington Irving. Greece, which was rebelling against the Turks, moved the hearts of such romantics as Lord Byron who went there to fight and die. The vastness of America, full of grandiosity and mystery, also became the setting for romanticism's fantasies.

The appraisement of the Middle Ages began. Classicism had turned its gaze toward Greco-Latin antiquity; romanticism looked to the Middle Ages. The exaltation of the Christian spirit replaced the evocation of pagan mythology. Gothic art, which had been considered barbarous by the neoclassicists, became the object of praise and enthusiastic acceptance.

Romanticism represents, thereby, a traditionalist and Christian movement of considerable importance in addition to its revolutionary liberalism.

Two distinct tendencies may be discerned in the romantic movement: (a) a liberal ideology which stemmed from the Encyclopedists, and (b) a certain traditionalist idealism which revalued the Christian spirit.

These two movements existed side by side with equal fervor and gave rise to the continuous political ups and downs of the nineteenth century.

To sum up the previously noted characteristics, we may say that romanticism imposes an idealistic concept of art and of life, which the individual believes or dreams and envisages will be as he wishes, i.e., subjectivism. Romanticism is the realm of fantasy and of dream and vision. Naturally the figure of Don Quixote, the hero who dreamed an impossible dream, became a very popular one in the period.

While new creative possibilities constantly invited poets to dream of fantastic and idealized worlds, reality presented itself as an ever-present source of disillusionment. This resulted in melancholy and the desperation and anguish which we find in almost all romantic writers and which the French designate with the term "mal du siècle."

Romanticism in Spanish Literature

Romanticism begins to come into being gradually during the last decades of the eighteenth and first decades of the nineteenth centuries—preromanticism—and does not triumph in a clear-cut manner until around 1835.

The word "romanticism" is derived, some assert, from the French word "roman" or novel, signifying accordingly a work that is novel-like or novelistic in nature. Others trace its development from the word "romance," alluding to the Medieval period when the languages of this designation were formed, as opposed to the classical Greco-Latin period which had served as a model up to this time.

Faced with the new style, neoclassical taste expressed its opposition through satires. In these works the characteristics of the new school may be studied.

The following is a fragment from Eugenio de Tapia; in it the author wittily satirizes the excesses of romanticism in the drama:

You can never imagine, good Prospero and dear,
How much good plays I like to hear . . .
Especially if the play is horrid,
Called by the masses Romantic, and florid,
Composed by an author, like the famous Dumas,
Whom you prefer calling the Gaul who's an ass.

. . . . .

There were decors and settings of type most exotic,
Thunder, lightning, a storm, a frightening night,
A convent, a pantheon, old ruins and cells
Brave warriors, some witches, and monks ringing bells.
No method or order in the work could I find,
The author, an anarchist, seemed sick in his mind.
He flitted at leisure with abandon of quill
Without troubling with reasons for good or for ill.
The performance itself full six years did fill,
The comic and tragic were completely mixed up,
There were terrible cries, and I, feeling ill,
Took out my kerchief to use as a cup.

When Spanish romanticism was introduced, with the two tendencies or directions also found in other earlier European movements, i.e., the traditional and the liberal, the writers of the latter group adhered to a regenerative and revolutionary romanticism which proclaimed liberalism in politics and advocated Europeanizing Spain. They asserted that traditionalism was the basic cause of the nation's decadence. On the other hand, the writers of the former persuasion advocated a conservative romanticism which defended the essential precepts of Christian civilization and turned for inspiration to models within the Spanish tradition.

In the first group were critics like Larra, poets like Espronceda, and orators like Castelar. To them are due the liberal and Europeanizing opinions which finally produced the founding of the Republic in 1931. In the second group appear politicians such as Donoso Cortés, philosophers such as Jaime Balmes, and scholars such as Menéndez y Pelayo. It is they who prepared the way for the traditionalists of today.

The problem of the nation was a serious concern for these men. The disintegration of the Empire, although not comprehended in its full gravity by the great majority of Spaniards, was a major preoccupation for those who were most aware. Already in the seventeenth century, Quevedo had sounded the alarm, pointing out the growing power of France.

We have seen how some writers in the eighteenth century— among them Cadalso and Jovellanos—analyzed the decadence of Spain and proposed formulas to remedy the situation. This patriotic preoccupation is closely related to the political ideas of these writers and resulted in a series of studies of spiritual and material problems relating to Spain.

The interest in French culture, which began as a literary Francophilia, became a political adherence, and thus we find that some well-known authors such as Moratín and Meléndéz-Valdés ended up in the service of Joseph Bonaparte. The energetic efforts of Jovellanos and of Quintana, however, served to reclaim the right to liberty of their invaded Fatherland.

Romanticism in the Realm of Ideas

Liberal Ideology

Just as in the eighteenth century there existed a certain unity in European tastes dominated by French neoclassical models, so in the nineteenth century each country searched out the patterns of its artistic creations in its own native tradition. Romanticism had taken the place of classicism, and if the latter had the characteristics of being uniform and European, romanticism everywhere is national and diverse in character. Consequently folk or popular material became increasingly important. On the other hand, the growing importance which the will of the people acquired in political life corresponds to the interest which writers showed in the life of the common people.

Precedents of this tendency in Spanish literature are not lacking. The drama, from Lope de Rueda to Ramón de la Cruz, and above all, the picaresque novel, show us an immense gallery of folk types and customs. Nevertheless it is during the nineteenth century that folk subject matter became especially important, not only because literature followed democratic tendencies but also because it was believed that the common people possessed a creative power, and thus, for example, the "old ballads" became the objects of study (by Agustín Durán and Nicolás Böhl de Faber) and were erroneously held to be "the work of the people." Moreover it is to Agustín Durán that we owe a magnificent defense of the Spanish national drama, disdained, as we know, by neoclassical theorists.

In the forefront, the nationalistic character of romanticism brought about an exaltation and evaluation of these elements which were most typical and picturesque in each country; popular elements which had retained their distinctive personality at a time when all of the European intellectual aristocracy were following uniform models. It follows from this that *costumbrismo* or prose vignettes reappeared with the advent of the romantic period, that writers became interested in popular and folkloric wisdom, and that songs, couplets, proverbs, and sayings preserved by people of humble origins were collected with loving care. As a consequence, literary language was enriched at this time by a multitude of typically native and plebeian expressions which the writers of the eighteenth century would not have accepted.

Logically this interest in the people was almost always closely related to forms of political liberalism. Writers, by means of the press and of politics, fought for their ideals. The figure of the conspirator who sacrificed everything in the struggle for liberty became especially attractive.

Mariano José de Larra exemplifies this. He was born in Madrid in 1809. His father was a doctor who served in Joseph Bonaparte's army. Because of this he had to leave Spain and subsequently entrusted the education of his son to an academy in Bordeaux. When he was able to return to Spain, young Larra completed his studies in Valladolid and Madrid. The influence of his European education is clearly visible in his work.

As a youth, Larra showed a misanthropic and introverted character; his love life was extremely unhappy. While still a youth he had an affair that left bitter memories; his marriage was unhappy; finally, an adulterous love affair brought him to desperation and death. All of this gave his character a bitterness full of violence.

Larra's life was both triumph and tragedy. As a writer he became known through journalism, gaining immediately great popularity and a secure position. He was elected deputy from Avila. In spite of all this, Larra, consumed with a deep pessimism over the ills of his country and in despair over the turn which his love had taken, committed suicide by shooting himself in the temple. He was only twenty-eight years old (1837).

The ideas expressed by Larra, or "Figaro" as he is often called, in his articles have considerable transcendence; they have deeply influenced posterity. Larra is a rebel who constantly collided with the reality surrounding him, which is, as we know, typical of the spirit of romanticism. However, whereas the romantic poets fled from reality on the wings of fantasy, Larra, of an excessively critical spirit, analyzed it and lashed out at it without pity, making its defects stand out starkly, even when he was not always able to point toward a remedy for the evils he was attacking. His criticism was, consequently, generally pessimistic, bitter, and negative and caused him wholly to lose hope.

In his political ideas, Larra was a disciple of the Encyclopedists; he belongs, thereby, to restorative and revolutionary romanticism. Loyal to the liberalism of his times, he was a lover of liberty. Larra was an enemy of the old Spanish traditions and believed that the influence of religion and of political absolutism had held back the progress of the nation. He argued that Spain had to redeem herself by following the progressive examples of foreign countries. His ideas have nourished the intellectual segment of Spanish liberalism.

Impassioned in his ideas, and perhaps wrong in them, no one could deny the sincerity and the patriotism of "Figaro" who, moreover, was faithful to the profound liberalism of his times.

> Liberty in literature as in the arts, as in industry, as in commerce, as in one's conscience. Here is the emblem of the epoch, here is our own device, here is the gauge by which we shall measure. In our critical judgments we shall ask: Do you teach us something? Are you the expression of human progress? Are you useful? Then you are worthwhile. We recognize no literary absolutism in any country; even less in any man, less so in any epoch, for taste is a relative thing; we recognize no school as exclusively good, because none is absolutely bad. Nor must it be thought that we shall assign to those who wish to follow us a less arduous task; no. We urge them to study, to learn to know man; it will not be enough, as for the Classicist, to open a volume of Horace and of Boileau, and to scorn Lope and Shakespeare; it will not be enough, as for the Romantic, to place himself under the banners of Victor Hugo and to lock up the rules with Molière and Moratín; no, because in our literature Ariosto will stand alongside Vergil, Racine alongside Calderón, Molière alongside Lope; at the same time, to put it briefly, Shakespeare, Schiller, Goethe, Byron, Victor Hugo and Corneille, Voltaire, Chateaubriand and Lamartine.

> —From the article: "Literature"

This same spiritual independence of Larra often caused him to attack those who judged Spain through some sort of system or those who attributed defects to her which were not exclusively Spanish.

> We were walking by one of those works that continually beautify this country and he blurted out:
> "What rubbish! In this country there are no police."
> In Paris houses that are built or are refurbished don't create dust.

He clumsily stepped into a puddle.
"There's no cleanliness in Spain!" he exclaimed.
In foreign countries there is no mud.
Some mentions a robbery:
"Ah! Land of robbers!" He shouted indignantly. Because in London no one robs; in London, where criminals attack pedestrians at midday in the streets on days when there is fog.
A beggar asked us for alms:
"In this country there's nothing but misery!" he exclaimed horrified. Because in foreign lands there is nary a poor man who does not have his coach.
We were going to the theater and, "Oh, what a horror!" said my friend Don Periquito with compassion, without ever having seen a better performance in his life. "There is no theater here!"
We went by a cafe: "Let's not go in. What cafes they have in this country!" he shouted.
Someone mentioned travel: "Heaven help us! You can't travel in Spain! What inns, what roads!"
Oh infernal itch, to revile this country which has been moving forward and progressing for some time past now, more rapidly than those model countries have to arrive at the vantage point at which they now stand."

—From the article: "In This Country"

Larra censured with unerring aim the defects of the society of his time: the lack of culture of the lower classes which found their pleasure only in bull fights and cheap dances; the indifference of the mass of people toward things that were supposedly for their betterment; the limited knowledge of the middle class; the uselessness of the young gentlemen; the laziness of bureaucrats (consider his article *Vuelva usted mañana* or "Come Back Tomorrow"); the lack of courtesy in the relationships between people (as in *El Castellano Viejo* or "A True Castilian Gentleman"). He also criticized the ignorance of actors (*Yo quiero ser cómico* or "I Want to Be a Comedian"); the absence of comfort in public inns (*La fonda nueva* or "The New Inn"); the denial of liberty in social customs (*Dos liberales, o lo que es entenderse* or "Two

Liberals, or What Understanding Each Other Means"), and so on.

Literature, according to Larra, should reflect truth and avoid artifice. He believed that the works of the Spanish classics were "more brilliant than solid" and that literature ought to be philosophical, useful, and progressive. Larra constantly lamented the scant appreciation accorded the writer by Spanish society.

"To write as we do in Madrid . . . is to realize a desperate and sorrowful monologue with one's self. To write in Madrid is to weep."

Larra was what we now call a "columnist." He was the first Spanish journalist in the modern concept of the word. His articles dealt with politics, manners, and literature, and were published under various pseudonyms such as "El Pobrecito Hablador," "El Duende Satírico" and, the one that became best known, "Figaro," the rebellious and popular character from the work of Beaumarchais. His journalistic style is reserved but expressive, often utilizing irony and satire to depict all he wants to combat.

Larra tried other genres as well, such as comedy of the type written by Moratín (*No más mostrador*), romantic drama (*Macías* —the troubador who is brought to his death by an impossible love affair; note that this is Larra's case), and the historical novel (*El doncel de Don Enrique el Doliente*) in the style of Walter Scott.

His crowning achievement is undisputedly his articles which have established him as the foremost critical *costumbrista* of the nineteenth century. Azorín writes of him imaginatively:

> In the dining room of a little inn in Madrid there sits, at a table, a young gentleman. The tablecloth is not very white; aging spots of coffee can be seen in its opaque whiteness. The youth has the stub of a cigar stuck to his lips and has just taken a knife out of his pocket; as he takes it out, some ashes from the cigar fall on him. The meal is eaten without haste. Now and then the young gentleman blandly strikes on the table with the handle of the knife. What is this gentleman like? His eyes, wide, sparkle with intelli-

gence, a shock of black hair lies on his forehead. Black hair, silken, frames his face and falls until it ends in a sharp point.

There is something in a human being which, from the very first moment, speaks to us of his temperament and of his intelligence. The bearing of this gentleman, his movements, his gestures, the tone of his voice when he orders or requests something, draw us deeply toward his person. We should like to speak with him, to question him, to know what he does, which are his favorite books. But let us observe him at a distance. The meal has come to an end. The dinner guest gets to his feet. Clean, fastidious and elegant is his suit. He leaves. Did he make, as he went out, as he cast a last look about the room, about the shabby room, did he make, we repeat, a grimace of resignation and of disdain? In the soul of this man there is a new force; all of the modern spirit of protest and of rebellion, of noble longing for a better Spain is in that imperceptible grimace."

—Azorín: *Larra*

Other *costumbristas* and satirists also characterize the style of the period.

Bartolomé José Gallardo was an astute scholar of Spanish literature, about whose bibliographical rarities he wrote a *Catalogue*, astounding for its erudition. Affiliated with liberalism, in the tradition of Voltaire, he expressed his ideas in a great number of articles and pamphlets. He edited a literary magazine entitled *El Criticón*.

Ramón de Mesoneros Romanos, a native and resident of Madrid (1803–1882), was a merchant by trade and a chronicler of the capital and of the court, to whose description and edification he devoted all of his enthusiasm and his inexhaustible talents. He collaborated on the magazine *Cartas españolas* and on the *Semanario Pintoresco Español,* signing his articles with the pseudonym *El Curioso Parlante*.

The Conservative Ideology

Even when the romantic tradition is, as we have said, predominantly liberal, there is no lack of strong voices raised in defense of traditional ways.

Juan Donoso Cortés, the Marquis of Valdegamas, is, as thinker, orator and politician, one of the most representative of the traditionalists. He was born in the Valle de la Serena (Badajoz) in 1809. He studied in Salamanca and Seville where he was imbued with the ideas of the Encyclopedists of the times. He went to Madrid in 1828. The death of one of his brothers for whom he cared deeply brought about a radical change in his ideas which he subsequently put at the service of Catholicism with extraordinary force.

Donoso was, above all, a formidable orator. Even those works written to be read display his rhetorical bombast, the hammering of his power of conviction which can be heard on page after page. His style is, consequently, declamatory and impassioned, shaped with the purpose of obtaining the approbation of the audience to which it was directed.

Donoso conceived the history of ideas as a struggle between Catholicism and philosophy (that is to say, rationalism). Out of this stuggle, Donoso believed—which he demonstrated to be fully evident—that the triumph of philosophical civilization was becoming more and more certain.

> I believe that Catholic civilization contains good without any mixture of evil, and that philosophy contains evil without any admixture of good whatsoever.
> Catholic civilization teaches that man's nature is ailing and fallen; fallen and ailing in a radical manner in its essentials and in all the elements which constitute it. Human understanding being ailing, man can neither invent truth nor discover it but only see it when it is placed before him; as his will is ailing, he can neither long for nor do good without help, and that he will not receive unless he is sub-

jected and repressed. Things being as they are, it is clear that freedom of discussion necessarily leads to error just as freedom of action leads necessarily to evil. Human reason cannot see truth if an infallible and educative authority does not disclose it; human will can neither desire good nor do good if it is not suppressed by the fear of God. When the will is cut free from God and reason from the Church, error and evil reign without counterbalance in the world,

Philosophical civilization teaches that man's nature is a whole and healthy nature: healthy and whole in a radical manner in its essentials and in all the elements which constitute it. Human understanding being healthy, man can see truth, discover it and invent it; as his will is healthy, he can long for and do good instinctively. Assuming this, it follows that the reason will come to know truth, all truth, all by itself, and that the will, left to itself, will inevitably make absolute good a reality. Things being as they are, it is clear that the solution of the great social problems lies in breaking all the bonds which repress and subject human reason and the free will of man; evil is not in free will nor in reason, but in the bonds. If evil consists of having bonds and good in not having them, perfection must consist in not having any ties of any sort. If that is the way things are, humanity will attain perfection when it denies Government, which is its political bond, and when it denies the family which is its domestic bond. Anyone who does not accept each and every one of these conclusions places himself outside philosophical civilization, does not enter into the Catholic fold, wanders in the deserts of emptiness.

From the theoretic aspects of the problem let us move on to the practical. To which of these two civilizations has time promised victory? I reply to this question without a moment's hesitation of the pen, without my heart skipping a beat or my mind becoming confused, that the triumph in time irrevocably will be that of philosophical civilization. Has man longed to be free? He shall be so. Does he abhor bonds? All of them shall fall in pieces at his feet. There was a time when, to take Liberty's pulse, he wanted to kill his God. Didn't he do so? Did he not hang Him on a cross between two thieves? Did the angels come down from heaven, by any chance, to defend the just man who was dyin politics, but while the social implications of his best-known plays, with their atmospheres of repression in a tradition-bound society, his so-called rural tragedies, *Bodas de sangre* [*Blood Wedding*, 1933], *Yerma* (1934), and *La Casa de Bernarda Alba* [*The House of Bernarda Alba,* 1936], together with *Doña Rosita la soltera* [*Doña Rosita the Spinster,* 1935], do not openly urge more "liberal" attitudes, there are clear thematic implications for a change of the rigid and frustrating moral codes of Spanish life. Certain political and social stances are also implicit in his poems, most notably in the *Romancero gitano* [*Gypsy Ballads*], published in 1928, with their powerful scenes of the brutal massacre of the gypsies by the Civil Guard, the ubiquitous police force in their patent leather tricornes that Arturo Barea, in his book *Lorca, the Poet and His People,* has called the keeper of the "black soul of Spain." Nevertheless, much of Lorca's great appeal before, during and since the Civil War, stems from the fact that he is deeply traditional. His love of his native land and of things Spanish is apparent throughout his works, as is his intimate knowledge of the history, music, poetry, drama and art of his country. His long poem, the *Llanto por Ignacio Sánchez Mejía,* usually translated as *Lament for a Bullfighter,* ranks with the *Coplas* of Jorge Manrique as one of the great elegies of Hispanic poetry.

If Lorca was the first important literary figure to fall a casualty to the destructiveness of war, he was not the last. Even Miguel de Unamuno, some would claim, was, in a sense, a victim. First declaring in favor of the Nationalist forces under Generalissimo Franco, he soon saw the anti-intellectualism of the Fascist right and spoke out. He died shortly after, in late 1936, while under house confinement. The poet Antonio Machado perished of illness a few days after going into exile in France after the fall of the last Republican forces in 1939. Miguel Hernández, died in prison at the tragically early age of 32 in 1942, a victim of tuberculosis and pulmonary complications brought on by suffering endured in political concentration camps. These are perhaps the best known, but to the list must be added the names of the many renowned writers who went into exile, the poets Jorge Guillén and Pedro Salinas who came to the United States, Juan Ramón Jiménez who, like world-famous cellist Pablo Casals, went to reside in Puerto Rico, Rafael Alberti who sought refuge in divine protection and that He entrusted to them the task of looking after the earth. And what happened to the rulers? What happened was that where they expected to end up as omnipotent they ended up on the guillotine. And what happened to the people? What happened was that where they expected to end up in complete emancipation, they ended up in absolute servitude.

Opposing both extremes, Donoso proposed the adoption of the spirit of the Church, following in this the doctrine of Pope Pius IX, who was reigning at that time.

2. Dictatorship as an extreme formula. The revolution which ended in France with the monarchy of Louis Philippe (February 1848) made a profound impression on Donoso. He subsequently proposed in Parliament that when "invading forces" which sought the destruction of society intensified their attacks, the "resisting forces," based on tradition, should concentrate their strength in a single hand. "When legality suffices to save a society, then legality; when it does not suffice, then, dictatorship." And in another place: "In these times of very frequent crises in the existence of peoples, dictatorship is the only thing that can serve as a shield for both liberty and law."

Jaime Balmés is another important figure of the conservative ideology in Spain. He was born in Vich (1810) and had considerable influence in the restoration of philosophical studies. He died in 1848.

Balmés gave a Christian content to the philanthropic feelings of the previous century and thus aspired to attain in society "the highest morality, the highest intelligence, the highest degree of well-being possible for the greatest possible number."

The following of his works are best known: *Filosofía fundamental* [*Fundamental Philosophy*], which is Thomistic in character; *El Criterio,* a treatise on logic; *El Protestantismo comparado con el Catolicismo* [*Protestantism Compared with Catholicism*], a polemical work. His style shows little flexibility but he is methodical and convincing.

Romanticism in the Theater

As we study the repercussions of romantic ideology in the Spanish theater we must point out two types of drama:

1. Idealistic and tragic dramas constitute the most ambitious and significant works of romanticism. They are characterized by their impassioned style and their tragic ending as well as their ostentatious staging (scenery, lighting, scenic effects).

2. Realistic and "costumbrista" dramas. Paralleling this grandiose and tragic theater there existed a minor theatrical school, the observer of the social reality of the middle and lower classes, which carried on the realistic traditions of Spanish literature.

Idealism and Tragic Drama

The tendency toward idealistic and tragic drama was inaugurated in 1834 (*La Conjuración de Venecia*), triumphed in 1835 with *Don Alvaro o la fuerza del sino* and attained a secure position in the theater in 1836 with *El Trovador* and, in 1837, with *Los Amantes de Teruel.*

Francisco Martínez de la Rosa, born in Granada, is a major figure in the origins of Spanish romanticism. His political activities took him to the highest posts of government. He negotiated the English-Spainsh alliance against Napoleon; he was a liberal deputy and therefore was persecuted and exiled in the absolutist period. During the reign of Maria Cristina, he was ambassador, Minister of State and President of the Council of State. He died in 1851.

Martínez de la Rosa was a cultured and elegant writer who never became an impassioned partisan of either contending group of classicists or romantics. Whenever possible he chose from each one the ideas or resources best suited to his needs.

In his lyric poetry he cultivated a neoclassical style, polished and restrained, but without personality. He composed a series of epigrammatic poems entitled *El Cementerio de Momo* [*The Cemetery of Momo*]. In his youth he wrote several comedies in the style of Moratín.

The most important part of his drama, nevertheless, may be classified as romantic. The opening, in 1834, of his work *La Conjuración de Venecia* [*The Conspiracy of Venice*] marks the triumph of the romantic school.

La Conjuración de Venecia is a historical drama in prose which takes place in the fourteenth century and is based on an episode of the political rivalries which ended in the death of Rugiero, the patriot who wanted to liberate Venice from the tyranny of the Council of Ten then presided over by Pedro Morosini. The tragedy acquires a sentimental character because the niece of the latter, Laura, is secretly married to Rugiero. As the height of ill fortune, we learn finally that the latter is nothing less than the son of Morosini himself. In spite of everything, Rugiero is taken to the scaffold.

The romantic color of the tragedy is accentuated by the tone of mystery which surrounds the conspiracy, the sepulchral atmosphere of several scenes, and the secret which hangs over the protagonists. It is a truly somber and strange work.

In his Moorish tragedy *Aben Humeya,* he develops an episode of the War of Alpujarras in which the protagonist is the noble Fernando de Valor who places himself at the head of the rebellious Moriscos in order to avenge the atrocities which the Christians have committed against his family. The work ends tragically with the death of the ringleader at the hands of his own vassals.

The Duque de Rivas is another major figure. His life as liberal aristocrat, as exile, and as prominent politician was an interesting one.

Don Angel de Saavedra y Ramírez de Baquedano was born in Cordova of an illustrious family in 1791. He was educated in the Seminary for Nobles and took part in the War of Independence, being wounded in the battle of Ocaña (1809). In Cadiz he showed himself to be an enthusiastic supporter of liberal ideas. When the absolutist reaction set in in 1823, Don Angel de Saavedra, seriously compromised, was forced to leave the country. He stayed in foreign lands for eleven years—in England, on the island of Malta (where he took a liking to the English romantics, and especially Lord Byron and Walter Scott), in Italy and in France, where he earned his living as a painter. Brought back to Spain, thanks to an amnesty (1834), he inherited from his brother the title of Duque de Rivas and was named Minister and later on ambassador. During the last years of his life, surrounded by the highest prestige, he held the position of President of the Royal Spanish Academy.

The Duque de Rivas merits the attention of literary historians as the consecrator of the triumph of romanticism in the Spanish theater. The opening of his tragedy *Don Alvaro o la fuerza del sino* [*Don Alvaro or the Force of Destiny*] in the Teatro del Príncipe in Madrid on March 22, 1835, heralds the definitive incorporation of the new school into Spanish dramatic literature.

All of the elements which constitute the well-known tragedy, *Don Alvaro* by the Duque de Rivas, may be considered as characteristic of the romantic school.

a He breaks, in fact, with neoclassic precepts. He dispenses with unities; he mixes prose and verse and utilizes all sorts of meters and verse lengths, and he alternates tragic with comic characters.

b Content. The work is lacking in logic and verisimilitude and, moreover, in didactic intent.

c Presentation. The action of *Don Alvaro* is presented with elaborate stage machinery. Each situation is prepared for by an atmosphere created through settings, strange noises, and lighting. The final tragic scenes are accompanied lugubriously by thunder, lightning, and funeral chants. This way of staging a work is characteristic of romanticism.

The work introduces the unlucky figure of Don Alvaro (who is of mysterious origin and perhaps a bastard) who is pursued by Fate to such a point that, without wishing to do so, he kills the father of his beloved Doña Leonor and then, in other quarrels, both of the latter's brothers. In fact, one of the two, Don Alfonso, has gone to seek vengeance against Don Alvaro who had taken refuge in a monastery; he challenges him and goads him until Don Alvaro kills him.

As Leonor's brother calls for confession, the door of a small chapel nearby opens and out comes Doña Leonor in the habit of a nun (for she had taken refuge there as an act of penitence);

Don Alfonso, dying, kills his sister, believing wrongly that she was living there with the murderer of her father. Don Alvaro, in despair at seeing such misfortune, commits suicide by throwing himself down a precipice.

Of less importance are other theatrical works by the Duque de Rivas, such as *El desengaño de un sueño* [*The Disillusionment of a Dream*], which seems to be an imitation of *La vida es sueño* of Calderón de la Barca; *Lanuza* and *El Duque de Acquitania* contain classical elements.

Also characteristic of the romantic tastes of the Duque de Rivas are his compositions on legendary themes, which we shall study later on.

Following the success of *La Conjuración de Venecia* in 1834, and of *Don Alvaro* in 1835, there came the resounding triumph of *El Trovador* [*The Troubador*] by Antonio García Gutiérrez which marks the definite advance of romanticism on the Spanish stage. The author went from obscurity to fame, the success of *The Troubadour* marking a complete change in his life.

Antonio García Gutiérrez was born in Chiclana (1813). The beginning of his literary career was beset with difficulties. A student of medicine, the author abandoned his studies and tried to gain entry to the literary groups of the capital without obtaining their protection or the attention of the theater managers. Discouraged, he enlisted as a soldier in the National Militia. Unexpectedly an actor chose *El Trovador* to be performed the night of his benefit (1836). The success was so resounding that the custom of having the author come out onto the stage to acknowledge the applause of the audience dates from that event. García Gutiérrez' popularity was immense and extended to Latin America which he visited in triumph.

The action of the play is very complex and imaginative. It is based on the unhappy love of the troubador Don Manrique, of mysterious origins, and the Lady Doña Leonor, who is being courted by the Count de Artal who, by his violence and his power, as he is Judge of Aragon, has the troubador condemned to death. Leonor commits suicide by taking poison. It is then revealed, by the gypsy woman Azucena whom the Troubador had supposed was his mother, that he and Count de Artal were brothers.

Don Juan Eugenio de Hartzenbusch, born in Madrid in 1806, a public official and a man of great erudition, wrote pleasant comedies in the style of Moratín. His outstanding work is his tragedy *Los Amantes de Teruel* [*The Lovers of Teruel*] (1837).

In the play, Don Diego Marsilla arrives after the time limit set by the father of his beloved, Doña Isabel de Segura, for acquiring a fortune because the Moorish queen of Valencia, Zulima, has fallen in love with the protagonist and prevents his return. Isabel has already married and the play ends with the tragic death of the two lovers.

The play contains some anachronisms. It is, nevertheless, the most harmonious, well balanced and believable of the major works produced in the Spanish romantic theater.

José Zorrilla was educated in the Seminary for Nobles and began the study of law, but he abandoned these studies in the hope of acquiring literary glory. The occasion presented itself in the tragic death of "Figaro" at whose burial he became known through the reading of a poetic composition (1839).

From that moment on, his life became agitated and picturesque. He started out as a journalist, he married and the marriage brought him nothing but misfortunes. He ran off to France and to Mexico where he was a protégé of the Emperor Maximilian. He returned to Spain and traveled to Rome. He lived once in France and finally returned to Madrid. His improvisation, his lack of orderliness, and the avarice of editors caused Zorrilla to live in a bohemian and irregular manner.

Back in Spain, his prestige at a high point, pensioned by parliament, crowned in Granada as Poet Laureate, Zorrilla passed his last years evoking the picturesque adventures of his life in the work *Recuerdos del Tiempo Viejo* [*Souvenirs of Former Times*]. He died in 1873.

The literary work of Zorrilla was received by the public with extraordinary popularity because of both its form and its content. Zorrilla is a master of music in verse; his style is clear and brilliant; the rhythms he employs—in all meters, forms, and strophes —are prodigies of verbal melody. At the same time, the themes he treats are all profoundly fitting to the Spanish spirit. Zorrilla con-

siders himself a troubador who sings for a people. The style of
Zorrilla is richer in music than in ideas.

Of his dramatic works, we shall discuss only the most characteristic:

1. In *Don Juan Tenorio* (1844), he takes the figure of Don
Juan of Seville, created by Tirso de Molina, and adapts it to his
own imagination, giving us a play essentially romantic in spirit.
In keeping with this spirit, Don Juan is saved, thanks to a woman,
Doña Inés.

Here is a description of the protagonist's exploits.

DON JUAN: Well, sir, leaving here
In search of greater space
For my adventures,
I went to Italy, for there
Pleasure has its palaces.
The ancient, classic land
Of war and joys of love,
Where Emperor and France's king
In battle rage,
"Where better go?" I said,
"Where soldiers go, there gaming,
Love affairs and fights go too."
In short I went to Italy.
In sword and flame sought out
Both duel and love's delights.
In Rome, to wager true,
Both amorous and hostile,
This sign upon the door I fixed:
"Here Don Juan Tenorio lives,
For anyone who seeks him out."
The story of my busy days
In detail I'll omit.
Suffice it said that there I left
For glory and for honor mine
Sufficient memory, and you
Can judge my exploits as you wish.
Those ways are most licentious,
I, high spirited and bold,

How reduce to numbers
The love adventures that I had?

. . . . . .

In every place I went
I trampled reason under foot,
I made a mockery of virtue,
The very laws to shame I put
And every woman left betrayed.
Down to peasant huts I went,
Up to the palace of a king,
Into cloistered walls did spring.
And in each place where time I spent
I left a bitter memory of me.

2. *Traidor, inconfeso y martir* [*Traitor, Unconfessed and Martyr*] (1849) is based on the life of a historical personage, the impostor called the *Pastelero de Madrigal* who posed as the King Don Sebastian of Portugal, although Zorilla gives a distinctive turn to the play in that he presents the true king as the man who, in disguise, is taken for the impostor and condemned to death.

3. *El Zapatero y el Rey* [*The Shoemaker and the King*] (1840) is one of Zorrilla's most dramatic works. Its central figure is Blas Pérez, the son of a shoemaker whom the King Don Pedro raises to the status of captain, counselor, and friend. When the war with Enrique de Trastamara breaks out, Blas Pérez finds that a daughter of his, whom Don Enrique had thought dead, is still alive. After the battle of Montiel is over, Blas Pérez offers his daughter to Don Enrique—who has fallen in love with her—in exchange for his captive king. When he finds out that Don Pedro has died, he has his daughter killed and thus sacrifices paternal love for loyalty.

Realistic and Costumbrista Drama

The realistic and *costumbrista* drama appeared simultaneously with the idealistic and tragic theater, personified in the authors we have just cited. There are two distinct tendencies in this movement:

1. *Comedy in the style of Moratín*. This tendency follows in the tradition of the wit and penetrating observation of the author of *El sí de las niñas* [*When a Girl Says Yes*]. It is exemplified by Bretón de los Herreros. Born in 1796, he participated in the War of Independence, was a journalist and a very prolific and popular writer of light drama; he was also an adapter and translator of French plays. An observer of life around him, he brought to the stage many a realistic portrait of picturesque types from the Spanish society of his times.

In *¿Marcela o cuál de los dos?* [*Marcela, or Which One of the Two?*] he holds up to ridicule three social types; the gossip, the conceited dandy, and the gloomy lover. In *Muérete y veras* [*When You Die You Shall See*] we find that the fiancée of a man who is presumed dead forgets the betrothed immediately, while the girl's sister remains faithful to the dead youth's memory.

2. The Independent Historical Theatre—Transition to Realism. As a derivation of the idealistic and tragic drama, but with a tendency toward the portrayal of persons and events of other epochs, there is a group of authors who may be considered as transitional—leading to, and forming part of, the realistic school. Thus Ventura de la Vega, who was born in Buenos Aires (1807) but lived in Spain, tried his hand at historical drama with a classical subject as in *La Muerte de César* [*Caesar's Death*], or a medieval one, as in *Don Fernando de Antequera*. In the latter he portrays the Castilian prince defending the Queen Mother, Doña Catalina of Lancaster, against the intrigues of the nobles. In *La Muerte de César*, Brutus, without knowing it, is supposedly the illegitimate son of Caesar himself, a situation which gives a grandiose and terrifying aspect to the tyrannicide. The following is a characteristic scene:

BRUTUS: A people in slavery cannot be happy.
CAESAR: It is not in slavery because of me;
No chains were forged by works of mine.
BRUTUS: Ah! your good works!
More ill-fated for our country have they been
than all the tortures of the blood-stained Silla!
If you refuse to hear my words, if tyrant be

you must, he is your model: pour forth
our blood in streams; perhaps to see it
Rome will waken from her lethargy
and rise at last, against you. But with
these wretched works of good, you lull the people,
traitor, and teach them love of bondage.
CAESAR: Not I who've made a slave of them.
BRUTUS: Then who?
CAESAR: Their wickedness.
BRUTUS: This wickedness that you, a hypocrite, lament,
combat them with examples you yourself do set.
You first of all: in this a task most noble
for a Caesar! Then renounce, renounce
your high authority; faced with the force
of this heroic virtue, you shall see that Rome
in awe shall bend itself on knee to honor you
not as a dictator but as numen come again!
CAESAR: It is too late.
BRUTUS: Not late! I beg of you to listen
to this Brutus here who kneels now at your feet.
For country and for glory' sake, renounce.
CAESAR: What do you ask, unhappy friend? If I renounce
what then of fatherland?
BRUTUS: Then enough! No more than one
in all this land now stands in shame for you
and Rome and turns to go in horror.
(He goes out.)
CAESAR: The wrath sublime! No master will he suffer!
My blood in him I see. This is the son of Caesar.

—From Scene IV

The most famous work of Ventura de la Vega, however, is
El hombre del mundo [*The Man of the World*] in which he portrays the figure of a libertine who, on marrying, is tormented by
jealousy.

Manuel Tamayo y Baus also follows in the tradition of historical themes and realistic settings. He was born in Madrid in
1829 and became very popular. He was a member of the Royal
Academy and Director of the National Library.

Tamayo worked in every form of drama, from the neoclassical tragedy *Virginia*, imitating Alfieri, to comedies of manners like *Lo positivo* [*The Affirmation*], a satire on modern materialism, or *Lances de honor* [*Affairs of Honor*], a strong attack on dueling. Nevertheless, his best works are those which evoke a specific historical moment.

Tamayo's greatest success came with the performance of *Un drama nuevo* [*A New Drama*]. This play tells the story of a comic actor, Yorick, who wants to play a tragic role (that of a deceived husband) in a work which his friend Shakespeare has just written. The dramatist refuses his request as he knows that the actor is being deceived by his wife Alicia. Finally he gives in, and Yorick learns the truth during the play's performance when the treacherous Walton hands him a letter from Edmundo, his wife's lover, a fellow actor and protégé of his, instead of a paper which he is supposed to read as part of his role. In despair, Yorick actually kills him on stage, to the astonishment of Shakespeare and of his friends and to the bewilderment of the audience who believes they are seeing the final episode of the play which is being performed.

In *Locura de amor* [*Love's Madness*], he portrays the queen, Doña Juana la Loca, known as Joan the Mad, torn by the terrible jealousies her husband, Felipe el Hermoso, causes her. The author interprets the madness of the queen as a desperate release from her terrible anguish.

"Mad! Mad! . . . If only it were true! And why not? The doctors say with certainty it is true, and all those here about me believe it. And so whatever I may do shall be the work of madness and of the perfidy of a beloved husband. That . . . that is as it should be. Felipe loves me; never have I been in an inn, nor have I seen a letter. That woman is not Aldare, but Beatrice. She is a ward of Don Juan Manuel and not the daughter of a Moorish king of Granada. How could I have believed such foolishness? All, all the effects of my delirium. Tell me, Marliano (*turning to each of the persons she names*), tell me, gentlemen, you Madam, you, Captain, you my husband: Is it not true that I am mad? It is certain, no one doubts it. What joy, eternal God, what joy! I thought I was a miserable wretch and it was not so. I was just crazy."

—From Act III, Scene XIV

3. The Tragic Realism of "High Comedy." The tendency toward realistic observation, and subsequent avoidance of romantic flights of fantasy, leads to the abandonment of historical subjects and to the study of contemporary society, materialistic and corrupt, which the dramatists subject to harsh criticism. This type of play, whose characters generally belong to the aristocracy, is called *alta comedia* or high drama.

Adelardo López de Ayala is one of the most characteristic writers of this movement. Born in 1828, he was a prominent figure both in literature and in politics. He took part in the September Revolution and became President of Congress. He died in 1879.

The society of his times is prominently portrayed in three major works: *El tejado de vidrio* [*The Roof of Glass*], in which an aging libertine initiates a young man into vice and thus causes the latter to bring dishonor to his own wife, *El tanto por ciento* [*The Percentage*], a study and satire of usury and materialism, and *Consuelo* [*Consolation*], in which the same theme is woven into a drama of love.

The desire to utilize a poetic tone for the most commonplace subject matter gave occasion for such unfortunate and ridiculous passages as the following one:

SABINO:	Sir,
	This gentleman awaits an answer.
PABLO (*to Roberto*):	You see my predicament?
ROBERTO:	What signature do you have?
PABLO:	My own.
ROBERTO:	Well, my friend, with no guarantee,
	five thousand duros, you can see . . .
PABLO:	Your friendly offer instills in me a sense of freedom . . .

ROBERTO: One thing is friendship
and something else, a business
deal.
The one that you propose me is
no good,
and what am I to do, in Heaven's
name?

PABLO: You know me well.

SABINO *(aside):*   Don Pablo's
look is thunderous.

PABLO: My honor.

ROBERTO: What can I do?
The most honorable of
gentlemen,
when he has no money . . .
has no money.

SABINO *(aside):*   And cannot pay.

ROBERTO: One must hock one's clothes
to pay one's debts.

ROBERTO: Well!

SABINO: Then you see what a frightening
state
we have come to here in Europe.

José Echegaray is the writer in whom the tragic realism of the *alta comedia* culminates. Born in Madrid in 1832, of excellent scientific and literary background, he had careers in both mathematics and politics. As a writer he has given us sensational and brilliant theater, but one with its roots in realism.

Echegaray was fundamentally a writer of melodramatic tragedy who liked to portray the conflicts of passion in all its brutality and violence. His milieu usually was the aristocracy of Madrid. Thus in *El gran galeoto* [*The Great Galeoto*] he utilizes a conflict provoked by slander. A gentleman named Don Julián feels toward a youth named Ernesto as toward a son, to the point of having him come to live in his home. He listens to the talk of persons who—like his brother Don Severo—ascribe to Ernesto an adulterous affair with Teodora, Don Julián's wife, who, the victim of a heart attack brought on by a fit of anger, falls dead.

The atmosphere of suspicion reaches such overwhelming proportions that it arouses violent passions in the characters in the play.

4. The *Sainete,* or One-act Farce. At the end of the nineteenth century there is a notable revival of the popular *sainete,* portraying scenes of Madrid, accompanied by melodious and typical music (Bretón, Chapí, Barbieri) which is known by the name of *género chico.* The best-known writers in this vein are Ricardo de la Vega, the author of *La verbena de la paloma;* Javier de Burgos, who wrote *El baile de Luis Alonso;* and López Silva and Fernández Shaw, creators of *La Revoltosa.*

Romanticism in Poetry

In studying the poetry of the Romantic school, we must take into account two fundamentally divergent tendencies: (*a*) that of those poets who follow in the pompous and rhetorical traditions of Lord Byron and of Victor Hugo—they cultivated external and brilliant form and wrote epic and descriptive poetry (The Duque de Rivas, Espronceda, la Avellaneda, Arolas, Zorrilla, Núñez de Arce); and (*b*) that of poets whose predilection is for subjective and sentimental themes expressed with sincerity and simplicity, more clearly lyrical (Bécquer, Carolina Coronado, Rosalía de Castro, and Nicomedes Pastor Díaz).

The Epic-Descriptive Tendencies

Within the epic-descriptive tendencies, the poetic work of the Duque de Rivas, whose importance in the creation of the romantic drama has been pointed out, won acclaim. Rivas' poems are notable for their evocative and descriptive force. One of them, *Al faro de Malta* [*To the Lighthouse of Malta*], a reminiscence of a tempestuous voyage of the poet, is one of the first fully romantic poems of Spanish literature. Because of this same power of description, his *leyendas* or legends are also noteworthy. In one of them, *El aniversario* [*The Anniversary*], he recounts how the skeletons of the conquerors of Bajadaz attend a commemorative mass in a year in which the city fathers, occupied with quarrels among themselves, have forgotten to hold it. In *La azucena mila-grosa* [*The Miraculous Lily*], he tells a tale of crime and expiation. Of his historical ballads (the interest in the ballad tradition be-came very intense), several have become well known, for example, *Una antigualla* [*An Ancient Custom*], on an episode in the life of Pedro el Cruel; *Don Alvaro de Luna,* which recounts the life of the Grand Constable; and *El solemne desengaño* [*The Solemn Disillusionment*], which concerns the conversion of Saint Francis of Borja.

El moro expósito [*The Moor in Danger*] is a long poem in hendecasyllabic ballad form in which the Duque de Rivas relates, with his own personal variations, the medieval legend of the Seven Infantes of Lara, their death at the instigation of Ruy Velázquez, and the vengeance which Mudarra, the "moro expó-sito," or bastard brother of the Infantes, exacts upon the latter. It is a work that has literary and historical worth but which, in final analysis, is monotonous. It was inspired by Sir Walter Scott.

Espronceda, in both life and works, exemplifies another phase of romanticism. The turbulent life of José de Espronceda is characteristic of the romantic excess of his times. He was born in Almendralejo (Badajoz) in 1808. He received a literary education under Don Alberto Lista, although he followed his teacher's precepts only in his youth. Of a fiery and impassioned temper-ament, he poured his intensity into both politics and love. His adventurous spirit carried him to different parts of Europe, and he died quite young, at the age of thirty-four, in 1842.

In politics Espronceda professed an ardent liberalism. As a child he was a member of a conspiratory society called *los Numantinos* whose discovery caused him to be banished to Gua-dalajara, and later to leave for Portugal. From there he traveled to England and after that to France where he took part in the Revolution of 1830, fighting behind the barricades. On his return to Spain, he was exiled once more (1833), but he found his place afterwards as a journalist, conspirator, Embassy Secretary and, finally, Deputy to Parliament as a militant member of the Pro-gressive Party and a defender of democracy.

One of his love affairs has become a sort of legend. In Lisbon while still quite young, Espronceda met and fell passionately in

love with Teresa Mancha, the daughter of a colonel who was also
an exile. When later on he went to England, he again met Teresa
who by this time was married, a fact which did not prevent the
poet's carrying her off with him to Paris. She became the heroine
of the famous *Canto a Teresa* [*Song to Teresa*]. Their love affair
had as its end a disastrous separation which their incompatibility
brought about and which deeply disillusioned Espronceda.

Espronceda personifies—in politics and love—the romantic
frenzy. Vehement and passionate, he wanted all his dreams to
become reality—but life with all its harsh and inflexible designs
only brought him disillusionment. Society was not good, as he
had envisaged it, and woman did not justify the faith placed in
her. It was this that was responsible for the poet's bitterness,
skepticism, and desperation.

> Flung as a rapid comet wide,
> on ardent fancy's wings I flew,
> where-er my wayward mind espied
> Or joys or triumphs to pursue.
> I launched myself, in daring flight,
> Beyond the world through heavenward space,
> And found but doubt, and all so bright
> That seem'd, illusive proved the chase.
>
> Then on earth I anxious sought
> For virtue, glory, love sublime;
> And my worn spirit found there nought
> But fetid dust and loathsome slime.
> Mid clouds with heavenly hues o'ercast
> Women of virgin lustre shone;
> I saw, I touch'd them, and they pass'd.
> And smoke and ashes left alone.
>
> I found the illusion fled; but rife,
> Unquench'd desires their longings crave;
> I felt the real, I hated life,
> And peace believed but in the grave.

—From "To Harifa in an Orgy"
Translation by James Kennedy

Espronceda's biography—aside from his humanistic education under the tutelage of Alberto Lista—is replete with the romantic psychology. As conspirator and exile, politics gave to him, in a collective sense, all the emotions of ambition and of nostalgia; in a personal sense, his love affair with Teresa Mancha came, as we know, to the disastrous end which so appropriately gave a "flavor of the times" to his anguish. The expression of these sentiments, consequently, mirrors the intensity of his brief existence, an intensity which is doubtlessly the primary characteristic of Espronceda's work.

The poet protests against social injustice and in his verses frequently portrays social outcasts such as the beggar and executioner. In his patriotic poems he defends liberty and exalts the uprising of *Torrijos* and *Joaquín de Pablo* (*Chapalangarra*), with whom he fought and was defeated. In his poem *Al dos de mayo* [*On the Second of May*], he does not limit himself to attacking the French invaders; he also lashes out against the Francophile aristocracy and points out that only the lower classes—the rabble —threw themselves without hesitation into the struggle against the enemies of the fatherland. The following poem represents the poet's spirit of rebellion:

Pirate's Song

With cannon on port and starboard,
Wind just aft and strong,
Flying the sea, not ploughing through,
A brigantine skims along.
She is called the Dreaded by a host
And feared on every side,
From the eastern to the western coast,
Wherever she may ride.

Across the sea the moonlight shines,
The wind goes wailing through,
Shrill the canvas, ruffling waves
Of silver and of blue.

There on the poop the captain sings
By whom the band is led,
With Asia left and Europe right
And Istanbul ahead.

Sail on, swift bark, at my command.
So brave and bold,
No warship by your foeman manned,
Nor storm, nor calm, nor any force
Shall turn you from your chosen course
Nor daunt your hardy soul.

A score of ships
We've seized aright
And this despite
The English fleet.
And I have forced
A hundred lords
To lay their swords
Beneath my feet.

My only treasure a pirate ship,
My god but liberty,
My law, brute force and a hearty wind,
My land, the open sea.

—From "Pirate's Song"
Translation by Alice McVan

Espronceda, along with Zorrilla, is one of the two most popular poets of the romantic movement. His style is direct and expressive. It describes with intensity and a powerful sense of imagination, and gives us an exact picture of the poet's visions. His themes are always suggestive and picturesque and are well fitted to the music of his verse. Among his famous works are the *Canción al pirata* [*Pirate's Song*], *Himno al sol* [*Hymn to the Sun*], *El reo de muerte* [*Death's Criminal,*] *A Jarifa en una orgía* [*To Harifa in an Orgy*], and *La vuelta del cruzado* [*The Return from the Crusade*].

Despite its power, however, Espronceda's poetic output was highly uneven. Along with magnificent successes, he shows lamentable carelessness and wrote tedious passages in poor taste. He imitated the English poet Byron and the Frenchman Alfred de Vigny.

Espronceda utilized from the very first a vocabulary typical of the period. He eventually became so fully a part of the spirit of his times that his literary diction is of an insurmountable effectiveness. Let us add to this that Espronceda was a penetrating observer; his sense of plasticity enabled him to focus on objects with the keen eye of a painter, or more precisely, of an engraver or an etcher. His imaginative tracings are indelible. Intense and plastic, the poet possessed the two major talents needed for being, as he was, the great popular poet of romanticism. He was of service to his epoch and to his people with his nervous gesticulating and direct style. Romantic and very Spanish, both to the very marrow of his bones, Espronceda is the typical example of the poet who felt no necessity to purge his work of all that was not strictly poetry. Lista said of him that he was "like a great bullring, but with a lot of rabble inside."

One of his best known works is *El estudiante de Salamanca* [*The Student of Salamanca*]. Utilizing the legend about a student named Lisardo who, as a punishment for his disorderly life, came face to face one day with the spectacle of his own funeral, Espronceda wrote an imaginative tale in verse whose protagonist, Don Félix de Montemayor, is portrayed in the following passage:

> A second Don Juan Tenorio,
> Of proud and insolent bearing,
> Blasphemous yet valiant,
> Haughty and to quarreling born.

The last and most terrible adventure of Don Félix (after seeing his own funeral procession go by) has him follow the silhouette of a woman, who, when she uncovers her face, is seen to be a frightful skeleton.

The tale is not a new one. Espronceda took it from an old

Spanish legend which had already been used by several writers
of the Golden Age. Zorrilla borrowed from the same story for his
El Capitán Montoya. It was Espronceda, however, who gave the
material its most impressively dramatic treatment. In the work
fantastic descriptions of an almost Surrealistic intensity abound.
In them, Espronceda utilized all sorts of metrical combinations,
ranging from the hendecasyllabic line to words of a single syllable.

The *Diablo mundo* [*This Devil World*] is the poet's most
extensive poem. Its development is extravagant and uneven. The
protagonist, named Adam, is miraculously restored to youth and
is thereby unspoiled by the evils and hypocrisy of society as he
re-begins life. Nevertheless, after a series of grotesque incidents,
he ends up in prison. The conclusion is arbitrary and questionable. Literarily, the *Diablo mundo* contains both successfully and
unsuccessfully executed passages. Within the length of the poem
one goes from the heights of imagination to the most coarse
sarcasms.

Although not belonging to the poem in structure or context,
Espronceda's masterpiece, the *Canto a Teresa* [*Song to Theresa*],
which may be considered the prototype of love poetry in Spanish
romanticism, is included in the *Diablo mundo*. The poet describes, on his part, the woman he loves with all the beauty of
love's early illusion; afterwards comes the anguish of disillusionment. The poem reflects, with its structural use of time past, time
present, love's happiness, and love's deceit, Espronceda's own experience with Teresa Mancha. The following is an illustrative
fragment of the poem:

> How then did you fall to earth,
> Bright star of radiant dawn?
> Angel of light, who cast you down
> From heaven to this vale of tears.
>
> . . . . .
>
> Alas, a fallen angel woman is,
> Or creature made of common clay,
> A being who was born to weep
> Or live an automaton in this world.

With fire from deepest hell,
The devil in his Eden lost,
Embraced our Mother Eve, and since
For womankind their heritage has been.

In *Sancho Saldaña o el castellano de Cuellar,* which is often called simply by the name of its protagonist, Sancho Saldaña, Espronceda tried his hand, with less success, at the historical novel of the type written by Sir Walter Scott. He also attempted the drama based on legendary material as in his *Blanca de Borbón,* and the epic poem, *Pelayo,* a work he never finished. His literary reputation has lived on for his poetry rather than his other works.

His natural instincts, his ideals, the circumstances of his hazardous life, the times in which he lived, took him down another path, and he expressed what he felt: pain and doubt, and he expressed them admirably, prodigiously, with more intensity than anyone else because he felt things more deeply. He was, to put it briefly, a Romantic, the first of Spanish Romantics in the technical as well as in the popularly accepted sense of the word.

—A. Bonilla y San Martín

Gertrudis Gómez de Avellaneda, who was born in Cuba in 1814, is generally considered a Spanish poetess both by inspiration and because of her residence in Madrid for the major part of her life. An impetuous and impassioned writer, she wrote poetry which are paeans to nature, such as *Al sol* [*To the Sun*] and *Al mar* [*To the Sea*], and poems of love. She also wrote, in keeping with the tastes of the times, several novels such as *Sab* whose protagonist is a mulatto slave who loves the daughter of his master, a theme typical of the type of sentimentality found in Rousseau. From her pen also came several historical dramas, one of the best of which is *Alfonso Munio.*

Juan Arolas, who was born in Barcelona in 1805, was a priest. His poetic work is characteristic of the romantic longing to forge worlds of fantasy and dream. Thus in his *Caballerescas* he evokes the splendor of the Middle Ages, peopling it with heroes, which has come down to us in the *Chronicles* and the *Ballads*. In his *Orientales*, which is his best work, Arolas describes for us, in magnificent colors, scenes of love and adventure whose protagonists are sultans, odalisques, and pirates. He places them in an environment both barbarous and refined, which oscillates between burning desert and a palace full of magnificence. His evocations show an easy and musical style. No doubt, the most important of these legends is the one entitled *Granada* in which the poet recounts, with great richness of form, the conquest of Granada by the Catholic Kings.

In these works of Zorrilla inspired by legend, we should note, along with the magnificence of the descriptions, the skill of the poet in creating interest, presenting his characters surrounded by intrigue and mystery, in picturesque and remote environments so that the reader's imagination is awakened to the plot which unfolds before him.

Gaspar Núñez de Arce, who was born in Valladolid in 1834, held important positions in Spanish political life and attained great literary prestige. The style of Núñez de Arce is, in general, rhetorical and grandiloquent, but his work is not lacking in expressive and rhythmical effectiveness although it is sometimes marred by mediocrity and commonplaces. Thematically, his poetic work shows great strength and a philosophical bent. His most famous work is entitled *Gritos de Combate* [*Battle Cries*].

Núñez de Arce also wrote historical drama in *El haz de leña* [*The Bundle of Firewood*], a play that treats the theme of the relationship between Philip II and Prince Don Carlos and that gives a version adjusted to historical fact and, thereby, different from the distortions of legend. A poem in tercets, *Raimundo Lulio*, centers on the figure of the great philosopher from Mallorca as the personification of human reason. In *La visión de fray Martín* [*The Vision of Fray Martín*], he deals with the doubts of Martin Luther. In *La última lamentación de Lord Byron* [*The Last Lament of Lord Byron*], he has the great English poet recount events of his life and describe the splendors of ancient Greece.

La selva oscura [*The Dark Forest*], an imitation of the *Divine*

Comedy, has a symbolic character. Núñez de Arce also wrote works based on legend. His *Vértigo* [*Vertigo*] enjoys a well-merited fame and is written in magnificent *décimas*.

As we stated when speaking of his dramatic works, José Zorrilla excels in epic rather than lyrical poetry, that is to say, he is far better at describing, with sensitive brush strokes, what he sees and imagines than what he feels. Because of this his narrations on legendary themes are justly famous, for example, *El Capitán Montoya* (whose plot recalls *El estudiante de Salamanca*), *Margarita la Tornera* [*Margarita the Turnkey*], or *A buen juez mejor testigo* [*Best Witness for the Judge*]. The last of these is the most popular of all, in which a saint's statue of Christ miraculously causes a man to keep the promise he had given to a young lady at the moment she asks for justice from the Governor of Toledo, Ruiz de Alarcón.

Subjective and Sentimentalist Tendencies

Gustavo Adolfo Bécquer is the purest and most sensitive of romantic poets. He is the poet who most fully characterizes the subjective and sentimental tradition.

Bécquer was born in Seville in 1836. His real name was Domínguez Bastida but he preferred to use Bécquer, the family name of his ancestors, a Flemish family which settled in Seville in the seventeenth century. His life was a continuous catastrophic encounter with the material world. He was orphaned while quite young and left for Madrid in search of glory while still a youth; he worked on publications and in offices as a journalist and bureaucrat, earning a modest living when he was not out of work. He traveled around Spain with his brother, the painter Valeriano Bécquer. Ill with tuberculosis and living a life of privation, Gustavo Adolfo died in Madrid at the age of thirty-four in 1870.

The best autobiographical work of Bécquer is the *Cartas desde mi celda* [*Letters from a Monastery Cell*], written from the Monastery of Veruela to which he had gone in 1864 to recuperate from his illness.

1. The *Rimas* or *Rhymes*. Bécquer's poetry is essentially a world of visions. Over this dramatic and commonplace world,

he created another that aspired to illusion and fantasy. Like a
good romantic, he evaded and scorned all that was prosaic in life.
For him poetry was the creation of an ideal kingdom where
everything is spirit and beauty because it is the fruit of sentiment.
He did not speak to the senses but to the heart. Because of this
his poetry is neither sonorous nor brilliant; it is simple and tender,
intimately subjective.

The Waiting Harp

There in the dusky alcove of the room,
Perchance forgotten by its covering of dust,
    The harp was seen.

How many a song was slumbering in its strings,
As some bird-breast sleeping on the boughs,
Waiting the snowy hand whose master touch
    Shall waken it!

Alas, me thought—how often genius halts
And drowses thus within the bosom's depth,
Hoping to hear a voice, like Lazarus,
To say its message—"Soul, arise and walk!"

—*Rima VII*
Translation by Thomas Walsh

Bécquer's basic theme is love. His *Rimas* are inspired by the
beloved woman, the symbol itself of poetry, as in *rima* XXI:

What is poetry, you say,
Holding my eyes with yours of blue,
What is poetry? . . . You ask that?
Poetry . . . it is you!

—Translation by Ina Duvall Singleton

Thus the loved one is something immaterial and perfect,
created in tender simplicity in the love-inspired mind of the poet.

The very atoms of the air
Seemed warmed and stirring everything;
The sky with golden light suffused;
The earth grown bright with dawn unused;
I hear in waves of carolings
The sound of kisses, sweep of wings;
I close mine eyes,—what happens there?—
—The passing-by of Love the Fair!—

—Translation by Roderick Gill

Reality, nevertheless, destroys the poet's dreams because the woman does not understand him or she forgets him. It is then that the writer expresses his disillusionment.

As the arrow from the flesh is torn,
So tore I from my breast her love. . . .

From there, the poet in his anguish turns to thoughts of death:

They closed her eyes
That were still open;
They hid her face
With a white linen,
And, some sobbing,
Others in silence,
From the sad bedroom
All came away.
The nightlight in a dish
Burned on the floor;
It threw on the wall
The bed's shadow,
One saw sometime
Drawn in sharp line
The body's shape.
The dawn appeared,
At its first whiteness
With its thousand noises
The town awoke.

Before that contrast
Of light and darkness,
Of life and strangeness
I thought a moment.
My God, how lonely
The dead are!

On the shoulders of men
To the church they bore her,
And in a chapel
They left her bier.
There they surrounded
Her pale body
With yellow candles
And black stuffs.
At the last stroke
Of the ringing for the Souls
An old crone finished
Her last prayers.
The doors moaned,
And the Holy place
Remained deserted.
From a clock one heard
The measured ticking,
And from a candle
The guttering.
All things there
Were so dark and mournful
So cold and rigid,
That I thought a moment:
My God, how lonely
The dead are!

—From *Rima LXXIII*
Translation by John Masefield

Only poetry remains forever, mysterious and beautiful:

Say not that, its treasure exhausted,
The lyre is mute, lacking a melody:

There may be no poets, but forever
   Poesy will be.
As long as the waves quiver glowingly
   At dawning's caress;
As long as the sun doth, with fire and gold,
   The flying clouds dress;
As long as the breezes are laden with
   Fragrance and harmony;
As long as the springtime comes to the earth,
   Poesy will be!

—From *Rima IV*
Translation by Young Allison

The poems of Bécquer, published under the title of *Rimas,* are of limited length and number (there are some seventy of them.) His style is simple and sincere, without artifice or rhetorical embellishment.

In some poems he was influenced by Lord Byron and Heinrich Heine.

2. The *Leyendas* or *Legenos.* Gustavo Adolfo Bécquer's prose works also answer to the desire to forget the coarseness of everyday life. In his *Leyendas* everything becomes extraordinary, fantastic and mysterious.

Remote environments, such as India; distant epochs, such as the Middle Ages; melancholy and magical scenes of castles in ruins and nymphs in sylvan pools bathed by moonlight. Apparitions from beyond the grave (*Maese Pérez el Organista* or *Master Perez the Organist*); fantastic women who incite men to sacrilege (*La ajorca de oro* or *The Necklace of Gold*), to madness (*El rayo de luna* or *The Moonbeam*) or death (*Los ojos verdes* or *The Eyes of Green*).

Describing picturesque or inaccessible places and heroic and gallant customs, Bécquer, in his narrative legends, shows a limitless imagination and an impressive prose style.

The night was a quiet and beautiful one, the moon shone down in all its fullness from the highest point of the heavens, and the wind whispered with the delicate rustle of the leaves in the trees.

Manrique came to the cloister, looked into its enclosure and peered between the massive columns of its archways. . . . . It was deserted.

He left it and turned his steps toward the shadowy poplar grove along the Duero and had barely stepped into it when from his lips there burst a cry of joy.

For one brief moment he had caught a fleeting glimpse of the white gown, the white gown of the woman of his dreams, of the woman whom he already loved to the point of madness.

He runs, runs in his search and comes to the place in which he has seen her disappear; but when he gets there, he stops, fixes his terrified gaze on the ground and stands a moment transfixed; a slight tremor which grows stronger, which grows stronger and takes on all the symptoms of a convulsion and finally breaks forth in a sonorous, strident, horrible laughter.

That object, white, filmy, floating, had shone again before his eyes; but it had shone at his feet for an instant, no more than an instant.

It was a moonbeam, a moonbeam which shone through the openings between the arched roof of the trees when the wind moved its branches.

—From *El rayo de luna*

The subjective and sentimental style of Gustavo Adolfo Bécquer, by its delicate tenderness, influenced two Spanish women poets, Carolina Coronado and Rosalía de Castro de Murguía.

The poetry of Carolina Coronado, who was born in 1823, is all sentiment and love. The object of this love, which at first is a human one, becomes increasingly more spiritual and profound, and finally acquires an almost mystical tone. The impassioned delicacy of her poetry is impressive.

Rosalía de Castro de Murguía reflects in her work the melancholy tenderness of the landscape of her native Galicia where she was born in Santiago de Compostela in 1837; her poetry evokes the mystery of things she perceives and cannot see and the sadness of loves that are past. Her poems in Spanish were published with the title *En las orillas del Sar* [*On the Banks of the Sar*].

Nicomedes Pastor Díaz, who was born in Vivero, Lugo, in 1811, is the poet of melancholy and torment, all the illusions that never can be or have been lost forever. The dead loved one, night bathed by a pale moonlight, a melancholy and solitary landscape and the unhappiness of his destiny are his favorite themes.

As a prose writer, he has left us a curious novel entitled *De Villa hermosa a la China* [*From Villahermosa to China*] and a series of critical studies called *Galería de españoles célebres contemporáneos* [*Portraits of Illustrious Spaniards of Our Times*] which are indispensable for anyone studying Spanish romantic literature.

Romanticism in the Novel

Interest in the medieval period, considered a mystical, impassioned, and chivalric period, appeared in Spanish romanticism through the advent of historical novels which, in imitation of Sir Walter Scott, began to be published in the Peninsula.

Ramón López Soler, the author of *Los Bandos de Castilla* [*The Factions of Castille*], introduced the genre. Among the best known writers of this type are Francisco Navarro Villoslada, author of *Amayo, o los vascos en el siglo VIII* [*Amayo, or The Basques in the Eighth Century*] and Enrique Gil Carrasco, who created the best Spanish historical novel, *El señor de Bembibre*. Larra also wrote historical works such as *El doncel de don Enrique el Doliente,* as did Espronceda in his *Sancho Saldaña.*

A common defect of these novels, which are based on legendary or little-known episodes of chivalric life with tourneys, adventures, abductions, is the artificiality of both the characters portrayed in them and the historical environment in which the action takes place, a result of a lack of sound knowledge about the Middle Ages.

There also appeared numerous serial novels which were

frequently sold to the public in cheap pamphlet form and were historical in theme. Many authors, like Manuel Fernández y González, wasted their literary talents in writing for a public avid for action and adventure. Among Fernández's many works are *El cocinero de Su Majestad* [*Chef to His Majesty*] and *Men Rodríquez de Sanabria*. The serial novel touched on social problems, but generally concentrated on facile and sentimental subject matter chosen for its appeal to a public of poor literary taste. This is true in the case of *María o la hija del jornalero* [*Maria or the Workman's Daughter*] by Wenceslao Ayguals de Izco.

There was also interest in tales based on folkloric materials, as has already been noted. This trend is reflected in the work of the *costumbrista* writers. In the novel it inspired stories from the oral tradition. Best known of the writers in this vein is Antonio de Trueba who was well acquainted with the poetry of the people (*Libro de los cantares*) and who left us in prose his *Cuentos campesinos* [*Country Tales*] and his *Cuentos de color de rosa* [*Tales the Color of the Rose*].

Literary *costumbrismo* resulted in the observation of reality. The writer took interest in what he saw about him, providing it was picturesque or evocative. This artistic procedure, based on observation, counterbalanced to a certain extent the longing of the romantics to feign worlds of fantasy. The novel is less adaptable than poetry for this type of writing. Consequently, *costumbrismo* rapidly adapted to narration and made an important contribution to the development of the modern novel.

The Spanish novel in the *costumbrista* tradition was created by Cecilia Böhl de Faber, who wrote under the man's name of Fernán Caballero. She was born in Switzerland, the daughter of the German Hispanist Nicolas Böhl de Faber who resided all his life in Spain, and she made the Spanish world the setting of her works. "The novel," the authoress tells us, "is not created; it is observed."

In speaking of the descriptive passages in Fernán Caballero's works, Emilia Pardo Bazán wrote: "A patio in Fernán Caballero's work comes to life before us and delights our eyes with its flowers, and our ear with the sound of water, the clucking of hens and the innocent chatter of children."

This description of environment is what interests us above all in her novels, as, for example, in the work which first brought her fame, *La Gaviota* [*The Sea Gull*]. The plot is as follows: Marisalada, a girl of humble background—who is called *la gaviota* or the Gull because of her gift for the imitation of the song of birds—marries a German doctor, Stein, who gives her social position and takes her to live in Madrid where she is known for the beauty of her voice. She falls in love with a bullfighter and is subsequently abandoned by her husband who leaves for America where he dies shortly afterwards. The bullfighter is killed in the bull ring and *la gaviota*, an outcast, returns to her native village and marries a barber.

Romanticism in Hispanic Literature

The interest in things medieval—characteristic of romanticism—aroused in Catalonia a curiosity about its own national period with a resultant dual linguistic-literary orientation similar to the one which occurred in Provence, thanks to the work of Frederick Mistral who became famous for his poem *Mireya*. In Catalonia, the tendency from the very first was toward restoring the vernacular, debased by rustic expressions, to the status of a literary language. This movement received the name of *Renaixence* (that is to say, Renaissance) and began with the *Oda a la Patria* [*Ode to the Fatherland*] (1832) of Buenaventura Carlos Aribau.

Actually Catalonian literature had never stopped being created, but the authors, including Vicente García, Rector de Vallfogona, did not have enough strength to invigorate the literature at the time it was eclipsed by the brilliance of the Golden Age of Spanish (i.e., Castilian) literature.

In the early years of the nineteenth century two famous periodicals made their appearance in Barcelona, *El Europeo* and *El Vapor*, which introduced romantic tastes in Spain as well as interest in the national period of Catalonia, a fact which had political, linguistic and literary consequences. In 1859 the institution of *Juegos Florales,* a type of poetry contest, like those of Provence, was reinstated and this had important results in stimulating the creation of new Catalonian poetry. Two poets soon emerged to preeminence, Joaquín Rubio y Ors and Victor Valaguer.

At the same time in Valencia there was inaugurated a group called *Lo Rat Penat* in which the Valencian poetry of Teodoro Llorente immediately became prominent. In addition scholarship in Catalonian and Provençal literatures gained in luster and value through the studies of Don Manuel Milá y Fontanals, the teacher of Menéndez y Pelayo. At the end of the century Catalonian literature counted in its ranks two major figures, Angel Guimerá and Jacinto Verdaguer.

Angel Guimerá (1847–1924) was the creator of a Catalonian theater which up to that time had been reduced to the trivial and commonplace works of Federico Soler who wrote under the name of Serafi Pitarra. Guimerá's theater compares favorably with the finest European theater of his time and includes (a) Plays of historical setting, such as *Gala Placidia, Rei i monjo, Judith de Welp;* (b) Naturalistic descriptions of rural life, such as *La Fiesta del Trigo* [*Wheat Festival*]; (c) The transformation of these descriptions into allegorical concepts including *Mar i cel*—the struggle between love and duty of a pirate, Said, and a Christian, Blanca, which ends in tragedy, and *Terra baixa (Tierra baja)* or *Lowland,* which portrays the social struggles of a humble shepherd named Manelic and the oppressor of his freedom and his feelings.

To this same period belong the dramas of the well-known painter Santiago Rusiñol who wrote tragedies such as *El Mistic,* sentimental plays such as *El pati blau,* and satirical works such as *L'Alegria que passa.*

The most outstanding figure of Catalonian literature in the nineteenth century is doubtless the priest Jacinto Verdaguer (1845–1902) who considerably enriched his native tongue with elements from his local home country (Vich). As a lyric poet he also stands out for the popular flavor which he imparted to his compositions, many of them truly songs of a folkloric character. His poetry is predominantly religious in theme.

The religious sense of Verdaguer recalls that of Saint Francis.

Animals, plants, and objects are the confidants of the poet who, through all of these, rises to the fervent heights of mysticism. His best works include *Flors del Calvari, El somni de Sant Joan,* and *Roser de tot l'any.*

Verdaguer wrote the most important Spanish epic poem of the nineteenth century, *La Atlántida,* a magnificent composition of more than twenty-five hundred lines which tell, in robust and resonant strophes, the sinking of the continent Atlantis of which today nothing remains but the Teide—"the finger of its ferrous hand, which seems to tell us: Atlantis stood here."

The sinking is due to divine punishment for the vices and ambitions of the Atlantians or Titans, the offspring of Atlas and Hesperis who sought to climb to the sky and dethrone God.

Another major epic poem of Verdaguer is *Canigó,* descriptive in character (it portrays the natural beauties of the mountain from which the poem takes its name) and legendary (the adventures of a knight, Gentil, who, charmed by a fairy, ceases his struggle and brings about a change in his uncle, Count Wilfredo, who repents and founds a monastery).

At the same time as this was occurring in Catalonia, romanticism was awakening in Galicia the memory of a glorious literary past and the desire to rejuvenate both language and literature.

Similarly, the establishment of *Juegos Florales* literary competition (1861) gave new impetus to poetry in the vernacular as in the case of the publication of the *Biblioteca Gallega,* a series of books in Galician.

The first major figures of the period are Manuel Curros Enríquez, a specialist in legendary materials and the country customs of Galicia (*Airiños da mina terra*) and Valentín Lamas Carvajal, the inspired singer in *Espiñas, follas e frores.*

In Portugal, meanwhile, as in the rest of Europe, boredom with Arcadian themes set in and a more idealistic environment and a taste for more independence began to grow. It was a youthful student who had emigrated for political reasons, Almeida Garret (1779–1854), who assimilated the new ideas current in England and in France. His best work, the play *Fray Luis de Sousa,* marks the triumph of romanticism in Portuguese literature.

The liberty which romanticism brings to the style and

thought of the writer had a productive influence in Latin America.

In Argentina liberal romanticism took the form of opposition to the tyranny of the dictator Rosas. Among the writers are José Mármol (1818–1871) whose vibrant lines, in the style of Byron, and whose novel, *Amalia,* in the style of Sir Walter Scott, expound his ideas; Esteban Echevarría (1805–1851), another poet of the style of Byron, who attacked tyranny in *El Matadero* [*The Slaughterhouse*], and Domingo Faustino Sarmiento, who in his book *Facundo o Civilización y Barbarie* [*Facundo, or Civilization and Barbarity*], masterfully describes the gauchos and the countryside of the pampas in the epoch of Rosas against whom he fought tenaciously. Sarmiento is Argentina's greatest educator.

The gaucho became hero and poet or *payador.* In the poem of José Hernández (1834–1886), *Martín Fierro,* the gaucho hero, in a witty colloquial style, tells the story of his life, happy at first and later disturbed by struggle and misfortune.

A place of honor in Latin American romanticism is also due to the Uruguayan Juan Zorrilla San Martín (1855–1931) who in his lengthy poem *Tabaré* portrays the figure of a sentimental Indian, educated to Christianity, who loves a Spanish woman. The poem ends with the tragic death of the protagonist. Also worthy of note is Florencio Sánchez, the creator of a popular theater with his *M'hijo el doctor* [*M'son the Doctor*].

In Peru, a deep sense of popular and humorous tradition, plus a major power of description, is to be found in *Tradiciones peruanas* [*Peruvian Traditions*] by Ricardo Palma (1833–1919).

Ecuador has a vibrant poet, classical in form and romantic in spirit, in José Joaquín Olmedo (1780–1847), the exalted singer of the victories of Bolívar in his *La victoria de Junín* [*The Victory of Junín*]. Also noteworthy is Juan Montalvo (1833–1899), a vigorous liberal in spirit, and formidable assimilator in the style of the Spanish classics in his book *Capítulos que se le olvidaron a Cervantes* [*Chapters That Cervantes Forgot*], a work which purports to continue the *Quixote.*

Colombia, in this period, produced two major poets in José Eusebio Caro (1817–1853), of an energetic and polished style, the exalted singer of liberty, and in Rafael Pombo (1833–1912), a lyric poet full of sentiment and melancholy. To Colombian literature we owe the most famous romantic novel of Hispanic America, *María* by José Isaacs (1837–1895).

Another important figure of this period is the Venezuelan Andrés Bello (1781–1865), an erudite Hispanist and scholar of the Castilian language who made major contributions to the knowledge of Medieval Spanish literature and wrote a long poem, *América*, with an introduction entitled *Alocución a la poesía* [*Allocution to Poetry*], and the famous *Silva a la agricultura de la zona tórrida* [*Silva on Agriculture in the Tropics*] in which he fuses his classical knowledge with the impassioned notes of color with which he exalts the natural beauty of the tropics.

The independence of Mexico also had its impassioned voices, in writers like Andrés Quintana Roo, from Yucatán, the exalter of liberty in his native land, and José Fernández de Lizardi, who, under the pen name of "El Pensador Mejicano," studied the problems and needs of his country. The latter also wrote a curious novel, picaresque in style, under the title of *El Periquillo Sarmiento* [*The Itching Parrot*].

In Cuba the romantic fervor in literature coincided with the most difficult period of her struggle for independence. Among many others is the romantic and patriotic writer, Gabriel de la Concepción Valdés, better known by his pseudonym of Plácido, a melancholy poet who vividly described the beauty of his native land. However, exceeding all others is José Martí (1853–1895), who died for the liberty of his country and who was an extraordinary orator who wrote *Versos sencillos* [*Simple Verses*] and a delightful book for children, *Ismaelillo*.

Even in the remote area of the Pacific, in the Philippines, Spain laid the fertile seeds of her language. By the nineteenth century a considerable literature already existed there in the Castilian tongue. The major figure is that of the poet José Rizal (1861–1896) whose most famous work is the novel *Noli me tangere*.

Reactions Against Romanticism

Ironical and Regional Poetry

The novel of sociological realism appeared as a logical reaction against the fantastic elements of the romantic historical novel. The writer, grown tired of remote, fictional worlds, set himself to observing the actual world, and the decline of romanticism began. Once more we are in the presence of a literary atmosphere which provided a new and completely antithetical feeling. The weariness with romanticism's modes and styles can be perceived in a series of symptoms which, with varying degrees of intensity, may be interpreted as reactions against the declining movement.

These reactions against romanticism can be perceived first of all in poetry where the new movement employed irony in place of surprise as used by the Romantics and skepticism in place of vehemence and passionate outburst.

In the area of lyrical poetry, emotive and sentimental expression became meditated statement, transformed by disenchantment and by an accurate observation of reality which no longer provoked a desperate gesture of disillusionment, but a bitter philosophical phrase.

This description fits the style of Don Ramón de Campoamor who was born in Navia in 1817 and died in Madrid in 1901. Early in his career, Campoamor wrote two epic poems, *Colón* [*Columbus*] and *El drama Universal* [*The Universal Drama*], the latter a daring imitation of Dante in which appear a series of legendary personages who symbolize human passions.

Campoamor's best known creations, however, are short poems. These do not sing of human passions; they make judgments on them. Human sentiments are analyzed in his verses and a moral lesson is drawn in them. His poems are marked by ingenuity and simplicity which made them very popular. Campoamor usually divided them into *humoradas, doloras,* and *pequeños poemas,* according to whether the narration was of lesser or greater length.

In almost all of them there is an emotional conflict which the poet enlarges upon and, ironically, resolves.

> Twenty years go by and he returns.
> Both he and she, they think by turns:
> "By all the saints! Could this be he?"
> "Why bless my soul! Could this be she?"

> —From the *Humoradas*

Other works of Campoamor, of philosophical and critical character, are of less importance than his poetry.

The poetry of Joaquín María Bartrina, who was born in Reus in 1850, shows a skepticism which is a similar reaction against romanticism. It is contained in his book *Algo* [*Something*]. Bartrina is the poet of doubt; love, progress, and his native land were the objects of his ironical disquisitions. There is, however, in the background of his skepticism a bitter but helpful lesson.

> To ascertain where someone's from,
> You know as quickly as he speaks.
> The Englishman will England praise,
> Of Prussia Frenchmen say it reeks,
> And Spaniards speak no good of Spain.

> —From *Arabescos*

The observation of reality that led to irony and skepticism as reactions against romantic fantasies also appears in the work of a group of poets who expressed another reaction through regionalism.

In Castile, José María Gabriel y Galán, the son of a farming family, was a teacher in the provinces of Salamanca and Cáceres from 1870 to 1905. While there he gained a thorough knowledge of the sayings and ways of shepherds and farm people. He entitled his poems *Campesinas* [*Country Verses*] and *Castellanas* [*Castilian Verses*]. They are characterized by:

1. A notable vigor in his descriptions of the Castilian plain, reflected in noble classical strophes. In *El Ama* [*The Housewife*], for example, the figure of the poet's wife presides over the serenity of the countryside.

2. A deep sense of tradition and of Christianity which teaches one resignation when faced with the hardships of country life.

One of his books of poetry, *Extremeñas,* is written in the country dialect of the northern parts of the province of Cáceres. His best known works are *El Embargo,* the tragedy of a humble man who is ruined to no purpose in the hope of saving his wife from death, and *El Cristu Benditu* in which the joys of fatherhood are extolled.

In Murcia, Vicente Medina (born in 1866) established his reputation with the publication of his *Aires murcianos* [*Airs of Murcia*]. Like Gabriel y Galán, Medina utilized the language of the people, but in describing the life of the humble country folk, he intensively depicts the suffering and helplessness of the poor.

In Valencia the most notable writers of the period are Vicente Wenceslao Querol and Teodoro Dorente.

Vincente Wenceslao Querol's best known work is his *Rimas* [*Rhymes*] which are characterized by ample phrasing and by the traditional themes of religion, family, and country.

Teodoro Llorente did a translation of Goethe's *Faust* and wrote several books of verse in Valencian dialect.

Andalusia is represented by Salvador Rueda. He was born in Malaga in 1857 and became enormously popular with his sonorous poetry, which is both rich and brilliant but a bit superficial. His verses are musical and take changing and new forms. His subject matter comes from the splendid spectacle of nature in Andalusia which he paints with all its light.

He is spoken of as a predecessor of the modernism of Rubén Darío which became the first characteristic school of twentieth-century poetry.

The Realistic and Psychological Novels

The failure of the historical novel and the sense of reality which the minor genre of "costumbrismo" had given made possible, along with what happened in the theater, the continuation of the realistic tradition in Spanish literature and the advent of the realistic novel.

Pedro Antonio de Alarcón was born in Guádix in the Province of Granada in 1833 of a good family of modest means. He studied law and theology but he succumbed to the lure of literature and left home and studies to go to Granada and later to Madrid. Imbued with revolutionary ideas, Alarcón became a fiery anticlerical polemicist. He was challenged to a duel by the writer Heriberto García de Quevedo who magnanimously shot his pistol into the air.

This was a decisive incident in Alarcón's life; henceforth he withdrew from political activity and his conservatism grew with his mature years. When war was declared in Africa, Alarcón enlisted as a volunteer. He took active part in the fighting and was wounded. Later he became affiliated with the monarchist party and actively combated political demagoguery. He was a deputy, a counselor of state and a member of the Royal Academy. He died in 1891.

The double ideological aspect of Alarcón's life, revolutionary youth and mature conservatism, is reflected in his novels. Frequently his characters are symbolic of good or of evil and the action is a conflict between the two tendencies. In some works, such as El escándalo [The Scandal], reason, i.e., goodness, triumphs; in others like El niño de la bola [The Child with the Globe], end with victory over passion and evil.

The short story is the genre which was primarily responsible for Alarcón's fame. This was due to the popular nature of his themes and the witty ingenuity with which he developed them. He took his stories from narratives he had heard as a child and which were derived from oral traditions or were the so-called romances de ciegos or blindman's ballads. Alarcón's short stories may be grouped in three series, love tales, stories from Spanish history, and improbable narratives. The delightful *El sombrero de tres picos* [*Three-Cornered Hat*] which tells the tale of the revenge which the miller takes on the *Corregidor* for having tried to seduce his wife, although not belonging to any one of these groups, is a sort of long short story.

The nucleus of the narrative is to be found as early as Boccaccio, but Alarcón became acquainted with it through songs and ballads like *El molinero de Arcos* [*The Miller of Arcos*] and *El Corregidor y la Molinera* [*The Miller's Wife*] of popular character.

Although Alarcón is inimitable in the simple and witty short story, he also excelled in longer narratives, nourished, as we have said, by his descriptive facility and his ideological preoccupations. In some works, as in *El Capitán Veneno,* he demonstrates the overpowering force of love while, in *La pródiga* [*The Prodigal Woman*] he depicts the difficulties caused by love which is not adjusted to normal standards.

The profound and dramatic shock of ideas is to be perceived in his two greatest novels, *El niño de la bola* and *El escándalo.*

The former portrays the triumph of passion and of evil. Manuel Venegas, the protagonist, goes to America before marrying his betrothed, Soledad. Eight years go by and Soledad marries someone else. When Venegas gets back to Spain, he searches out Soledad. A priest tries to calm him before an image of Jesus and recommends that he leave the town. He learns, however, that his love is still returned and he goes in search of his former sweetheart whom he strangles during a public dance. He is killed in his turn by a dagger blow from Soledad's husband.

El escándalo is a complex and extensive narrative. The central episode concerns the conversation between a young libertine, Fabrián Conde, and a Jesuit priest, Father Manrique, to whom he recounts his life of sin redeemed by the virtue and love of Gabriela, the heroine of the work.

Alarcón's ability as a chronicler was also a major part of his talent. He was helped by his magnificent powers of description which enabled him to evoke his native country, in *La Alpujarra,* and the many lands of Europe where he had traveled, in *De Madrid a Nápoles.* His war writings were published under the title *Diaro de un Testigo de la guerra de Africa* [*The Diary of a Witness of the War in Africa*].

The significance of Alarcón's work lies in the fact that it marks the transition between the simple descriptive narrative of *costumbrismo* and the thesis novel which embodies philosophy and a moral lesson.

The major figure, however, was Benito Pérez Galdós. Although he was born on the Canary Island of Las Palmas in 1843, he spent most of his life in Madrid. It was there that he studied law, only to become first a journalist and later on one of the most popular, and the most controversial, writers of his time. He was active in liberal and republican politics. He died in 1920.

Galdós inherited Larra's preoccupation for the national good. In his view, Spain should have become a progressive and modern nation. Galdós saw the possibility of this in political liberalism and the development of the applied and mechanical sciences. Hurtado and González Palencia in their *Historia de la literatura española* wrote of him that "his characteristic types are, one, attractive, who represents progress, light, affability, or the youthful engineer; another, disagreeable, the symbol of obscurantism, as Galdós interprets it, as the priest." His characters attack or defend the traditional ideas of Spanish society. The novelist himself took part in the polemics and opted for liberalism. In several works the love misfortunes of the protagonists are blamed on religious intransigence This is what happens in *Doña Perfecta* which depicts the shock between a youthful freethinker and a very conservative provincial society. A similar problem is central to *La familia de León Roch* [*Leon Roch's Family*]. In *Gloria,* a love affair between a Jew and a Christian comes to a tragic end.

Clarity and simplicity are the essence of Galdós' style. His novels have become famous through his great gifts of observation and the telling accuracy with which he describes hundreds of human types, in particular the men and women of the people from the poor sections of Madrid, and for the wealth of situations in which his characters find themselves. His descriptions oscillate between an overt realism and a certain sentimental idealism.

In the *Episodios Nacionales* [*National Episodes*], Galdós gives proof of his extraordinary powers for evoking a vision of the past. Pérez Galdós, without a shadow of a doubt, is the most productive Spanish writer of the nineteenth century. More than a hundred volumes of novels, drama, literary criticism, and travel articles make up his work. Forty-six of these volumes constitute the four series of his *Episodios Nacionales,* the most extensive work, if considered as a continuous whole, in Spanish literature.

More than five hundred characters move through the pages of its volumes, to give us a novelistic portrayal of the history of Spain from the Battle of Trafalgar to the Restoration period under Cánovas del Castillo. Galdós uses the device of having a protagonist, Araceli in the first series, Monsalud in the second, and Carpena in the third, present at the scene of the major events in Spanish nineteenth-century history. Each episode or historical event is woven around the hero's travels. The first series is the most exciting and the most national in character. The culminating events of the War of Independence are its focal point, as the titles with their well-known dates and place-names of the separate volumes indicate: *El diecinueve de Marzo y El Dos de Mayo* [*The Nineteenth of March and the Second of May*], and *Bailén, Zaragoza, Gerona.* The later three series have a more pronounced political bias and narrate episodes from the endless struggles between progressives, i.e., believers in parliamentary government, and moderates, i.e., believers in absolutism, and the civil wars of the century. Galdós always favored those persons who defended parliamentary and liberal ideas.

Nevertheless, Galdós always succeeded in giving a sense of living history to these novels. His prodigious powers of description gave the *Episodios* as well as his other novels a striking sense of immediacy. The following passage taken from *El diecinueve de Marzo y El Dos de Mayo* illustrates this trait:

The youth stumbled as he came up the staircase. Most people would have said that he was afraid; for me it was excitement. When we went to where Inés and Don Celestino were, we found them as happy as could be to see me unharmed. Inés pointed to a statue of the Virgin before which she had lighted two candles. Juan de Dios was standing in the doorway, half in and half out of the room. He held his hat in his hand and his face was pale and contracted. He seemed undecided whether to say something or to go back inside. Inés, who had eyes only for me, paid no attention to him whatsoever.

"We have seen some acts of great heroism here, Gabriel," said the priest. "The French have been driven back. All of Madrid is rising against them."

Just as he had said this, a terrible explosion shook the whole house.

"The French are coming back! That shot came from our side. We won't surrender. May God and His Holy Mother assist us!"

Juan de Dios was still standing in the doorway, while my friends, whose attention was completely absorbed in the new moment of danger, did not notice that he was there.

"It is starting up again!" exclaimed Inés who had hurried to close the window. "I thought it was all over. There was one explosion after another, and such shouting! And the cannons! I thought the world was being torn to shreds. I knelt down and didn't stop praying. If you had seen, Gabriel! . . . First some soldiers came and pounded on the park gates. Then there was a crowd of men and some women who came to ask for arms. Inside the patio a Spaniard in a green uniform argued with another in a blue uniform. Finally they threw their arms around each other and opened up the gates. What shouting there was then! My uncle began to cry and shout, 'Long Live Spain' three times. . . ."

As we have already pointed out, one of the characteristics of Galdós's style is the oscillation between overt realism and sentimental idealism. Almost all of his novels participate in this but they may be grouped according to what predominates in them:

a Realistic novels. Galdós depicts reality for us as it would present itself before our very eyes. He frequently describes the poorer districts of Madrid, as in *Miau* [*Meow*], the hardships of the middle class in *Lo prohibido* [*Forbidden*], the persistent pursuit of an honest woman by a lecherous man; in *Fortunata y Jacinta,* the longest novel of all, the adulterous love affair of Fortunata and Juan Santa Cruz, Jacinta's husband. The best novel of all is perhaps *Misericordia* whose major characters are the beggars and urchins of the capital city. The protagonist is the memorable figure of Benigna whose humility and goodness soften the suffering of others.

b   Ideological and sentimental novels. Works in which sentiment or ideology predominately constitute another group of novels. This is the case with *Doña Perfecta, La Familia de León Roch,* and *Gloria* which we have already mentioned.

Marianela should also be spoken of here. The heroine, whose name gives the title to the work, is a wretched and homely girl whose goodness of heart wins her the love of a blind youth. When the latter recovers his sight, Marianela runs away so that he will not be disillusioned. The youth marries another girl and the heroine dies of grief.

The following is a conversation between the blind boy and the girl:

"Is the sun shining brightly, Nela? Even though you tell me that it is, I won't be able to understand for I don't know what to shine is really like."

"It is shining brightly indeed, dear friend. But what difference does that make to you? The sun is very ugly. You can't look it in face."

"Why not?"

"Because it hurts."

"What hurts?"

"Your eyes. What do you feel when you are happy?"

"When the two of us are alone out in the fields?"

"Yes."

"Well, I feel a sort of freshness, a good warm feeling inside of me. . . ."

"Don't say you don't understand. You know very well what sunshine is like."

"Like a freshness!"

"No, silly."

"Like what then?"

"Like this."

"Like this? And what is this?"

"This," said Nela once again with firm conviction.

"I see now that these things can't be explained. Before
I had formed an idea of day and night. Like this: It was
daytime when people talked. It was nighttime when people
stopped talking and the cock crowed. I don't make the same
comparisons anymore. The daytime is when you and I are
together and night is when we are separated."

"Sweet Mother of Heaven!" exclaimed Nela, "For me
who might have my eyesight it is exactly the same."

The four novels of the *Torquemada* cycle, a profound analysis
of avarice, and *El amigo Manso,* which is the story of an introspective man who meditates and an extrovert who expresses
himself through action, may also be included here. The bias of
the author sometimes affects the veracity of these works.

Several of Galdós' novels were also rewritten in the form of
plays. Among those originally written to be performed on the
stage is his *Electra,* a drama of revolutionary tendencies. *La de
San Quintín* is the tale of the efforts of some impoverished
aristocrats to redeem themselves. *Santa Juana de Castilla* brings
the figure of Queen Juana the Mad to the stage.

José María de Pereda (1833–1905) was born, lived, and died
in the province of Santander. He is the undisputed novelist of
his native region. His work is based on the observation of the
reality of the life around him in his native province which he
knew thoroughly. He describes:

a Customs. Pereda once wrote, "A slave to truth when I
copied the customs of the Montaña region. I copied them from
life." The figures portrayed in his novels appear as they were
in reality, with their picturesque language and customs, their
vices and virtues.

b The Landscape. Pereda is a great literary landscape artist.
He has given us many memorable depictions of the region around
Santander. In his *Peñas arriba* [*Cliffs Aloft*] and *El sabor de la
tierruca* [*The Flavor of the Soil*], he describes the mountains, while
in *Sotileza* seascapes predominate.

Many of Pereda's novels embody a thesis of moral or satirical
character. In *El buey suelto* [*The Ox Let Loose*], he attacks im-
penitent bachelors; in *De tal palo tal astilla* [*Like Father, Like*

Son], free thinkers; in *La Montalvez,* certain aristocrats; and in *Los hombres de pro* [*Men of Note*] and *Nubes de estí* [*Summer Clouds*], he attacks unscrupulous and ambitious men.

Pereda paints portraits of irreproachable morality, as Emilia Pardo Bazán wrote:

> Pereda is the living sign and palpable demonstration that realism did not enter Spain as contraband merchandise from France. On the contrary, those who love both the literary traditions and living traditions (of Spain) have resuscitated it. It is something that will not fool intelligent people again, except for the innumerable mob who counts the Realist era from the advent of Zola.

Father Luis Coloma, (1851–1914) who was a Jesuit, followed in the novelistic footsteps of Fernán Caballero. His *Pequeñeces* [*Trifles*], an accurate portrayal of Madrid aristocracy with satirical and moralizing overtones, had considerable success. His novel *Boy* was also widely read, as were such short stories as *La Gorriona* [*The Sparrow*], *!Era un Santo!* [*He was a Saint!*], and *Juan Miseria.* In his later years Coloma cultivated the historical novel and published such works as *Jeromín,* concerning Don Juan de Austria; *Fray Francisco,* of the times of Cardinal Cisneros; and *La reina mártir* [*The Martyred Queen*], about Mary Stuart.

The study of the human reality of fictional characters led to an increasingly complete analysis of their ideas and feelings and developed into the so-called psychological novel.

Juan Valera was born in Cabra in the province of Cordova in 1827, the son of the Marquis de la Paniega. He was a career diplomat and held posts in the principal legations of Europe and America. He died in 1905.

He received a sensitivity of spirit from his Andalusian and aristocratic family. His profession provided elegance and a knowledge of the world. All of this was fused into a vast culture which, like his polished tastes, is clearly discernible in his works.

Valera was a writer of many facets. He wrote articles of literary criticism and of philosophy. His letters are a model of ingenuity and style. He wrote a series of short stories which are full of ironic observations. At the age of forty-seven he published his first novel, *Pepita Jiménez,* which is an extraordinary study of the psychology of love.

The protagonist of this novel is Don Luis de Vargas, a seminary student who feels his mystical fervor transform itself into the human love for Pepita Jiménez, a young widow who was to have married Luis' widowed father, but who ends up preferring the son. Valera reveals the evolution of his protagonist's feelings in letters which the young man writes to his uncle who is also his spiritual mentor.

A letter from Luis de Vargas to his uncle:

Hardly anyone here understands what they call my mania for becoming a priest. These good people, with their rustic candor, tell me I should hang up my habits, that the priesthood is fine for poor folk, but that I as heir to an estate should get married and be a consolation to my father in his old age and give him a half dozen happy and healthy grandchildren.

To flatter me and to flatter my father, everybody says that I am a fine fellow, full of spirit and a lot of feeling, that my eyes are full of the devil and other silly things that annoy me and disgust me and upset me. Not that I'm shy. After all I know the miseries and the follies of this world and do not allow anything to shock me or to frighten me.

The only defect they find in me is that I am too skinny from too much studying. They don't want me to study or read a thing while I am here so I will fatten up and they are going to fix every kind of special dish they prepare around here, I know what they want to do, get me fat. There is not a family we know which has not sent something to our house. One sends a fruit tart, another some cheese or some nuts or a jar of syrup.

The attentions they show me don't stop there. Three or four of the most important people here have asked me to dinner.

Tomorrow we are invited to the house of Pepita Jiménez, of whom you have undoubtedly heard people speak. Everyone hereabouts knows my father is courting her.

My father, despite his fifty-five years is still so vigorous that he is the envy of the liveliest young men of our town. His past conquests and his renown as a sort of Don Juan Tenorio make him all the more attractive and even irresistible for some women.

I have not met Pepita Jiménez yet. Everyone says she is very pretty. I suspect she is a local beauty and somewhat countryfied. From what I have heard said about her I can't decide whether she is a good person or bad, but she must be naturally intelligent. She is about twenty years old. She is a widow and was married only three years. She is the daughter of Doña Francisca Gálvez, the widow, as you know, of a retired captain.

> "Who in his will
> left only his sword and his honor"

as the poet says.

Valera is known as the great expert in matters concerning women. As in *Pepita Jiménez,* there is also a conflict between sacred and profane love in his *Doña Luz. Juanita la Larga* is the seductive figure in another novel while in *Genio y figura* it is Rafaela who personifies Andalusian grace and fiery wit.

Among Valera's masculine creations is the memorable protagonist of *Las ilusiones del Doctor Faustino* [*The Illusions of Doctor Faustino*] in whom the author wished to embody "a combination of vices, ambitions, dreams and skeptical attitudes, which afflict the youth of my times." He has also left us an excellent study of *El Comendador Mendoza.*

The novel, according to Valera, should avoid romantic fantasies, but it cannot be a mere recounting of observed reality. It must be rooted in a reality whose interest is heightened by art but which shuns what is ugly or disagreeable. For Valera, the foundation of narrative is the analysis of the characters' feelings, and in this sense, we must consider him as the creator of the psychological novel in Spain.

The Naturalistic Novel

Despite Valera's psychological essays, the vogue in Europe for deeper and more penetrating observations of life brought about the development of a movement called naturalism, which also had its exponents in Spain.

Emilia Pardo Bazán, a countess, was born in La Coruña in 1852. She traveled widely throughout Europe. Her residence, however, was in Madrid where her literary accomplishments earned for her the title of Secretary of Public Instruction and a Chair of Literature at the University. She died in 1921.

Under the title of *La cuestión palpitante,* translated as *The Burning Question,* Doña Emilia Pardo Bazán published a book on the French naturalistic movement which Emile Zola headed and which was causing considerable interest among Spanish writers. For Zola, art was no more than reality as seen through a temperament. The artist's task was to depict life without letting his imagination enter into it. Doña Emilia had already foreseen the defects inherent in the movement and in 1881 wrote in the prologue to her book *Un Viaje de novios* [*A Honeymoon*]: "I do not reprehend the patient, thorough, exact observation which distinguishes this modern French literary movement. On the contrary, I praise it, but I disapprove of the systematic reading and preference for repugnant or shameful subject matter, the tediousness and sometimes boredom of the descriptions and, more than anything else . . . the perennial solemnity and sadness, all of which I consider artistic faults."

The Countess conceived of a truly Spanish realism, one following in the tradition of such works as the *Quixote* and the *Celestina,* and of such authors as Tirso de Molina and Ramón de la Cruz, in which happiness and pathos would both have a place, as in real life. She wrote, "As the novel is likeness of human life, par excellence, as in our existence, tears and laughter, the background of the eternal tragicomedy of the world, should come by turns." In *La cuestión palpitante,* she attacked naturalism for wanting to forge an art dedicated overwhelmingly to what was ugly and distorted. Nevertheless she defended realistic literature which drew its nourishment from observation of nature and intelligently balanced the elements found there.

Emilia Pardo Bazán valiantly confronted the problem she elucidated in *La cuestión palpitante,* making use of an energetic and positive style that can best be described as masculine in its strength.

The following are her own descriptions of her work:

> In *Pascual López,* I gave an idea of the life of a scholar in Old Galacia, medieval and represented by Santiago; in *La Tribuna,* of modern Galicia, industrial and productive, where I was born, La Coruña; in *El Cisne* I studied a small town with its intrigues and its politics in miniature; in *Bucólica,* a village girl named Graziella, poor, ignorant and a creature of instinct; in *Los Pazos de Ulloa,* the Gallegan mountain country with its local bosses and the decay of a noble family. In *La Madre Naturaleza* I give rein to my liking for the countryside, for the earth and landscape.

She wrote other memorable works as well. *Morriña* gives an excellent portrayal of the melancholy of the Gallegans. *La Quimera* [*The Chimera*] tells of the role ambition played in the society of the times, and *La sirena negra* [*The Black Siren*] has the presentiment of death as its theme.

The naturalistic movement in Spain found an eminent spokesman in the critic and novelist Leopoldo Alas who wrote under the pseudonym of Clarín. His novel *La Regenta* [*The Professor's Wife*] dissects the society of Vetusta (Oviedo) where the author was a member of the faculty of the university. The work attacks and satirizes provincial society. Clarín's short stories are more idealistic and sentimental in content, as in *¡Adiós, Cordera!*

As a sharp and implacable critic, Leopoldo Alas won fame with his articles such as *Paliques* [*Chitchat*].

The work of Armando Palacio Valdés (1853–1938), even where his descriptions are clearly in the vein of naturalism, retains his own individualism through his subtle sense of humor and his knowledge of human feelings. His novels are a mine for the student of Spanish life. He depicts Asturias in his *El idilio de un enfermo* [*The Idyl of a Sick Man*] and in *José*, Seville in *La Hermana San Sulpicio* [*Sister San Sulpicio*], and Valencia in *La alegría del Capitán Ribot* [*Captain Robot's Joyousness*]. In other works a tendency toward ideology predominates. In *Marta y María* he combats false mysticism; in *La aldea perdida* [*The Lost Village*], he attacks the civilization which erodes the traditional country virtues; in *Tristán* he develops the theme of pessimism. Palacio Valdés' studies of women are notable for the sensitivity and accuracy of their psychological penetration.

Vicente Blasco Ibáñez was born in Valencia in 1867 and died in 1929. His novels stand out for the vigorous naturalism of their descriptions and the dramatic interest engendered by their plots. He is a true. painter who reflects with brilliant and living color the world in which his characters move.

His work, which is very extensive, may be classified as follows:

1. Regional novels of Valencia, including *Arroz y tartana* [*Rice and Tartans*], *Flor de mayo* [*Flower of May*], *La barraca* [*The Cabin*], and *Cañas y barro* [*Reeds and Clay*], which describe with great forcefulness the life of the peasants and fishermen of the Valencian region.

2. Revolutionary novels which are four in number. They show the influence of Zola and depict the rebellion of the common people. They comprise *La Catedral* [*The Cathedral*], *La bodega* [*The Wine Cellar*], *El intruso* [*The Interloper*], and *La horda* [*The Horde*].

3. Novels of sociological realism, such as *Sangre y arena* [*Blood and Sand*] which portrays the world of bull fighting; *La maja desnuda* [*The Nude Maja*] which shows the world of artists; *Los muertos mandan* [*The Dead Command*], a novel of the *chuetas* or descendants of Jewish families in Mallorca.

4. Cosmopolitan novels. Some portray the international world of the First World War and include such works as *Los cuatro jinetes del Apocalipsis* [*The Four Horsemen of the Apocalypse*], *Los enemigos de la mujer* [*The Enemies of Woman*], and *Mare Nostrum*. Other books have Hispanic America as a

setting: *La tierra de todos* [*Land for All*] and *La Reina Calafia* [*Queen Calafia*].

5. Lastly, there are his historical novels such as *Sónnica, la cortesana* [*Sonnica the Courtesan*] which is set in the epoch of Carthage; and *El papa del mare* [*The Pope of the Sea*], the story of the antipope Luna.

6

The Twentieth Century

Prolegomena to Contemporary Literature

European romanticism, by its revaluation of Spanish authors of the Golden Age such as Calderón and Lope, aroused the interest of such scholars as the Schlegel brothers, and Bouterweck and Tickner, who laid the foundations for the traditions of Hispanic studies that have lasted down to the present. In Spain itself, historians including Martínez Marina, the Count of Toreno, and Modesto Lafuente, analyzed the historical past of the Peninsula, while Amado de los Ríos and Milá y Fontanals studied Spanish Medieval literature.

Menéndez y Pelayo is a major figure in the scholarship of Spanish letters. He was born in Santander in 1856. He, like Milá y Fontanals, studied in the school of Philosophy and Letters at the University of Barcelona. At the age of twenty-two, after brilliantly passing the examinations, he obtained the chair of Spanish literature at the University of Madrid. During the last years of his life he was Director of the National Library. He died in 1912.

Menéndez y Pelayo was a man of vast knowledge. Gifted with a prodigious memory and an incredible capacity for work, he made such a brilliant display of culture in his works that he astonishes us still today. He had a thorough knowledge of ancient and modern literatures and a command of the major languages. His knowledge of philosophy was also extraordinary.

Menéndez y Pelayo put his knowledge at the disposal of his country and reconstructed for all time the spiritual history of the Spanish people. In addition he gave all his enthusiasm and wisdom to the task of defending Spain against attacks by other nations. From the time of his early *La Ciencia Española* [*Spanish Science*] on—in the work he presented a formidable catalogue of scientists, a fact which certain authors had denied existed in Spain—all of Menéndez y Pelayo's labors tended toward an evaluation of the great importance of the Spanish spirit in the history of the world. This traditional spirit, he felt, was the only one that could serve the regeneration of Spain. For Menéndez y Pelayo, Spanish greatness lay politically in unity and spiritually in Catholicism. When Spanish culture became separated from these two roots, decadence resulted. This is the concluding thought of his major work, *Historia de los heterodoxos españoles* [*The History of the Spanish Heterodoxes*], from which the following selection comes:

What can be deduced from this history? In my opinion, the following:

Neither by the nature of the soil where we live, nor because of race or character did we seem destined to form a great nation. Without unity of climate or of products, without unity of customs, without unity of cults, without unity of rites, without unity of family, without consciousness of our brotherhood nor sense of nationhood, we succumbed before Rome, tribe by tribe, city by city, man by man, fighting each on his own with great heroism but showing himself impassive before the ruin of the bounding city and even delighting in it. Except for these innate traces of savage and ferocious independence, the Spanish character did not begin to manifest itself until the Roman occupation.

Rome, without completely wiping out the old customs, brought us legislative unity. It brought together the distant regions of our soil with a network of military roadways. Within the mesh of this network it planted the seed of settlements and cities. It reorganized property and family on such firm foundations they have subsisted in their essential forms down to the present day. It gave us unity of language and mixed Latin blood with ours. It confounded its gods with ours and it put on the lips of our orators and our poets the sonorous speech of Marcus Tullius and Virgilian hexameters. Spain owes Rome a debt for unity of language, of art, of law.

But one other more important unity was lacking: the unity of belief, of faith. Only through it can a people acquire its own life and a consciousness of its full strength. Only through it do its institutions acquire roots and become legitimate. Only through faith does the sap of life reach the furthermost branches of the social tree. Without the same God, without the same altar, without the same sacrifices, without considering themselves all the sons of the same father and regenerated by a common sacrament, without seeing the visible protection of the Almighty, without feeling every single day in their children, in their homes, in the circle of their inheritance, in the public square of their native town, without believing that this same favor of heaven which bestows the ties of law among brothers, and consecrates with the oil of justice the power which He delegates for the good of the community . . . what people can be great and strong?

Menéndez y Pelayo had a through knowledge of Greco-Latin writers and literary tastes that leaned to what was balanced and classical. He made studies of the influence of ancient writers in *Horacio en España* [*Horace in Spain*], the evolution of Spanish poetry in *Antología de poetas líricos* [*Anthology of Lyrical Poets*], and of the novel in *Orígenes de la novela* [*Origins of the Novel*]. He made an impressive study of the theater of Lope de Vega and of Calderón de la Barca. His critical work grew out of his research in the artistic theories of all times in his *Historia de las ideas Estéticas* [*A History of Aesthetic Theories*], while his stated means of evaluating a literary work was to base his conclusions on a knowledge of "the literary atmosphere the author breathed, the ideas which nourished him and the influence of the philosophical currents of the times."

The finest prose stylist of didactic writing in the nineteenth century, Marcelino Menéndez y Pelayo owes the liveliness of his writing to his enthusiastic expression and to his desire to convince. These give the tension of a balanced oratorical paragraph to his sentence, backed by the solid argumentation of his immense culture.

By education and by personal preference, he was an active champion of classicism in matters of language. His model was Fray Luis de León whose language was composed, he said, of "sobriety and purity." It is understandable, in view of this, that he reacted against the style of other didactic writers who ignored the example of classical writers and who blemished their work, as he tells us in his *Discurso en contestación al musicógrafo Barbiere* [*Speech in Answer to the Musicologist Barbiere*] with a "dense thicket of unpolished phrases, of grating Gallicisms and of insufferable pedantries."

He also refers to scientific books which he found singularly careless in matters of style because of the influence of the many incorrect translations with which new scientific works came into Spain from other countries.

Menéndez y Pelayo also wrote some poetry on didactic and love themes. Their elevated and serene style is reminiscent of the neoclassical poets. He translated numerous works from Latin into Spanish.

While Menéndez y Pelayo was reconstructing the intellectual past of Spain, others continued their efforts at analyzing the problems of looking clearly at their native land and searching for solutions. Great orators brought their points of view to platform and Parliament. On the Conservative side, Aparisi Guijarro and Vázquez Melba gained considerable recognition, while among the Liberals appeared the famous and grandiloquent Emilio Castelar and Joaquín Costa.

Joaquín Costa was born in Graus in the province of Huesca in 1846. His primary interests lay in juridical and political literature. He wrote numerous works on social and agricultural institutions, a history of law, on pedagogy, and so on. His writings tend to polemics and are marked by their great patriotic fervor.

Costa counseled the reorganization of Spanish economic life, and of the educational system, and the abandonment of all imperialistic ambitions: the larder, the school, and seven locks on the Cid's tomb.

Angel Ganivet was born in Granada in 1862. He studied law and served as consul in Antwerp, Helsinki, and Riga. It was in the latter city that he committed suicide in 1898 by throwing himself into the Dwina River for causes still unknown. His humanistic background and his travels contributed to making him a writer of imposing stature.

Ganivet, like Larra, who was also a suicide, made a penetratingly sharp analysis of the Spanish character and deeply felt the problem of his country's decadence in his *Idearium español* [*The Conception of Spain*]. The following are characteristic aspects of his work:

1. Senecan stoicism. The spirit of Spain, according to Ganivet, is embodied in mysticism and in the dignity with which Spaniards bear adversity, which he denominates *senequismo*.

When we examine what constitutes the idealogical makeup of Spain, we find that the moral element, and to a certain extent the most profoundly religious, which serves as a sort of over-all base, is stoicism. It is not the brutal and heroic stoicism of Cato, nor the serene and majestic stoicism of Marcus Aurelius, nor that of a rigid and extreme kind of Epictetus; it is the natural and human stoicism of Seneca. Seneca is not a son of Spain by accident, he is Spanish in his very essence. Nor is he Andalusian, for at the time of his birth the Vandals, who gave their name to the region, had not yet come to Spain. Indeed if he had been born in the Middle Ages it probably would have been in Castile. All of Seneca's doctrine may be condensed in the following words: Do not let yourself be vanquished by anything which is foreign to your spirit. Keep in mind, that despite the uncertainty of life, you have within you a primordial force, something as strong and indestructible as a core of diamond around which swirl the petty events which make up the drama of everyday life. Whatever happens to you, whether things which prosper you or are unfavorable or even those which degrade you, stay firm and erect so that the least that can be said of you is that you are a man.

2. Strong individualism led Spain into colossal undertakings for which insufficient preparations were made. Because of this he proposed an inner reconstitution of the nation.

The following is a significant passage from Ganivet's *Idearium:* "A reconstitution of the whole of the life and history of Spain can have no other point of departure than the concentration of our energies within our own territories."

Colonialization is sensitively satirized in two works whose protagonist is "Pío Cid": *Conquista del Reino de Maya por el último conquistador Pío Cid* [*The Conquest of the Kingdom of Maya by the Last Conqueror, Pío Cid,* sometimes called in English *The Labors of the Tireless Creator, Pio Cid*]. His study of his native city, *Granada la bella* [*Granada the Beautiful*] and his *Cartas finlandesas* [*Letters on Finland*] are both notable works.

In the middle of the nineteenth century a Spanish professor, Julián Sanz del Río, introduced to Spain the theories of a mediocre German philosopher named Krause. These consisted of a vague pantheistic nationalism. Because of their lack of conventionality, Sanz del Río's disciples were removed from their faculty positions and founded the "Institución Libre de Enseñanza" at whose head was Francisco Giner de los Ríos. The group became known as "Krausistas." These writers had considerable influence during the first decades of the twentieth century.

The Turn of the Century

The Generation of 1898

With the defeat of Spanish arms at Cavite and Santiago de Cuba in 1898, Spanish overseas power came to an end. Internal conflicts, political improvisation, and a clear industrial and economic disadvantage coupled with the great distances from the homeland to the fighting fronts, made the results of a highly unequal struggle inevitable.

All those who sustained the thesis that Spanish politics had to change course used the depressive atmosphere following the defeat to demand, as Costa did, the internal reconstruction of the country and the abandonment of imperialistic designs.

Along with this came the desire to downgrade Spanish cultural history. The "Institution Libre de Enseñanza" aimed at creating a youth of liberal and Europeanized outlook, and while bringing in knowledge and methods from other countries, the school tended to neglect the more traditional aspects of Spanish culture in favor of a more cosmopolitan outlook.

In the literary field a group of writers known as the Generation of '98 took advantage of the confusion occasioned by the spiritual commotion of the military disaster to change the character and style of Spanish literature. Some critics have doubted the existence of this so-called "generation," saying that the authors who made up the group had nothing more in common than a negative gesture of protest. Nevertheless we can find the following attitudes characterizing the Generation:

1. Patriotic pessimism. The pessimistic mood which grew out of the defeats Spain had suffered led to two postulates:
   a. Patriotism should not be shouted from the rooftops. It should not consist of a rhetorical exaltation of all things Spanish. Quixotic exaltations lead only to calamity.
   b. Spain should recapture a sense of its forgotten beauties. Authors such as Azorín, Machado, and Unamuno rediscovered the landscape of Castile and the artistic and literary values of El Greco, Berceo, and the Archpriest of Hita.

The preoccupation with Spain and its problems is fundamental to almost all of the writers of the Generation of '98.

2. Europeanization. The patriotic pessimism of the men of '98 led them to import the literary, political, and philosophical ideas of *fin-de-siècle* Europe. Spanish culture lost its traditional character and took its orientation from foreign models—German, English and French.

Later on many of the writers of the Generation rectified their ideas along more nationalistic lines. Unamuno, for example, ex-

alted Spanish moral values to such an extent that he proposed the
Hispanization of Europe.

3. Autodidacticism. In general, the major figures of the
Generation of '98, insatiable readers, organized their knowledge
to fit their temperaments. The later leaders of Spanish culture
were clearly of university background, but the members of the
Generation of '98 were self-taught. They were also embattled
writers who carried their ideas and doctrines to the press, the
rostrum, and the printed page. This formation brought great
popularity to these authors.

4. Influences. In spite of their liberal educational formation, the influence of Larra and of the German philosophers
Schopenhauer and Nietzche was common to all of the writers of
the Generation.

5. Rebelliousness. The Generation of '98 broke with the
preceding generation. It satirized the bombastic oratory of Castelar, the showy drama of Echegaray, the sentimentalism of Campoamor and the conformism of the politicians of the Restoration
period. All of their labors were oriented by a profound desire to
renovate Spain.

6. Style. Romantic rhetoric and exaggeration had worn out
expressive formulas. Consequently the writers of '98 began a con-
scientious study of style. They made use of the etymological
meaning of words, as in Unamuno's case, or, as in Azorín's case,
took expressions whose force had not diminished from the classical
writers and from the everyday speech of the people.

The Generation of '98 bequeathed a new beauty and efficacy
to the Castilian language.

As a whole, it may be said affirmatively that the Generation
of '98 attained an enormous importance and an undeniable tran-
scendency. As a literary group, along with the modernists whom
we shall study later on, it constitutes one of the most brilliant
movements in the history of Spanish literature. As an ideological
group it may be said that the writers of '98 gave an orientation
to all the political and intellectual life of Spain in the twentieth
century. Whether right or not, it is evident that they studied
Spain's problems with a tremendous passion and that they were

THE TWENTIETH CENTURY 315

devoted in their search for solutions to them, as Pedro Laín
Entralgo has pointed out:

> The men of '98, whatever the visible image of their
> conduct may have been—at times totally in disagreement,
> at others partially in accord, and at still others, misguided—
> have lived with dignity and have dreamed their dreams with
> nobility and without blemish. That part of their lives that
> was not dream will be judged in diverse ways and will pass;
> what was dream lives and will always live in the brother-
> hood of all men who dream today or tomorrow of the
> existence of a pure and exemplary Spain.

Miguel de Unamuno was born in Bilbao in 1864 and died
in 1936 in Salamanca where he was a professor and then Rector
of the University. He was the most forceful personality of the
Generation of '98.

This "forceful personality" led him to mysticism, of which
we can discern three types, and to satire.

1. Religious mysticism. The exaltation of religious mysticism
caused him, on occasion, to affirm what some considered heretical
opinions. His lengthy poem, however, *El Cristo de Velázquez*
[*The Christ of Velazquez*] is justly famous, of which the following
is a brief passage:

> Like the white snow is the garment
> Of the soul, O Nazarene, you yielded up;
> Like the snow; here on earth
> No cleanser that can make such white is there: it shines
> Like snow, a mirror to the light, an invitation
> To remain upon the mount and there encamped
> To savor of its whiteness.

2. Sentimental mysticism. Unamuno exalted human love,
honest and homely, in works like *El Rosario de sonetos líricos*
[*The Rosary of Lyrical Sonnets*] and *Teresa,* from which the
following is taken:

Far off, the laughter of my children;
I, in comfort, sitting on my couch;
Herodotus offers me the richness
Of his wisdom . . .
                    Before me in her chair,
She sews, and for a bit retains
My gaze with hers, and in my glory,
I reflect upon what secrets history holds
And in this blessed peace the house enfolds,
To the quiet rhythm of the sound of breath,
Thoughts, like the ox the fertile earth,
Plow their sweet and silent furrows.

—From *Teresa*

The following passages depict Unamuno's love of landscape:

Castile

O, land of Castile, you do raise me up
to the sky in the rough palm of your hand;
to the sky that burns and refreshes you,
            the sky, your master.
Parched land, sinewy land and land of clear
horizons, mother of hearts and of arms,
the present takes in you the ancient coloring
            of long past glories.
At their outer edges, your bare brown fields
touch heaven with its concave meadow of sky,
the burning sun has its cradle in you,
            its tomb, its sanctuary.

Salamanca

Tall grove of towers that as he goes down
back of the trees that embellish the cloudscape
the father sun of Castile doth touch with
            his golden rays;

Great forest of stone that drew the history
from the deep recesses of mother earth,
backwater of quietude, I bless thee,
            my Salamanca!

. . . and when the sun as it sinks to its rest
kindles the age old gold that adorns thee,
In thy tongue of eternal herald tell
    what I have been.

—Translation by Eleanor L. Turnbull

3. Patriotic mysticism. Unamuno said, "Spain pains me"—
to signify his patriotic preoccupation. Influenced by pessimistic
philosophies current in his time, he wrote an article entitled
"Muera Don Quijote" ["Down with Don Quixote"] although, as
we have said, he later asserted that Spain should Hispanize Europe with its moral values.

In his magnificent commentary on the *Quixote, Vida de Don
Quijote y Sancho* [*The Life of Don Quixote and Sancho*], Unamuno made a religion of Quixotism:

Your people has been called a dying race, Don Quixote
mine, by those who are drunk with transitory triumphs and
who forget that fortune takes more turns than this earthly
sphere and that what makes us less adaptable for the type
of civilization which prevails today may be exactly what is
necessary for our adaptation to the civilization of tomorrow.
The earth makes many a turn and fortune even more.

We must aspire, nevertheless, to become eternal and
famous, not only in our own times but also in epochs to
come. No people can subsist whose pastors, its conscience,
do not have a sense of its historical mission, a sense of its
ideal to be realized on earth.

Go on your way! Where are you going? The star will
tell you: to the tomb of Don Quixote! What are we going to
do while we march? What? Fight! Fight! And how?

How? If you meet someone who lies? Shout in his face:
Lies, and march on! If you meet someone who robs? Shout
to him: Robber, and march on! If you meet someone who
is saying stupid things and the crowd stands agape before
him? Shout to them: Idiots, and march on! Always march
onward!

4. Satire. Unamuno, with a spirit ever young and fighting, was constantly taking part in literary or political struggles. His major weapons were paradox, which he defined as the means of attacking "the platitudes of common sense," and satire.

Unamuno had a thorough knowledge of the Spanish language and often utilized etymology as the point of departure for his ruminations. His style is always impassioned and vehement. Unamuno was one of the Spanish writers most deeply concerned with the Castilian tongue. One of his linguistic ideas was that the language must be made more flexible. Instead of the "old Castilian" which was "rigid and emphatic," there should be a language that is "more agile and more precise at the same time, somewhat disarticulated since today the tendency is toward ankylosis." Grammar should not be an obstacle to expression. The writer should express himself "with a natural grammar, in the speech which most readily comes to mind," seeing that needless forms will be automatically eliminated.

He believed also that Spanish should incorporate American forms. Unamuno wrote: "It seems ridiculous to me that the Spaniards of Spain should want to exercise complete control over literary language as though it were a feudal right." And again, "The Castilian language must undergo some profound modifications to become truly Spanish or Hispanoamerican."

Unamuno, for whom language was life itself, did not oppose the renovation of the lexicon by the introduction of neologisms and Gallicisms. Neologisms enrich language and consequently are never without some utility, he believed. "Two words never have a double usage without producing duality of form and thus a differentiation in meaning."

Unamuno's essays and philosophical meditations are indubitably his most important works. Nevertheless, these constitute only a part of his literary production:

1. His novels. He wrote novels on various subjects. His youth during the Siege of Bilbao by the Carlist insurrectionists appears in *Paz en la guerra* [*Peace in War*]; *Abel Sánchez,* and *Amor y pedagogía* [*Love and Pedagogy*] are sentimental in character; *Tres novelas ejemplares* [*Three Exemplary Novels*] and *San Manuel Bueno, Mártir* [*Saint Manuel Bueno, Martyr*] are short narratives. His most famous novel is *Niebla* [*Mist*].

In this work, Unamuno, like Pirandello, asserts that every literary character has a life that is independant of his creator. Therefore, the protagonist of *Niebla* makes a call on Unamuno to protest the turn of events in the book.

2. His dramatic works. Many of the author's ideas are expressed in his plays, including *Fedra* [*Phaedra*], *Sombras de sueño* [*Dream Shadows*], and *Todo un Hombre* [*Every Bit a Man*], which he adapted from a short novel.

Ramiro de Maeztu is another important figure of the period. He was born in 1875 of a Basque family. His early work was progressively modern and followed patterns of English and German ideologies. He was the author of penetrating literary studies in works such as his *Don Quijote, Don Juan y la Celestina*. His later literary output drastically changed course. His *Defensa de la Hispanidad* [*Defense of Hispanism*] (1934) is a magnificent exaltation of the mission of Spain which he calls the creator of a Christian civilization based on the brotherhood of man, without prejudices of race or of class.

José Martínez Ruiz, who is best known under the pseudonym of Azorín, another important member of the Generation, was born in Monovar in the province of Alicante in 1874. He resided in Madrid, dying in 1968.

Azorín opposed oratorical style and lengthy sentences. He wrote, "The more simply we write, the better we write." His style is characterized by short sentences, separated by semicolons or by periods.

> Style consists of writing in such a way that the reader thinks: "There's nothing to this." So that he thinks: "I could write like that." And so that, nevertheless, he cannot create this nothing that seems so simple; and so that this little nothing be the most difficult, the most laborious and the most complicated.

Azorín continually commented on the Spanish classics which he knew thoroughly.

> We do not feel, esteemed compatriot, that literary values are something immoble and unchangeable. Anything which

does not change is dead. We want our classical past to be something living, palpitating, vibrating. Let us see in our great authors the reflection of our present day sensitivity.

As he evokes their habits and describes their landscapes, the classics take on new life in his works *Los valores literarios* [*Literary Values*], *Al márgen de los clásicos* [*On the Fringes of the Classics*], and *Rivas y Larra.*

Azorín loved the Spanish landscape, and above all, Castile. He liked to evoke its ancient towns and the poetry of its fields, and this he did in *Castilla, Los pueblos* [*Towns*] and *La ruta de Don Quijote* [*The Route of Don Quixote*]. He also wrote about the luminous landscapes of Alicante.

Azorín's novels tend to be essays and meditations in dialogue. His pessimism, recalling Gracián's in the seventeenth century, manifests itself in *La Voluntad* [*Will Power*]. Other notable works are the autobiographical *Antonio Azorín,* and *Don Juan, Doña Inez,* and *Félix Vargas.*

Azorín attempted unsuccessfully to renovate the Spanish stage. The characters in his plays are cerebral types who ponder over their actions and have little corporeal reality. This is the case with the figure of *La Muerte* [Death] in *Lo invisible* [The Invisible], *"Tiempo"* [Time] in *Angelita,* and *"el Ensueño* [The Illusion] in *Cervantes or the Enchanted House.*

Pío Baroja, to whom Hemingway paid high tribute, was born in San Sebastián in 1872 and died in 1957. He was the author of an extensive number of novels, primarily descriptive of the Basque countryside, as in *El mayorazgo de Labraz* [*The Firstborn of Labraz*] and *Zalacain, el aventurero* [*Zalacain the Adventurer*].

Baroja is another characteristic writer of the Generation of '98. His style is unadorned, clear and expressive.

> My literary ideal is rhetoric in a minor tone. By that I mean a form so well adjusted to thought and to feeling that it in no way exceeds them. If I were an architect, I would make a beam look like a beam no matter what occasion I had to disguise it.
> Logic is a sort of foundation for all beauty.

I do not believe you can go very far in the correcting of languages.

His attitude toward society is skeptical. His novels are dynamic, and may be grouped into the following categories:

1. Social novels, revolutionary and cynical in outlook. In the trilogy, *La Busca* [*The Search*], *La mala hierba* [*The Bad Seed*], and *Aurora roja* [*Red Dawn*], he portrays life in the poor sections of Madrid, full of vice and misery.

2. Psychological novels, in which he makes a painstaking study of persons who reflect his own thinking as in *Camino de perfección* [*The Road to Perfection*] and *El Arbol de la cienca* [*The Tree of Knowledge*].

3. Historical novels, which is the most extensive series, and treats of various episodes in Spanish history, from the War of Independence at the beginning of the nineteenth century down to our own times. The best known of this series are the earlier novels, the *Memorias de un hombre de acción* [*Memories of a Man of Action*], whose protagonist, Eugenio de Aviraneta, a guerrilla fighter, conspirator and plotter, actually did live.

Antonio Machado, who is often called the poet of the Generation of '98, (1875–1939) was born in Seville and was a teacher in Soria, Baeza, and Segovia. He brought to his poetry all the patriotic love of country typical of the Generation.

Machado countered the dying and frivolous Spain of brass band and tambourine with the industrious Spain of chisel and hammer of the future. He was the great singer of Castile whose noble serenity he exalted in verses of sobriety and great beauty. The landscapes he describes glow with the typical somber chromatism of the Castilian countryside.

> Silvered hills,
> gray heights, dark violet rocks
> where the Duero twists
> a bow around Soria, somber oaks,
> fierce stony ground, bald peaks,
> white roads and river poplars,
> Sorian afternoons, mystical and warlike,

today I feel deep sadness for you,
sadness of love. Fields of Soria
where the rocks seem to dream,
come with me. Silvered hills,
gray heights, dark violet rocks!

—Translation by Willis Barnstone

His poetic style is grave and reflective. He prefers sincerity
and emotion to external perfection. His language is notable for
its sobriety. In his poetry he often philosophizes utilizing the
style of popular proverbs or sayings. He also expresses his thoughts,
however, in prose, through the fictitious poet, Juan de Mairena.
    The following may be considered a sort of lyrical autobiography,

Am I classic or romantic? I don't know.
I would leave my verse as a warrior his blade:
known for the manly hand that made it glow,
not for the smithy's famous mark or trade.

I chat with a man who goes with me to the end—
who speaks alone and hopes to speak to God one day—
my soliloquy is talk with this good friend
who showed me the secret of philanthropic ways.

In the end I owe you nothing. You owe me what I write.
By my work I pay the house I rent,
the clothes that cover me, my bed at night,
the plain bread that gives me nourishment.

And when the day for my last trip arrives,
and the ship, never to return, is set to leave,
you will find me on board with scant supplies,
almost naked, like the children of the sea.

—Translation by Willis Barnstone

The preoccupation with "preciousness" of form which characterized his contemporaries of the modernist movement was of
no interest to him. Machado, on the contrary, was a pensive and
serious poet who wrote of the passage of time in human life and
was not preoccupied with niceties of style.

> I walk dreaming roads
> of afternoon. The hills
> of gold, the green pines,
> dusty evergreen oaks!
>
> Where does the road go?
> I am singing, a traveler
> following the path . . .
> —Afternoon is fading—
>
> "I had the thorn of
> a passion in my heart.
> One day I pulled it out
> and cannot feel my heart."
>
> And the whole field is
> momentarily still and shadowy,
> meditating. Wind sounds
> in poplars by the river.
>
> The afternoon grows dim,
> and the road that winds
> and weakly blurs in white
> gets hazy and disappears.
>
> My song starts up again:
> "Sharp thorn of gold,
> in a punctured heart,
> who can feel you now?"

—Translation by Willis Barnstone

Modernism

Parallel to the great ideological revolution undertaken by the Generation of '98, there appeared a tendency of a primarily aesthetic nature involving the renovation of theme and form and which was named "modernism."

In matters of form, modernism permitted the writer complete liberty in the writing of his poems, provided that he gave them a personal stamp and a studied beauty. In this aspect the major influence was the French Parnassian school of Leconte de Lisle, who cultivated poetry solely for its perfection of form.

In matters of content, the poet's preference was for unusual or exotic subjects which permitted the creation of spectacles of exquisite beauty through the use of new rhythms and metaphors. In this aspect of the movement's development, the principal influence was the French Symbolism of Paul Verlaine who wrote of the seductive beauty of the remote and ineffable.

Modernism was primarily a Spanish-American literary phenomenon, introduced to Continental Spain by a poet from America. "Modernism," wrote Juan Ramón Jiménez, "was not only a literary movement. It touched on everything. It was a new encounter with beauty which had been concealed during the nineteenth century by the general tone of Middle Class poetry. This is what Modernism is: a great movement of enthusiasm and liberty toward beauty."

Rubén darío, the outstanding figure of modernism, was born in Metapa, Nicaragua, in 1876. He traveled incessantly throughout Europe and America as a part of his professional duties as a journalist and a diplomat. He died in 1916.

Rubén Darío has been called the most important Hispanic poet of the twentieth century. His work may be construed as a recapitulation of the whole of Spanish poetry, from whose most neglected pages he was able to draw new delights. At the same time, his work was the point of departure for a movement of renovation which, despite variations, dominated the first thirty years of the present century.

Darío was initiated in the reading of the Spanish classics as a child. He later took a special interest in the French literary schools of the period, Symbolism and the Parnassus, whose innovations he wished to transmit to Spanish. In an attempt to explain the multiplicity of his interests, Darío wrote:

> My Spanish grandsire with his white beard points out a series of portraits to me. This one, he says, is the great Don Miguel de Cervantes Saavedra, genius with a crippled hand. This is Lope de Vega, this, Garcilaso, this, Quintana. I ask for the noble Gracián, for Saint Teresa, for the fearless Góngora and for the strongest of them all, Don Francisco de Quevedo y Villegas. Afterwards I cry out: Shakespeare! Dante! Hugo! And to myself, Verlaine!

After several youthful works in which the influence of Spanish poetical works of the nineteenth century is in evidence, Darío produced the books which brought about the triumph of the new movement. The first of these was *Azul* [*Blue*] which was published in 1888, and the culminating ones were *Prosas profanas* [*Profane Prose Works*], 1896, and *Cantos de vida y esperanza* [*Songs of Life and Hope*], 1905.

Darío accomplished a remarkable metrical revolution based on musicality. He wrote verses of from two to twenty-one syllables and made combinations of accentuation and of rhyme at will. Sometimes he utilized metrical feet, as in Latin.

The following is an example of an amphibrach which is made up of short, long, short: Ya pásan / debájo / los árcos / ornádos / de bláncas / Minérvas / y Mártes."

His thematic material may be grouped as follows:

1. Collective expression. Darío wrote patriotic works which exalt the Hispanic peoples. For example, in the sonnet *España* [*Spain*], he lamented the world's lack of comprehension of Spain's historic mission.

At other times he extolled Hispanic values as opposed to the "Yankee" world of the United States, as in his *A Roosevelt:*

'Tis only with the Bible or with Walt Whitman's verse,
That you, the mighty hunter, are reached by other men.
You're primitive and modern, you're simple and
    complex—
A veritable Nimrod with aught of Washington.
You are the United States;
You are the future foe
Of free America that keeps its Indian blood,
That prays to Jesus Christ, and speaks in Spanish still.

—Translation by Elijah Clarence Hills

His unending quest for beauty brought him in touch with
a multiplicity of subjects. As a poet who became the voice of his
people he may be considered an impassioned spirit of Hispanic
values. This can be found in sonorous verses of his *Salutación
del optimista* [*Salutation of the Optimist*], written in a dactylic
rhythm that had long been unused.

2. Evocations. Figures of indigenous America as in *Caupolicán,* of heroic Spain as in *Cosas del Cid* [*Tales of the Cid*],
Letanía de Nuestro Señor Don Quijote [*Litany for Our Lord
Don Quixote*], of eighteenth century France as in *El clavicordio
de la abuela* [*The Grandmother's Clavichord*] or of lands of
fantasy and imagination as in *Sonatina* appear in Darío's works.
The following is the famous *Sonatina:*

The Princess mourns—Why is the Princess sighing?
Why from her lips are song and laughter dying?
Why does she droop upon her chair of gold?
Hushed is the music of her royal bower,
Beside her in a vase, a single flower
Swoons and forgets its petals to unfold.

The fool in scarlet pirouettes and flatters,
Within the hall the silly duenna chatters;
Without, the peacock's royal plumage gleams.
The Princess heeds them not; her thoughts are veering
Out through the gates of Dawn, past sight and hearing,
Where she pursues the phantoms of her dreams.

Is it a dream of China that allures her,
Or far Golconda's ruler who conjures her
But to unveil the laughter of her eyes?
He of the island realms of fragrant roses,
Where treasure flashing diamond hoards discloses,
And pearls of Ormuz, rich beyond surmise?

Alas! The Princess longs to be a swallow,
To be a butterfly, to soar, to follow
The ray of light that climbs into the sun;
To greet the lilies, lost in Springtime wonder.
To ride upon the wind, to hear the thunder
Of ocean waves where monstruous billows run.

—Translation by John Pierrepont Rice

3. Intimate tone. The poet's intimate tone appears in poems of gallantry as in *Margarita,* nostalgia as in *Poema de otoño* [*Poem of Autumn*], and sorrow as in *Lo fatal.* The following strophes from the *Canción de otoño en primavera* or *Song of Autumn in Springtime* exemplifies this:

Days of youth, my sacred treasure,
Unreturning ye pass by!—
Would I weep?—No tears I measure;—
Then my tears—I know not why!

. . . . .

Vain my search for that high lady
For whom I have awaited long.
But life is hard and grim and shady,—
There was no princess, save in song!

In spite of Time's unyielding measure,
My thirst for love has never died,—
My gray head bends to scent with pleasure
The roses of the garden-side—

Days of youth, my sacred treasure,
Unreturning ye pass by!—

Would I weep?—No tears I measure;—
Mine is still the Dawn of golden treasure!

—Translation by Thomas Walsh

Rubén Darío's work has had an extraordinary influence on Spanish-American poetry.

Don Ramón María del Valle Inclán was a follower of Darío in his lyrical poetry. He was born in Villanueva de Arosa in 1869. He spent his youth in Galicia in the area around Salués until he went to Mexico in 1892. He was a journalist and soldier while in America. When he returned to Spain, he gained a reputation in Madrid as a novelist and a singular personage in the world of literary Bohemia. He died in Santiago de Compostela in 1936.

The following is Valle Inclan's literary self-portrait:

The person you see here with the Spanish face à la Quevedo, with the black locks and the long beard, is I, Don Ramón del Valle Inclán.

The outset of my life was full of hazards. I was a lay brother in a Carthusian monastery and a soldier in New Spain (Mexico).

A life like those of second-born sons of aristocratic families who enlisted in the regiments in Italy, there to seek their fortunes in love or in battle . . ."

Two tendencies stand out in Valle Inclán's poetic work: (a) a mystico-legendary tone as in *Aromas de legenda* [*Aromas of Legends*] and *El pasajero* [*The Traveler*], and (b) a humorous and caricaturesque tone, as in *La pipa de kif.*

These two tendencies are also traceable in his prose. His four *Sonatas,* of spring, summer, autumn, and winter; his *Comedias bárbaras* [*Barbarous Plays*], including *Aguila de blasón* [*The Armorial Eagle*], and *Romance de lobos* [*The Ballad of the Wolves*]; his *Novelas de la guerra carlista* [*Novels of the Carlist Wars*], including *El resplandor de la hoguera* [*The Radiance of the Bonfire*], *Los Cruzados de la Causa* [*The Crusaders of the*

Cause], and *Gerifaltes de autaño* [*Gerfalcons of Yesteryear*] have an aura of legend about them and of heroism and gallantry which the poet evokes with a noble nostalgía.

The following is from *The Carlist War*:

The Castilian youth was handsome and had the same impressive stature as Don Diego. Doña Serafina asked him:
"Where are you from, son, to have such an impressive way?"
"From Viana del Prior."
"And what part of Spain is that?"
"Near Santiago in Galicia."
Don Diego smiled condescendingly: "You are a Gallegan. Why do they call you Castilian?"
The soldier looked straight at the father and his children and said, "Because I had servants at home! Because I make my own decisions! Because when a soldier goes into the world he is naturally from Castile!"

On the other hand, such farces as *La reina castiza* [*The Pure-Blooded Queen*] and *El Terno del difunto* [*The Clothes of the Dead Man*] and his caricatures of Spanish and Spanish-American political life, such as *El ruedo ibérico* [*The Iberian Arena*] and *Tirano Banderas* [*Tyrant Banderas*] are overtly satirical. Valle categorized this group with the name of *esperpentos,* a word that carries the sense of "absurdities" or "nonsense."

Manuel Machado (1874–1947), was the brother of Antonio Machado. He also was a poet and gave to his poems, which were modernist in tone, the musical themes of his native Andalusia whose popular gracefulness he sang in sonorous verse. Native Spanish elements frequently combined with the influence of French Symbolism, especially in his earlier works. As he grew older, however, his interest turned more and more to religious and traditionally patriotic subjects.

Wine, sentiments, guitar and poetry
Make up the songs of my native land.

Songs . . .
Who speaks of songs, says Andalusia.

Juan Ramón Jiménez, who received the Nobel Prize in 1956, was born in Moguer in the province of Huelva in 1881 and died in 1958. He is one of the most renowned of all contemporary poets in the Spanish tongue.

He left a very extensive work. In the following poem, the poet outlines the development of his poetry through different stages:

Pure and Innocent She Came

Pure and innocent she came
In robes of whitest candour.
And I loved her like a child.

But then she began to dress herself
In all sorts of gala showy things.
And I began to hate her and I knew it not.

Pompous in her jewels
A queen she had become . . .
What wrath of cold senselessness!

But bit by bit she bared herself
and I smiled at her again.

She stood there in the tunic
of her innocence of yore.
I believed in her once more.

And off she took the tunic
and appeared before me wholly bare.

Oh passion of my life, oh poetry
stripped bare, all mine forever!

These verses annotate the evolution of his earlier work: a The postromantic period. Ingenuous and sentimental, the primary influence was Bécquer, in *Rimas,* 1903, and *Jardines le-janos [Distant Gardens],* 1904.

b The modernist period. The modernist period, influenced by Rubén Darío and the Frenchman Francis Jammes, is characterized by a sense of musicality and an appreciation of tranquil nature, as in *Pastorales,* 1905. This stage in his development ended with a delightful work in prose, *Platero y yo [Platero and I],* 1914.

c The quest for "pure poetry." Jiménez's book, *Diario de un poeta recién casado [The diary of a Newly-Married Poet],* dating from 1916, marks the poet's quest for a poetry of essence, or "pure poetry," which stresses content over versification. The French poet Valéry's influence is strong in this period of his work, which shows a tendency toward a deeper and more difficult expression, a sort of "hermetic" poetry.

Juan Ramón Jiménez's poetic creation became increasingly difficult to comprehend. The following poem, replete with musical and popular overtones, belongs the the second period:

Green

Green was the maiden, green, green!
Green were her eyes, green her hair.

The wild rose in her green wood
was neither red nor white, but green.

Through the green air she came.
(The whole world turned green for her.)

The shining gauze of her garment
was neither blue nor white, but green.
Over the green sea she came.
(and even the sky turned green then.)

My life will always leave unlatched
a small green gate to let her in.

—Translation by J. B. Trend

Latin American Literature

In Latin America the triumph of Rubén Darío and of modernism was resounding. Three of its most outstanding representatives were, in Argentina, Leopoldo Lugones, in Peru, José Santos Chocano, and in Mexico, Amado Nervo.

Leopoldo Lugones (1874–1928) wrote with a cosmopolitan elegance. His poems are subtle evocations of landscapes, movements, or figures, in which delicacy and refined restraint predominate. José Santos (1875–1924) was a strong, vibrant political poet who wrote nostalgically of the brilliant potential of Incas and Viceroys and who considered himself the singer of a violent and sensitive America. Amado Nervo (1830–1919) was a pensive and sentimental lyricist whose work is elegant in form and sometimes touched by vague mysticism.

The more recent tendencies of Latin-American literature appear to have been inspired by the desire to abandon the cosmopolitan modernism in favor of native, indigenous subject matter, the racial conflicts and the study of landscape and creole language. Thus Ricardo Güiraldes has given us novels of gaucho life in *Don Segundo Sombra;* Rómulo Gallegos, novels of the tropics such as *Doña Bárbara;* and José Eustacio Rivera in *La Vorágine* [*The Vortex*], and Mariano Azuela, in *Los de abajo* [*The Underdogs*], a panorama of the life and times of the Mexico of the 1910 Revolution.

The so-called *poesía negra* or Negro poetry also may be considered under the general heading of indigenous movements. This poetry comes mostly from the Antilles. It is marked by a use of themes and vocabulary from Negro terminology and has produced such poets as the Puerto Rican Luis Palés Matos, the Cuban Nicolás Guillén with his *Songoro Cosongo,* and Emilio Ballagas with his *Cuaderno de poesía negra* [*Notebook of Negro Poetry*].

The historical novel, as in Enrique Larreta's *La Gloria de Don Ramiro,* set in the Avila of the period of Philip II, and the psychological novel, such as those of Eduardo Mallea, are also found in twentieth century Latin-American literature.

Contemporary Spanish Literature

Ideology

Unlike the ideologists and essayists of the Generation of '98, the generation that followed had a rigorous and systematic university training in its ideology and educational formation. At the head of the intellectuals or the "new" generation stood José Ortega y Gasset and Eugenio d'Ors.

Ortega, along with Eugenio d'Ors, gave direction to Spanish intellectual life. Born in 1883 he occupied the chair of Metaphysics at the University of Madrid for many years. He died in 1955.

Ortega y Gasset was a tireless worker for the spiritual Europeanization of Spain. The articles and books published by the *Revista de Occidente*, of which he was director, incorporated in the Spanish soul the great values of Germanic culture, by means of careful translations.

Aside from this, Ortega y Gasset was an original thinker of the first magnitude. His philosophy is rooted in a new spiritual consideration of the values of human existence (*vitalismo*) in relation to the world about us. "I am myself and my circumstances," says Ortega.

Ortega's studies brought him to the political problem of Spain in *España invertebrada* [*Invertebrate Spain*] and *Rectificación de la República* [*Rectification of the Republic*], and, in the broader context of the world, in *La rebelión de las masas* [*The Rebellion of the Masses*]. In both areas he succeeded in giving us a penetrating diagnostic of the most serious problems of our times.

It may be said, however, that his major preoccupation lay in the understanding of Spain through her history and her landscape.

Gifted with great elegance and purity of style, Ortega wrote a series of articles included under the title of *El Espectador* [*The Spectator*], and in other books discoursed on literature and on contemporary or on traditional art and artists. These works comprise *Ideas sobre la novela* [*Ideas on the Novel*], *El espíritu de la Letra* [*The Spirit of the Letter*], *La deshumanización del arte* [*The Dehumanization of Art*], and *Papeles sobre Velázquez y Goya* [*Papers on Velazquez and Goya*].

Ortega y Gasset was one of the most brilliant of all Spanish essayists, interpreting, as he did, the form as a peripatetic intellectual expression whose ingredients were an original point of view and profound interpretatio.

Eugenio D'Ors, who became famous under the pseudonym "Xenius," was born in 1882. His early work was written in Catalan because of his journalistic work. This consisted of a daily commentary, called "Glosari" of current events and gave him the role of an intellectual orientor which he maintained and increased with his writings in Castilian Spanish. He died in 1954.

His philosophy was dubbed *Novecentismo* and was a complete reaction against romanticism. In his *Estética* [*Aesthetics*], he rejected all forms of sentimental or spontaneous expression and proposed in its stead a free and intellectualistic art called *Arbitrarismo*. In *Política* [*Politics*], he defended intellectual concepts such as the State and Empire, against the sentimentalistic concept of Nation. In his *Historia de la Cultura* [*History of Culture*], D'Ors also showed himself to be an impassioned defender of clarity and reason. His intellectualism led him to the concept of unity; man's culture is a unity, and his historical evolution is rooted in a series of repeated spiritual happenings *(eones)*.

The study of these "constants" is the object of the "science of culture." Works of this type include *Las Ideas y las Formas* [*Ideas and Forms*] and *Lo Barroco* [*The Baroque*] in which he analyzes artistic phenomena in the aspect of their fundamental attitudes which appear repeatedly, though with different names, throughout history.

His "Glosas" ["Glosses"] consist of elevating the commentary of a concrete fact to the level of general and philosophical terminology, or as d'Ors himself put it, to pass from Anecdote to Category.

The *Glosario* is, consequently, of a critical nature. By means of it the enormous variety of the world of culture may be reduced to formulas. There are three series of them, *Glosari, Nuevo glosari,* and *Novisimo glosario*.

D'Ors wrote also many books on art, painting in particular, and architecture. Among the best known are *Tres horas en el Museo del Prado* [*Three Hours in the Prado Museum*], *Cezanne*, *Picasso*, and so on.

D'Ors utilizes, in his history of art, the criterion of the painting's proximity to sculpture, in such artists as Mantegna and Poussin who accentuate drawing, or to music, as in El Greco and the Impressionists in whose works form becomes evanescent. At the center of this line of development, in complete equilibrium, he places Velázquez.

Eugenio D'Ors' work has become of considerable use in the education of young people because of its clarity of judgment, desire for systematization, and breadth of culture. For example, his book *El Valle de Josefat* [*The Valley of Josephat*] gives a judgment, in a terse and telegraphic style, of the most lofty figures of humanity. He also wrote magnificent biographies of Ferdinand and Isabella as in *Los Reyes Católicos* [*The Catholic Kings*], of Goya, and others.

His anti-romanticism is apparent in the following literary caricatures:

Bécquer—Bécquer's poetry is like an accordion played by an angel.

Espronceda—On the contrary, Espronceda sounds like a piano played with one finger.

The image is absolutely exact when he offers us those monosyllabic verses which, as poetic treatises so aptly make evident, sound like bisyllables. Moreover, Espronceda's piano is in need of repair work. Every note is seconded by some inner dry, strange notes that come from the case.

Zorrilla—As for him, it is evident that we are talking in terms of a pianola. And Zorrilla is the person who is tired of all the pedaling.

Eugenio D'Ors was an excellent narrator and wrote fictional works. His novel *La Bien Plantada* [*The Jilted Woman*] describes, with a rigorous intellectual observation, a young woman named Teresa in whom D'Ors symbolizes the harmonious classicist spirit of Mediterranean Catalonia.

Other stories of his include *Oceanografía del tedio* [*Ocean-ography of Tediousness*], *Jardín de Plantas* [*The Plant Garden*], and *El sueño es vida* [*Dream is Life*]. His desire was to write a type of novel that, for harmony and clarity, would be the an-tithesis of the brutal and pathological novel made fashionable by the works of Dostoievsky.

Ortega had various followers. Being a professor at the uni-versity, Ortega y Gasset was able to group around himself a number of thinkers who have continued his philosophical en-deavors. Among these followers, the best known is probably Xavier Zubiri, for his work *Naturaleza, historia, Dios* [*Nature, History, God*], 1944.

Other notable thinkers of this group are Julián Marías who studied the works of Ortega and of Unamuno and has written various brilliant philosophical essays, and Pedro Laín Entralgo who has done research on Menéndez y Pelayo and the Genera-tion of '98.

The essay of philosophical and historical interpretation has a long history in Spanish letters. In this tradition, we might point out such eminent figures as Salvador de Madariaga who has made important studies in the history of Latin America and of English literature, José María de Cossío who has done masterly studies of themes related to tauromachy and poetry, and Angel Valbuena Prat, literary historian who has done notable research in the field of the Spanish classics.

In contemporary literature, journalistic writing has also ac-quired considerable importance.

In addition to the aforementioned magazine, the *Revista de Occidente*, which was liberal and European in orientation, there were other noteworthy publications including *Cruz y Raya* which was predominantly Catholic, and other magazines like *La Gaceta Literaria* and *Escorial*. The daily press itself has considerable literary importance. The literary sections of many papers have, or have had, much prestige, including *El Imparcial, El Sol, El Debate, ABC,* all of Madrid, and *La Vanguardia,* of Barcelona.

Among the many names known for journalistic excellence we might mention Mariano de Cavia, José María Salaverría, Gabriel Alomar, Eugenio Montes, Ernesto Jiménez Caballero, Pedro

Mourlane Michelena, Rafael Sánchez Mazas, and Víctor de la Serna.

Research

One of the hallmarks of the contemporary period is the increase in critical activity. This is true of Spain as well as of other Occidental countries.

The study of the past was made under rigorously exacting conditions. In the second half of the nineteenth century, José María Quadrado devoted himself to a study of Spanish art in his *Recuerdos de España* [*Memories of Spain*]. Vicente Lampárez has done valuable research on architecture and Manuel B. Cossío has drawn world attention to the figure of El Greco. José Pioján has made important historical synthesis and José Camón Aznar has made penetrating interpretations of Spanish art.

New histories of literature appeared. The gigantic work of Menéndez y Pelayo opened up the way for critical and literary erudition. Some of his disciples followed closely in his footsteps. Among them are Antonio Rubio y Luch who has made studies of the works of Calderón, Cervantes, and Fray Luis; Francisco Rodríguez María who has done important work on folklore and literature; Pedro Sainz Rodríguez, the author of works on Spanish mystical and scholarly literature; Emilio Cotarelo, a scholar of the drama; Miguel Artigas who has done a definitive study of Góngora; and Angel González Palencia, an outstanding Arabist and tireless scholar and critic.

There is also a group of literary scholars who have worked under Ramón Menéndez Pidal, the most profound and well informed scholar of the Spanish epic tradition, the editor and researcher of the *Poema del Cid* and of the chronicles and ballad tradition, and, undoubtedly, the master of Spanish philology. Among his disciples may be numbered Dámaso Alonso who has renovated and definitively resolved the problems of style in Góngora.

The following is a passage from Ramón Menéndez Pidal's study of the Cid:

A hero whose fame rests on his dedication to an arduous purpose, who tenaciously rebuilds what has been destroyed time and again and was always threatened by the wrath of the king, who struggled against the extensive empire of the Moors and against the elusive armies of jealousy and envy, an historical Hercules who overcame the stubborn enmity of the gods and the fury of monsters, he will always be a powerful example for young people.

Several writers are not strictly in the field of literature. For example, Santiago Ramón y Cajal, the illustrious neurologist of world-wide renown, wrote several interesting autobiographical books including *Recuerdos de mi vida [Memoires]* and *El mundo visto a los ochenta años [The World Seen at the Age of Eighty]* and the important *Reglas y consejos sobre investigación [Rules and Advice Concerning Scientific Investigation]*.

Comparably, Dr. Gregorio Marañón, in addition to his pro-digious scientific work, cultivated historical research up until his death in 1960. Among his books are *Luis Vives, Las ideas biológicas del Padre Feijóo [The Biological Ideas of Father Feijóo]*, *El Conde-Duque de Olivares*, and *Antonio Pérez*. The equilibrium of his judgment is particularly noteworthy.

The Novel

In the contemporary novel we can find the following directions:

1. Preoccupation with style. The novelists of the turn of the century—Palacio Valdés, Blasco Ibáñez, and Baroja, for example —are characterized by their sense of observation of reality. At the same time, they were careless in matters of style. The polished work of Azorín, on the one hand, and the care devoted by the modernists to matters of form, brought about a preoccupation with style which is to be observed in the novelists studied below.

Ricardo León (1877–1943), for example, liked to evoke the heroic Castile of untouched little villages like Santillana del Mar in his novel *Casta de hidalgos [Aristocratic Lineage]*, or in the traditional and religious customs of *El amor de los amores [The*

Love of Loves]. His ideals embody a noble defense of the Spanish tradition, one of exaltation that contrasts with the pessimism of '98.

> Good Castilians never close up the tombs of our paladins. . . . One day our Lord the Cid Rodrigo de Vivar, who knows how to win battles long after death, will awaken in his grave and after cleaning the rust off his sword will mount his nervous steed and will tear away the shrouds from sepulchers and cradles. And he will swear by the cross on his sword to rid Spain of renegades and of thieves.

Nevertheless, his style is heavy and declamatory and, in final analysis, artificial. Archaisms and rhetorical sentences, which make his work empty and tiresome, abound. His preoccupation with style impairs the spontaneity of phrasing. In his later novels he is more realistic and objective.

Ramón Pérez de Ayala was born in 1880 and educated in Oviedo. Even when the basic theme of his works is the psychology of his characters who are often strange in temperament or extravagances, the cities and countryside of Asturias appear in the pages of his novels. This is true of *La pata de la raposa* [*The Fox's Paw*], *Belamino y Apolonio,* and *Tigre Juan.* In some of his works he is tendentious and exaggerated.

He has published works of poetry of a modernistic type but with a certain archaic flavor, and of a literary criticism that is generally rigorous and well informed.

Pérez de Ayala's style, although abounding in archaisms, is polished and complete and demonstrates a profound knowledge of language. At times he delights in mixing scholarly words with everyday phrases, manipulating puns and contrasts, sarcasm and irony, showing his admirable acquaintance with the Spanish classics.

Gabriel Miró (1878–1931) has captured in his novels all the light and color of his native region of Alicante, in *El libro de Sigüenza* [*The Book of Sigüenza*] and *Años y leguas* [*Years and Leagues*], or of its cities as in *Nuestro Padre San Daniel* [*Our*

Father Saint Daniel] and *El Obispo Leproso* [*The Leprous Bishop*]. Of particular beauty are the descriptive passages of his *Figuras de la Pasión del Señor* [*Figures of the Passion of the Lord*].

His novels are of greater value for their descriptive elements than for the interest of their plots which digress into long contemplative paragraphs or into inner monologues. As a result the books of greatest interest are those in which the author recalls the psychological and sensory memories of childhood. In these the manner in which the author writes is more important than what he tells.

His style is slow-moving and tractable. He has a liking for developing before the eyes of his reader the image of his sensations; the color, the odor, the sounds of each landscape find the perfectly adequate adjective. Often Miró gives life to things which, on being described by him, begin to have movement and strike postures. He is one of the most artistically successful Spanish writers of the century.

2. The continuation of the naturalistic tradition. In search of a wider public appeal, many novelists sacrificed preoccupation with style to portray, with varying degrees of rawness, the reality of their times.

Such authors as Felipe Trigo, Alberto Insúa, Eugenio Noel, and Alejandro Pérez Lugín became very popular.

The naturalistic vision is surpassed by means of poetical and human emotion in the writings of Concha Espina (1871–1955) who evoked the life of a small village of Castile in *La esfinge maragata* [*The Sphinx of Maragatería*] and the beauty of Covadonga in *Altar Mayor* [*High Altar*].

3. Humorists. Another means of going beyond naturalism is found in humorists like Wenceslao Fernández who was born in La Coruña in 1885. In his novels *Fantamas* [*Phantoms*] and *Los que no fuimos a la guerra* [*Those of Us Who Did Not Go to War*] he makes us smile, while in *El bosque animado* [*The Animated Woods*] he makes us dream. Another Gallegan, Julio Camba, who was born in Villaneuva de Arosa in 1886, was the author of *Aventuras de una peseta* [*Adventures of a Peseta*] and sparkling travel tales. Alvaro Cunqueiro, born in Mondoñedo in

1910, was another Galician. His formidable powers of imagination which invented innumerable incredible episodes can be observed in *Merlín y familia* and in *Las crónicas del sochantre* [*The Chronicles of the Subchanter*].

Ramón Gómez de la Serna is one of the major renovators of Spanish prose. He was born in Madrid in 1888. His style matured, within his humorous vision of the world, in the captivation of small observations to which the author gave the name of *greguerías*.

Present-day life, he says, "has broken new ground, has divided up styles, has opened holes in them and has given them a rhythm that is freer, lighter and more odd."

His novelistic production is enormous. Among his works are the memorable *El dueño del átomo* [*The Master of the Atom*], *El caballero del hongo gris* [*The Gentlemen with the Gray Derby*], *La mujer de ambar* [*The Woman of Amber*] and whole books of *greguerías* and of observations of Madrid's "flea market," as in *El Rastro*, and the circus in *El Circo*, in addition to his autobiography, *Automoribundia*.

4. The return to naturalism, the *Tremendistas*. The fundamental characteristic of the contemporary novel in Spain is the analysis of the rawest aspects of reality, whether in the life that surrounds the novelist, as in Carmen Laforet's *Nada* [*Nothing*], which was published in 1944, or one that is invented and accumulates harsh and disagreeable details as in Camilo José Cela's novel of 1942, *La familia de Pascual Duarte* [*Pascual Duarte's Family*]. Another type describes the vignettes of everyday life in all their color and movement as in the novels of Juan Antonio de Zunzunegui: *Las ratas del barco* [*The Rats of the Ship*] of 1950 and *La vida como es* [*Life as It Is*] of 1953.

This means of enlarging the negative aspects of existence is called *tremendismo* and is characterized, in its spiritual aspects, by a desolate pessimism. Literally the "movement" offers estimable successes, especially in those aspects concerning the study of language.

5. The historico-documentary novel. In addition there has been a series of novels on the Spanish Civil War: in 1943, *La fiel infantería* [*The Loyal Infantry*] by Rafael García Serrano; in 1954, *Cuerpo de tierra* [*Body of Earth*] by Ricardo Fernández de la Reguera; and the major historico-documentary cycle begun by José María Gironella with his *Los cipreses creen en Dios* [*The Cypresses Believe in God*], 1953, and *Un millón de muertos* [*A Million Dead*], 1961.

Poetry

From the time of the First World War on, the Spanish literary panorama underwent a radical change. Spanish poetry had exhausted the possibilities of modernism and a series of literary schools which mirrored similar movements in European literature came into existence.

In poetry several movements left their mark:

Ultraismo. Under this name and that of *Futurismo,* there appeared, shortly after the First Great War, a literary movement whose subject matter was mechanical objects and war.

In search of novelty, the "Ultraist" poets turned to *caligramas,* a form of poetry made fashionable by the French poet Apollinaire. Its subject matter is machines, planes, factories, conflict and, in general, the manifestations of the contemporary cosmopolitan spirit. The poems were written in an "expressionistic" typography.

The models for this poetry were the American Walt Whitman, the poetry of the workaday world, the Frenchman, Guillaume Apollinaire whose *caligramas* were widely read, and Filippo Tommaso Marinetti who provoked incredible turmoil in Italy to publicize his theories on "Futurism."

Gerardo Diego was born in Santander in 1896. He was a professor at the Institute and a member of the Academy. He began his poetic work partially within the Ultraist movement, orienting his poetic line toward a *creacionism* with very personal strophes or metaphors. We find this exemplified in his poem *Rosa Mística* [*Mystical Rose*]:

It was she
                    And no one knew it
But when she passed
the trees fell to their knees
There nestled in her eyes
                    the avemaria
and in her hair
                    were plaited distant places
It was she
                    It was she
I swooned in her hands
like a fallen leaf

                    her gothic hands
                    that fed the stars

Through the air flew
romance without sound

                    And on her pillow of dreams
                    I fell asleep.

Gerardo Diego's work evolved with the new poetic schools, of which he became an outstanding figure.

2. "Neopopularismo." As a reaction against this purely descriptive and impersonal literature, a group of Andalusian poets turned to the poetry of the people. They took its turns of phrase and its form but kept the taste for daring metaphors of modernism and ultraism. The movement also drew on the traditional and sensitive poetry of the *cancioneros* of the fifteenth century.

Ultraism like modernism was cosmopolitan, which is to say, both aspired to be an art that was remote from local color. The neopopularist reaction possibly had as a precedent music of Andalusian theme, as from Albéniz, Falla, and Turina, and turned to the most typical and picturesque types and landscapes.

Federico García Lorca (1898–1936) was from the province of Granada. Although an important dramatist, Lorca initiated his work within modernistic tendencies with his *Libro de poemas* [*Book of Poems*]. He went on to become in *Canciones* [*Songs*],

344 History of Spanish Literature

Romancero Gitano [Gypsy Ballads], and Poema de Cante Jondo [Poem of the Deep Song], the finest interpreter of the Andalusian soul, which he saw with a profound and elegant sense of drama coupled with an intuition of sorrow and foreboding. His preferred poetic form was a short verse line, either the copla or the popular ballad or romance to which he added daring metaphors. The following passage is an example of this:

The Rider's Song

Cordova.
Alone and far away.

Black my mare is, full the moon,
Olives in my saddle-bag are stowed.
Although I know the roadway well,
I'll never get to Cordova.

Across the plain and through the wind,
Black my mare is, red the moon,
Death is looking down at me,
Down from the towers of Cordova.
Ay, how long the roadway is!
Ay, my valorous black mare!
Ay, Death is looking out at me,
Before I get to Cordova.

Cordova.
Alone and far away.

3. *Superrealismo. Superrealismo,* a type of surrealism, frequently depicted the illogical and fantastic world of dreams and the subconscious with complete independence of the rules of art and the poetic tradition.

The French surrealistic school was given form and definition by the poet André Breton who, in his book *Manifeste du Surréalisme,* tells us that the new school should transmit to the page by automatic writing those images of the world of dreams or of the subconscious which the poet receives.

Rafael Alberti was born in 1903. He is Andalusian as was Lorca, and like the latter cultivated neopopular themes and forms in *Marinero en tierra* [*Mariner on Land*] and *El alba del alhelí* [*The Dawn of the Gilliflower*]. His most ambitious work, however, is Surrealist and is entitled *Sobre los ángeles* [*About the Angels*]. The poet imagines the conflict of his inner drives, his angels, as in the following passages:

> Angel of light, shining,
> O come, and with your sword
> light up the deep abyss where lies
> My subterranean angel of the mists.
> O sword-low in the shadows:
> Multiply the sparks,
> driving themselves into my body,
> into my featherless wings,
> into what no one sees,
> life.
>
> You are burning me alive.
> Flee from me, dark
> Lucifer of quarries without sand,
> of wells that hold no water,
> of chasms without dreams,
> already charcoal of the spirit,
> sun, moon.
>
> My anguish and my locks of hair,
> Give me distress, Oh burn me!
> More, more, yes, yes, more. Burn me!
>
> Burn it, Angel of light, my guardian,
> you who weeping move among the clouds;
> you without me, you for me,
> cold angel of dust, your glory sped,
> thrown into the darkness!
>
> Burn it, angel of light,
> burn me and flee!

In its evasion of reality, surrealism is a sort of new romanticism which takes delight in the world of the dream. The greatest poet of the movement today is Vicente Aleixandre.

4. *Poesía pura* or pure poetry. The quest for a sincere poetic expression which would reflect the deepest being of the author led the poets, as we noted in speaking of Juan Ramón Jiménez (1881–1958), to write works in form, as rhythm and rhyme did not count; what was important were the ideas or feelings stripped bare of all but the most important elements. It was this orientation which began the talk of the so-called "pure poetry."

The desire for a "pure poetry" developed out of a quest for the true profundities of poetry which are neither the musicality of the verses nor the superficial "plot" of the poem.

Pedro Salinas (1891–1951) wrote a deeply intimate poetry full of feeling in which the subjective vision of the loved woman appears as in Bécquer; the loved one is a figure which the poet must constantly recreate, at times without anyone's knowing it, by struggling with reality itself.

The sensory contact of the poet with the multiple image of the world is the keynote of the poetry of Jorge Guillén (b. 1893) which is a perpetual exaltation and which he has entitled *Cántico*. In the following passages, translated by Richard Wilbur, reality issues forth before the poet's eyes:

The Horses.

Shaggy and heavily natural, they stand
Immobile under their thick and cumbrous manes,
Pent in a barbed enclosure which contains,
By way of compensation, grazing-land.
Nothing disturbs them now. In slow increase
They fatten like the grass. Doomed to be idle,
To haul no cart or wagon, wear no bridle,
They grow into a vegetable peace.

Soul is the issue of so strict a fate.
They harbour visions in their waking eyes,
And with their quiet ears participate
In heaven's pure serenity, which lies
So near all things—yet from the beasts concealed.
Serene now, superhuman, they crop their field.

Death, from a Distance.

> *Je soutenais l'éclat*
> *de la mort toute pure.*
> —Valéry

When that dead-certainty appals my thought,
My future trembles on the road ahead.
There where the light of country fields is caught
In the blind, final precinct of the dead,
A will takes aim.
　　　But what is sad, stripped bare
By the sun's gaze? It does not matter now,
Not yet. What matters is the ripened pear
That even now my hand strips from the bough.

The time will come: my hand will reach, some day,
Without desire. That saddest day of all,
I shall not weep, but with a proper awe
For the great force impending, I shall say,
Lay on, just destiny. Let the white wall
Impose on me its capricious law.

　　　　　—Translations by Richard Wilbur

5. Poetical trends since the Spanish Civil War. The period
begins in 1939, at the end of the Spanish Civil War, and has the
following characteristics:

1. The peak of the poetic mastery of such poets of the movements of the Generation of '98 and of modernism, and especially
of Antonio Machado and Juan Ramón Jiménez, as well as of
Vicente Aleixandre, who published his most important books in

this period, including *Sombra del Paraíso* [*Shadow of Paradise*] (1944) and *Historia del corazón* [*Story of the Heart*] (1954).

2. A return to an unadorned classicism in the group called "Garcilaso," whose major figures are José García Nieto, born in 1916, and Dionisio Ridruejo, born in 1912. Both are concerned with the perfection of form and are partial to the sonnet.

3. An intensification of expression and a quest for the sorrows of existence. This is what we find in the poetry of Miguel Hernández (1910–1942) in his *Viento del pueblo* [*Wind from the Village*], 1937, and of Dámaso Alonso in his *Hijos de la ira* [*Children of Anger*], 1944. In Alonso's *Hombre y Dios* [*Man and God*], 1955, existential anxiety is transformed into a religious sublimation.

4. A spiritualistic tendency, Catholic in orientation, the mark of another group of contemporary poets among whom is José María Valverde, who was born in 1926, the author of *Hombre de Dios* [*Man of God*] (1945) and whose work is characterized by a return to the more tender themes of everyday life. Another member of this group is Luis Rosales who wrote *La casa encendida* [*The Burning House*] (1949).

5. A lyrical tendency which sees man as a social being who suffers from the injustice of other men. One of the representative writers of this school, Gabriel Celaya, has written, "Poetry is not an end in itself. It is an instrument for the transformation of the world." In addition to Celaya two other members of the group are Blas de Otero and Angela Figuera Aymerich.

Drama

On the contemporary stage several tendencies are discernible: (1) the social drama of the playwright Jacinto Benavente, (2) poetic drama, (3) realistic drama, (4) comedy, (5) the drama of evasion, (6) the drama of attestation and of denunciation.

1. Jacinto Benavente was born in Madrid in 1866 and died in 1954. He was the most important Spanish playwright of his time. His work is very extensive, with over a hundred titles, and very popular. It is characterized, in style, by a reaction against the declamatory and solemn drama of Echegaray. His characters speak in prose and with complete naturalness. His satires are created

with delicate ironical shadings without recourse to violent expression. His language generally is that of the cultured society of Madrid.

His best-known work is entitled *Los intereses creados* [*Vested Interests*]. Using the traditional characters of the Italian *commedia dell'arte*, Benavente analyzed the double planes of the human psyche.

COLOMBINA: And who is your master, if you don't mind telling me?

CRISPIN: The most noble of gentlemen and the most powerful. Forgive me if right now I don't pronounce his name. You will know it soon enough. My master wishes to greet the Lady Sirena and to attend her party tonight.

COLOMBINA: The party! How did you find out . . . ?

CRISPIN: I know. My duty is to find everything out. I know that there have been certain inconveniences that could spoil things, but there will be none for everything has been taken care of.

COLOMBINA: How did you know that . . . ?

CRISPIN: I can assure you that nothing will be lacking. Sumptuous refreshments, illuminations and firework displays, musicians and singers. It will be the most brilliant party ever held . . .

COLOMBINA: Are you some sort of magician by any chance?

CRISPIN: You will get to know me. I can only tell you that for some good reason destiny has brought together here today people of such clear understanding and incapable of being unsuccessful because of idle scruples. My master knows that Polichinela and his daughter, the lovely Silvia, the best match in the city, will be here tonight. My master intends to win her love, my master intends to marry her and my master will know how to properly reward the kind help of the Lady Sirena and your own if you decide to favor him.

COLOMBINA: Don't beat about the bush. Your outspokenness should offend me.

CRISPIN: The time is too short to permit the usual courtesies.

COLOMBINA: If one is to judge the master by the servant . . .

CRISPIN: Have no fear. You will find my master a most kind and courteous gentlemen. My lack of scruples allows him to feel shame. The harsh necessities of life can force even the noblest of men to the acts of a ruffian, as they can oblige the noblest of ladies to undertake the lowest of functions and this mixture of baseness and of nobility in the same person can bring discredit in the world. The real feat is to divide in two different people what normally is found in only one. My master and I, being one and the same, are each a part of the other one. If only it could always be that way!

We all carry within us a great gentleman of lofty thoughts, capable of all that is admirable and beautiful. . . . And at his side is the humble servant, he of the degrading acts, he who devotes himself to the base undertakings which life forces on us all. . . . The trick is to separate the two in such a way that when we fall into some base deed we can always say: That's not mine, that's not I, it was my servant. In the deepest misery of our life there is always something that wants to feel itself superior to ourselves. We would despise ourselves too much if we did not think ourselves of greater worth than the life we live. . . . You already know who my master is. He is the person of elevated thoughts, of idealistic dreams. You already know who I am: the person with the demeaning jobs, the one who always moves along the ground and digs into every lie and indignity and misery. There is only one thing in me that redeems me and lifts me in my own eyes. This loyalty of my servitude, this loyalty which humbles itself and abases itself so that the other can take wing and can always be the gentleman of lofty thoughts, of the most idealistic dreams.

—From *Vested Interests*

In content, Benavente criticizes the vices, and above all the apathy and pride, of the Spanish aristocracy in such plays as *La comida de las fieras* [*The Beasts' Meal*] and *Campo de armiño* [*Ground of Ermine*]. In other works his satire has a broader national sense, as in the aforementioned *Intereses creados* and in

La ciudad alegre y confiada [*The Happy and Confident City*] in which he underscores the dangers inherent in the Spanish character and the tendency to inaction.

Benavente also wrote plays with a rural setting, *Señora Ama*, and *La Malquerida*, sometimes translated as *The Passion Flower*, both works strongly dramatic and centered on secret passions.

2. Poetic drama. Along with the depiction of everyday life as represented in Benavente, there also appeared a drama in verse whose first author in this period was Eduardo Marquina (1879–1946).

His work may be divided into two groups: historical drama and realistic drama in a rural setting. In the former category, the best-known work is *En Flandes se ha puesto el sol* [*The Sun Has Set in Flanders*] (1911).

A Spanish captain, Diego Acuña de Carvajal, has a Flemish wife who shelters relatives who conspire against Spain. He decides to help the latter despite the fact that his act will bring him imprisonment and dishonor, and as a result he breaks his sword:

> With the breaking of my sword, broken is my life.
> Heaven shall my fate henceforth dispose.
> Now you know what I am like, and Spain!

Of realistic drama in a rural setting, Marquina has bequeathed us, in the field an excellent work, *La ermita, la fuente y el río* [*The Hermitage, the Fountain and the River*] (1922).

The plays of the modernist poet Francisco Villaespesa (1877–1936) were contemporary with the early productions of Marquina.

The poetic drama has continued to be cultivated in Spain, notably by José María Pemán, who was born in 1898, an orator and excellent articulator. Among his most successful works are *El divino impaciente* [*The Impatient Saint*], the story of Saint Francis Xavier's evangelization; *Cuando las Cortes de Cádiz* [*In the Days of the Parliament of Cadiz*], which takes place in the time of the Spanish War of Independence against Napoleon; and *La Santa Virreina* [*The Holy Viceroy's Wife*], which is a tale of Spanish colonization of America.

352 *History of Spanish Literature*

3. Realistic drama. Realistic plays were written by Manuel Linares Rivas with his *La Garra* [*The Claw*], Joaquín Dicenta with his *Juan José,* and Gregorio Martínez Sierra with his *Canción de cuna* [*Cradle Song*].

The tradition of plays which show the life of the people of Madrid has been continued in the witty sainetes or short interludes of Carlos Arniches. A similar type of realism showing Andalusian life dominates the sparkling scenes of the brothers Joaquín and Serafín Alvarez Quintero.

In the post-Civil War period, Joaquín Calvo Sotelo (in *La muralla* or *The Wall*), Juan Ignacio Luca de Tena, Alfonso Paso, and others have carried on the tradition.

4. Comedy. One interesting aspect of the Spanish stage tradition is that of comedy which has taken on different characteristics in the work of Pedro Muñoz Seca (1881–1936) with his *astracán* and Enrique Jardiel Poncela (1907–1952) and Miguel Mihura with their sense of humorous absurdity.

5. The drama of evasion. Another group of authors tends to elude everyday reality in its quest of poetic or dream-like settings. This is true of a part of the works of Alejandro Casona as in *Otra vez el diablo* [*The Devil Again*] and *La sirena varada* [*The Stranded Mermaid*], of José López Rubio in his *Celos del aire* and *Alberto,* and of Victor Ruiz Iriarte in his *El landó de seis caballos* [*The Landau With Six Horses*].

6. The drama of negation and of denunciation. Another characteristic of the Spanish drama of our time is the appearance of works which protest life about us, for example, the harsh reality faced by the humble people of *Historia de una escalera* [*Story of a Stairway*] by Antonio Buero Vallejo. He has also applied his critical attitude to the past in *Las Meninas* [*The Ladies in Waiting*] (about the Court of Philip IV), in *Un soñador para un pueblo* [*A Dreamer for a People*] (about the Spain of the eighteenth century).

The drama of Alfonso Sastre is of similar intent. In *Escuadra hacia la muerte* [*Squadron Against Death*], he expresses his anguish when faced with the bloodshed of a new world conflict.

Addendum on Contemporary Spanish Literature

Despite over thirty years since the conflict came to an end, the Civil War of 1936–1939 remains a central fact of Spanish life to the present day. Those who lived through it still discuss it with vividness and vehemence. Every aspect of Spanish life either directly or indirectly has been effected by it. No historian, literary or otherwise, can avoid its consequences. On what might be called the positive side, the war has become an important and lasting topic and theme of prose fiction. On the debit side, it resulted in death or exile for some of Spain's major artistic and intellectual figures and has been the justification for a government censorship which has been practiced with varying degrees of severity and overtness down to the present time. As in the case of every war, we can never know how many of the young who perished might have made major contributions to the intellectual life of their nation had they lived. As it was, a period of literary and intellectual creativity second only to the great Golden Age of the sixteenth and seventeenth centuries was brought to a sudden and brutal halt.

The most widely known and perhaps the most tragic loss to Spanish literature was the murder, in the opening days of the war, of Federico García Lorca whose poetry has been discussed above. His death was long thought to have been political in origin. However, it has since been fairly well established to have been an act of personal revenge carried out during the confusion that prevailed at the beginnings of the conflict. Nevertheless, the Republicans and their sympathizers outside of Spain soon saw in Lorca a martyr and a symbol of the struggle against Fascism. In the post-Civil War period, Lorca's works were difficult to obtain in Spain. This situation has changed in the last two decades, however, as there has been a slowly growing governmental policy of liberalization in many regards. Lorca's friends have frequently repeated the fact that Lorca had little direct interest in politics, but while the social implications of his best-known plays, with their atmospheres of repression in a tradition-bound society, his so-called rural tragedies, *Bodas de sangre* [*Blood Wedding*, 1933], *Yerma* (1934), and *La Casa de Bernarda Alba* [*The House of Bernarda Alba*, 1936], together with *Doña Rosita la soltera* [*Doña Rosita the Spinster*, 1935], do not openly urge more "liberal" attitudes, there are clear thematic implications for a change of the rigid and frustrating moral codes of Spanish life. Certain political and social stances are also implicit in his poems, most notably in the *Romancero gitano* [*Gypsy Ballads*], published in 1928, with their powerful scenes of the brutal massacre of the gypsies by the Civil Guard, the ubiquitous police force in their patent leather tricornes that Arturo Barea, in his book *Lorca, the Poet and His People,* has called the keeper of the "black soul of Spain." Nevertheless, much of Lorca's great appeal before, during and since the Civil War, stems from the fact that he is deeply traditional. His love of his native land and of things Spanish is apparent throughout his works, as is his intimate knowledge of the history, music, poetry, drama and art of his country. His long poem, the *Llanto por Ignacio Sánchez Mejía,* usually translated as *Lament for a Bullfighter,* ranks with the *Coplas* of Jorge Manrique as one of the great elegies of Hispanic poetry.

If Lorca was the first important literary figure to fall a casualty to the destructiveness of war, he was not the last. Even Miguel de Unamuno, some would claim, was, in a sense, a victim. First declaring in favor of the Nationalist forces under Generalissimo Franco, he soon saw the anti-intellectualism of the Fascist right and spoke out. He died shortly after, in late 1936, while under house confinement. The poet Antonio Machado perished of illness a few days after going into exile in France after the fall of the last Republican forces in 1939. Miguel Hernández, died in prison at the tragically early age of 32 in 1942, a victim of tuberculosis and pulmonary complications brought on by suffering endured in political concentration camps. These are perhaps the best known, but to the list must be added the names of the many renowned writers who went into exile, the poets Jorge Guillén and Pedro Salinas who came to the United States, Juan Ramón Jiménez who, like world-famous cellist Pablo Casals, went to reside in Puerto Rico, Rafael Alberti who sought refuge in

Argentina, the novelists Ramón Sender, who lived in New Mexico, and Arturo Barea, who died in England, the poet-playwright-novelist Max Aub who lives in Mexico, León Felipe who died in Mexico in 1969, and the dramatist Alejandro Casona who long made his residence in Buenos Aires but who returned and died in Madrid in 1965, to mention only some of the best known.

After the brilliance of literary activity in the Spain of the first decades of the twentieth century, literature herself seemed a victim in the immediate post-Civil War period. While such major novelists as Baroja and Azorín, and poet-scholars as Dámaso Alonso and Vicente Aleixandre, continued to live and write in Spain, it was not until 1942 with the publication of Camilo José Cela's controversial and brutal *Familia de Pascual Duarte* that a literary renaissance began. The impulse once given, prose fiction began appearing in great abundance. Cela's influence has been a lasting one. The number of his published works is too great to list here. Some of the best known are: *Nuevas andanzas y desventuras de Lazarillo de Tormes* [*New Wanderings and Misfortunes of Lazarillo de Tormes*, 1944], *Pabellón de reposo* [*Rest Home*, 1943], *La colmena* [*The Hive*, 1951], *Baraja de invenciones* [*A Pack of Tales*, 1953], *Mrs. Caldwell habla con su hijo* [*Mrs. Caldwell Talks with Her Son*, 1953], *Judíos, moros y cristianos* [*Jews, Moors and Christians*, 1956], *Primer viaje andaluz* [*First Andalusian Journey*, 1959], *Nuevas escenas matritenses* [*New Scenes of Madrid*, 1965, 1966], *La Familia del héroe* [*The Hero's Family*, 1965], and the amusingly satirical *Viaje a U.S.A.* [*Journey to the U.S.A.*, 1967]. Cela founded and edits the prestigious literary review, *Los Papeles de Son Armadans*.

The great number of excellent novelists who have appeared on the literary scene in the intervening years makes accurate evaluation of the quality of contemporary Spanish literature difficult. Critics, by the very nature of their work, must make value judgments. The scholar, as investigator and elucidator, frequently avoids overt evaluation. After all, in one's own times it is often hard to see the forest for the trees; we lack the perspective of time. Furthermore tastes in literature change just as styles do, and the authors who loom large on the literary horizon today might seem to have relatively little intrinsic importance or value a generation from now. Nevertheless, some attempt at systematizing the very recent past must be made, with or without well-defined canons to guide us. One contemporary critic-scholar whose influence is steadily growing, Juan Luis Alborg, currently living and teaching in the United States—a book could be written about the major twentieth-century literary figures who have come to America to teach and to live, men like Francisco Ayala, Joaquín Casalduero, Francisco García Lorca, Jorge Guillén, José F. Montesinos, Federico de Onís, Angel del Río, Fernando de los Ríos, Ramón Sender, among others—devotes, in his two-volume study, *Hora actual de la novela española* [*The Current Spanish Novel,* 1958 and 1962], a chapter each to twenty-nine different novelists. These include: Camilo José Cela, Ignacio Agustí, Carmen Laforet, José María Gironella, Miguel Delibes, Pedro de Lorenzo, Ana María Matute, Elena Quiroga, Ricardo Fernández de la Reguera, Tomás Salvador, Alejandro Núñez Alonso, Ignacio Aldecoa, José Luis Castillo Puche, Rafael Sánchez Ferlosio, Antonio Prieto, Ramón J. Sender, Max Aub, Juan Antonio Zunzunegui, Manuel Halcón, Arturo Barea, Gonzalo Torrente Ballester, Sebastían Juan Arbó, Darío Fernández Flórez, Luis Romero, Dolores Medio, Elena Soriano, Jesús Fernández Santos, Mercedes Salisachs, and José María Castillo Navarro. Many of these writers first came to prominence by winning the coveted *Premio Nadal* or Nadal Prize for the novel. This award was first given in 1944 to Carmen Laforet for her now famous *Nada* [*Nothing*], the story of Andrea, a young woman of eighteen, who goes to Barcelona two years after the Civil War to live with relatives while she goes to college. Much of the interest of the novel lies in the descriptions of the nightmarish and sordid lives of her family, their hopes, frustrations and conflicts, in which some critics have seen a portrayal of the decadence of postwar Spain. Laforet has continued to publish various works, both short stories published in *La muerta* [*The Dead Woman,* 1952], and *La llamada* [*The Call,* 1954], and novels such as *La isla y los demonios* [*The Island and the Demons,* 1952], and *La mujer nueva* [*The New Woman,* 1955], the recipient of two literary prizes.

Probably the most widely read of the novelists studied by Alborg is still José María Gironella who wrote penetrating novels centered on the Civil War period. Others who have received considerable critical attention and who have published numerous works, are Juan Antonio Zunzunegui, born in 1902, recipient of the Fastenrath Prize for his *Ay estos hijos* [*Oh These Children*] in 1943 and named to the Spanish Academy in 1957; Miguel Delibes, born in 1920, who won the Nadal Prize in 1947 for his tragic tale of an orphan youth in *La sombra del ciprés es alargada* [*The Shadow of the Cypres Tree is Lengthy*]; Elena Quiroga, born in 1921, whose novel about a Galician nobleman who marries a servant girl, *Viento del norte* [*Wind From the North*], was the Nadal winner in 1951; Ana María Matute, born in 1926, and also recipient of the Nadal Prize in 1952 for her *Fiesta al noroeste* [*Party to the Northwest*], and Rafael Sanchez Ferlosio whose *El jarama* received the Nadal Prize in 1955.

Even this list, however, is not currently adequate, for in the decade since the publication of Alborg's studies, other novelists have made their mark. One of the most notable of these is Juan Goytisolo, considered by some to be the most promising of the "new generation" that began publishing in the 1950s. He was born in Barcelona in 1931 and now lives most of the time in Paris, making frequent trips back to his native land. *Juegos de manos* [*The Young Assasins*], published in 1954, brought him immediate recognition. The story is one of the tribulations of adolescents in the Spanish Civil War and the corrupting influence of war; it paints a vivid picture of the sordid conditions of life in the period shortly after the conflict's end. The theme of the war and its effects on Spanish life have persisted in Goytisolo's work to the present, in such works as *Duelo en el paraíso* [*Duel in Paradise*, 1955], which won the *Indice* Prize, *Fiestas*, which was banned in Spain and first published in Buenos Aires, *Fin de fiesta* (1962), translated as *The Party's Over*, which is a collection of four short *novellas*, and more recently, *Señas de identidad*, translated as *Marks of Identity* in 1969, in which the author purportedly speaks for those Spaniards who, children during the Civil War, grew up during Generalissimo Franco's "twenty-five years of peace and prosperity."

Another novelist who came on the literary scene in the 1950's is Angel María de Lera, who although born in 1912, did not publish his first novel, *Los olvidados* [*The Forgotten Ones*], until 1957. This was followed in rapid succession by a series of works: *Los clarines del miedo* [*The Trumpets of Fear*, 1958], *La boda*

[*The Wedding*, 1959], *Bochorno* [*Hot Wind*, 1960], *Trampa* [*Trap*, 1962], *Hemos perdido el sol* [*We Have Lost the Sun*, 1962], a story of Spanish workers living in Germany, *Tierra para morir* [*Land in Which to Die*, 1964], which won two major literary prizes, *Las últimas banderas* [*The Last Flags*, 1967], based on the last week of the siege of Madrid in 1939, plus various articles for magazines and newspapers. Two of his novels, *Los clarines del miedo* and *Bochorno*, have been made into motion pictures. His works have been translated into a number of languages.

Three older writers also deserve mention here: Max Aub, born in 1903, Arturo Barea, 1897-1957, and Ramón Sender, born in 1902. Both Aub and Barea gained prominence in the post-Civil War period while living in exile. Aub's novels, *Campo cerrado* [*Closed Field*, 1939], and *Campo de sangre* [*Field of Blood*, 1943], concern the Civil War, while his short work of 1960, *La verdadera historia de la muerte de Francisco Franco* [*The True Death of Francisco Franco*] is humorously satirical. Barea is best known for his trilogy, *La forja de un rebelde* [*The Forging of a Rebel*], first published in English in 1944 as *The Forge, The Track* and *The Flash*. These works are autobiographical as well as novels and go from the author-protagonist's childhood and adolescence in Madrid, through his experiences as a soldier in the war in Morocco in 1921, and finally recount the seige of Madrid and subsequent exile in France after the conflict's end. Sender, who lived for some time in New Mexico, became famous with the publication in 1929 of his story of military service in Morocco, *Imán*, translated as *Earmarked for Hell* in 1934. In 1935 he won the National Prize for Literature with his *Mister Witt en el cantón* [*Mr. Witt among the Rebels*]. Other well-known works of his are *Crónica del alba* [*Chronicle of Dawn*, 1942], *El verdugo afable* [*The Affable Hangman*, 1952], *Los cinco libros de Ariadne* [*The Five Books of Ariadne*, 1957] and *Novelas ejemplares de Cíbola* [*Tales of Cíbola*, 1961]. Most of Sender's works have been translated into English.

To these names should be added that of another famous exile, Salvador de Madariaga, born in 1886. He has lived most of his adult life in England. He, like Barea, has frequently published his works first in English and then in Spanish. While not a

THE TWENTIETH CENTURY 359

novelist, Madariaga has made many notable contributions in the field of Spanish culture, such as *Shelley and Calderón* (1920), *The Genius of Spain* (1923), *Ingleses, franceses, españoles* (1929), translated as *Englishmen, Frenchmen and Spaniards,* and various other works on figures such as Christopher Columbus, Cortez and Bolivar. He also wrote the informative *Guía del lector del "Quijote,"* an analysis of Cervantes' immortal masterpiece.

The works of those playwrights mentioned earlier continue to be presented on the stage, both those of the older generation, such as Jacinto Benavente, (1866–1954) and Alejandro Casona (1900–1965), Juan Ignacio Luca de Tena (b. 1897), José María Pemán (1897), Enrique Jardiel Poncela (1901–1952), Edgar Neville (b. 1899), José López Rubio (b. 1903), Miguel Mihura (b. 1903), and such comparatively younger dramatists as Alfonso Sastre (b. 1926), Victor Ruiz Iriarte (b. 1912), Alfonso Paso (b. 1926), and Antonio Buero Vallejo (b. 1916). Mention should also be made of Jacinto Grau (1877–1959).

An interesting recent development in the drama has been the creation of an "underground" theater, which, due to censorship, could not, until recently, be either produced or published inside Spain. Of the authors, one, Alfonso Sastre (born 1926), is already known to the Spanish stage for such plays as *Escuadra hacia la muerte* [*Squadron Toward Death,* 1953], *La mordaza* [*The Gag,* 1954], *El cuervo* [*The Raven,* 1957], *La cornada* [*The Horn Thrust,* 1960] and *En la red* [*In the Net,* 1961]. Others of Sastre's plays, however, have not been performed in Spain, including *Guillermo Tell tiene los ojos tristes,* published in English in 1970 as *Sad Are the Eyes of William Tell, Muerte en el barrio* [*Death in the District*], *Tierra roja* [*Red Earth*], and *Asalto nocturno* [*Night Assault*]. The names of the other authors writing in the vein of political and social protest, the "underground," are less familiar: Antonio Martínez Ballesteros, born in Toledo in 1929, who has written two plays now published in English, *The Hero* and *The Best of All Possible Worlds;* José María Bellido, born in 1922, from San Sebastían, whose *Tren a F . . .* [*Train to H . . .*] and *El pan y el arroz o Geometría en amarillo* [*Bread and Rice, or Geometry in Yellow*]; and José Ruibal, a Galician now residing in Madrid, who has been successful as a writer for cabaret theatre and whose *El hombre y la mosca* and *El asno* have been translated as *The Man and the Fly* and *The Jackass.*

Poetry in the post-Civil War period has perhaps not reached the heights it did in the so-called "Generation of 1927." Some think it has continued on an ascendent lyrical curve, only just interrupted by the war, with a few excursions into so-called "realist" poetry. Nevertheless, various poets have come to the fore, Germán Bleiberg (b. 1915), Carlos Bousoño (b. 1923), José Luis Cano (b. 1912), Vicente Gaos (b. 1919), Blas de Otero (b. 1916), Gabriel Celaya (b. 1911), José Hierro (b. 1923), Eugenio de Nora (b. 1923), Leopoldo Panero (b. 1909), Luis Felipe Vivanco Bergamín (b. 1907), Victoriano Crémer (b.   ), José Luis Hidalgo (1919–1947), and Luis Rosales Comacho (b. 1910), to name only some whose names are well known, both for poetry and, in many cases, literary scholarship.

Many contributions to literary and cultural scholarship have and are being made. In Spain itself, various professor-scholars have published notable contributions, men such as José Manuel Blecua, José Luis Cano, Carlos Clavería, Luis Granjel, Ricardo Gullón, Rafael Lapesa, the Marqués de Lozoya, Gonzalo Torrente Ballester, José Antonio Maravall and Martín de Riquer. An equally impressive group of Spaniards residing and teaching in the United States includes such writer-scholars as Francisco Ayala, Carlos Blanco Aguinaga, Manuel Durán, Francisco García Lorca, Jorge Guillén, Juan Marichal and Juan López Morillas, plus those mentioned earlier, José F. Montesinos, Federico de Onís, Angel del Río and Fernando de los Ríos.

Three Spanish writers have been awarded the Nobel Prize for Literature: José Echegaray (1832–1916), in 1904, Jacinto Benavente (1866–1954), in 1922, and Juan Ramón Jiménez (1881–1958), in 1956. Two Latin American writers have also been recipients of the prize: Gabriela Mistral, the Chilean poetess (1899–1957), who received the award in 1945, and Miguel Angel Asturias, the Guatemalan novelist (b. 1899) who won it in 1967.

Suggested Readings*

Paperbacks

General

Adams, N. B. and Keller, J. E. *A History of Spanish Literature* (Littlefield).

Bell, Aubrey F. G. *Cervantes* (Collier Books).

Borkenau, Frank. *The Spanish Cockpit* (University of Michigan Press).

Brenan, Gerald. *The Face of Spain* (Grove Press).

————. *The Literature of the Spanish People* (Meridian Books).

————. *South from Granada* (Grove Press).

————. *The Spanish Labyrinth* (Cambridge University Press).

Chase, Gilbert. *The Music of Spain* (Dover Books).

Davies, R. T. *The Golden Century of Spain 1501-1621* (Harper Torchbooks).

————. *Spain in Decline 1621-1700* (Papermac. St. Martin).

Durán, Manuel. *Lorca, A Collection of Critical Essays* (Spectrum Books).

* This selective bibliography has been prepared primarily as a guide for the English speaking reader who wants to know more about Spanish literature and does not in any way purport to be a complete listing of Spanish works in English translation. It is a suggested list of works that are reasonably available at the present time. Paperbacks are stressed, as they are less expensive. Many less recent translations exist, and for example the works of Blasco Ibáñez which were very popular in the 1920's, will be found on many a local library shelf. I suggest you consult the librarian or the card catalogue by author.

Elliott, J. H. *Imperial Spain 1469-1716* (Mentor Books).
Eoff, Sherman H. *The Modern Spanish Novel* (New York University Press).
Honig, Edwin. *Federico García Lorca* (New Directions).
Keny, Michael. *A Spanish Tapestry* (Harper Colophon Books).
Unamuno, Miquel de. *The Tragic Sense of Life* (J. C. Flitch, tr., Dover Books).
Matthews, Herbert L. *The Yoke and the Arrows* (George Braziller).
Michener, James A. *Iberia* (A Fawcett Crest Book).
Nelson, Lowry Jr. *Cervantes, A Collection of Critical Essays* (Spectrum Books).
Northup, George Tyler. *An Introduction to Spanish Literature* (University of Chicago Press).
Ortega y Gasset, José. *The Dehumanization of Art and Other Writings on Art and Culture* (Anchor Books).
Orwell, George. *Homage to Catalonia* (Beacon Books).
Payne, Robert (ed.) *The Civil War in Spain* (A Premier Book).
Peak, J. Hunter. *Social Drama in Nineteenth Century Spain* (University of North Carolina).
Rennert, Hugo A. *The Spanish Stage in the Time of Lope de Vega* (Dover Publications).
Roth, Cecil. *The Spanish Inquisition* (W. W. Norton).
Sitwell, Sacheverell. *Spain* (W. W. Norton).
Thomas, Hugh. *The Spanish Civil War* (Harper Colophon Books).
Watt, W. M. *A History of Islamic Spain* (Anchor).

Drama
Calderón de la Barca, Pedro. *Four Plays* (Edwin Honig, tr. and introd., Hill and Wang).
García Lorca, Federico. *Three Tragedies* (O'Connell and Graham-Lujan, trs., New Directions).
———. *Masterpieces of Modern Spanish Theatre* (Robert W. Corrigan, ed., Collier Books).
———. *Five Plays: Comedies and Tragic Comedies* (O'Connell and Graham-Lujan, trs., New Directions).
The New Wave Spanish Drama (George E. Wellwarth, ed., The Gotham Library).
Six Spanish Plays (Vol. 3, Classic Theatre, Eric Bentley, ed., Anchor Books).
Spanish Drama (Angel Flores, ed., Bantam Books).
Three Classic Spanish Plays (Hyman Alpern, ed., Washington Square Press).

Poetry

There is a book edited by Charles David Ley: *Spanish Poetry Since 1939* (Washington, 1962).

Anonymous. *The Poem of the Cid* (Lesley Byrd Simpson, tr., University of California Press).

Also in paper:

Madariaga, Salvador de. *Spain: A Modern History* (Praeger Paperbacks).

Whitaker, Arthur P. *Spain and Defense of the West* (Praeger Paperbacks).

Feis, Herber. *The Spanish Story* (The Norton Library).

An Anthology of Spanish Poetry from Garcilaso to García Lorca: In English Translation with Spanish Originals (Angel Flores, ed., Anchor Books).

García Lorca, Federico. *Gypsy Ballads of García Lorca* (R. Hemphries, tr., Indiana University Press).

———. *Poet in New York* (in Spanish and English; Ben Belitt, tr., Grove Press).

———. *Selected Poems* (In Spanish and English; New Directions).

Guillén, Jorge. *Cántico: A Selection* (Norman Thomas de Giovanni, Ed., Little, Brown).

Jiménez, Juan Ramón. *The Selected Writings of* (H. R. Hays, tr., Evergreen Books).

Modern Spanish Prose and Poetry (G. W. Andrian, ed., Macmillan).

The Penguin Book of Spanish Verse (Span. with Prose Tr., J. M. Cohen, ed. and tr., Penguin Books).

Ten Centuries of Spanish Poetry, An Anthology in English Verse with Original Texts (Eleanor L. Turnbull, ed., Grove Press).

Prose Fiction

Alarcón, Pedro Antonio de. *The Three Cornered Hat* (Barron's Educational Series).

Anonymous. *The Life of Lazarillo de Tormes* (W. S. Merwin, tr., Anchor Books; also, H. de Onis, Barron's Educational Series).

Caballero, Fernán. *The Sea Gull* (Joan McLean, tr., Barron's Educational Series).

Cela, Camilo José. *The Family of Pascual Duarte* (Anthony Kerrigan, tr., Avon Books).

———. *The Hive* (J. M. Cohen, tr., Signet Books).

Cervantes, Miguel de. *The Deceitful Marriage and Other Exemplary Novels* (Walter Starkie, tr., Signet Classics).
———. *Don Quixote* (J. M. Cohen, tr., Penguin Books; also, Walter Starkie, tr., Signet Classics).
———. *Exemplary Novels of Cervantes* (Perpetua Books).
———. *The Portable Cervantes* (Samuel Putnam, tr. and ed., Viking Portable Series).
———. *Six Exemplary Novels* (H. de Onis, tr., Barron's Educational Series).
Great Spanish Short Stories (Angel Flores, ed., Dell Books).
Masterpieces of the Spanish Golden Age (Angel Flores, ed., Rinehart and Company).
Pérez Galdós, Benito. *Doña Perfecta* (H. de Onis, tr., Barron's Educational Series).
———. *Marianela* (H. W. Lester, tr., Translation Publishing Company).
———. *Miau* (Penguin Classics).
———. *Tristana* (R. Selden Rose, tr., Peter Smith Publisher).
Rojas, Fernando de. *The Celestina* (M. Singleton, tr., University of Wisconsin Press).
———. *The Spanish Bawd, La Celestina* (J. M. Cohen, tr., Penguin Books).
Spanish Stories: A Bantam Dual-Language Book (Angel Flores, ed., Bantam Books).
Spanish Stories and Tales (H. de Onis, ed., Washington Square Press).

Hardbacks

Alberti, Rafael. *Selected Poems* (Ben Belitt, tr., University of California Press).
An Anthology of Spanish Literature in English Translation, 2 vols. (Seymour Resnick and Jeanne Pasmantier, eds., Ungar Publishing Company).
Cervantes, Miguel de. *Don Quixote* (Samuel Putnam, tr., Modern Library).
Chandler, Richard E. and Schwartz, Kessel. *A New History of Spanish Literature* (Louisiana State University Press).
Goytisolo, Juan. *Marks of Identity* (Gregory Rabassa, tr., Modern Library).
———. *The Party's Over* (José Yglesias, tr., Grove Press).

Gironella, José María. *The Cypresses Believe in God* (Harriet de Onis, tr., Knopf).
———. *One Million Dead* (Joan MacLean, tr., Doubleday).
Green, Otis H. *Spain and the Western Tradition* (University of Wisconsin Press).
Guillén, Jorge. *Affirmation: A Bilingual Anthology, 1919-1966* (Julian Palley, tr., University of Oklahoma Press).
An Introduction to Modern Spanish Literature, An Anthology of Fiction, Poetry and Essay (Kessel Schwartz, ed., Twayne Publishers).
Lovett, Gabriel H. *Napoleon and the Birth of Modern Spain* 2 vols., New York University Press).
Machado, Antonio. *Eighty Poems of* (Willis Barnstone, tr., Las Américas Publishing Company).
Mariejol, Jean H. *The Spain of Ferdinand and Isabella* (Rutgers University Press).
Matute, Ana María. *The Lost Children* (Joan MacLean, tr., Macmillan).
Quevedo y Villegas, Francisco de. *The Dog and the Fever* (William Carlos Williams and Raquel Helene Williams, trs., Shoe String Press).
———. *The Scavenger* (Hugh A. Harter, tr., Las Américas Publishing Company).
———. *The Visions* (J. M. Cohen, ed., Southern Illinois University Press).
Sender, Ramón. *The Affable Hangman* (Florence Hall, tr., Las Américas Publishing Company).
———. *Before Noon* (Florence W. Sender, tr., University of New Mexico Press).
———. *Tales of Cibola* (Florence W. Sender et al, trs., Las Américas Publishing Company).

Index of Authors

Acuña, Hernando de, 87, 100
Adams, Nicholson B., 40
Aesop, 34
Agustí, Ignacio, 356
Alarcón, Juan Ruiz de, see Ruiz de Alarcón, Juan.
Alarcón, Pedro Antonio de, 293-295
Alas, Leopoldo, see Clarín.
Alberti, Rafael, 345, 355
Alborg, Juan Luis, 356, 357
Aldana, Francisco de, 100
Aldecoa, Ignacio, 356
Aleixandre, Vicente, 346, 347, 355
Alemán, Mateo, 137, 186, 187
Alfieri, Count Vittorio, 239, 265
Alfonso, Pedro, 34
Alfonso X, the Wise, 12, 22-27, 33, 34, 75, 79-81
Allison, Young, 281
Alomar, Gabriel, 336
Alonso, Dámaso, 174, 337, 348, 355
Alvarez de Vallasandino, Alfonso, 54
Alvarez Quintero, Joaquín, 352
Alvarez Quintero, Serafín, 352
Anacreon, 185, 206
Aparisi Guijarro, Antonio, 310
Apollinaire, Guillaume, 342
Arbó, Sebastián Juan, 356
Aribau, Buenaventura Carlos, 285
Ariosto, Ludovico, 211, 248

Aristotle, 104, 105, 208
Arniches, Carlos, 352
Arolas, Juan, 268, 275-276
Artigas, Miguel, 337
Asturias, Miguel Angel, 360
Aub, Max, 355, 356, 358
Aurelius, Marcus, 311
Avellaneda, Alonso Fernández de, 155
Avellaneda, Gertrudis Gómez de, 268, 275
Avila, Juan de, 124
Ayala, Francisco, 356, 360
Ayguals de Izco, Wenceslao, 284
Aznar, José Camón, 337
Azorín (José Martínez Ruiz), 251, 313, 314, 319-320, 338
Azuela, Mariano, 332

Baena, Juan Alfonso, 54
Ballegas, Emilio, 332
Balmes, Jaime, 245, 255
Barea, Arturo, 354, 355, 356, 358
Barnstone Willis, 322, 323
Baroja, Pío, 320-321, 338, 355
Bartrina, Joaquín María, 291
Beaumarchais, Pierre Augustin, 250
Bécquer, Gustavo Adolfo, 268, 277-282, 331, 335, 346
Bell, Aubrey F. G., 117, 119

367